79.95

P9-AOI-738

Alphonse
Dell'Isola, PE

Value
Engineering:
Practical
Applications

*... for Design,
Construction,
Maintenance &
Operations*

RSMeans
CMD Understanding your craft.
Advancing your business.

Alphonse
Dell'Isola, PE

Value Engineering:
Practical
Applications

*.... for Design,
Construction,
Maintenance &
Operations*

Copyright 1997

R.S. Means Company, Inc.
Construction Publishers & Consultants
Construction Plaza
63 Smiths Lane
Kingston, MA 02364-0800
(800) 334-3509

The editors for this book were: Mary Greene, managing editor, Robin MacFarlane and Suzanne Morris, manuscript editors. Book production was managed by Karen O'Brien and coordinated by Marion Schofield; Michele Able supervised electronic publishing. Book design by Norman R. Forgit.

Printed in the United States of America

10 9 8 7 6 5

Library of Congress Catalog Number 98-106185

ISBN 0-87629-463-8

Table of Contents

List of Figures

Preface and Acknowledgements

This book presents the significant advances made since the publication of the previous three editions of *Value Engineering in the Construction Industry*. In lieu of publishing a fourth edition and repeating the basics, the author and publisher decided a new text would better present the innovative VE concepts developed in the last decade. This reprint includes an updated diskette with additional VE tools and automated formats.

Since the first printing, a complement of clean discipline-oriented workbooks that are linked to provide a quick, accurate summary of recommendations have been developed and included in the new diskette. Also since the first printing, additional VE tools have been developed. These are also provided in the new diskette. These include:

- Automated weighted evaluations worksheet in Excel
- General purpose linked cost model
- Excel-oriented spreadsheets for building-oriented conceptual estimates
- VE report formats for organizing a VE study report
- An Excel spreadsheet for collecting and evaluating creative ideas

The integration of VE methodology into the design and project construction/management processes is an important focus of this book. Supporting techniques are illustrated, and the text includes topics such as expanded initial and life cycle costing input, use of Quality Modeling, integrating VE and risk analysis, and greater use of computerized formats and linkages. A VE goal change emphasizes optimizing decision making rather than reducing unnecessary costs, which was the initial VE objective.

The text outlines a VE Job Plan, which is supported by a system of electronic, integrated spreadsheet templates that are provided on disk as a basic tool. Easily used on IBM-compatible computers with Lotus 1-2-3 or Excel, the disk includes formats developed during the completion of over 500 major project VE studies. Optional tools, offered as an aid to advanced practitioners, were developed especially for use in the VE process. These applications include a parameter-based cost-estimating system tied to the Cost Model and a life cycle costing system. The disk interfaces with a workbook, included as part of the text, that guides practitioners through application of the Job Plan during the performance of a VE study.

Seven case studies illustrate the range of application for value engineering techniques, which evaluate total building costs over the economic life of a facility. The case studies make use of excerpts from actual VE study reports for buildings and process projects to demonstrate application of value engineering concepts, the VE Job Plan, and life cycle costing methods.

Many people participated in the development of this new book by providing important information, and acknowledgment of their contributions is made with appreciation. The principal contributor was the architectural/engineering firm of Smith, Hinchman & Grylls Associates (SH&G), where the author worked for some twenty years. The firm offered the environment in which to practice and implement new ideas. Special thanks go to Nancy Gladwell, the office manager, who gave her wholehearted support throughout the ups and downs of the consulting business. Dr. Stephen Kirk, who now heads his own office, whose efforts provided valuable input into the development of life cycle costing, quality modeling, and the concepts underlying the integration of VE into the design process. Mr. Don Parker offered his insight and experience in the development of the project cost control and value management aspects.

Other key contributors were located in New York City (NYC). Jill Woller and Bill McElligot, in the NYC Office of Management and Budget, provided opportunities to implement VE studies and explore new ideas. Similarly, the former employees of the Port Authority of NY/NJ, Robert Harvey and David Kirk (formerly at the World Trade Center) provided the opportunities and proving grounds to apply innovative methodology to many challenging and varied projects.

During the past ten years, the author has performed over 50 VE studies in the Middle East and United States. These studies constitute some of the most diverse and complex projects in 35 years of experience.

In particular, the author would like to thank the Abdul Latif Jameel Real Estate Investment Co., Ltd., headquartered at Jiddah, Saudi Arabia, for the opportunities to work for them. General Manager Mohammed Ibrahim Al-Abdan and Engineering & Projects Director Mohammed M. Abdul Qadir were exceptional people to work with. Currently, the author represents several consulting firms in the U.S. and abroad. With their encouragement, the author has developed various digital applications of VE methodologies that function as basic tools in the performance of value engineering studies.

As a final note, by utilizing the methodology and tools illustrated in this book, in 2001, the author worked on two New York City projects valued at $5 billion. He had the good fortune of acting as VE coordinator where $1 billion in savings were achieved with enhanced design in both projects. These results followed being recognized the the International Society of American Value Engineers by receiving their highest award, the Lawrence D. Miles Award, culminating a most productive year in retirement.

The proceeds of the book are dedicated to my wife, who has the unenviable task of taking care of the author in retirement.

About the Author

Alphonse J. Dell'Isola, PE, RICS, FCVS, is currently president of Projacs USA, a subsidiary of Projacs of Kuwait, Saudi Arabia, and Emirates. Projacs offers consultant services for project management, value engineering, life cycle costing (LCC), and cost control. For the twenty prior years, Mr. Dell'Isola was director of the Value Management Division of the large design firm Smith, Hinchman & Grylls in Washington D.C. Previous experience was in field construction as a materials and cost engineer, principally on overseas airfields.

Mr. Dell'Isola has been working full-time in construction management and value engineering since 1963, conducting over 1,000 contracts for various organizations and agencies on projects totalling more than $50 billion dollars in construction that has resulted in implemented savings of some $3.5 billion. In addition, the author has conducted workshops, seminars, and briefings on value engineering, construction management, and project cost control for over 15,000 professionals.

Serving as director of value engineering for the Naval Facilities Engineering Command, Specifications & Estimates Branch, and for the Army Corps of Engineers in Washington, D.C., Mr. Dell'Isola introduced VE programs in some 30 government agencies, and in an equal number of corporations in the U.S. and abroad. Many of his overseas efforts were in the Middle East, where he is currently involved with projects.

Engineering News-Record cited the author in 1964 for outstanding achievement in value engineering; in 1980, the Society of Japanese Value Engineers (SJVE) presented him with a Presidential Citation; and in 1993, he was given an Exceptional Service Award for his active role in the disaster reconstruction of the World Trade Center. In 1994 The Royal Institute of Chartered Surveyors (U.K.) elected Mr. Dell'Isola an Honorary Associate, and in 1996, SAVE International recognized his achievements by establishing a new honor and award for outstanding achievement, the Alphonse J. Dell'Isola Award for Construction. He has presented expert testimony to several (U.S.) Senate and House committees and was a consultant to the Presidential Advisory Council on Management Improvement. These testimonies were instrumental in leading to the adoption of VE for construction in federal government agencies.

The author's publications include over 100 articles on VE, LCC, and cost control, as well as several professional texts: *Value Engineering in the Construction Industry, Third Edition* (Smith, Hinchman & Grylls, 1988); *Life Cycle Costing for Design Professionals, Second Edition* (McGraw-Hill, Inc., 1995), with Dr. Stephen J. Kirk,

AIA, CVS; *Life Cycle Cost Data* (McGraw-Hill, Inc., 1983), with Dr. Stephen J. Kirk, AIA, CVS; and *Project Budgeting for Buildings* (Van Nostrand Reinhold, 1991), with Donald E. Parker.

Al Dell'Isola is a graduate of the Massachusetts Institute of Technology, a Certified Value Specialist (CVS-Life), a Fellow in the Society of American Value Engineers, an Associate of the Royal Institute of Chartered Surveyors (RICS) in London, England. He is a professional engineer licensed in the Commonwealth of Massachusetts, the District of Columbia, and the state of Florida.

Among the author's many projects, the following represent a cross section of the more significant.

- Supersonic Wind Tunnel and Large Rocket Test Facility, Corps of Engineers ($700 million)
- Atlanta Airport, Airport Authority ($400 million)
- North River & Newtown Creek plus several other Water Pollution Control Plants (WPCPs), NYC. ($5 billion)
- Artery (Highway) Project and Deer Island WPCPs, Massachusetts Bay Authority, Boston, MA ($2 billion)
- Government Complex (Amiri Diwan), Kuwait ($500 million)
- Rapid Transit System, Taipei, Taiwan, ROC ($1 billion)
- Offshore Drill Platform, North Sea ($1 billion)
- Al Kharj Air Force Base, Kingdom of Saudi Arabia ($3 billion)
- Hotel & Apartments (8,000 rooms) and Shopping Complex, Kingdom of Saudi Arabia ($1 billion)
- Modernization Upgrades and Disaster Relief, World Trade Center, NYC ($1.5 billion)

Introduction

A Briefing

Traditionally, construction projects have been developed by generating a program of needs, using in-house personnel or outside consultants to develop necessary documents, and subsequently awarding the projects. This approach has fulfilled managers' requirements for presenting and controlling capital expenditures.

However, the traditional approach does not allow for programmed input to implement any kind of quality control/value assurance program. In most areas of the industrial field—computers, steel, automobiles, aircraft, etc.—formal quality control/value assurance programs are a basic part of management controls over production. Yet, large corporations have implemented very few formal quality control/value assurance programs for construction-related procurement.

Value Engineering (VE) is a methodology that is known and accepted in the industrial sector. It is an organized process with an impressive history of improving value and quality. The VE process identifies opportunities to remove unnecessary costs while assuring that quality, reliability, performance, and other critical factors will meet or exceed the customer's expectations. The improvements are the result of recommendations made by multidisciplinary teams representing all parties involved. VE is a rigorous, systematic effort to improve the value and optimize the life cycle cost of a facility. VE generates these cost improvements without sacrificing needed performance levels. A wide range of companies and establishments have used VE effectively to achieve their continuous goal of improving decision making.

Life Cycle Costing (LCC), as practiced in VE, is an economical assessment of competing design alternatives using the concept of equivalent costs. LCC focuses on the total costs (initial cost + follow-on costs). Follow-on costs are all the associated costs of running the facility. LCC concentrates on optimizing energy consumption, maintenance and operations costs, replacement and alterations expenses, and staffing costs, including the time value of money. These items can account for over 60% of the total cost of running a facility. See Figure I.1, "Life Cycle Costs for a Typical Residential/Office Building."

Many owners, especially federal government construction agencies, have found the techniques of VE and life cycle costing to be successful in optimizing value and improving the return on investment (ROI) for a given project. These objectives are accomplished through systematic application of VE and

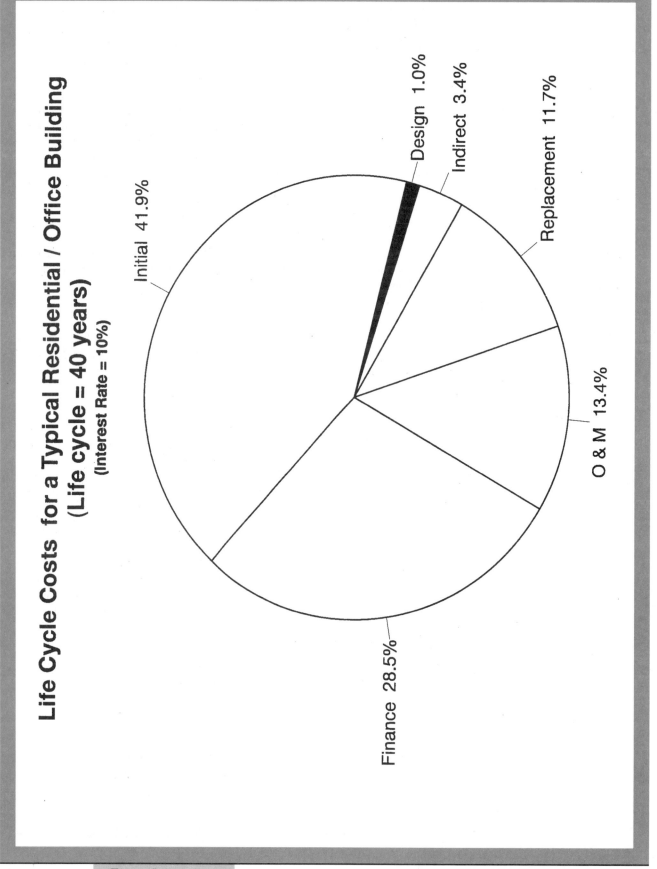

Life Cycle Costs for a Typical Residential / Office Building
(Life cycle = 40 years)
(Interest Rate = 10%)

Design 1.0%

Indirect 3.4%

Replacement 11.7%

Initial 41.9%

O & M 13.4%

Finance 28.5%

Figure I.1

LCC techniques during design as a counterpoint, or "second look," at major decisions affecting the initial investment and operating costs of a facility.

Most facility owners would identify long-term profitability as their main objective. They would also quickly point out that high quality and competitively priced facilities, products, or services are essential to achieve this goal. Of course, these must be produced economically in quantities consistent with demand. The coordination and communication necessary to accomplish these complex and seemingly conflicting tasks are often difficult to achieve. To keep pace with the ever-changing business climate, companies must better utilize their most important resource—their people. This has been demonstrated through the recent quality revolution experienced in companies in many advanced countries. Management has learned that when personnel are involved in the decision-making process and committed to a goal, significant improvements can be realized. The quality revolution has demonstrated that waste and inefficiency are unacceptable anywhere in the organization. Also, companies have learned that they must offer users products and services that satisfy their needs in a timely and responsive manner. Responsible decision makers have realized that they must better meet owners'/users' needs at optimum value.

VE can play a critical role in managing value to meet these goals. It can provide the networking required for improving coordination and communication. In other words, VE facilitates management of both value and costs. Using the VE methodology will result in improved profit, and it will continue to pay dividends for years to come.

The Objectives of Value Engineering

VE techniques can be used to achieve a number of objectives. They can save money; reduce time; and improve quality, reliability, maintainability, and performance. VE can also make contributions to improve human factors, such as attitudes, creativity, and teamwork.

Value engineering can also extend the use of financial, manpower, and material resources by eliminating unnecessary or excessive costs without sacrificing quality or performance. Decision making can be improved by using the team approach. Each person has an opinion regarding what affects the value of a product or service. Often, decisions are made by one dominant individual, who bases the choice on just one criterion, such as cost, quality, or reliability. Decisions like these lead to less than optimal overall decisions. A decision that improves quality but increases cost to a point where the product is no longer marketable is as unacceptable as one that reduces cost at the expense of required quality or performance. It is important to avoid confusing cost with value. If added cost does not improve quality or the ability to perform the necessary functions, then value is decreased.

Three basic elements provide a measure of value to the user: function, quality, and cost. These elements can be interpreted by the following relationship:

$$\text{Value} = \frac{\text{Function} + \text{Quality}}{\text{Cost}}$$

Where:

Function = The specific work that a design/item must perform.

Quality = The owner's or user's needs, desires, and expectations.

Cost = The life cycle cost of the product.

Therefore, we can say that:

Value = The most cost-effective way to reliably accomplish a function that will meet the user's needs, desires, and expectations.

The Reasons for Unnecessary Costs

The main objective of VE is to improve value, and VE techniques can overcome many of the roadblocks to achieving good value. Unnecessary costs that lead to poor value are generally caused by one or more of the following:

- **Lack of information.** Insufficient data on the functions the owner/user wants or needs and information on new materials, products, or processes that can meet these needs, within the required cost range.

- **Lack of ideas.** Failure to develop alternate solutions. In many cases, decision makers accept one of the first workable solutions that come to mind. This tendency invariably causes unnecessary costs, which can be eliminated by requiring the development of additional alternate ideas and then making choices based on economics and performance.

- **Temporary circumstances.** An urgent delivery, design, or schedule can force decision makers to reach a quick conclusion to satisfy a time requirement without proper regard to good value. These temporary measures frequently become a fixed part of the design or service, resulting in unnecessary costs.

- **Honest wrong beliefs.** Unnecessary costs are often caused by decisions based on what the decision maker believes to be true, rather than on the real facts. Honest wrong beliefs can impede a good idea that would otherwise lead to a more economical decision or service.

- **Habits and attitudes.** Humans are creatures of habit. A habit is a form of response—doing the same thing, the same way, under the same conditions. Habits are reactions and responses that people have learned to perform automatically, without having to *think* or *decide*. Habits are an important part of life, but one must sometimes question, "Am I doing it this way because it is the best way, because I feel comfortable with my methods, or because I have always done it this way?"

- **Changes in owner requirements.** Often, the owner's new requirements force changes during design or construction that increase costs and alter the schedule. In too many cases, the owner is not cognizant of the impact of the desired change.

- **Lack of communication and coordination.** Lack of communication and coordination are principal reasons for unnecessary costs. VE opens channels of communication that facilitate discussion of subjects and allows the expression of opinions without undue concern about acceptability. Also, it creates an environment that promotes listening and responding to varying points of view without becoming defensive.

- **Outdated standards and specifications.** Many of the standards and specifications in use in large construction programs are at least ten years old. As technology progresses, continual updating of data is required, but it is often not accomplished. VE helps to isolate and focus on new technologies and standards in areas where high costs and poor values may be incurred.

Each reason for poor value provides an opportunity for improved decision making and an area where a value engineering effort is appropriate.

An initial VE program study was conducted in 1965 by the United States Department of Defense to determine the sources of opportunity for VE. The aim of the study was to obtain an indication of range and degree of application from a sample of 415 successful value changes. The study identified seven factors that were responsible for about 95% of the savings. Predominant among these were excessive cost, additional design effort, advances in technology, and the questioning of specifications. See Figure I.2, "The Seven Most Significant Factors Responsible for Savings Actions."

The Department of Defense study revealed that a VE action was usually based on several factors rather than on a single aspect. In addition, the change was rarely a result of correcting bad designs. Second guessing designs to find them deficient

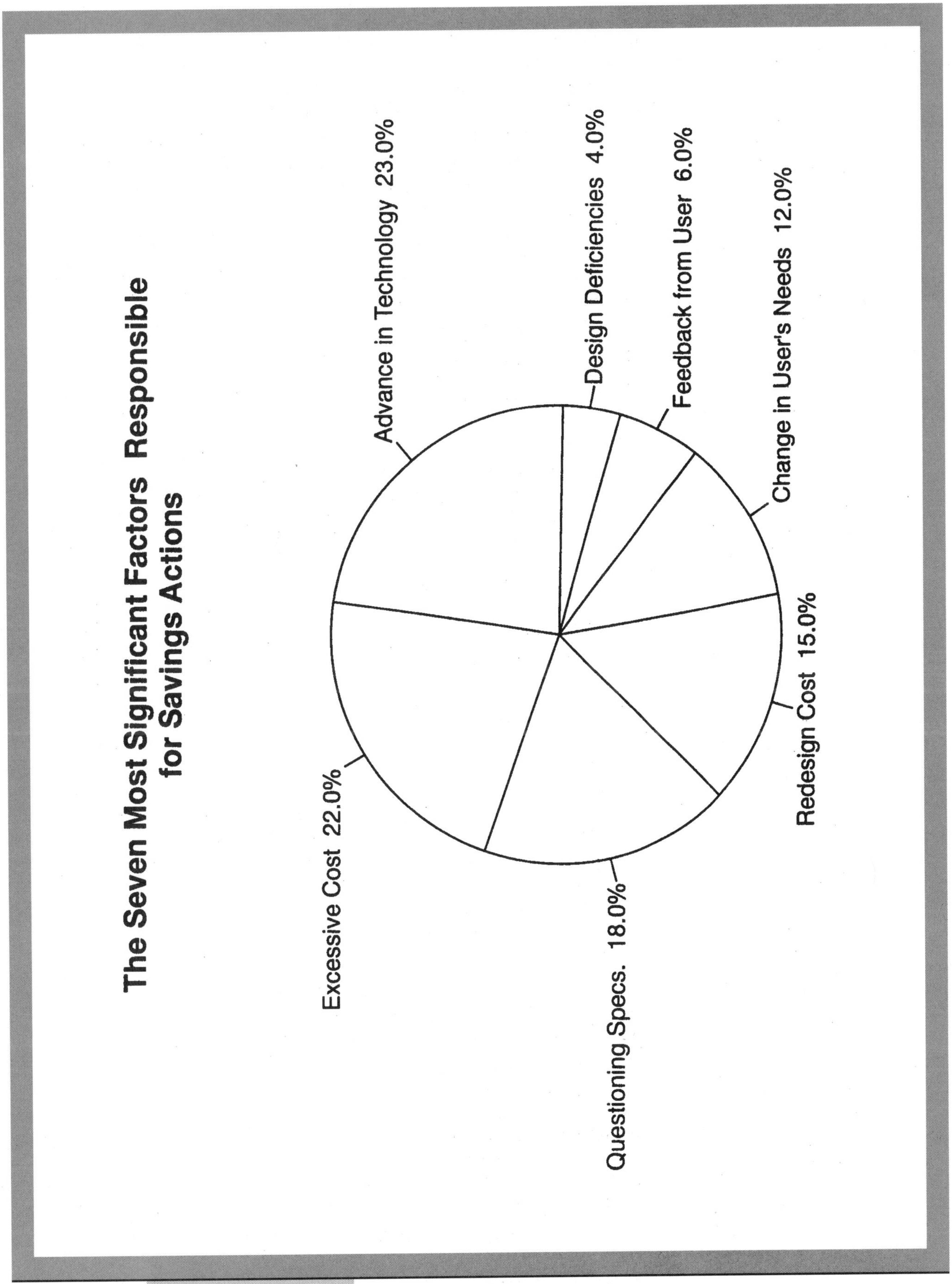

The Seven Most Significant Factors Responsible for Savings Actions

Advance in Technology 23.0%

Design Deficiencies 4.0%

Feedback from User 6.0%

Change in User's Needs 12.0%

Redesign Cost 15.0%

Questioning Specs. 18.0%

Excessive Cost 22.0%

Figure I.2

Introduction   A Briefing

xxi

provides little value opportunity. Most designs still work as the designer intended, following incorporation of VE study results. However, most designs can be enhanced, thereby providing an opportunity for value improvement.

When to Apply Value Engineering

VE should be performed as early as possible—before commitment of funds, approval of systems, services, or designs—to maximize results. The potential for savings, as illustrated in Figure I.3, "Potential Savings from VE Applications," is much greater the earlier VE is applied. When VE is applied later, two things increase: the investment required to implement any changes, and resistance to change.

Figure I.4, "Major Decision Makers' Influence on Facility Costs," shows whose decisions have the most influence over the expenditure of funds during the life cycle of a facility. The owner and consultants are the major decision makers. To ensure optimal results, it is essential to involve the owner and consultant in the VE process.

Regarding total costs for a facility, the consultant's fee represents the smallest expenditure of all of the initial costs. Consultants' decisions influence about 50% of the facility's total costs. Therefore, the optimum results can be expected when resources are set aside for VE early in the design process, focusing on owner and consultant impact. Owners who delight in squeezing design fees invariably promote poor value design decisions. Prudent expenditures during design to improve design decisions can return significant initial and follow-on cost and quality improvements.

VE Methodology and Techniques

Several factors or roadblocks lead to unnecessary costs. Use of the team approach is a proven way of overcoming many of these roadblocks. See Figure I.5, "The Conventional Approach vs. the VE Approach." Individual efforts can be costly, inefficient, and incomplete. A team effort, on the other hand, concentrates on problem-solving techniques to break through obstacles. VE develops a cohesive team of self-motivated achievers committed to a common objective.

The planned VE effort consists of using the *VE Job Plan*. The Job Plan fosters improved decision making to realize the optimal expenditure of owner funds, while meeting required functions at most favorable value. At the same time, the owner's desired tradeoffs, such as aesthetics, environment, safety, flexibility, reliability, and time, are considered.

Assembling the VE Team

It takes time and effort to assemble the expertise to conduct an in-depth review using the Job Plan. The importance of selecting appropriate team members cannot be overemphasized. A typical VE team consists of a mix of personnel, as illustrated in Figure I.6, "VE Methodology & Techniques." A good rule to follow is to seek out team members with equal or better qualifications than the original design team. Specialty areas—such as fire protection, material handling, elevators, food preparation equipment, and landscaping—offer unusual potential on large projects. To improve implementation, a decision-making representative for the owner should attend, or at least be on call, during application of the Job Plan. Initially, design personnel brief the team on major system selection; then review and offer comments on the team's ideas before a proposal is developed. Several hundred studies have shown that a well-selected team that follows the organized VE approach, always produces savings. The order of magnitude of the results is the only variable.

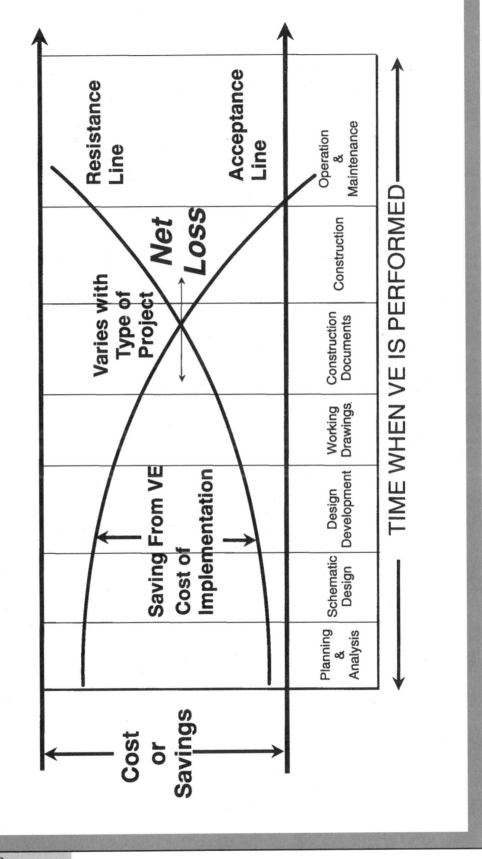

Potential Savings from VE Applications

Figure I.3

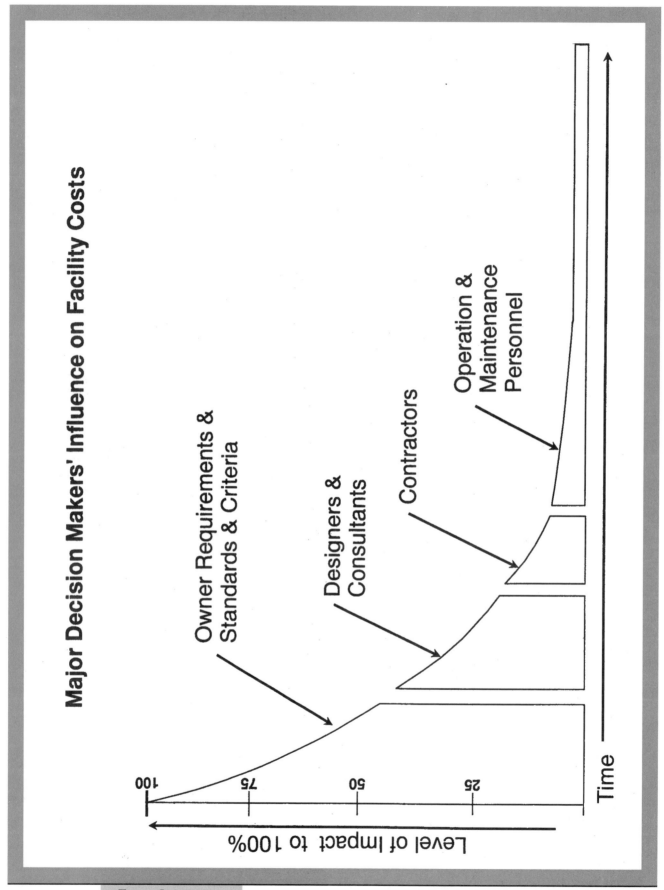

Figure I.4

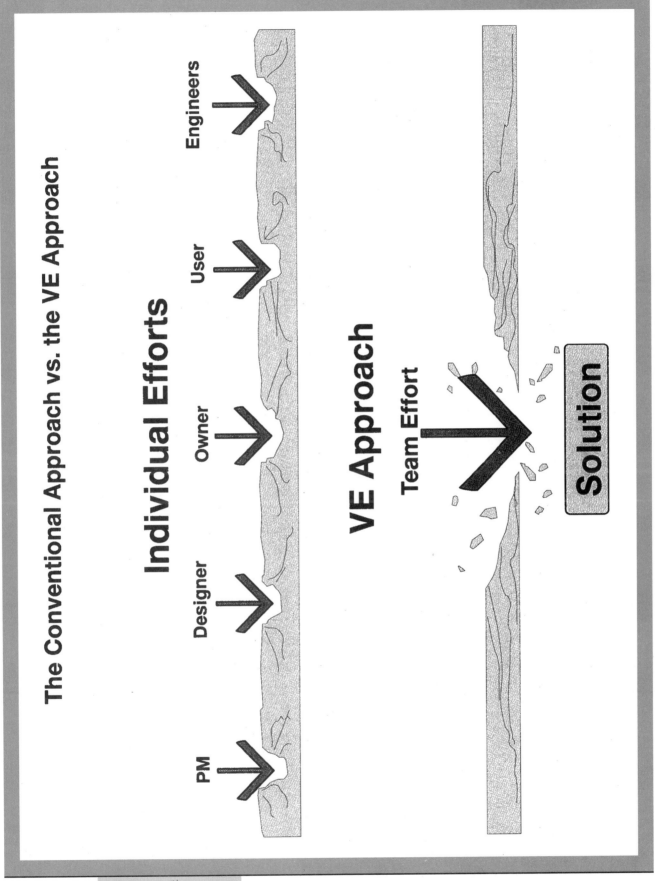

Figure I.5

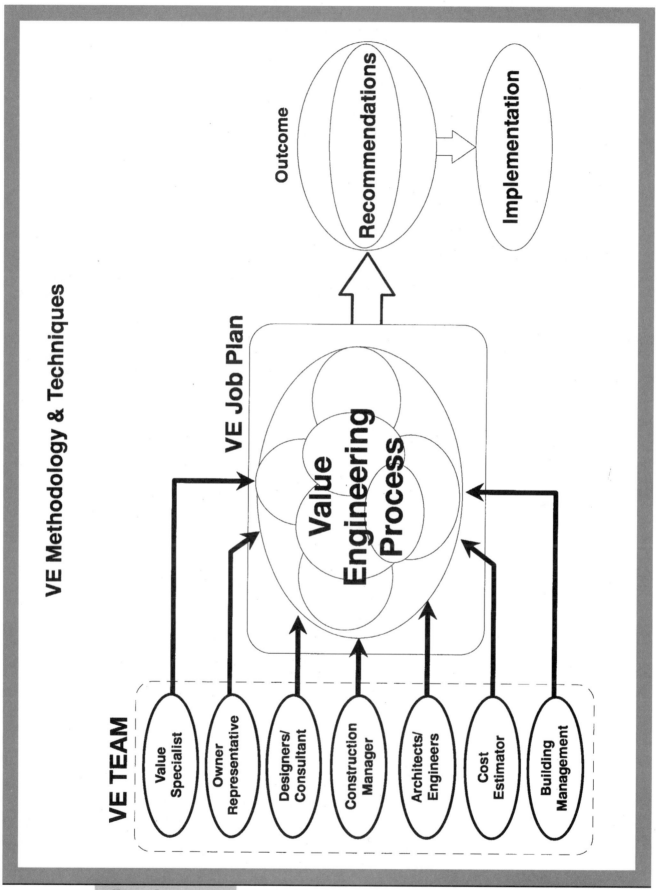

Figure I.6

VE techniques create changes to optimize design on purpose rather than letting changes occur by accident. The VE Job Plan is built around the scientific approach to problem solving. The process follows a well-documented, proven strategy comprised of the following structured phases:

- Information Phase
- Creative Phase
- Analytical Phase
- Proposal/Presentation Phase
- Implementation Phase

Figure I.7, "Value Engineering Job Plan," illustrates the interaction and steps of the Job Plan methodology. See Chapter 4 for a more detailed definition of each phase of the Job Plan.

Interface With Other Programs

Managers' responsibilities include the protection, conservation, and constructive utilization of the resources entrusted to them. The mechanisms available to managers to meet these objectives can be categorized in two basic groups: static and dynamic. *Static mechanisms* are devices built into the process of doing business, such as guidelines, regulations, and laws. These devices are always in force. Costs to achieve these benefits involve hidden resources, but they are rarely measured. Figure I.8 shows some examples of static mechanisms intended to set overall policies and guidelines. While it is important to recognize that these mechanisms exist and affect the project, they are outside the scope of what can be affected by VE.

It is the *dynamic mechanisms* that are involved in our subject. The principal strategies, listed in Figure I.8, all compete for management resources. Their dynamic quality is determined by several factors.

- Emphasis on and utilization of dynamic mechanisms fluctuates with changes in organizations and economics.
- The level of use by managers and employees is limited by understanding, experience, training, and preconceived notions.
- Appreciation of dynamic mechanisms as a resource is dependent on staff perception of top management's interest in them.

Selecting a Program

Among the dynamic mechanisms that conserve and protect resources, one program—value engineering (VE)—best meets management needs. Following are several reasons that support this contention:

1. VE has universal application in all of the areas in which dynamic mechanisms operate. The objective of VE is to improve value. Improving value can be achieved in the following ways:

   - Raise productivity
   - Improve management
   - Improve LCC
   - Improve quality
   - Reduce paper
   - Simplify work
   - Conserve energy
   - Reduce paperwork
   - Reduce cost
   - Audit decisions

2. VE has the advantage of advocating or concentrating on techniques that focus on the relationship of cost and worth to function. It teaches and supports the utilization of all *existing* techniques in application to the proper problem. Figure I.9 shows how VE methodology interfaces with the utilization of the other dynamic mechanisms.

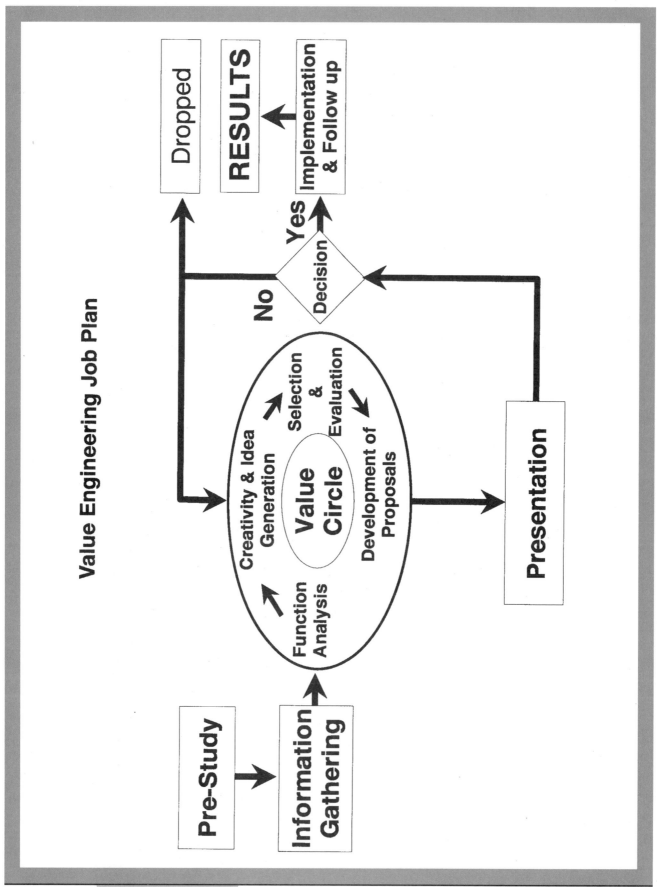

Figure I.7

Static and Dynamic Mechanisms

for an
Operational Mission Related to Responsibility
to Conserve & Protect Resources

Static Mechanisms

- Personnel Ceilings
- Budget Limitations
- Competitive Procurement
  Regulations
- Laws from Congress
  - Davis-Bacon Act
  - Economy Act
  - Other

Dynamic Mechanisms

- Productivity Programs
- Work Simplification
- Cost Reduction
- Paperwork Management
- Life Cycle Costing
- Management by Objectives
- Employee Suggestions
- Management Improvement
- Zero Based Budgeting
- Total Quality Management
- Value Engineering
- Energy Conservation
- Risk Analysis
- Systems Analysis

Figure I.8

Relationship of Current Activities with VE and Other Techniques

Supporting Activities Useful as Information Sources	VE Methodology	Supporting Techniques for Redesign, Development Work and Selection of Alternatives	Results
• Audits • Management Surveys • Management Improvement • Management by Objectives • Zero-based Budgeting • Employee Suggestions • Energy Program • Performance Indicators • Contractor Ideas • Paperwork Management • Productivity Measurement • Complaints	Function Analysis (Cost) vs. (Worth) Function Analysis System Technique (FAST) Diagramming	• Work Simplification • Economic Analysis • Life Cycle Costs • Design-to-cost • Management Analysis • Flow Charting • Weighted Evaluation • Trade-off Analysis • Systems Analysis • Cost Reduction • Risk Assessments • Total Quality Management	Optimize Value Cost Savings Time Savings Manpower Savings

Figure I.9

3. VE is a universal problem-solving methodology that can be taught and used at all levels.

4. Its applicability allows VE to improve all related studies. Through the Job Plan, VE provides a system to ensure that approved studies reach a definitive conclusion that includes implementation, while it improves quality. Too many studies are subject to one or several of the following pitfalls:
   - Definition of the incorrect problem.
   - Recommendation of unworkable solutions.
   - Failure to gather all necessary information.
   - No demonstration of creativity.
   - Failure to include implementation actions.
   - Failure to quantify benefits.

The VE Job Plan specifically addresses each of these issues.

VE is one of the few programs a manager can initiate that generates more savings than cost! After an initial expenditure to launch a VE program, value engineering pays for itself. Return on investment (ROI) can be measured and monitored.

Application to Facility Programs

Under several mandatory federal statutes (Office of Management and Budget OMB Circular No. A-131—Value Engineering, June, '93 and Defense Authorization Act, February, 1996), all major United States government agencies employ full-time value engineers. In addition, most major government suppliers and contractors have VE staffs. There are formal programs in the Department of Defense and in the Departments of Environmental Protection, Transportation, General Services, Veterans Administration, and Energy. Outside the federal government, the leader in VE application is the City of New York, where teams include a representative from the mayor's office. The Port Authority of New York/New Jersey was very active, especially in front-end type applications, until a change in administration reduced their program. In all cases, significant savings and reductions in project budget overruns have been realized. Other areas with programs include cities such as San Diego, Boston, Philadelphia, Chicago, Orlando, Seattle, and Miami; and the states of Washington, Wyoming, Florida, Maryland, and Virginia. In the private sector, Chevron, United Technology, Digital, Ciba Geigy, IBM, Chrysler, FritoLay, and Owens Corning Fiberglass all have applied the technique.

There are several excellent VE consultants available through SAVE International, "The Value Society," located in Northbrook, Illinois.

Outside of the United States, approximately twenty countries have active VE practitioners. One of the leaders is Japan. There are more members in the Society of Japanese Value Engineers (SJVE) than SAVE International members in the United States. SAVE International chapters are located in Korea, India, France, Germany, Hungary, Saudi Arabia, and Australia. In addition, there are currently programs throughout Europe, Canada, South America, Taiwan, and South Africa. In Saudi Arabia, the General Directorate of Military Works (GDMW), under General Otaishan, retired, of the Saudi Arabian Ministry of Defense and Aviation (MODA), has had a fulltime program for more than eight years. The GDMW has saved from $30 million to $75 million per year. Through the efforts of the GDMW, the VE concept has spread in Saudi Arabia. Recently, a Saudi chapter of SAVE International was established which includes three Saudi professionals who are Certified Value Specialists (CVS), and eight Saudi Associated Value Specialists (AVS). In the government sector, the Ministry of Municipalities, Saudi Arabian Basic Industries (SABIC), GOSI—the Saudi Agency of Social Security, High Commission for Development of Arriyadh, and Saudi Consolidated Electric Company have initiated programs. In the private sector, Saudi Aramco and several other private investors (e.g., ALJ Real Estate Development, Jeraisy Corporation and Saudi German Hospital) have used VE.

Typical Results

The results of over 500 studies show a 5-35% reduction in initial costs and widely differing results for follow-on costs, depending on emphasis. When initial costs are critical, owners place less emphasis on follow-on costs, especially if no project will materialize unless the initial cost budget is realized. Owners who both build and maintain their facilities usually require a balanced emphasis on seeking out initial and follow-on savings. There have been several studies where operations and maintenance costs have been solely targeted.

With emphasis on follow-on costs, annual savings have ranged from 5-20% of annual costs. Best results have been attained on large municipal projects. A classic example is the City of New York Office of Management and Budget, which has often experienced $100 in savings for each $1 invested in the VE study. Their ROI on wastewater treatment plants, as well as other large projects, have averaged an $80 to $1 return on investment. In the process area, one large oil producer started a VE program about four years ago. Over that time, approximately 60 studies were done on projects worth over $3 billion. The oil producer's ROI was substantial, with a 10% average reduction in initial and follow-on costs.

VE has the potential for savings in any entity that spends money. The potential for savings will vary directly in proportion to the amount of spending and the types of expenditures. Larger, complex facilities offer the greatest potential. Results of recent programs with large facility expenditures are illustrated in Figure I.10, "Results of VE Programs." Typical requests for proposals and scopes of work that generated these savings are illustrated in Chapter 8.

Demonstrated Impact of VE

Value engineering is effective in many areas of the construction industry, and it can be utilized at different stages in the life of a building project. Applied with flexibility and creativity, VE is almost unlimited in its ability to indicate areas of potential savings that were not readily apparent.

Often, VE can generate significant funds in initial installation and operating costs. For example, as part of a planned design approach, VE was integrated with the cost and quality control program for a courthouse facility that resulted in $1,500,000 in initial cost savings and $150,000 in annual cost savings for maintenance and operations.

In addition to identifying specific items that promote cost efficiency, VE can provide objective scrutiny of a project to (1) determine cost-effectiveness within a planned time frame or (2) identify improved processes and performance. In one actual instance, the VE team questioned the economic feasibility of a building project. When the plans were reevaluated, the return on investment was marginal at best. As a result, the scope of the project was reduced to be more cost-effective, and the money saved was used to fund several critical projects that had been on hold.

An important aspect of value engineering lies in its ability to respond with timeliness, flexibility, and creativity. After the terrorist bombing of the World Trade Center in New York City, time was critical, since occupancy would be adversely affected if the project was drawn out. A VE/LCC/cost group responded quickly to maximize decision making and document actions. The team provided an overview for each major expenditure to optimize first-time and secondary costs, tracking both time and costs. Risk analysis techniques were used to mitigate potential catastrophic results. These efforts resulted in a savings in time and costs, and helped achieve an 80% occupancy rate within three months. In addition, the document/cost trails developed by the team were invaluable in explaining and justifying owner actions during negotiations with the insurance companies.

Results of VE Programs (Million U.S. $)

Agency	Annual Approximate Expenditure	Period	Annual Program Cost	Annual Savings	% Savings
EPA	1,100	1981 – Present	3 – 5	30	2 – 3
Federal Highways	10 – 20,000	1981 – Present	Varies Widely	150 – 200	1.5
Corps of Engineers	3,400	1965 – Present	3	200	5 – 7
Naval Facilities – Engineering Command	2,400	1964 – Present	2.5	100	3 – 5
Veterans Administration	200	1988 – Present	0.5	10	3 – 5
School Facilities State of Washington	200	1984 – Present	4	5 – 10	3 – 5
Office of Management and Budget, NYC	2,000 1,700	1984 – 87 – 88 Present	1 to 1.5	80 200 – 400	3 – 5 10 – 20
Design & Construction United Technology	300	1984 – 1985	0.5	36	12
GDMW – MODA Saudi Arabia	2,000	1986 – Present	3	150	5 – 10

Figure I.10

Conclusion

Based on 35 years of experience, the following guidelines are recommended for setting up an effective value engineering program.

- Establish a mandated program for VE to realize savings not only for initial capital costs, but also for follow-on (LCC) costs. There is as much or greater potential in follow-on cost savings as in initial cost savings.

- Focus on an organizational unit with overall fiscal responsibility to oversee the application and implementation of the program. Establish the organizational unit at a management level with responsibility for both initial expenses and operations and maintenance costs.

- Fund the program automatically as a percent of capital expenditures. In addition, integrate the program into the design process. See Figure I.11, which illustrates how a large design firm integrated VE into its approach.

- In establishing requirements for implementing VE programs, top management should set the goals and objectives. These goals and objectives should focus on optimizing decision making, including project enhancements.

- Work to change personnel's attitude from the beginning. A training program can create positive attitudes and set incentives for generating savings within the organization. When needs increase and available funds decrease, no organization can afford to waste money while critical projects are lacking in funds.

- In large construction agencies, expect program costs of 0.1-0.3% of total project costs for an effective program. These funds should result in a minimum of 5-10% savings in initial costs and 5-10% follow-on cost savings in annual maintenance and operations costs. As for timing, VE efforts are most effective when applied early during the design process.

With all of its potential and no sacrifice of needed requirements, why not accept the challenge and implement a VE program!

Note: The disk that is part of this book package provides, as a basic tool, a system of electronic, integrated spreadsheet templates. Optional applications, offered as an aid to advanced practitioners, include a parameter-based cost-estimating system that is tied to the Cost Model and a life cycle costing system.

The disk can be used on IBM-compatible computers, with Lotus 1-2-3 or Excel.

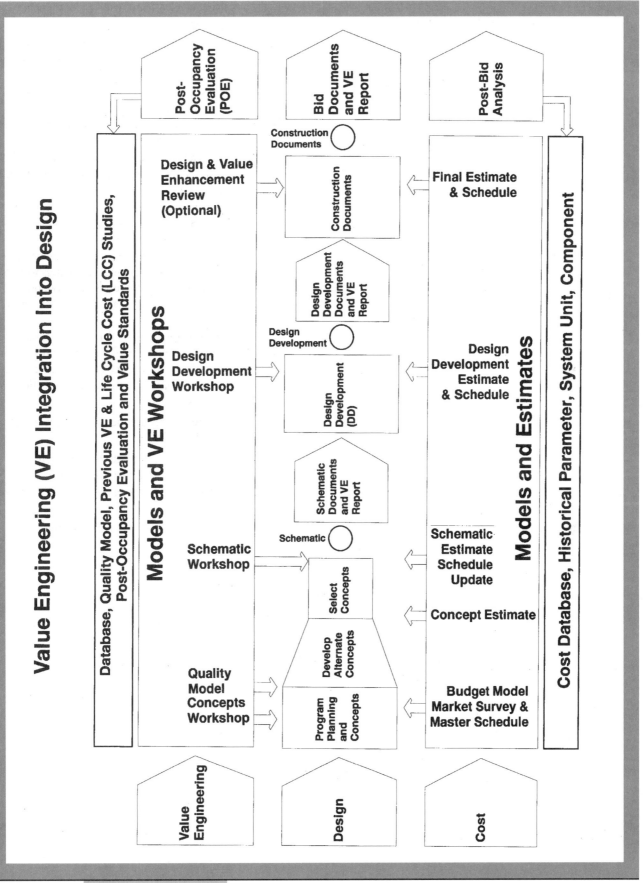

Value Engineering (VE) Integration Into Design

Figure I.11

Part One

Value Engineering: Practical Applications

Chapter One

Project Scope and Budget

When agreeing to perform value engineering (VE) for a project, the team coordinator should first determine whether the budget for the project can be used as a baseline for a VE study. Otherwise, a VE study might identify potential savings of $500,000, only to find out later that the project is really $2 million over budget. This would result in wasted effort. To prevent this occurrence, the value engineer must have expertise available within the team to review budgets, especially for early concept studies in which budgets are notoriously problematic. This chapter's discussion on project scope and budget will help to illustrate potential problems and areas for improvement.

Project budget development is the process of predicting (or forecasting) within acceptable variances what the actual project cost will be when the project is completed. Once a budget for a project is established, the goal is to control costs to stay within the budget.

Previously, when facilities were less complex and prices were more stable, costs were less of a problem. Cost took the number-three position in its triad relationship with performance and schedule. The number-one position was performance at any price. After all, the best-performing design was the end objective. Schedule was in second place. Generally, a project had to be on schedule, or it was not useful. In the rush to meet schedules, designs were frozen as soon as they were created, and fast track construction came into vogue. The cost of construction was not as important as generating income from the building or getting the facility on line at a certain time. On top of this, project managers were evaluated using delivery time as the key factor.

Times have changed. Cost is in the uncomfortable position of being equal to, or in some cases more important than, schedule and performance. Owners are sometimes required to make tradeoffs among these three factors. Designers sometimes make tradeoffs in performance to control costs. Uncontrolled costs influence schedules through delays caused by high bids, lack of funds, or projects that show poor return on investment (ROI) after the initial commitment of funds.

Social values are also changing. As costs go up, many seem to grudgingly accept less in terms of value and performance. Project features, qualities, and amenities are often sacrificed to control cost overruns. Bid alternates, some even deducting desired work, are introduced by design professionals and accepted by owners because the whole project can no longer be obtained within budget.

Problems concerning budgeting and cost control generally fall into the areas of "before" and "after" budget approval. Following are the key items in both areas:

How can budgets be wrong at the start?

- Owner requirements are not fully known.
- Initial planning and design programming are inadequate.
- The design and construction schedule is not established.
- Estimators have obtained requirements in piecemeal fashion.
- Too many requirements are lump summed; requirements need to be better defined.
- Owner politics force budgets to match a predetermined figure rather than reflect actual requirements.

How can budgets go astray after approval?

- Project scope is misunderstood by owner and users.
- Requirements are not clearly communicated to the designer.
- The designer is not monitored.
- User changes are not controlled.
- Project cost is not properly evaluated during reviews.
- The schedule is not met.

Each of the above items represents a potential problem, whether real or imagined, to the client. VE must contribute solutions for the effort to be deemed a success.

In order to judge its validity, the value engineer should know the components of a proper budget. Proper budget preparation is necessary for management to make sound investment decisions related to the worth of the project. Once the investment decisions are made, the budget can be used through VE as a vehicle to control project scope and design decisions before experiencing a cost overrun.

Elements of the Project Budget

Project budgets have a number of cost elements. An understanding of the various elements is essential in providing the baseline needed for VE.

Figure 1.1, "Program Budget Elements," illustrates the five budget elements used by the General Services Administration (GSA)[1] to compute program costs for a project. These costs occur in all projects, both government and private sector. For a private sector project, additional items would need to be added to the Estimated Reservation Cost (ERC) element to include costs for financing, taxes, insurance, titling fees, and permits.

The method used to develop the project budget must be precise enough to provide a basis for monitoring throughout the detailed design process. A good budget should be supported by established design parameters and quality levels, then priced on a conceptual basis in enough detail to allow the control process to be effective. If the budget used to seek the project financing cannot be used in this fashion, control during execution will be difficult or impossible to achieve, and the effective performance of VE will be in jeopardy.

Prevalent Budgeting Techniques

A survey conducted by the Veterans Administration[2] in 1974, which the author still believes is valid, indicated that the square foot method of estimating was used by 82% of all architect-engineer (A/E) firms to prepare budget estimates. The result of these budgets, when compared to the actual construction low bid for the projects for the agency, showed the following ranges:

Extreme deviation range = 66% (28% above low bid, 38% below low bid)

Program Budget Elements

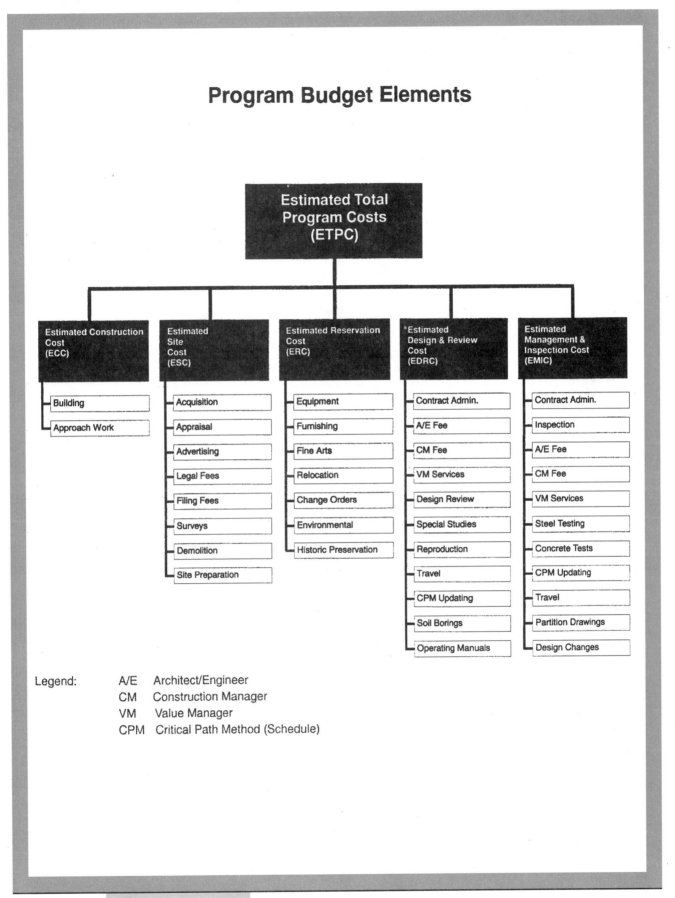

Estimated Total Program Costs (ETPC)

Estimated Construction Cost (ECC)	Estimated Site Cost (ESC)	Estimated Reservation Cost (ERC)	Estimated Design & Review Cost (EDRC)	Estimated Management & Inspection Cost (EMIC)
Building	Acquisition	Equipment	Contract Admin.	Contract Admin.
Approach Work	Appraisal	Furnishing	A/E Fee	Inspection
	Advertising	Fine Arts	CM Fee	A/E Fee
	Legal Fees	Relocation	VM Services	CM Fee
	Filing Fees	Change Orders	Design Review	VM Services
	Surveys	Environmental	Special Studies	Steel Testing
	Demolition	Historic Preservation	Reproduction	Concrete Tests
	Site Preparation		Travel	CPM Updating
			CPM Updating	Travel
			Soil Borings	Partition Drawings
			Operating Manuals	Design Changes

Legend: A/E Architect/Engineer
         CM   Construction Manager
         VM   Value Manager
         CPM Critical Path Method (Schedule)

Figure 1.1

- Mean deviation range = 29% (13% above low bid, 16% below low bid)

About 12% of the A/E firms surveyed used a modular quantity takeoff method for budget preparation. This method was somewhat more accurate than the square foot method. When compared to bid results, the deviations were as follows:

Extreme deviation range = 31% (21% above low bid, 10% below low bid)

Median deviation range = 24% (14% above low bid, 10% below low bid)

One of the largest variables in budgeting is effective cost control through design development. The above data illustrates that cost control using a square foot budget as a basis is virtually impossible. The ability to control costs to a budget seems to improve as the definition of the budget basis improves.

The survey also indicated that the budget technique most commonly used for facilities is one that employs the following elements:
- Identify the type of facility.
- Budget the cost per gross square footage ($/GSF).

The minimum amount of information necessary for this type of budget is:
- Historical cost for the facility type.
- Desired gross square footage.
- Geographical location.
- Desired completion date.

Often, this minimal information is all that is known or used when budgets are prepared. Project budgets developed on this basis are inadequate for controlling costs during subsequent design stages. Further, this method cannot fairly represent the cost of the project at the budget stage. One cannot judge the adequacy of a budget unless the owner's requirements are clearly defined.

For example, construction budgeting publications[3] show a wide variation in historical $/GSF, depending on the type of building. Within building types, cost ranges similar to the following sample data are typical:

Offices (5 to 10 story)	$59.15–$98.15/GSF
Parking Garages	$20.15–$46.25/GSF
Auditoriums	$62.35–$114.00/GSF
Courthouses	$93.55–$125.00/GSF

Budgeting on this basis might be called "pick a number." When budgeting is performed in this manner, one is limiting or selecting, without documentation, factors such as facility quality level, program content, space efficiency, facility configuration, and future life cycle cost (LCC) experience. Because these elements are undocumented, they cannot be controlled against the budget.

Cost Control

There is a difference between managing costs and controlling costs. Management is the act or manner of handling, directing, or supervising something. To manage something is to succeed in accomplishing it. Thus, to manage costs is to succeed in accomplishing a cost objective.

Many talk about cost control as if they can control costs through some tangible, prescriptive means such as VE. Because people are involved, however, the situation is not that simple. Individual attitudes, feelings, and concerns change with time.

Cost control does not promise an end to the problems of management, whether they are inflation or design related. Control is a process; in other words, a systematic series of actions directed toward a desired result. To exercise cost control, one must have a budget baseline against which to compare, so that management can spot deviations in time to take corrective action. The strong assumption in the term *control* is that management is willing to exercise authority—to make a decision.

The Cost Control FAST Diagram

Many feel that *cost control* means the control of money or a budget review. In fact, when cost control is mentioned, the first thing project managers do is consult the estimate to see what prices can be cut. VE does not control costs by looking solely at estimates, money, or cash flow. As Figure 1.2, "Cost Control FAST (Function Analysis System Technique) Diagram," indicates, the key to controlling cost is to control scope. The diagram assumes that the function of cost control is a critical management objective consistent with the overall goals and objectives of the owner.

The FAST Diagram illustrates the relationship of cost control to other procedural functions. This diagram considers cost control as one basic function of the organization (this restriction excluded listing other basic functions not germane to the issue). It indicates only major goals and objectives, with a few of the basic methods necessary to achieve cost control. Higher-order functions appear to the left of the figure, with lower-order functions to the right. Critical path activities are located on the centerline. The figure may be read by inserting any of the verb-noun activities into one of the following two questions:

"Why is it necessary to _____ ?"
"How is _____ accomplished?"

The answer to the "why" question appears in function form to the left of the activity inserted. The answer to the "how" question appears to the right of the activity inserted.

Achievement of the cost control function depends on successful achievement of all functions shown to the right of it. The FAST Diagram indicates that one controls cost by controlling scope, not dollars. See Chapter Five, "Function Analysis," for a more detailed description of the FAST Diagram.

Designing to Budget versus Improving Value

The task of holding project costs at the level initially accepted by the owner depends on a team effort, an effort identified by the term *project cost control*. The project cost control team members are the project manager, the cost engineer, the design professionals, and the owner's representative.

Simply achieving the budget does not mean, however, that optimum value is achieved. VE is a technique directed toward improving value. This can be achieved by providing more building scope (if needed by the owner) for the same budget, the same building scope for a cost below budget, or less building scope (if approved by the owner) for a reduced budget.

Thus, the information needed to control design is the same information needed to improve its value. Basic design parameters and quality levels should have been established during budgeting. If they were not, then the value engineer must determine what they are before beginning his work. These parameters must then be used as guidelines in supporting the ultimate VE recommendations for value improvement. See Chapter Three, Figure 3.16.

Defining Project Scope

For a construction project, scope is defined by words, drawings, and cost figures. To most designers, scope consists merely of the owner's program needs for net square feet of space. If square feet is all that is specified, there is a wide range of opportunity for freedom of choice of everything else in the project. With such maneuvering room, cost will also have a wide variance.

The key to achieving cost control through scope control lies in the definition of scope. The old-fashioned idea of viewing scope as building square feet is not sufficient. Scope control is achieved by identifying essential requirements and generating a baseline document to record them. Such a system requires close

Cost Control FAST Diagram

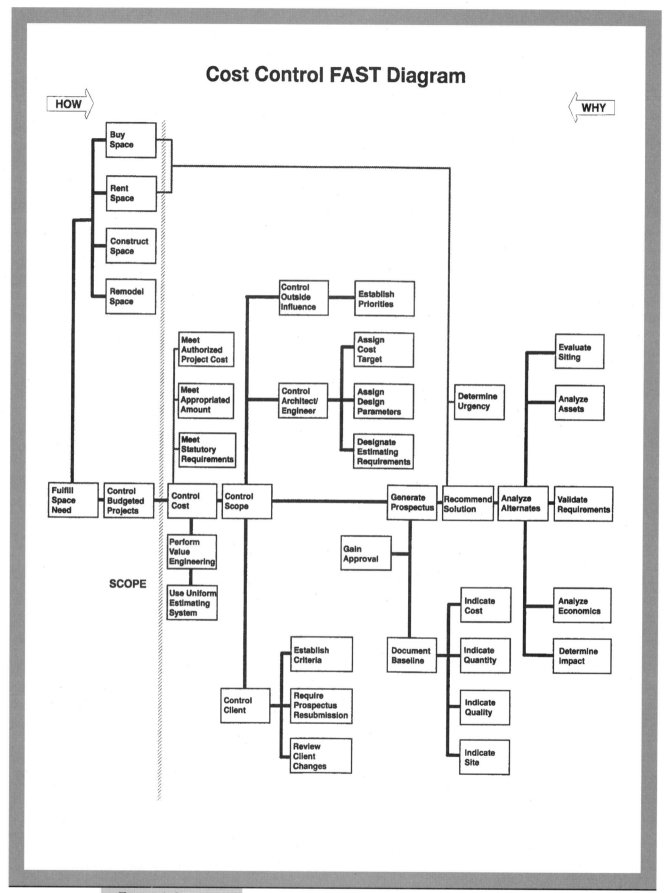

Figure 1.2

monitoring by management, but it does permit verification to take place in order to regulate, thereby achieving the control function.

The scope of a project includes three elements: Project Cost Plan, Project Management Plan (schedule), and Design Basis, as shown in Figure 1.3, "Elements of a Project." Each of these represents "values" thought to be desired by the owner.

Key Scope Drivers

Seven broad areas, when established, are key in determining the project cost for any type of facility. These are as follows.

Functional Areas

The net square feet of each space to be provided in the project should be listed by type. The sum of all this space should represent the owner's requirements for the facility. Knowledge of these quantities of space facilitates the budgeting of equipment, finishes, and various system quantities (such as for power, lighting, heating, air conditioning, plumbing and ventilation) for each space type.

Occupancy

Many features of a facility depend on the number of occupants who will use it, as well as the operating profile of the facility. The following information should be known:

- Number of permanent employees
- Number of part-time employees
- Number of visitors
- Operating hours
- Number of shifts
- Number of employees per shift

This data influences the necessary amounts of plumbing; circulation for stairwells and exits; elevatoring; parking to meet local zoning; and support space such as lunchrooms, auditoriums, and so on.

The type of functional space planned for a facility will also determine the number of visitors it will draw. For example, space to accommodate tour groups, shopping, theater, training, and large conference facilities can increase building system requirements at a higher budget than if they were not provided.

Configuration

Configuration data does not refer to the process of designing the building. It does mean indicating the number of floors, height, perimeter, and volume.

Design Parameters

Once a program and configuration are established, one can estimate the design parameters for the major systems of a process facility or building. The parameter quantity for each system depends on the criteria used or assumed.

Generally, four major systems depend on engineering calculations based on design criteria. These are the structural, mechanical, plumbing, and electrical systems.

Special Systems

Special systems involve the identification and quantification of all special systems and features to be provided, uninterruptible power supply, emergency power, generation, and communications systems. Normally, the decision to include them is a simple "yes-no" decision by the owner.

Geographical Location

Knowledge of the geographical location provides essential data for use in developing project scope. It provides structural criteria (seismic and wind loading) and mechanical criteria (outside winter and summer design temperatures).

Elements of a Project

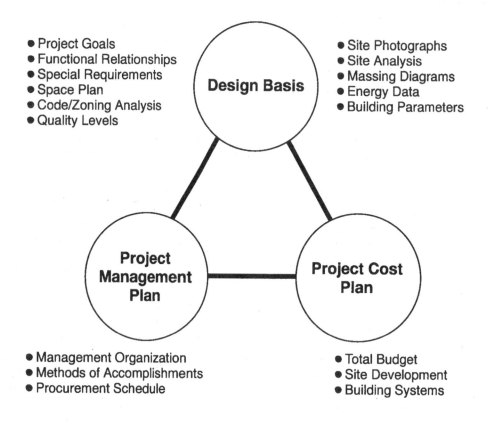

- Project Goals
- Functional Relationships
- Special Requirements
- Space Plan
- Code/Zoning Analysis
- Quality Levels

Design Basis

- Site Photographs
- Site Analysis
- Massing Diagrams
- Energy Data
- Building Parameters

Project Management Plan

Project Cost Plan

- Management Organization
- Methods of Accomplishments
- Procurement Schedule

- Total Budget
- Site Development
- Building Systems

Figure 1.3

Geographical information is also important for determining necessary index adjustments to labor, material, and equipment costs. Geological data is also necessary for basic drainage and foundation information.

System costs known for one location can be indexed to another location and, if the location is remote, budget elements can be added for transportation of materials and labor per diem.

Schedule

Key milestone dates must be fixed or assumed to provide the scheduling data for a controllable budget.

Parameters and Parameter Cost

Parameters are good indicators of worth for the value engineer. However, the term *parameter cost* is often misunderstood and misused. A parameter is an arbitrary constant whose values characterize an element of a system.

The most common way to estimate a new building is by the cost per square foot. This classical parameter is really not a parameter at all. Cost is not constant; it does not vary in a consistently predictable pattern; it does not characterize any particular system.

The major problem with using costs per square foot as a parameter to determine function worth is that the cost for that unit of measure is constant for only one class or type of building at a particular time. Retrieval and reapplication of $/GSF data requires extreme care, good judgment, and complete understanding of the separation of classes inherent between differing $/GSF statistics.

The user of $/GSF data must know more about the basis for the data to separate its applications between the buildings inherent in the statistics. For example, knowing the $/GSF for constructing a residence does not help when pricing a ten-story office building. Parameters at the building level are difficult to develop, qualify, quantify, and store for future use. Similarly, $/GSF pricing for systems such as exterior closure, plumbing, mechanical, and electrical systems is not very helpful. However, parameters at the systems level are easier to develop in a meaningful way than is $/GSF.

Generally, parameter units of measure can be developed based on some term or characteristic of the system to be priced. Figure 1.4, "Units of Measurement," provides some common system-level parameters used for building construction. Figure 1.5, "Construction Cost Summary," represents a recent parameter-based cost estimate developed for a hospital in Saudi Arabia. A program for aiding the efforts has been developed by Saudi Projacs, a company offering consultant services for project management, value engineering, life cycle costing, and cost control. A parameter budget based on this figure can then be used effectively to control costs. For example, if the budget were based on 1,200 fixtures for plumbing and the subsequent estimate indicated 1,676 fixture units, one could assume that either the budget was in error or too many fixtures were specified.

Related Ratios

Parameter measurements result in the development of quantities associated with each system. These quantities can vary widely depending on the efficiency of design. System quantities can often be increased or decreased without affecting basic system function. For example, a pencil can be long or short, or you can buy one dozen or two dozen at a time. Over time, related ratios for system quantities have been developed that provide a value standard to judge parameter quantity.

Units of Measurement

System	Unit Measure	Definition
01 Foundations		
011 Standard Foundation	FPA	Footprint Area (square feet)
	KIP	1,000 pounds
02 Substructure		
021 Slab on Grade	SFSA	Square Foot of Surface Area
022 Basement Excavation	CY	Cubic Yard
023 Basement Walls	SFSA	Square Foot of Surface Area
03 Superstructure		
031 Floor Construction	SFA	Supported Floor Area (square feet)
032 Roof Construction	SRA	Supported Roof Area (square feet)
033 Stair Construction	LFR	Lineal Feet of Riser
	FLT	Flight
04 Exterior Closure		
041 Exterior Walls	XWA	Exterior Wall Area (square feet)
042 Exterior Doors & Windows	XDA	Exterior Door/Window Area (square feet)
05 Roofing	SQ	Square (100 square feet)
06 Interior Construction		
061 Partitions	PSF	Partition Square Feet
062 Interior Finishes	SFSA	Square Foot of Surface Area
	GSF	Gross Square Feet
07 Conveying Systems	LO	Landing Openings
08 Mechanical		
081 Plumbing	FU	Fixture Unit
082 HVAC	TONS	One Ton = 12,000 BTUH
	MBH	1,000 BTUH (heating system measure)
083 Fire Protection	HEAD	Number of Sprinkler Heads
	STA	Stations (for standpipe systems)
09 Electrical		
091 Service and Distribution	AMP	Amperes of Connected Load
092 Power & Lighting	NSF	Net Square Feet
10 General Conditions & Profit	PCT	Percent
11 Equipment	EA	Each
12 Site Work		
121 Site Preparation	ACRE	Acre
122 Site Improvement	SY	Square Yard
	SF	Square Foot
123 Site Utilities	LF	Lineal Foot

Figure 1.4

Construction Cost Summary
General Hospital in Saudi Arabia
180 Bed Hospital and Supporting Facilities: 33,007 Sq. M.

Nov-96

DIV. NO.	SYSTEM	Total Cost Per System		Subsystem	UOM-Unit of Measure	Quant.	Total Cost Per UOM	Total Cost $ US	Cost Per Sq. M
	DEMOLITION			Demolition	GSM				
01	FOUNDATION	1,701,845	011	Standard Foundations	MPA	3,548	51	179,765	5.45
			012	Special Foundations	MPA	6,342	240	1,522,080	46.11
02	SUB STRUCTURE	960,557	021	Slab on Grade	MPA	3,548	39	137,357	4.16
			022	Basement Excavation	BCM	43,500	13	580,000	17.57
			023	Basement Walls	BWA	2,400	101	243,200	7.37
03	SUPER STRUCTURE	3,129,387	031	Floor Construction	UFA	31,482	93	2,938,320	89.02
			032	Roof Construction	MS	770	173	133,467	4.04
			033	Stair Construction	FLT	54	1,067	57,600	1.75
04	EXTERIOR CLOSURE	1,816,320	041	Exterior Walls	XWA	9,160	160	1,465,600	44.40
			042	Exterior Doors & Windows	XDA	2,192	160	350,720	10.63
05	ROOFING	408,787	05	Roofing	MS	9,890	41	408,787	12.38
06	INTERIOR CONSTRUCTION	7,882,597	061	Partitions	PSM	47,530	64	3,038,240	92.05
			062	Interior Finishes	TFA	149,600	24	3,577,333	108.38
			063	Specialties	GSM	31,938	40	1,267,024	38.39
07	CONVEYING SYSTEM	1,123,200	071	Elevators	LO	39	28,800	1,123,200	34.03
			072	Escalators & Others	LS				
08	MECHANICAL	8,526,653	081	Plumbing	FXT	1,676	1,328	2,225,867	67.44
			082	HVAC	TON	1,725	2,647	4,566,667	138.35
			083	Fire Protection	AP	31,610	25	800,787	24.26
			084	Special Mechanical Systems	LS	1	933,333	933,333	28.28
09	ELECTRICAL	7,262,112	091	Service & Distribution	KVA	4,070	212	862,667	26.14
			092	Emergency Power & UPS	KVA	8,800	238	2,093,333	63.42
			093	Lighting & Power	GSM	32,252	40	1,292,779	39.17
			094	Special Electrical Systems	LS	3	1,004,444	3,013,333	91.29
10	GEN. CONDITIONS & PROFIT	10,096,692	101	Site Overhead	MOS				
			102	Head Office Overhead & Profit	PCT	20%	50,483,459	10,096,692	305.90
11	EQUIPMENT	17,672,000	111	Fixed Equipment	LS	1	1,938,667	1,938,667	58.74
			112	Furnishings	LS				
			113	Special Construction	LS	1	15,733,333	15,733,333	476.67
12	SITE WORK	520,000	121	Site Preparation	MS				
			122	Site Improvements	MS				
			123	Site Utilities	MS				
			124	Off-Site Work	LS	1	520,000	520,000	15.75

Cost Including Office Overhead & Profit	61,100,150	1851.13
Escalation 13.00%	7,943,020	
Total Estimated Construction Cost	**69,043,170**	**2,092**

Abbreviations

AP	Area Protected	PSM	Partition Square Meter	LM	Linear Meter
BCM	Basement Cubic Meter	TFA	Total Finishes Area	LO	Landing Opening
BWA	Basement Wall Area	TON	12,000 Btuh	LS	Lump Sum
FLT	Flight	UFA	Upper Floor Area	MOS	Months
FXT	Fixture Count	XDA	Exterior Doors & Window Area	MPA	Meter Print Area
GSM	Gross Square Meter	XWA	Exterior Wall Area	MS	Meter Square
KW	Kilowatts Connected			PCT	Percent

Figure 1.5

Figures 1.6 through 1.12 are tables of various related ratios that can be used in making initial judgments of system worth regarding designed quantities. Also included are Figure 1.13, "Total Energy Budget Levels," and Figure 1.14, "Conveying System Quantities."

Conclusion

During the initial VE application from 1964 to 1965 at the Naval Facilities Engineering Command in Washington, D.C., the major problem encountered was the lack of realistic cost estimates broken into a useful format. As a result, considerable energies were expended working with the cost groups to refine procedures for estimating. The same problem occurs today in trying to set up VE programs, for example, for municipalities in the U.S. and government agencies overseas. This chapter illustrates some key ingredients of project cost control that enables a complementary cross-feed to the VE program. They have been used and work well.

References

1. GSA Handbook, *Value Management*, PBS P8000.1A.

2. G.M. Hollander, "Ingredients for Accurate Construction Cost Estimating," *Actual Specifying Engineer*, June 26, 1974.

3. R.S. Means Company, Inc., *Means Assemblies Cost Data*, 1997.

Building Perimeter per Linear Foot

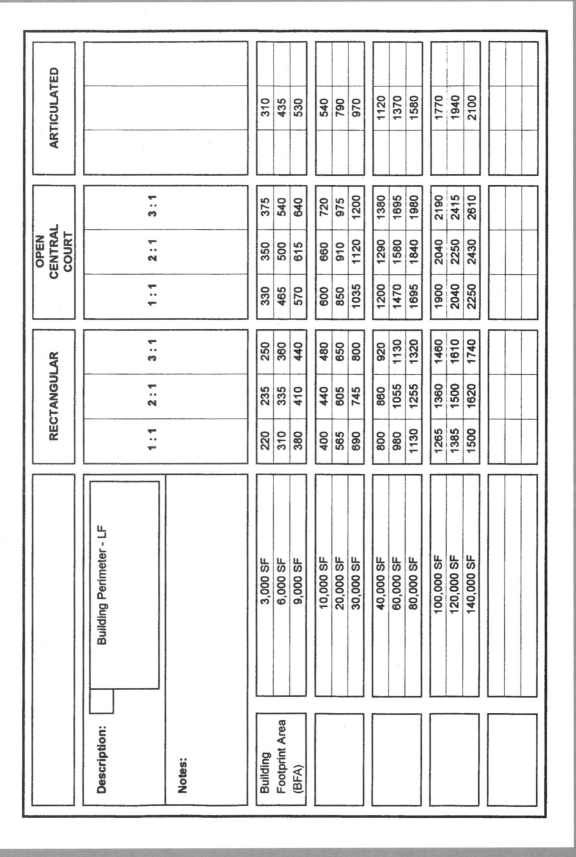

Description:	RECTANGULAR			OPEN CENTRAL COURT			ARTICULATED
Building Perimeter - LF	1:1	2:1	3:1	1:1	2:1	3:1	
Notes:							
Building Footprint Area (BFA)							
3,000 SF	220	235	250	330	350	375	310
6,000 SF	310	335	360	465	500	540	435
9,000 SF	380	410	440	570	615	640	530
10,000 SF	400	440	480	600	660	720	540
20,000 SF	565	605	650	850	910	975	790
30,000 SF	690	745	800	1035	1120	1200	970
40,000 SF	800	860	920	1200	1290	1380	1120
60,000 SF	980	1055	1130	1470	1580	1695	1370
80,000 SF	1130	1255	1320	1695	1840	1980	1580
100,000 SF	1265	1360	1460	1900	2040	2190	1770
120,000 SF	1385	1500	1610	2040	2250	2415	1940
140,000 SF	1500	1620	1740	2250	2430	2610	2100

Figure 1.6

Configuration Factor–Space

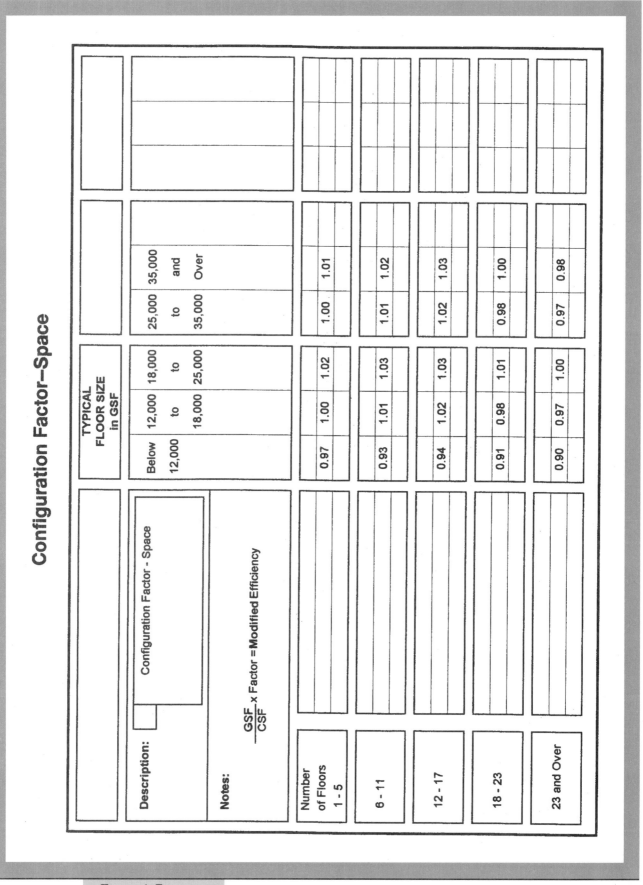

Description: Configuration Factor - Space

Notes:

$$\frac{GSF}{CSF} \times Factor = Modified\ Efficiency$$

Number of Floors	TYPICAL FLOOR SIZE in GSF			
	Below 12,000	12,000 to 18,000	18,000 to 25,000	25,000 to 35,000	35,000 and Over
1 - 5	0.97	1.00	1.02	1.00	1.01
6 - 11	0.93	1.01	1.03	1.01	1.02
12 - 17	0.94	1.02	1.03	1.02	1.03
18 - 23	0.91	0.98	1.01	0.98	1.00
23 and Over	0.90	0.97	1.00	0.97	0.98

Figure 1.7

Space Efficiency Factors

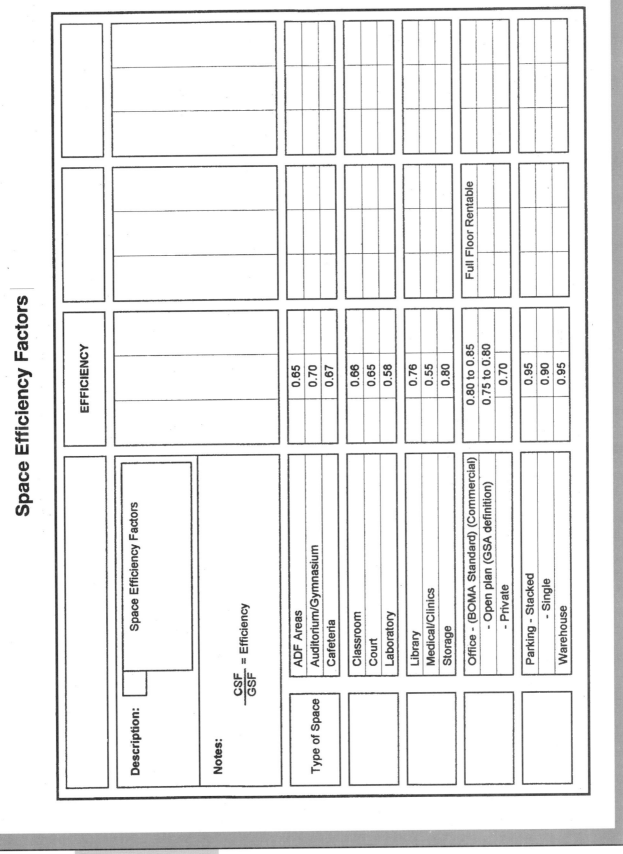

Description: Space Efficiency Factors

$$\frac{CSF}{GSF} = \text{Efficiency}$$

Notes:

Type of Space	EFFICIENCY
ADF Areas	
Auditorium/Gymnasium	0.65
Cafeteria	0.70
	0.67
Classroom	0.66
Court	0.65
Laboratory	0.58
Library	0.76
Medical/Clinics	0.55
Storage	0.80
Office - (BOMA Standard) (Commercial)	0.80 to 0.85
- Open plan (GSA definition)	0.75 to 0.80
- Private	0.70
Full Floor Rentable	
Parking - Stacked	0.95
- Single	0.90
Warehouse	0.95

Figure 1.8

QUANTITIES

Description: 01 | Whole Bay Working Loads — KIPS/Floor/Bay

Notes: Add 10% per floor for column load.

FLOOR SYSTEM TYPE — LL Range Recommended

Live Loads	Bay Size	Waffle Slab 50-200 psf LL	Joist Slab 200 psf LL	Joist Slab 50 psf LL	Flat Slab 150 psf LL	Flat Slab 50 psf LL	2-way Slab 200 psf LL	2-way Slab 100 psf LL	1-way Slab 200 psf LL	1-way Slab 50 psf LL
50 psf	20 x 25	113	118	108	138	120	120	113	132	98
	30 x 35	270	285	250	335	320	-	-	-	-
	35 x 40	389	439	384	-	-	-	-	-	-
80 psf	20 x 25	138	143	-	163	-	153	138	138	-
	30 x 35	321	336	-	386	-	-	-	-	-
	35 x 40	461	511	-	-	-	-	-	-	-
100 psf	20 x 25	155	160	-	180	-	170	155	155	-
	30 x 35	355	370	-	420	-	-	-	-	-
	35 x 40	508	558	-	-	-	-	-	-	-
125 psf	20 x 25	176	101	-	201	-	191	-	176	-
	30 x 35	397	412	-	462	-	-	-	-	-
	35 x 40	567	627	-	-	-	-	-	-	-
200 psf	20 x 25	198	203	-	-	-	213	-	198	-
	30 x 35	440	455	-	-	-	-	-	-	-
	35 x 40	627	677	-	-	-	-	-	-	-

Figure 1.9

Plumbing Fixture Units

Description: 081 | Plumbing Fixture Units — FU/Floor or Area

Notes: Add private toilets as necessary.

			FLOOR SIZE - OSF							
			0 - 1,000	5,000	10,000	15,000	20,000	25,000	30,000	40,000	50,000
Office Space	Commercial	160 OSF/Person	5	7	10	12	16	20	24	28	32
	Federal	100 OSF/Person	6	9	13	16	20	25	30	34	42
Other Space	District Courthouse	(per each)	15	-	-	-	-	-	-	-	-
	Auditorium	(per each)	5	15	30	-	-	-	-	-	-
	Support Space	(per each)	2	2	2	3	4	5	6	8	10
	Warehouse		6	6	6	6	6	6	6	6	6
	Parking - Floor Drainage		1	1	2	3	4	5	6	8	10
Rough-in	Cafeteria		10	20	-	20	25	30	35	40	45
	Co-operative Use		5	10	15	20	25	30	35	40	45
Roof Drainage	Metal Surface	2,500 SF/FU	2	3	4	6	8	10	12	16	20
	Built-up Surface	3,000 SF/FU	2	2	3	5	7	8	10	13	17

Figure 1.10

HVAC–Cooling

QUANTITIES

Description: | 082 | Cooling | GSF/Ton

Notes: - Based on 78°F inside temperature energy efficient

$$\text{Tons} = \frac{\text{GSF}}{\text{GSF/Ton}}$$

By Region		Open Space	Closed Office	ADP	Cafeteria	Conference	Auditorium	Court	Co-op Use	Support Space
Boston	1	594	518	92	324	232	117	173	405	648
New York	2	600	523	93	327	234	118	174	409	654
Philadelphia	3	578	504	89	315	224	115	168	394	670
Atlanta	4	567	494	88	309	221	111	165	386	610
Chicago	5	583	509	90	318	228	114	170	398	634
Kansas City	6	545	475	84	297	213	107	158	371	594
Forth Worth	7	528	461	82	288	204	104	154	360	576
Denver	8	572	499	88	312	224	112	173	390	624
San Francisco	9	638	557	99	348	249	125	186	435	696
Seattle	10	664	562	99	351	252	126	187	439	702
Washington, DC	NCR	550	480	85	300	215	108	160	375	600
Anchorage	Alaska	770	672	119	420	301	151	224	525	640
Saudi Arabia		392	342	61	214	153	77	114	267	427
(Now in Energy Conservation)										

Figure 1.11

HVAC–Heating

QUANTITIES

Description: | 082 | Heating BTU

Notes:
- Based on 68° F inside temperature energy efficient
- For non-energy efficient, multiply by 1.86
- 1MBH = 1,000 BTU

By Region		Up to 500,000	500,000 - 1,000,000	1,000,000 - 3,000,000	3,000,000 - 7,000,000	7,000,000 - 10,000,000	Over 10,000,000
Boston	1	0.69	0.56	0.40	0.33	0.31	0.29
New York	2	0.67	0.33	0.39	0.32	0.30	0.28
Philadelphia	3	0.63	0.30	0.37	0.30	0.28	0.26
Atlanta	4	0.56	0.44	0.32	0.27	0.25	0.23
Chicago	5	0.76	0.40	0.44	0.36	0.34	0.32
Kansas City	6	0.73	0.58	0.43	0.33	0.33	0.31
Forth Worth	7	0.52	0.41	0.30	0.23	0.23	0.21
Denver	8	0.78	0.62	0.46	0.37	0.33	0.33
San Francisco	9	0.34	0.27	0.20	0.16	0.13	0.14
Seattle	10	0.63	0.50	0.37	0.30	0.28	0.26
Washington, DC	NCR	0.59	0.47	0.34	0.26	0.26	0.24
Anchorage	Alaska	1.04	0.82	0.60	0.50	0.47	0.43

(Building Volume Above Grade Cubic Feet)

Figure 1.12

Total Energy Budget Levels
Commercial & Residential Facilities
(in MBTU/SF/Year)

State	SMSA	Clinic	Community Center	Gymnasium	Hospital	Hotel, Motel	Multifamily - High Rise	Multifamily - Low Rise	Nursing Home	Office Large	Office Small	School Elementary	School Secondary	Shopping Center	Store	Theater/Auditorium	Warehouse
Arizona	Phoenix	146	133	152	406	196	131	136	192	134	119	100	137	212	171	168	49
California	Los Angeles	112	101	115	364	157	103	103	151	106	91	74	106	171	132	126	42
	San Francisco	108	92	109	353	150	103	94	143	101	87	76	103	165	125	119	51
Colorado	Denver	122	98	123	338	162	119	100	156	109	100	97	118	178	137	135	71
D.C.	Washington	127	107	129	353	169	120	109	164	115	104	96	121	185	144	142	63
Florida	Miami	152	142	161	406	203	133	147	201	140	125	103	141	219	179	178	41
Georgia	Atlanta	122	106	125	353	165	114	108	160	112	100	88	116	180	141	138	53
Illinois	Chicago	127	102	129	338	167	124	103	161	113	104	103	123	183	142	141	75
Louisiana	New Orleans	144	129	149	406	194	130	133	189	132	118	100	135	210	168	164	52
Massachusetts	Boston	125	101	126	338	165	121	102	159	111	102	99	121	181	140	139	72
Michigan	Detroit	129	103	130	338	168	126	104	163	114	106	105	125	185	143	143	77
Minnesota	Minneapolis	142	109	144	335	180	140	110	175	123	117	122	138	198	155	157	93
Missouri	Kansas City	133	110	136	353	175	127	112	162	119	109	104	128	191	150	149	70
Montana	Great Falls	131	102	132	335	170	129	102	163	115	107	110	127	186	144	144	85
New York	New York	126	105	128	353	168	120	107	162	114	103	96	121	184	143	141	66
Oklahoma	Oklahoma City	129	110	132	353	172	121	112	167	117	106	97	123	187	147	146	61
Pennsylvania	Philadelphia	131	107	133	353	173	126	109	160	117	107	102	126	189	147	146	71
So. Carolina	Charleston	124	110	128	358	168	114	113	163	114	102	88	118	183	144	141	49
Tennessee	Memphis	126	109	129	353	169	117	111	164	115	103	92	120	184	145	142	56
Texas	Dallas	131	116	136	358	175	119	119	171	120	107	94	124	190	152	150	50
	Houston	145	130	150	406	195	130	134	190	133	118	100	136	211	169	166	51
Washington	Seattle	119	96	119	353	160	116	97	153	107	96	91	115	176	134	130	69

Note: Figures include design energy requirements for heating, cooling, domestic hot water, fans, exhaust fans, heating and cooling auxiliaries, elevators, escalators and lighting.

Note: Space is reserved in this table for restaurants and industrial buildings.

*Federal Register Vol. 44. No. 230 Wednesday, November 28, 1979: Proposed Rules

Figure 1.13

Conveying System Quantities

Passenger Elevator

High Level of Service: 1 Elevator per 500 people
Fair Level of Service: 1 Elevator per 750 people

General Formula:

$$N = \frac{P \times f \times T}{300 \times E}$$

Where:
N = Number of Elevators
P = Design Population
f = Peak factor
> f = 14.5% of building population when
> > all occupants start work at staggered time.

> f = 16.5% of building population when
> > all occupants start work at same time.

T = Round trip time (seconds) on morning peak
E = Normal number of persons per car at peak:

$$E = \frac{0.8 \times C}{150}$$

C = Car capacity in pounds

Freight Elevator

1 per 75,000 net square feet of space, or
1 for every 3 passenger elevators

Escalator

Used to carry 600 people or more between floors
Capacity = 5,000 to 8,000 people per hour

Electrical System Requirements

Energy conservation design standards of GSA for office space
limits the installation of lighting and power to 7 watts per
square foot, broken down as follows:

Lighting	2.0
Power	1.0
HVAC	2.0
Elevators	1.0
Spare	1.0

Figure 1.14

Chapter Two

The Capitalized Income Approach to Project Budgeting (CIAPB)

The private sector has used the **capitalized income approach to project budgeting (CIAPB)** for many years as a building investment analysis technique to evaluate the economics of constructing property for owning and/or rental purposes. The value engineer's understanding of CIAPB can result in an overall indicator of the required functions and the worth of a project.

CIAPB Objectives

The value engineer can use the CIAPB to achieve several objectives:

- Identify and consciously reaffirm or waive specific requirements that exceed the value provided by equivalent or alternate income sources.
- Propose realistic, lower attainable budgets for provision of space for a specific project.
- Early in the project cycle, establish the financial relationship between income and costs for each proposed capital expenditure.
- Provide a performance indicator for cost control early in the project cycle to alert management to the need for value improvement.
- Facilitate treatment of each building, and/or each income-producing element, as an individual cost center.

If the designer has a "costing out design" rather than a "design to cost" philosophy, the owner should be made aware of the differences in cost when compared with the owner's attainable rental income in the marketplace. Otherwise, the owner will be unaware of the consequences of a financially unsound project. If the owner wants to achieve a certain return on investment (ROI) for his partners or himself, then cost control and value engineering (VE) to prevent cost overruns is a sound approach.

Measuring Property Value

Real estate developers use three separate techniques for measuring property value. These are the cost, market, and income methods. Each method may serve as an independent guide to an estimation of property value, or as in the case of a developer, as an indicator of how much to spend in constructing or improving a piece of property.

Cost Approach

The cost approach (or replacement method) measures property value with an estimate of the dollar outlay necessary to replace the land and building with improvements or equivalent utility under current conditions. Costs are generally arrived at by market comparison, using historical cost experience of recently completed buildings of the class, style, and quality level desired, considering depreciation.

Market Approach

Using the market approach to property value, price data are gathered from recent transactions in which similar properties have been sold. These properties must be comparable in condition and location to the proposed property.

Income Approach

The income technique to measuring property value centers around the thesis that "value is the present worth of future rights to income." This approach requires the owner or his representative to determine the revenues that may reasonably be anticipated during the estimated economic life of the property. The gross income is reduced to net income and then capitalized (discounted) at a market rate of interest, including recapture (capitalization rate), which reflects the quantity, certainty, and quality of the anticipated income stream. This approach is represented by the following generic equation:

$$\text{project value} = \frac{\text{net income}}{\text{capitalization rate}}$$

The CIAPB process is based on the income approach to determine project value. Thus the generic equation to determine estimated total program costs (ETPC) for budgeting purposes is:

$$\text{ETPC} = \frac{\text{net income}}{\text{capitalization rate}}$$

The Meaning of Capitalization

The capitalization rate—also known as the going rate of interest, cost of money, or market rate of interest (plus recapture provisions)—constitutes a ratio of income to value at which property is exchanging in the market. This ratio, or rate of capitalization, is generally accepted as a guide in the conversion of anticipated income into a sum of present value, especially when the property is acquired for income or investment.

Here is an example of capitalization in its simplest form: Suppose a rich uncle left you a sum of money in trust, but he did not tell you how much. However, every year you receive a check from the bank. This year's check is for $10,000. You are curious to know how much money is left for you in the trust fund. You call the bank, and they tell you they are paying an interest rate of 8%. Now you have all the information you need to capitalize the net income received into a present value for the trust fund:

$$\frac{\$10,000 \text{ (net income)}}{.08 \text{ (rate paid)}} = \$125,000 \text{ (trust)}$$

For real estate transactions, however, determining the capitalization rate is a bit more complex.

Rate of Interest

The rate of interest consists of four factors:

- Pure interest—interest that can be secured on government bonds.
- Rate of management—the rate necessary to process and administer the investment.
- Rate for nonliquidity—the rate necessary to compensate for relative inability to "cash in" the investment.
- Rate of risk.

The risk rate varies with the type of investment. A city-guaranteed mortgage is relatively risk free. However, noninsured mortgages are high risk, and may mean losses for the investor or lender. Such losses are reflected in the applicable rate of interest.

The capitalization rate could be indicated in tabular form as follows:

Pure interest	9.00%
Management	.50%
Nonliquidity	1.00%
Risk	1.00%
Recapture (40 years)	2.50%
Suggested capitalization rate	14.00%

Such a "built-up" rate, however, does not accurately reflect the motivations, cost benefits, or other considerations of real property investors.

Modified Band Rates

The next generation of capitalization theory developed the Modified Band of Investment Theory based on more realistic assumptions:

Ratio of equity × equity dividend rate (ROR) + Ratio of loan × amortization constant (CRF) = Weighted capitalization rate

This formula simply states that most properties are heavily mortgaged, and the investor wants coverage of the mortgage amortization plus an adequate return on his or her equity investment. When placed into the generic formula, the following is derived:

$$\text{ETPC} = \frac{\text{net income}}{(1-K)\,(\text{ROR}) + K\,(\text{CRF})}$$

Where:

K = Ratio of mortgage to total project cost

ROR = Rate of return on equity

CRF = Capital recovery factor; amount to retire a one dollar mortgage with interest over a specified term at a constant annual payment.

Third- and fourth-generation capitalization techniques have continued to expand this basic formula to account for such attributes as equity build-up, possible property appreciation over an ownership period, and other considerations. The use of these advanced techniques is encouraged with expert advice from an appraiser who is knowledgeable about the property. However, for purposes of gross estimates of value, the basic formula is reliable and does not unduly skew results.

The Capitalization Process

The process of the CIAPB analysis involves three steps:

1. **Obtain Market Data**

    First, research the community where the project is located. Data collection from the market area is essential. Such data would include potential rental rates and other costs near the location where the facility will be constructed. Local banks can provide the area norms for desired rates of return on building projects, available financing terms, interest rates, tax incentives, and other available investment incentives. Finally, the desired rates can be obtained by asking what rates the owner is willing to accept in the analysis.

2. **Compute Net Income**

    Second, reduce estimated potential gross annual income to net annual income. This computation requires subtracting annual fixed expenses and operating expenses from estimated annual gross income. Fixed costs are the expenses necessary to own and manage a property even if it is not occupied, including insurance, taxes, management costs, and reserves for repair and replacement. Operating costs are the expenses incurred when a facility is used, including utilities, custodial, preventative maintenance, security, and so on. A good source of data for expected income and expense for office type space is published by the Building Owners and Managers Association (BOMA).

3. **Determine Maximum Construction Cost**

   Next, capitalize the net income, which indicates the maximum amount of capital that a prudent investor would put into the project. From this, determine the maximum construction cost for the project by subtracting the other project budget centers from the capitalized project value.

An Example Using CIAPB Analysis

Assumptions for this example are as follows:

Gross building area = 315,000 square feet

Site area = 100,000 square feet

Rentable space = 250,000 square feet

Rent = $21.77 per square foot per year

Expenses = $8.36 per square foot per year

Financing = 100% (30 years at 9%)

CRF = .097336

Land cost = $15.00 per square foot

The procedure outlined in items a through f below illustrates the sequence of steps used in applying the process of CIAPB analysis.

a. The gross annual income will be: $250,000 \times \$21.77 = \$5,442,500$

b. Total expenses will be: $250,000 \times \$8.36 = \$2,090,000$

c. Net income will then be: $5,442,500 - 2,090,000 = \$3,352,500$

d. The maximum estimated total program costs (ETPC) will be:

$$\frac{3,352,500}{.097336} = \$34,442,550$$

e. The maximum estimated cost of construction (ECC) will be computed as follows:

ETPC	34,442,550
Estimated site cost (ESC) (land)	− 1,500,000
Estimated design and review cost (EDRC) (7%)	− 2,411,000
Estimated management and inspection cost (EMIC) (4%)	− 1,377,700
Estimated reservation cost (ERC) (6%)	− 2,066,550
Estimated construction cost (ECC)	$ 27,087,300

f. This example provides a construction budget of $86.00/GSF for the building, computed as follows:

$$\frac{27,087,300}{315,000} = \$86.00$$

General Application

The CIAPB analysis can be applied to all forms of construction even when the owner is not in the rental business or actually receiving income. The basis of capitalization can be imputed income using avoided expenditures. For example, if you plan to build a new house, you can base your budget on the unit costs to rent similar homes in the area. Figure 2.1 illustrates various types of imputed income for a wide range of projects.

Imputed Income

Type of Construction	Possible Methods for Computing Income
Public School	Cost per pupil based on payment of private tuition
Wastewater Treatment Plant	Community sewage charge Cost per million gallons
Prison	Cost per prisoner to house elsewhere
Office	Cost per square foot to rent space elsewhere
Court House	Cost per square foot to rent office space and to renovate it for court use
Computer Space	Cost to contract out computer processing
Hotel and Motel	Conference, food service and room income
Cafeteria	Equivalent restaurant expense or loss of employee time to go outside
Auditorium	Equivalent theater income

Figure 2.1

Before spending capital for any project, the value of the budgeted amount can be checked against its economic benefits. The CIAPB determines the worth of the project, which can be reviewed on a cost per square foot basis. The income must produce a budget sufficient to construct the quality desired to justify itself.

The Need for Cost Control

Owners have a critical need for cost control when they have justified a project budget to receive a certain ROI. Figure 2.2 provides the economic summary of a project that was budgeted to provide a ROI of 18.1%.

The figure presents several scenarios to show what would happen if construction and operating cost vary from budgeted costs:

- In the first case, project construction costs rose 10% over what was originally planned. This increase in initial cost reduces the ROI to 12.1%.
- In the second situation, the designed facility operating costs are 10% higher than planned. If this were the case, the ROI would be 13.4%.
- In the third situation, both the construction costs and the operating costs are 10% higher than originally planned. The net result is an ROI of only 9.6%.

In all three cases, the resulting ROI is less than the owner would have accepted during the planning phase and certainly represents a poor ROI for the risk and effort involved. Considering how easily 10% changes can creep into a project, the importance of an effective cost control effort is apparent. The entire financial feasibility of a project can be drastically altered long before anything is in the ground.

- In the final situation, both planned initial cost and ownership cost are reduced by 5%. This result can easily be achieved by monitoring project costs throughout design and applying both VE and LCC techniques. The result is an ROI of 30.2%—**an increase of 66%.**

Conclusion

Typically, owners purchase insurance on their facilities to safeguard against catastrophic losses. VE/LCC efforts would effectively dovetail with the purchase of property insurance and bring owners the knowledge that they are insuring a worthwhile investment. In many instances, actual application of the capitalized income approach to project budgeting and follow-on VE have resulted in doubling of the ROI.

Economic Impacts of Cost Changes
Hypothetical Office Building

	As Planned (Budgeted)	Construction Cost + 10%	Operating Cost + 10%	Construction +10% Operating Cost + 10%	Economic VE-Studies Construction -5% Operation- 5%
Total Construction Cost	34,757,000	38,233,000	34,757,000	38,233,000	33,020,000
Indirect Cost	9,249,000	9,711,000	9,249,000	9,711,000	9,062,000
Land Cost	4,480,000	4,480,000	4,480,000	4,480,000	4,480,000
Total Project Cost	48,486,000	52,424,000	48,486,000	52,424,000	46,562,000
Less Mortgage Loan*	40,583,235	40,583,235	38,384,387	38,384,387	41,686,194
Equity Investment Required	7,902,765	11,840,765	10,101,613	14,039,613	4,875,806
Gross Income	8,850,000	8,850,000	8,850,000	8,850,000	8,850,000
Operating Costs	3,110,000	3,110,000	3,421,000	3,421,000	2,954,000
Net Income	5,740,000	5,740,000	5,429,000	5,429,000	5,896,000
Less Mortgage Payment (Debt Service)	4,305,000	4,305,000	4,072,000	4,072,000	4,422,000
Before Tax Stabilized Cash Flow	1,435,000	1,435,000	1,357,000	1,357,000	1,474,000
Return of Equity Investment(ROI)	18.16%	12.12%	13.43%	9.66%	30.23%

*Loan amount determined by 75% of net income capitalized @ 10% interest over 30 years.

0.75 x $ 5,740,000 x 9.427 (PWA) = $ 40,583,235
0.75 x $ 5,429,000 x 9.427 (PWA) = $ 38,384,387
0.75 x $ 5,896,000 x 9.427 (PWA) = $ 41,686,194

Figure 2.2

Chapter Two   The Capitalized Income Approach to Project Budgeting (CIAPB)

Chapter Three

Preparation of Cost Models

Preparing a cost model from a detailed estimate is a common practice in value engineering (VE) construction work. Costs are the foundation of value analysis. The **cost model** is a tool that assembles and breaks down total facility costs into more functional units that can be quickly analyzed. Experience has proven that the act of preparing the model is more important than actually having the model. Preparing the model forces the preparer to become more knowledgeable about the size, content, and scope of the project; it is an excellent way to document the effort of a prestudy VE review. Preparing a cost model contributes immensely to the "mind setting" and "mind tuning" that Larry Miles, the founder of VE, found so important to value work.[1]

Once a model is prepared, other benefits include:

- Increasing cost visibility, enabling one to see the high cost areas.
- Helping to identify VE potential.
- Providing a baseline reference for use in comparing alternatives.

Making Models

A model is an expression of the distribution of costs (or other resources) associated with a specific project, system, or item. All models generically represent a work breakdown structure in which each part works in relationship with the other parts, or through levels of indenture. These relationships are illustrated in Figure 3.1, "Work Breakdown Structure."

Models for any subject matter can be developed by obtaining cost or other resource information at the first level of indenture, then logically breaking down that information to subsequent levels. Some of the rules for making models are as follows:

- Work from the top down.
- Identify cost centers at each level of indenture.
- Organize the model so items above depend on items listed below.
- Make the total cost of items equal to the sum of each level.

As a further enhancement, the cost model includes two types of costs: the actual/estimated cost and the target costs. The value review team, augmented with cost expertise as required, develops cost breakdowns of each component or project element. Each element is assigned a specific block on the model. The team adjusts the model blocks for each facility to better reflect the appropriate functional areas and estimating techniques. Normally, the team uses available estimating data. However, whenever data is lacking or its validity is suspect, the study input is augmented by a cost validation effort to secure more meaningful costs.

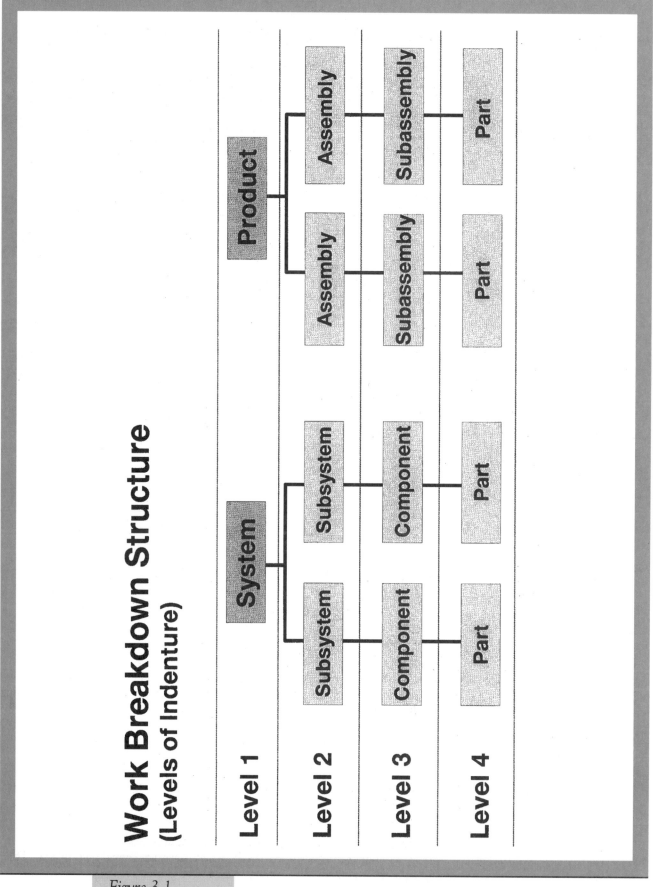

Work Breakdown Structure
(Levels of Indenture)

Figure 3.1

Subsequently, target costs for each project element are developed and listed below the estimated cost. These idealized costs are based on team expertise and a functional analysis of each cost block. The costs represent the minimum cost believed possible for each block, based on team experience with similar elements, cost files on similar facilities, and/or previous VE study results. With a cost model, it is possible to develop a one-page visual analysis of the costs for the total facility. *Note: A general purpose cost model in Excel format is included on the book's diskette.*

Construction Cost Models

The most common work breakdown structure for a construction cost model of a building is based on the UniFormat system. For other types of heavy construction (e.g., wastewater, plants, dams, highways, and airfields), the value engineer must create a special work breakdown structure for the model.

UniFormat for buildings has become a standard in the construction industry because it is based on a building systems level of detail rather than on a trade breakdown, as used by the Construction Specifications Institute (CSI). Building systems can be directly related to one or two basic functions for each system. Also, building systems are adaptable to parameter cost measurements.

The UniFormat standard has resulted in a library of historical experience of the square foot cost of various systems as well as parameter costs. This body of knowledge relates worth (target) to the system functions at the system cost level of detail.

Figures 3.2 through 3.8 demonstrate several cost models for a variety of projects.

Figure 3.2 illustrates a typical UniFormat building systems level cost/worth model for a pretrial service center building. This model indicates that the architectural area has the greatest savings potential.

Figure 3.3 illustrates the same UniFormat level of detail for a manufacturing plant expansion project. Figure 3.3 was prepared using Microsoft Excel computer software. The program totals both cost and worth input at the lower levels of indenture. The cost blocks were developed in collaboration with owner cost personnel using functional analysis concepts. This function-cost-worth approach is essential to the VE process. This model indicates that the HVAC area has the greatest savings potential.

Figure 3.4 is a cost model of a large wastewater treatment facility. In this case, the goal was to isolate functional cost elements, thereby enhancing the team's ability to review function-cost-worth. The cost model was developed using the Function Analysis System Technique (FAST) Diagram concept (see Chapter 5). From the VE study, some $150 million was saved, and several areas of design concerns were isolated.

Figure 3.5 shows a computer-generated cost model of a large city highway network. The model was generated by breaking the project into component parts. The concern was several high-cost areas that were not related to basic function; for example, secondary function ramps DN and CD. The model isolated several major areas of cost savings, some of which involved the impact of political concessions made by municipal officials. The major cost was a special ramp into one neighborhood. Implementation actions were lengthy, with actual savings hard to identify. Some $50 million of initial cost savings were initially implemented. However, several months after the study illustrated in Figure 3.5, a state financial review committee questioned why more of the identified savings were not implemented. As a result, a more intense appraisal—with costs upgraded as a basis for selection and political goals decreased—doubled the savings. (See Case Study Six for an in-depth analysis.)

Figure 3.6 shows a cost model of a large dam. The cost model isolates several secondary function areas as high costs; namely, diversion tunnel and spillway. This model was developed from function analysis data gained from Figure 5.4. Some

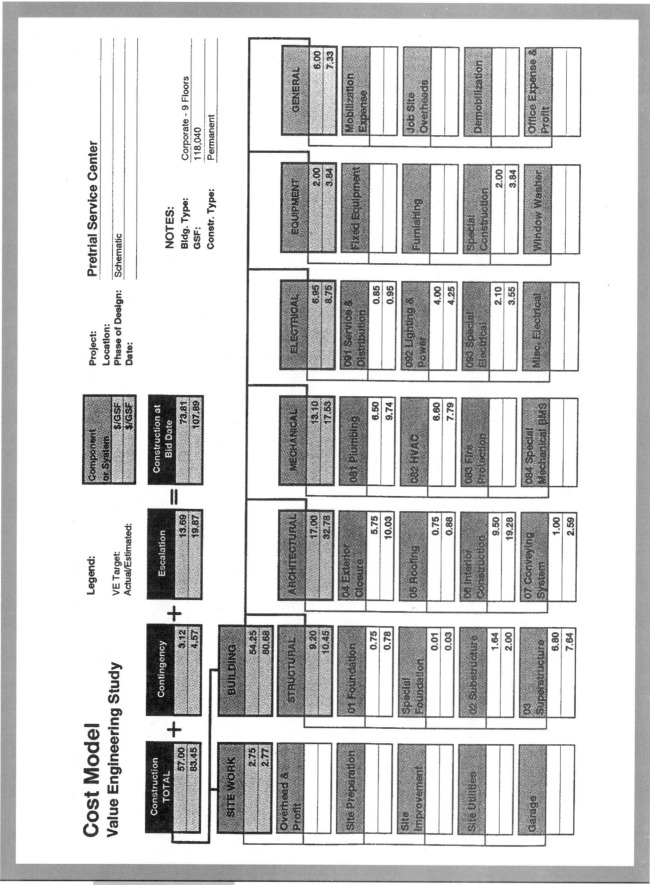

Figure 3.2

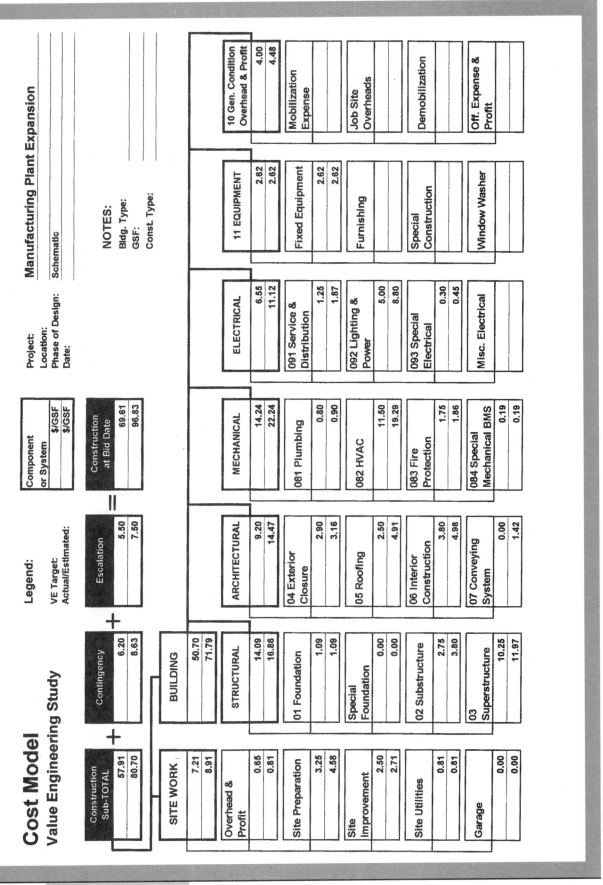

Figure 3.3

Cost Model
Value Engineering Study

Project: Wastewater Treatment Plant
Location:
Phase of Design: Conceptual
Date:

Legend:
VE Target:
Actual/Estimated:

Area: ___ $ (US) / ___ $ (US)

TOTAL COST
1,378,105,000
1,581,172,000

GENERAL & SITEWORK — 93,607,000 / 94,778,000

Item	VE Target	Actual/Estimated
Temp./Const. Facilities	7,500,000	7,500,000
General Requirements	12,080,000	12,080,000
Landscape	5,530,000	5,530,000
Roads and Paving	14,060,000	14,060,000
Demolition and Removal	20,724,000	20,724,000
Earthwork	27,673,000	27,673,000
Miscellaneous Site Work	6,040,000	7,211,000

PROCESS SYSTEM — 663,789,000 / 859,293,000

PUMPING / PRETREAT — 99,769,000 / 152,081,000

Item	VE Target	Actual/Estimated
N. Main Pump Station	12,000,000	18,933,000
Headworks	7,546,000	9,612,000
N. Flow Conduit	10,000,000	14,947,000
Grit Facility	10,000,000	16,627,000
Headworks	29,025,000	53,462,000
S. System Pump Station	31,198,000	38,500,000

PRIMARY TREATMENT — 87,900,000 / 149,058,000

Item	VE Target	Actual/Estimated
Influent Conduit	6,400,000	10,705,000
Primary Clarifiers	81,500,000	133,384,000
Screening and Odor Control	0	4,969,000

SECONDARY TREATMENT — 303,000,000 / 365,596,000

Item	VE Target	Actual/Estimated
Anaerobic Selectors	40,000,000	45,349,000
Aeration Basins	45,000,000	50,570,000
Secondary Clarifiers	190,000,000	227,216,000
Oxygen Gener. Facility	28,000,000	42,361,000

RESIDUALS — 162,120,000 / 162,120,000

Item	VE Target	Actual/Estimated
Gravity Thickener	3,288,000	3,288,000
Sludge Pump Station	2,733,000	2,733,000
Digesters and Storage	104,725,000	104,725,000
Process/Thick. Facility	37,849,000	37,849,000
Tunnels and Galleries	9,443,000	9,443,000
Odor Control Facility	4,082,000	4,082,000

OTHERS — 11,000,000 / 30,438,000

Item	VE Target	Actual/Estimated
Disinfection Basins	4,000,000	10,307,000
Sodium Hypo Tank	0	1,880,000
Sodium Metal Tank	0	1,880,000
Primary Odor Control Facility	6,000,000	12,329,000
Secondary Odor Control Facility	1,000,000	4,082,000

OPERATIONAL SUPPORT FAC — 65,336,000 / 71,728,000

Item	VE Target	Actual/Estimated
Primary Operation Bldg.	13,473,000	13,473,000
Secondary Operation Bldg.	6,850,000	6,850,000
Administration Building	4,349,000	4,349,000
Laboratory Building	4,650,000	5,166,000
Maint. Building & Warehouse	16,500,000	21,079,000
Dry Storage	7,300,000	8,177,000
Vehicle Maint. Building	3,000,000	3,420,000
Plant Water Pump Station	6,464,000	6,464,000
Potable Water Tank	2,750,000	2,750,000

INTERFACE — 555,373,000 / 555,373,000

Item	VE Target	Actual/Estimated
Interisland Tunnel	66,780,000	66,780,000
Temporary Effluent Conduit	9,796,000	9,796,000
Effluent Tunnel	348,607,000	348,607,000
Main Substation & XFMR Yard	5,767,000	5,767,000
Power Plant	42,742,000	42,742,000
Yard Piping	840,000	840,000
Site - Electrical	39,477,000	39,477,000
Utility Corridor	36,364,000	36,364,000
Control and Instrumentation	5,000,000	5,000,000

Figure 3.4

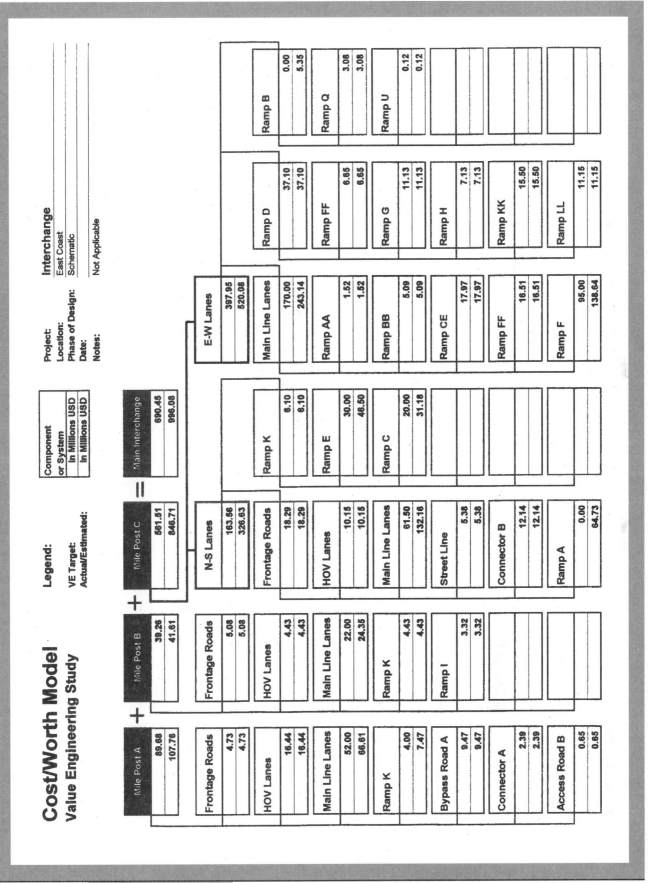

Cost/Worth Model
Value Engineering Study

Figure 3.5

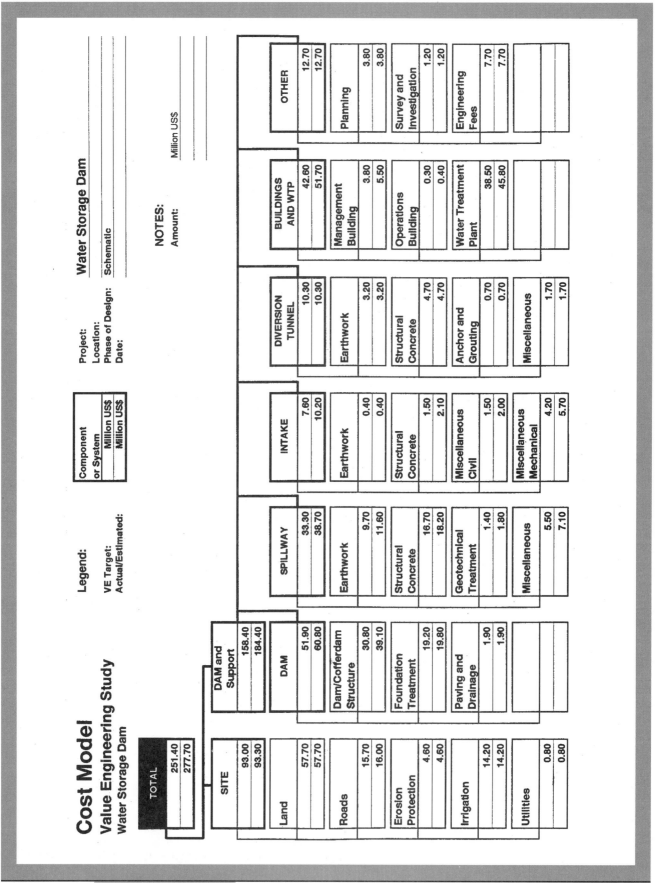

Figure 3.6

$20 million in savings were implemented by the chief engineer, who attended the final presentation.

Figure 3.7 illustrates a cost model of a large offshore oil/gas platform. This model restructures the project estimate into more functional lines using FAST Diagrams of process and layout. The worth targets were established after team review of the project documents and function analysis, using some initial ideas developed by the team. The model isolated high-cost areas: the design, structural, equipment, and piping costs. The jack-up platform is a temporary unit used to house workers and supplies during construction. Actual implemented savings were approximately $30,000,000. The savings were low because the design was over 50% complete, and the study was conducted as part of a training effort.

Figure 3.8 is a cost model of a prototype air separation facility. Once the team realized that a general cost savings appeared feasible, they focused mainly on a revised layout of air compressor, piping, electrical, and instrumentation equipment. Again, this model was developed along functional cost lines by using a FAST Diagram (see Figure 5.7). The savings generated—about $500,000—may not seem significant, but the facility was scheduled to be built in several locations. Thus, the savings were multiplied.

Other Resources

Although cost is the most common, it is not the only resource to which VE applies. Certainly, cost is not the full measure of value. Other resources that represent value to an owner are space, time, utilities, labor, quantity of materials, and aesthetics. The VE process can be as effective if cost is measured in some of the following ways:

- Square feet of space
- Weeks of time
- Kilowatt hours of energy
- Labor-hours
- Risk assessment

In addition, all the parameter measurements of quantity for a facility are resources such as:

- Tons of air conditioning
- MBTU of heating
- Fixture units of plumbing
- Kips of structural load
- kW of connected load

Note: Excel spreadsheets for conceptual estimating are included in the VE tools section of the attached diskette.

Types of Models

When resources other than costs are important, models can be generated to assist in optimizing the impact of these resources on the project. The following are examples of models that address space, energy, life cycle costs, and quality.

Space Model

Preparation of a space model is highly recommended when a VE study is being performed at the programming or conceptual stage of facility design. In the early project phase, all one knows about the project, or all one can measure, is the area of various types of functional space. Often, only lump sum cost data exist that are not really suitable for allocation to function without an extensive effort to generate additional data.

Figure 3.9 illustrates a typical space model. It shows the gross square feet (GSF) of space originally programmed for a new manufacturing plant, and the actual gross area based on a takeoff of areas from delivered design work. In this case, "worth" was established by the owner as the programmed amount of space, and the VE team was asked to identify and isolate the apparent 30% space overrun.

Cost Model
Value Engineering Study

Project: **Offshore OIL-GAS Platform**
Status: SAMPLE DESIGN
Phase of Design: Front End
Date:

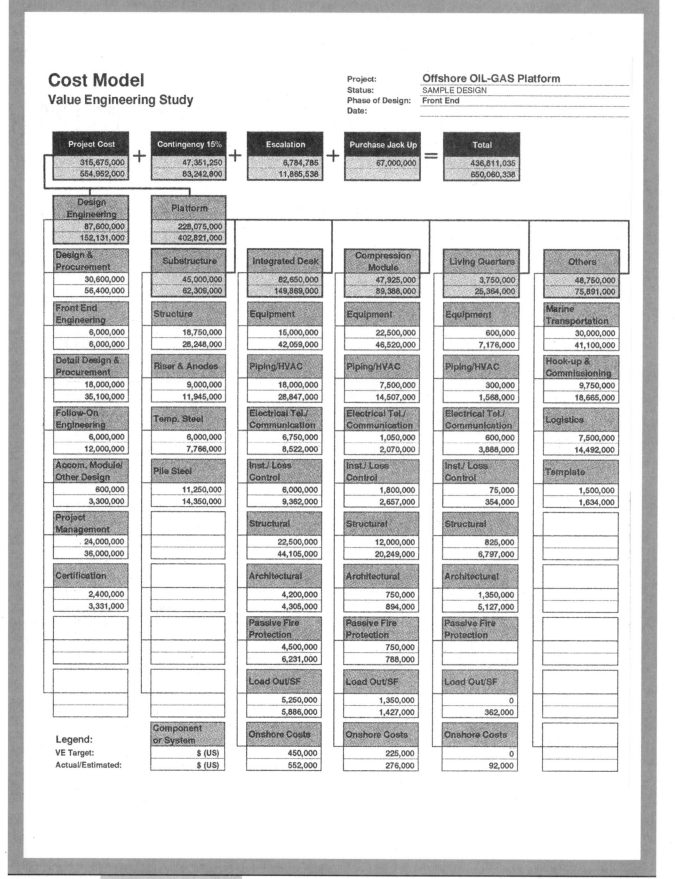

Project Cost		Contingency 15%		Escalation		Purchase Jack Up		Total
315,675,000	+	47,351,250	+	6,784,785	+	67,000,000	=	436,811,035
554,952,000		83,242,800		11,865,538				650,060,338

Design Engineering	Platform
87,600,000	228,075,000
152,131,000	402,821,000

Design & Procurement	Substructure	Integrated Desk	Compression Module	Living Quarters	Others
30,600,000	45,000,000	82,650,000	47,925,000	3,750,000	48,750,000
56,400,000	62,309,000	149,869,000	89,388,000	25,364,000	75,891,000

Front End Engineering	Structure	Equipment	Equipment	Equipment	Marine Transportation
6,000,000	18,750,000	15,000,000	22,500,000	600,000	30,000,000
6,000,000	28,248,000	42,059,000	46,520,000	7,176,000	41,100,000

Detail Design & Procurement	Riser & Anodes	Piping/HVAC	Piping/HVAC	Piping/HVAC	Hook-up & Commissioning
18,000,000	9,000,000	18,000,000	7,500,000	300,000	9,750,000
35,100,000	11,945,000	28,847,000	14,507,000	1,568,000	18,665,000

Follow-On Engineering	Temp. Steel	Electrical Tel./ Communication	Electrical Tel./ Communication	Electrical Tel./ Communication	Logistics
6,000,000	6,000,000	6,750,000	1,050,000	600,000	7,500,000
12,000,000	7,766,000	8,522,000	2,070,000	3,888,000	14,492,000

Accom. Module/ Other Design	Pile Steel	Inst./ Loss Control	Inst./ Loss Control	Inst./ Loss Control	Template
600,000	11,250,000	6,000,000	1,800,000	75,000	1,500,000
3,300,000	14,350,000	9,362,000	2,657,000	354,000	1,634,000

Project Management		Structural	Structural	Structural	
24,000,000		22,500,000	12,000,000	825,000	
36,000,000		44,105,000	20,249,000	6,797,000	

Certification		Architectural	Architectural	Architectural	
2,400,000		4,200,000	750,000	1,350,000	
3,331,000		4,305,000	894,000	5,127,000	

		Passive Fire Protection	Passive Fire Protection	Passive Fire Protection	
		4,500,000	750,000		
		6,231,000	788,000		

		Load Out/SF	Load Out/SF	Load Out/SF	
		5,250,000	1,350,000	0	
		5,886,000	1,427,000	362,000	

Legend:

	Component or System	Onshore Costs	Onshore Costs	Onshore Costs	
VE Target:	$ (US)	450,000	225,000	0	
Actual/Estimated:	$ (US)	552,000	276,000	92,000	

Figure 3.7

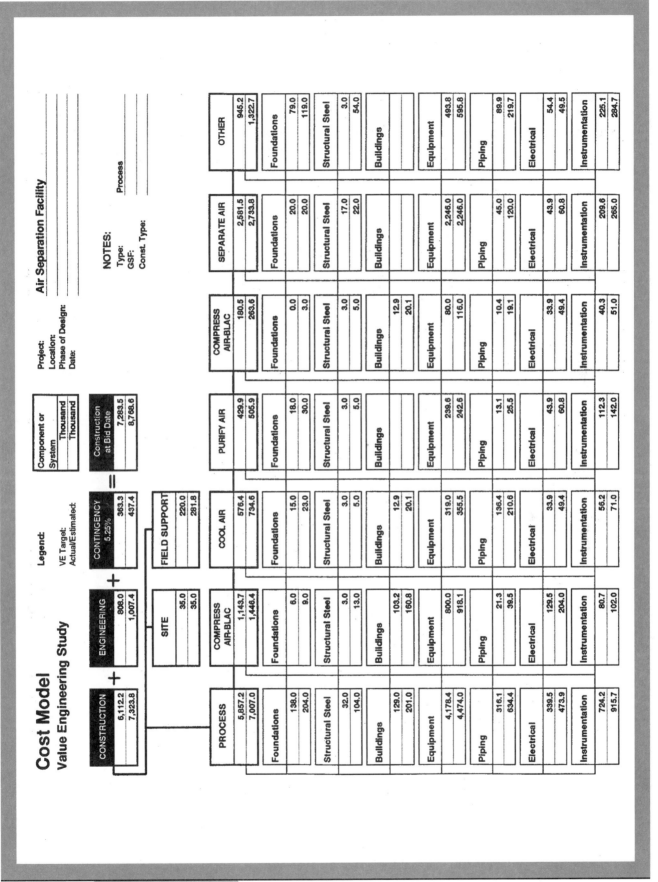

Figure 3.8

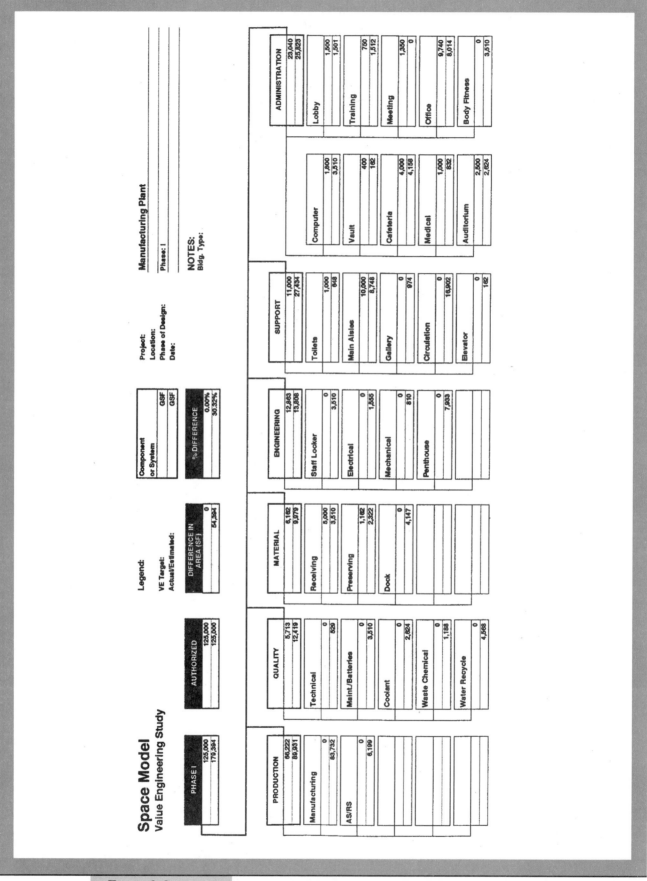

Figure 3.9

Worth of space functions can also be established through historical data, space performance standards, and elimination of secondary function space. For example, space for stairwells is always a secondary function as required by the codes). However, lower floor-to-floor height and/or discreet layout changes would reduce this area.

When function analysis worksheets are completed, cost is typically allocated to each function. At the concept stage of design, this worksheet can be completed using areas of space in the cost and worth role.

Another area of concern that has surfaced over the years is the lack of a standard approach to gross area takeoff. An architect may sometimes be reluctant to indicate to the owner that the owner's space program is being exceeded. When this occurs, there is no recognition of a standard method of space takeoff. When the takeoff method for calculating area is not standardized, confusion often is the result. For standardization, the American Institute of Architects (AIA) method is used. Figure 3.10, "AIA Area Take-off Standards," illustrates the association's approach.

A function analysis of space performed for a new sports stadium is illustrated in Figure 3.11. It was prepared at the concept stage of design, where the resource used was measured in square meters. Worth was taken from the *AIA Graphic Standards* using the Los Angeles Forum (basketball stadium) as a function comparison. The value index can be determined for each function because the units of measurement for cost and worth are the same. In the process of doing the space model, the VE team uncovered several significant areas of confusion between user requirements and designer space interpretation, especially in regard to seating capacity and type of parades. See Figure 5.2 in Chapter Five, "Function Analysis," for a detailed description of the process.

Construction Worth Model

In performing studies, cost improvement targets can be developed by assigning worth to system functions. This normally will account for targeted potential changes to either or both of the following:

- System quantities.
- System characteristics, as represented by the type of system specified and the type of materials used.

What happens if the amount of space can also be changed? Would a 5% reduction in floor area represent a 5% reduction in project cost? Probably not. For example, a 5% reduction in floor area would probably not change the number of elevators in the building. The conveying system component of the cost model would be unchanged.

In addition, merely selecting the high value indices as indications of poorest value from a unit priced cost model might not lead to working on the area with the highest potential magnitude of savings. For example, in Figure 3.3, *Substructure* has a value index (VI) of 1.38, and *Superstructure* has a VI of 1.17. Yet the potential savings per GSF is:

Substructure = $1.05

Superstructure = $1.72

When both cost and space models were developed in the past, they normally stood in isolation from each other. Now the combined effect of both space and system changes must be analyzed.

Energy Model

Another resource that can be modeled is energy. Figure 3.12 illustrates an energy model for a shopping center project based on kilowatt-hours per year (kWh/yr.). One of the features of the energy model is the need to show the operating hours

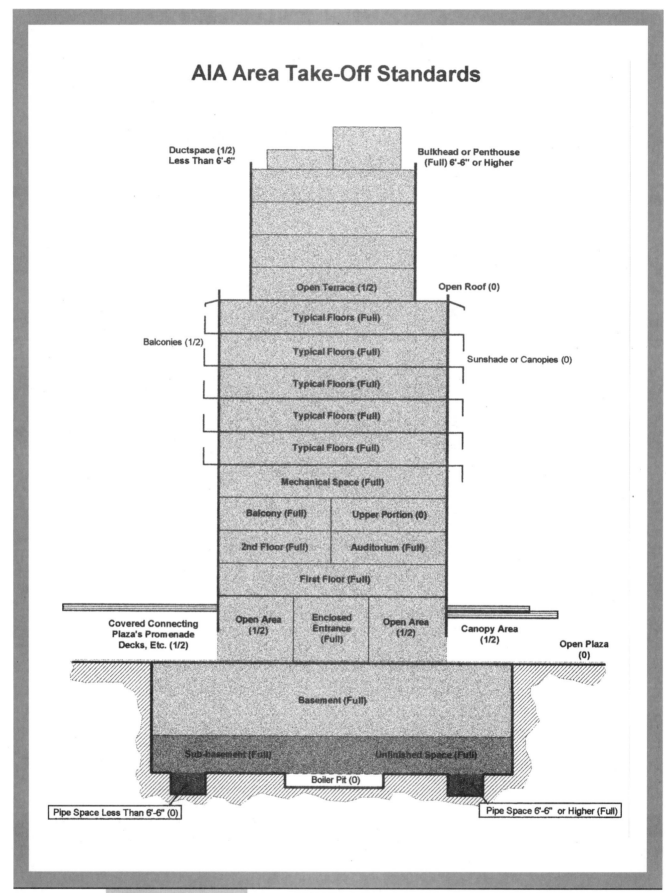

AIA Area Take-Off Standards

Ductspace (1/2) Less Than 6'-6"

Bulkhead or Penthouse (Full) 6'-6" or Higher

Open Terrace (1/2)

Open Roof (0)

Typical Floors (Full)

Balconies (1/2)

Typical Floors (Full)

Sunshade or Canopies (0)

Typical Floors (Full)

Typical Floors (Full)

Typical Floors (Full)

Mechanical Space (Full)

Balcony (Full)

Upper Portion (0)

2nd Floor (Full)

Auditorium (Full)

First Floor (Full)

Covered Connecting Plaza's Promenade Decks, Etc. (1/2)

Open Area (1/2)

Enclosed Entrance (Full)

Open Area (1/2)

Canopy Area (1/2)

Open Plaza (0)

Basement (Full)

Sub-basement (Full)

Unfinished Space (Full)

Boiler Pit (0)

Pipe Space Less Than 6'-6" (0)

Pipe Space 6'-6" or Higher (Full)

Figure 3.10

Function Analysis - Space   Stadium

Component	Function Verb	Noun	Kind	Cost M2	Worth M2	Value Index	Remarks
TEAM SPACE, SIDE A							
Lockers	Store	clothes	B	132	66	2.00	Reduce lockers by 50%
Toilet	Dispose	waste	RS	132	66	2.00	See above
Waiting & Activity	Instruct	team	RS	216	111	1.95	Size of LA Forum
First Aid	Treat	players	RS	50	35	1.43	Combine spaces
Referee Room	Store	clothes	RS	50	35	1.43	Combine spaces
Entrance Toilet	Dispose	waste	S·	16	1	16.00	Delete
Coach Room	Plan	game	S	40	30	1.33	Reduce size
Office	Meet	players	S	77	1	77.00	Delete
Coach Toilet	Dispose	waste	S	18	1	18.00	Delete
Supply Room	Store	equipment	RS	36	36	1.00	
Circulation	Connect	space	RS	84	40	2.10	10% allowance
Total				**851**	**422**	**2.02**	
PUBLIC AREA, SIDE A							
Kiosk	Serve	beverages	S	55	55	1.00	
Public Toilets	Dispose	waste	RS	138	414	0.33	Size of LA Forum
Store Space	House	equipment	RS	345	60	5.75	Two spaces/side
Concourse	Route	spectators	S	1,350	515	2.62	Walk in on grade
Service Corridor	Connect	space	S	99	1	99.00	Delete enclosure
Circulation	Connect	space	S	63	63	1.00	
Total				**2,050**	**1,108**	**1.85**	
VIP, SIDE B							
Reception Hall	Entertain	VIP	RS	66	40	1.65	Size for 50
Prayer Hall	Say	prayers	RS	39	25	1.56	Size for 50
Tea Room	Prepare	tea	S	5	5	1.00	
Ablution	Wash	feet	RS	6	6	1.00	
Toilet	Dispose	waste	RS	9	9	1.00	
Boxes	View	game	B	43	30	1.43	Size for 50
Patio	Connect	space	S	51	20	2.55	Reduce size
Circulation	Connect	space	RS	97	50	1.94	
Total				**316**	**185**	**1.71**	
PUBLIC AREA, SIDE B							
Kiosk	Serve	beverages	S	59	40	1.48	Reduce size
Public Toilet	Relieve	waste	RS	50	150	0.33	Size of LA Forum
Concourse	Route	spectators	S	420	1	420.00	Enter on grade
Corridor	Connect	space	S	195	1	195.00	Delete
Store Space	House	equipment	RS	388	60	6.47	Two spaces/side
Circulation	Connect	space	RS	52	51	1.02	
Total				**1,164**	**303**	**3.84**	
SPECTATOR AREAS, A, B, C							
Seating	View	game	B	5,726	3,972	1.44	Reduce capacity=10,000
Aisles	Access	seats	RS	728	655	1.11	Delete dead end aisles
Circulation	Access	seats	RS	782	391	2.00	Elimin. one crossover
Stairs	Access	seats	RS	340	255	1.33	Use ramps at row 1
Entrance Booth	Control	access	RS	51	25	2.04	Provide one side only
Total				**7,627**	**5,298**	**1.44**	
PLAYING AREA							
Field	Play	soccer	B	6,400	6,400	1.00	Use National Standards
Track	Conduct	meet	S	4,416	3,200	1.38	Delete ends
Inner Area	Hold	team	RS	4,296	800	5.37	Remove concrete rail'g
Outer Area	Permit	view	S	5,412	541	10.00	
Total				**20,524**	**10,941**	**1.88**	

Figure 3.11

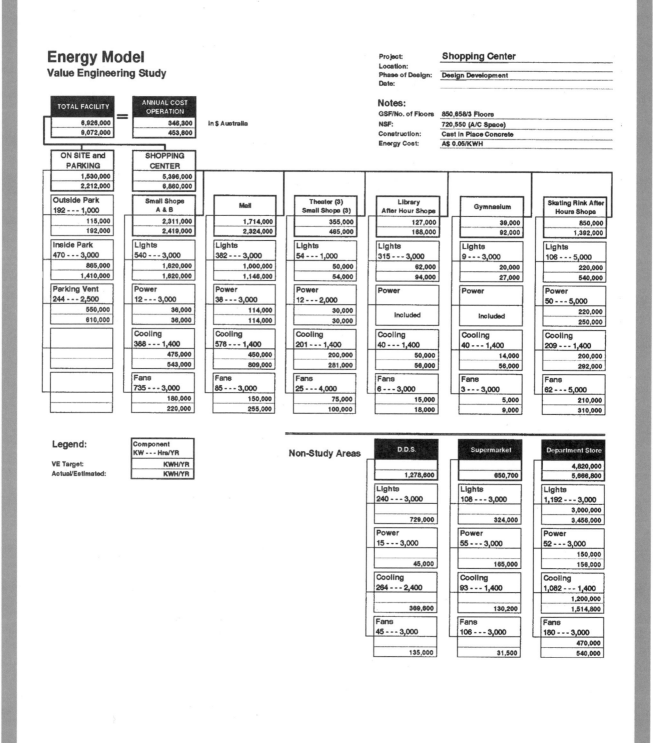

Figure 3.12

per year for the various types of space as well as the unit rate: 1kW/hr. or kW/S.F. In the preparation of the energy model in Figure 3.12, the cooling load was isolated as a key area of potential savings.

Worth is determined by asking "What if?" about potential elimination of the function, changes to operating hours, use of utilization rates for energy efficiency, reductions in square footage, changes in system types, and elimination of energy sources.

Figure 3.13 is an energy model for the oil/gas platform shown in Figure 3.7. From this model, the team focused on energy savings for the compressors and heaters/driers. The results indicated that to first have an excess of heat and then to run heaters/driers appeared questionable.

Figure 3.14 is an energy model for an administrative building measured in BTUs per square foot per year (BTU/S.F./yr.). This unit of measurement is often desirable because it facilitates comparison with "worth" set in that unit of measurement in published energy standards (see Figure 1.13). The model highlights the heating and office lights as the two significant high energy use areas. For conversion between the two types of models, the following information is useful.

1 watt = 3.412 BTUH

1 kW = 3,412 BTUH

Life Cycle Cost (LCC) Model

The LCC model is the ultimate indicator of value to the client. It encompasses both initial costs and running costs. The LCC model considers optimum value because it takes into account all probable costs over the life of the facility. The LCC model can be based on either the annualized cost or the present worth approach. That is, all costs shown in the model can be equivalent annual or present worth costs. If desired, the costs can be converted by using a simple conversion factor.

Figure 3.15a is the LCC summary sheet from a recent study. This sheet is used for present worth analyses of all costs. Figure 3.15b presents the LCC model (discussed in greater depth in Chapter Two and Chapter Seven), which outlines these costs and sets targets for analysis.

Worth for annual expenditures such as maintenance, alteration, replacement, security, and so on, can be judged from historical data like that published by the Building Owners and Managers Association (BOMA). Worth for the facility cost can be taken from the cost model. Worth for the energy consumed can be taken from the energy model.

Thus a full value picture of a facility is born. This LCC Model (Figure 3.15b) shows the capital costs for construction to be the area of greatest LCC savings potential.

Quality Model

The quality model illustrated in Figure 3.16 provides a thorough definition of the owner's project performance expectations. These expectations must result in a consistent definition and understanding between the owner and the design team. This consistency helps to ensure that original owner expectations in terms of functional performance are indeed met when the project is delivered and the facility is operating. The quality model defines the overall expectations of the project representatives regarding project goals, image concerns, design criteria, and performance standards. The information is established from an interactive Quality Model Workshop at the concept stage, in which owner representatives of the facility are polled for their concerns and opinions regarding their desired minimum, balanced or maximum response, for the twelve major planning elements shown in Figure 3.16. The center of the circle represents the minimum response.

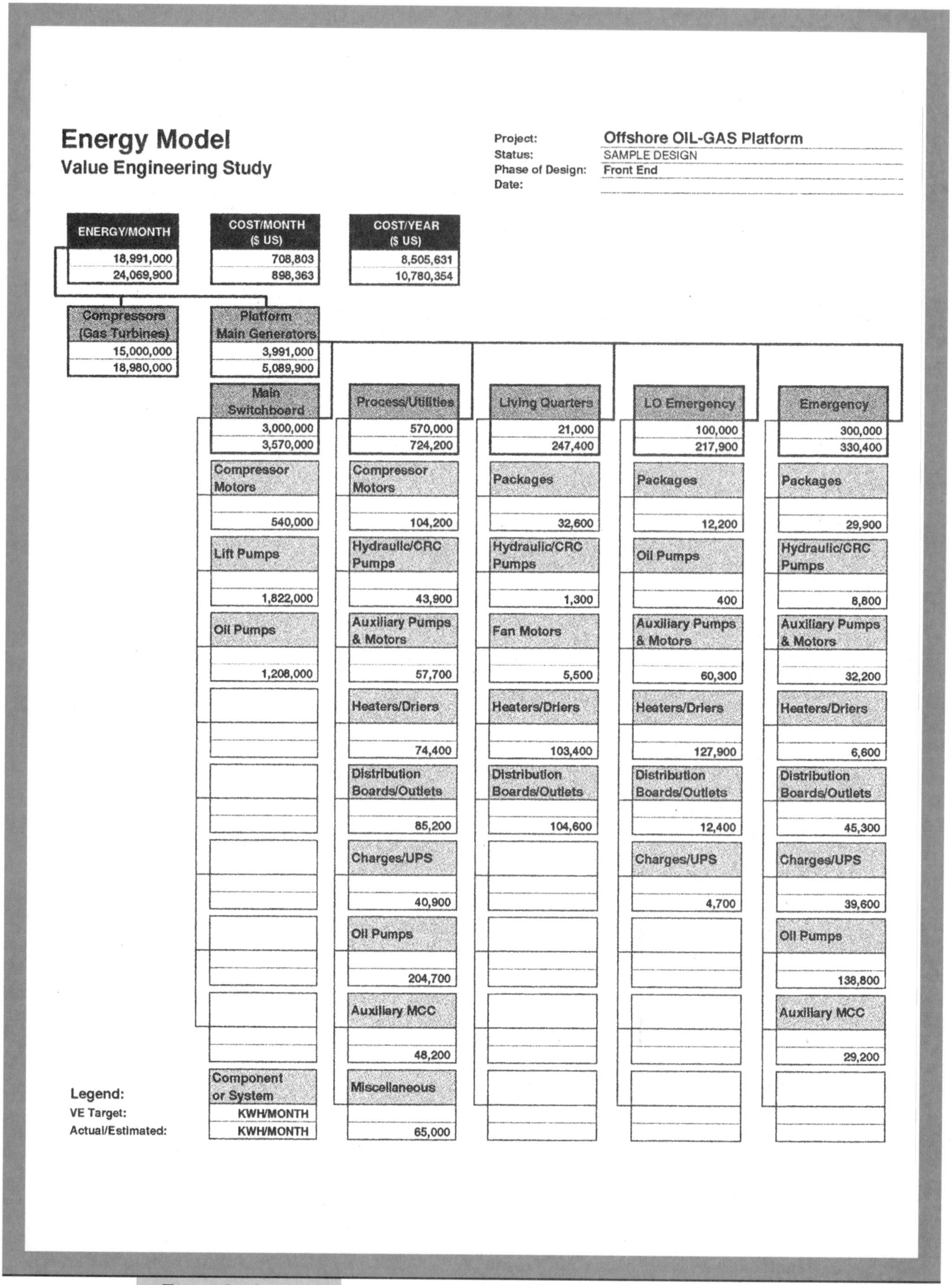

Energy Model
Value Engineering Study

Project: **Offshore OIL-GAS Platform**
Status: SAMPLE DESIGN
Phase of Design: Front End
Date:

ENERGY/MONTH	COST/MONTH ($ US)	COST/YEAR ($ US)
18,991,000	708,803	8,505,631
24,069,900	898,363	10,780,354

Compressors (Gas Turbines)	Platform Main Generators
15,000,000	3,991,000
18,980,000	5,089,900

Main Switchboard	Process/Utilities	Living Quarters	LO Emergency	Emergency
3,000,000	570,000	21,000	100,000	300,000
3,570,000	724,200	247,400	217,900	330,400
Compressor Motors	**Compressor Motors**	**Packages**	**Packages**	**Packages**
	104,200	32,600	12,200	29,900
Lift Pumps	**Hydraulic/CRC Pumps**	**Hydraulic/CRC Pumps**	**Oil Pumps**	**Hydraulic/CRC Pumps**
1,822,000	43,900	1,300	400	8,800
Oil Pumps	**Auxiliary Pumps & Motors**	**Fan Motors**	**Auxiliary Pumps & Motors**	**Auxiliary Pumps & Motors**
1,208,000	57,700	5,500	60,300	32,200
	Heaters/Driers	**Heaters/Driers**	**Heaters/Driers**	**Heaters/Driers**
	74,400	103,400	127,900	6,600
	Distribution Boards/Outlets	**Distribution Boards/Outlets**	**Distribution Boards/Outlets**	**Distribution Boards/Outlets**
	85,200	104,600	12,400	45,300
	Charges/UPS		**Charges/UPS**	**Charges/UPS**
	40,900		4,700	39,600
	Oil Pumps			**Oil Pumps**
	204,700			138,800
	Auxiliary MCC			**Auxiliary MCC**
	48,200			29,200
Component or System	**Miscellaneous**			
	65,000			

Legend:
VE Target: KWH/MONTH
Actual/Estimated: KWH/MONTH

Figure 3.13

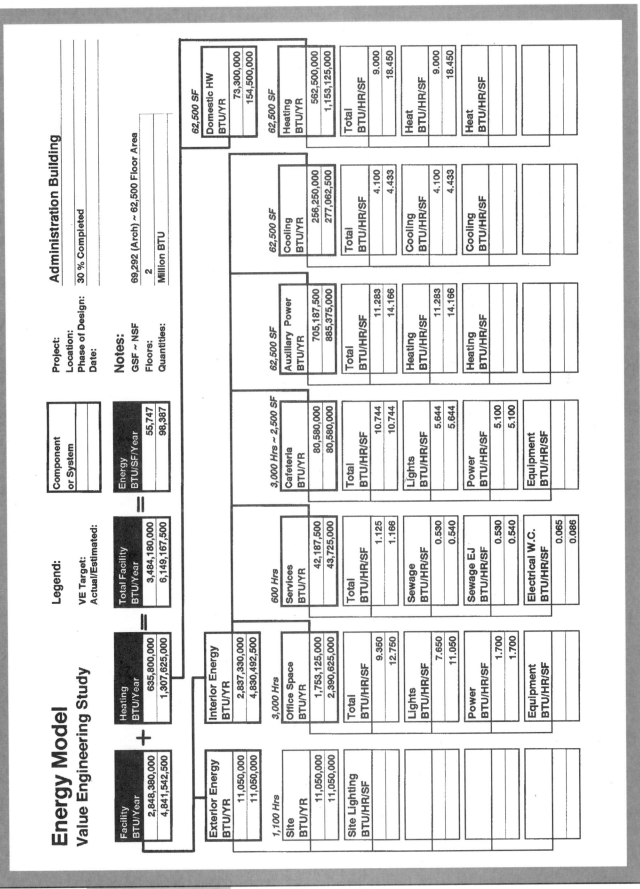

Figure 3.14

Development Phase
Life Cycle Cost (Present Worth Method)

Court House			Original		Alternative 1	
Date:						
Project Life Cycle (Years)	30					
Discount Rate (Percent)	10.00%					

Capital Cost			Estimated	PW	Estimated	PW
A) Design			987,900	987,900	987,900	987,900
B) Construction			13,499,410	13,499,410	10,000,000	10,000,000
C)				0		0
D)				0		0
E)				0		0
F)				0		0

Other Initial Cost						
A)				0		0
B)				0		0

Total Initial Cost (IC) Impact				14,487,310		10,987,900
Initial Cost PW Savings						3,499,410

Replacement/Salvage Costs	Year	Factor				
A) Cooling Towers	10	0.3855	43,800	16,886	43,800	16,886
B) Other Renovation (%)	10	0.3855	80,000	30,843	80,000	30,843
C) Chillers	15	0.2394	657,000	157,280	657,000	157,280
D) Cooling Towers	20	0.1486	43,800	6,510	43,800	6,510
E) Other Renovation (%)	20	0.1486	80,000	11,891	80,000	11,891
F)		1.0000		0		0
G)		1.0000		0		0
Salvage (neg. cash flow)	30	0.0573	(3,000,000)	(171,925)	(3,000,000)	(171,925)

Total Replacement/Salvage PW Costs				51,485		51,485

Operation/Maintenance Cost	Escl. %	PWA				
A) Utilities	3.000%	12.677	169,110	2,142,199	150,000	1,900,123
B) Cleaning	0.000%	9.427	71,490	673,930	60,000	565,615
C) Maintenance	0.000%	9.427	80,720	760,941	75,000	707,019
D) Building Management	0.000%	9.427	62,260	586,920	62,260	586,920
E) Security	0.000%	9.427	38,440	362,371	38,440	362,371
F) Trash Removal	0.000%	9.427	3,840	36,199	3,840	36,199
G) Domestic Water	0.000%	9.427	3,000	28,281	3,000	28,281

Total Operation/Maintenance (PW) Cost				4,590,841		4,186,528

Total Present Worth Life Cycle Costs				19,078,151		15,174,428
Life Cycle (PW) Savings						3,903,723

PW = Present Worth

PWA = Present Worth of Annuity

Figure 3.15a

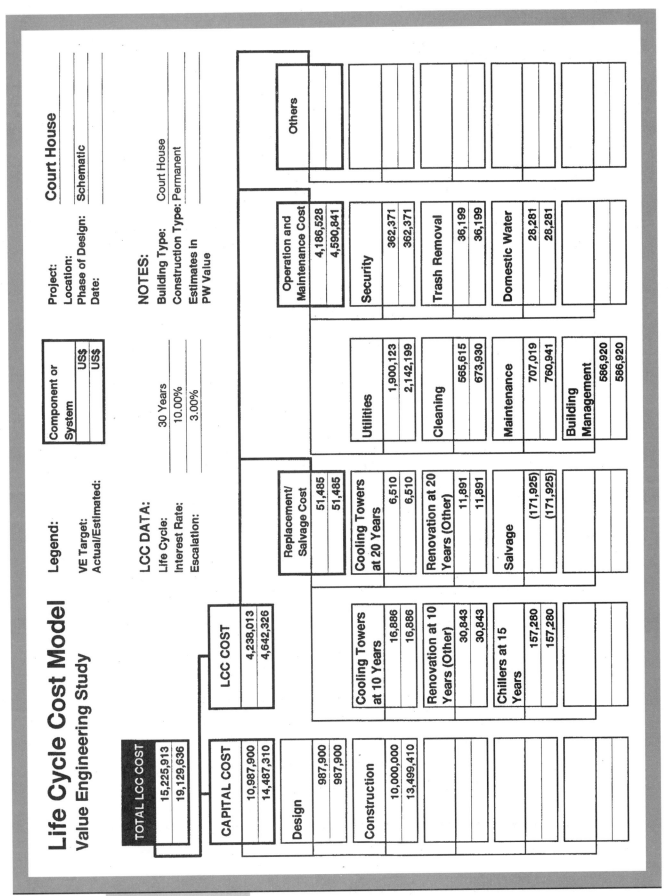

Figure 3.15b

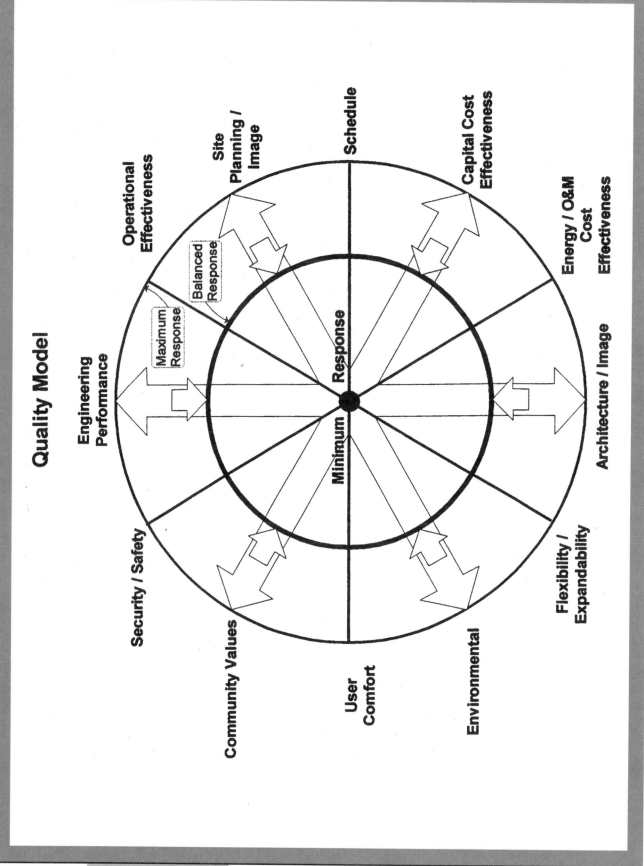

Quality Model

Figure 3.16

The quality model then serves as the foundation for the VE application. Attitudes and expectations regarding operational and technical performance—having been clearly defined, understood, and documented—become the yardstick by which decisions are made.

As design proceeds, the quality model is used to ensure that VE design alternatives are consistent with original owner expectations. During the early design phases, the VE team explores a number of alternatives that seek to optimize owner expectations. These alternatives are then reviewed in the workshop session. During the workshop, the owner and design team compare the alternatives with the quality model. The alternative that most closely matches the owner's functional performance needs is selected for further development.

The number of participants in the Quality Model Workshop should represent five points of view: financial, users, facility operations, design, and construction. The objective is to determine and document through group dynamics a consensus directive that will guide all subsequent decision making in the development of the design.

The document that results from the Quality Model Workshop is the Quality Model Diagram, which is illustrated in Figure 13.17. Along with a narrative, the Quality Model Diagram records the relative choices of importance between the twelve major planning elements. Those items of greatest concern are indicated on the outer edges of the diagram, those of lesser concern toward the center, and a neutral opinion between the extremes. Each of the twelve major elements may consist of 20 to 50 subcategories, depending on the complexity of the project. Figure 3.17 is a Quality Model Diagram from a recent workshop on a research project. The model shows that the owner places high emphasis on operational effectiveness, site planning/image, capital cost effectiveness, and architectural/image. User comfort, community values, security/safety, energy, and schedule are placed at lesser response.

Conclusion

Modeling to graphically express the distribution of costs associated with a specific project, system, or item was an important feature of VE in construction from its earliest stages. Among the advantages construction has over the industrial sector is the availability of cost estimating resources and bid data. The opportunity to utilize this resource and to combine it with the functionally cost-oriented value engineering is enhanced by application of the modeling methodology. Models can be developed that optimize the impact on a project of resources other than cost, for example, space, time, energy, and risk. Finally, modeling is useful in the development of a design-to-cost philosophy set up by functionally oriented blocks. Project managers will find far-reaching usefulness in a tool like modeling.

References

1. Lawrence D. Miles, *Techniques of Value Analysis and Engineering, Second Edition*, McGraw-Hill, 1972.

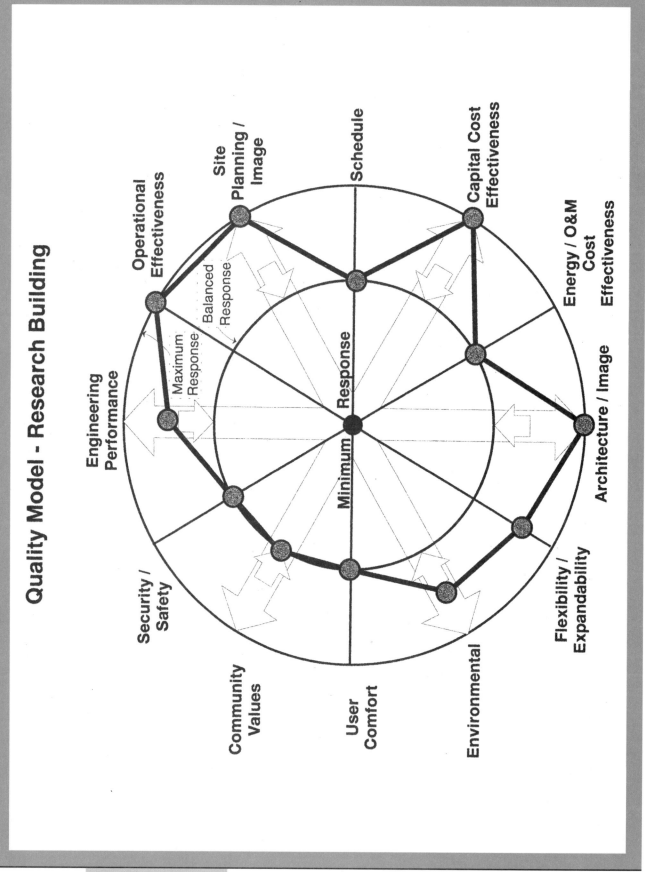

Quality Model - Research Building

Site Planning / Image

Schedule

Capital Cost Effectiveness

Energy / O&M Cost Effectiveness

Operational Effectiveness

Architecture / Image

Engineering Performance

Balanced Response

Maximum Response

Minimum Response

Flexibility / Expandability

Security / Safety

Community Values

User Comfort

Environmental

Figure 3.17

Chapter Four

Planning for Value Engineering Services

In today's climate, both public and private sector organizations are requesting value engineering (VE) services at an increasing rate. Some of these parties are very sophisticated in their knowledge of VE, what services they want, and what they expect of the service. However, many are not.

Some requests for proposals (RFPs) for VE services indicate very little comprehension of value engineering. It behooves those who respond to offer nothing less than professional-level VE services. These services should use the VE methodology, follow the Job Plan, and apply function analysis and creativity, regardless of whether specifically requested. The value engineer can educate the client subtly, by the manner in which the response to the RFP is structured, and the VE services are planned and presented. The response can:

- Structure the proper number of teams and select team staffing to provide a quality study.
- Phase the work, following the Job Plan.
- Schedule services to allow time to perform all desired tasks, such as collection of information, preparation of models, and life cycle costing (LCC), without adversely affecting the overall project schedule.
- Ensure that the fee quoted is commensurate with the project value and size to offer a reasonable return on investment (ROI).

VE Objectives

VE is a systematic, organized approach to obtaining optimum value for each dollar spent. Through a system of investigation using trained, multidisciplined teams, both value and client requirements are improved by one of the following:

- Eliminating or modifying elements not essential to required functions.
- Adding elements that achieve required functions not attained.
- Changing elements to improve quality or performance to more desirable levels established by the owner/user.

By using creative techniques, the VE team develops alternative solutions for specific functions.

The objective of a VE study should be to obtain the optimum functional balance among construction costs, user requirements, and life cycle costs. This action should result in savings in the following areas:

- Initial capital construction costs, without detriment to costs of operations and maintenance and/or income.
- Predicted follow-on costs, such as facility staffing, operation, and maintenance.

- Either or both of the above, when results indicate an overall savings under conditions established by the owner/user.

Level of Effort

The appropriate level of effort for a given construction project is a function of several factors; mainly project size, project complexity, constraints such as cost versus time, and the degree of completion of the design. The major elements to be determined for a given study are:

- Total manpower and number of studies required.
- Number and composition of the VE team(s).
- Anticipated cost versus anticipated return on investment (ROI).

One method of computing the study cost is to establish a savings goal for the project. Experience has shown that 5% savings of initial cost and an additional 5% savings (present worth) of follow-on LCC are reasonable initial goals for a well-planned VE effort. Consider the following example on a $10 million project.

$$\text{Savings goal} = \begin{array}{ll} \$\,500,000 & \text{(initial cost)} \\ \underline{\$\,500,000} & \text{(LCC present worth)} \\ \$1,000,000 & \text{(Total)} \end{array}$$

Note: Using a 10% interest rate, the $500,000 in Present Worth of follow-on costs would equate to:

$$\frac{\$500,000 \text{ PW}}{10.0 \text{ PWA}} = \$50,000/\text{yr. in annual savings. (See Chapter Seven for further explanation.)}$$

The average implementation rate, based on results of approximately 500 projects, is 50% of the recommendations. Therefore, initial cost potential savings of at least $1,000,000 must be isolated to realize $500,000 in implemented savings. Equally, the isolated follow-on cost savings should be $100,000/year to realize $50,000/year in implemented savings. Initial cost savings are used to establish a fee target, since follow-on costs do not affect initial fees. Based on a 10:1 ROI (a conservative ratio based on experience that would result in a 20:1 ROI for total savings), the target fee for a study cost can be computed as follows:

$$\frac{\text{Initial Savings}}{\text{ROI}} = \$500,000/10 = \$50,000$$

This fee is based on a one-study effort on a fairly complex project.

Fees vary depending on the complexity, stage of design, and owner fee constraints. If the study is at early design documents, less material needs to be covered than at working drawings. If the project is less complex and repetitive, less time is required. Therefore, fees for that project would be lower.

As a range, fees for a $10,000,000 project of one study would vary from $25,000 to $50,000.

When planning for VE services, separate plans are required for large, multiproject programs versus plans for individual projects. Planning for programs is based on:

- Program expenditures
- Budget and time constraints
- Desired results

For example, total costs for implementing a VE program range from 0.1% to 0.3% of program costs (over $200 million). If an owner wants to maximize savings, more money (up to 0.3%) must be allocated.

Figure 4.1 provides a nomograph based on a one-study effort that can be used to make a rough judgment regarding the affordable level of VE effort based on project size. However, VE study costs should always be computed based on the estimated amount of work needed to provide proper services. Subsequently, the cost should be checked for logic and reasonableness against the project cost as shown above.

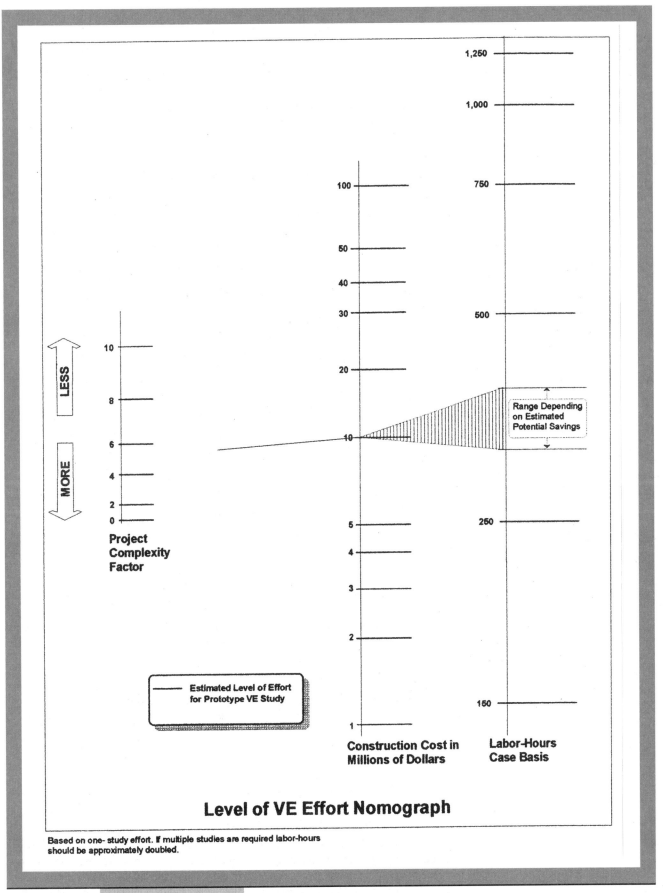

Level of VE Effort Nomograph

Based on one- study effort. If multiple studies are required labor-hours should be approximately doubled.

Figure 4.1

Normally, it is desirable to conduct two VE studies for any major project. In such cases, the first study would be conducted during the design programming/schematic/concept stage of design (+15%) completion. The second study would be conducted at the tentative/preliminary/intermediate stage of design (40%-60%) completion.

Figure 4.2 illustrates typical study areas for buildings at various stages of design. The number of teams necessary to perform each study depends on the complexity of the project and the extent of preselection of potential study areas by the value engineer and the client. For example:

- Projects that consist of multiple large buildings with different functions might require one team per structure.
- If all external wall systems are similar on all buildings regardless of their function, one team could be established to study that subject across all buildings on the project.
- Teams can also be established to study related disciplines on large projects; e.g., civil/site work team, architectural/structural team, mechanical/electrical team.

Standard teams generally consist of three to six members who conduct a 40-hour study (not counting prestudy and poststudy work). For a five-member team, this represents 5.0 labor-weeks or 200 labor-hours of effort per team, plus 80 to 100 labor-hours (professional only) for pre- and poststudy efforts.

In general, a five-day formal study yields the best results. However, for early stage effort when there is minimal documentation, a two- or three-day VE study can be considered. Under time and budget constraints, these minimal workshops may be an option, though a difficult one.

Figure 4.3 provides an approximate level of VE effort as a function of the number of teams and number of studies.

VE and Total Project Management

VE used in conjunction with total project management is most effective when VE, cost, schedule, and design review efforts are linked using common personnel. The result is usually significant savings in manpower and improved service.

The following two case studies are based on the author's experience.

Case 1

A government agency has an annual construction program of $200,000,000, involving some 150 projects. The owner has decided that projects under $10 million will have only one VE study, and projects over $10 million will be scheduled for two studies; the initial study will be a three-day formal study and the follow-on efforts will be a five-day formal study. What would be a reasonable VE program cost, and how should it be planned?

Using Pareto's Law as a basis, the sizes of the projects should be analyzed to determine the number of projects (20%) that have the bulk of expenditures (80%). In this case, some 18 projects involve approximately $160,000,000 of the total program. The lower threshold indicated a project cost of $2,000,000.

The proposed planning budget would be the following:

Level	Project Cost	Approx. No. of Projects	Approx. VE Cost/Project	Total
A	Over $20 Million	2	$55,000	$110,000
B	$10-20 Million	6	47,500	285,000
C	$2-10 Million	10	22,500	225,000
D	In-house Proj. Mgmt. and Admin.			130,000
Total Cost				$750,000

Areas of VE Study by Design Stage

Areas of Study	Conceptual	Schematic	Design Development
General Project Budget Layout Criteria & Standards	• Design Concepts • Program Interpretation • Site/Facility Massing • Access, Circulation • Project Budget • Design Intentions • Net to Gross Ratios	• Schematic Floor Plans • Schematic Sections • Approach to Systems Integration • Floor to Floor Height • Functional Space	• Floor Plans • Sections • Typical Details • Integrated Systems • Space Circulation • Specifications
Structural Foundation Substructure Superstructure	• Performance Requirements • Structural Bay Sizing • Framing Systems Exploration • Subsurface Conditions • Underground Concepts • Initial Framing Review • Structural Load Criteria	• Schematic Basement Plan • Selection of Foundation System • Structural System Selection • Framing Plan Outline • Sizing of Elements	• Basement Floor Plan • Key Foundation Elements, Details • Floor & Roof Framing Plans • Sizing of Major Elements • Outline Specifications
Architectural Exterior Closure Roofing Interior Construction Elevators Equipment	• Approach to Elevation Views to/from Building • Roof Types & Pitch • Interior Design • Configuration of Key Rooms • Organization of Circulation Scheme • Need & Types of Vertical Circulation • Impact of Key Equipment on Facility & Site • Passive Solar Usage	• Concept Elaboration • Selection of Wall Systems • Schematic Elevations • Selection of Roof Systems • Room Design • Selection of Partitions • Circulation Sizing • Basic Elevator & Vertical Transportation Concepts • Impact of Key Equipments on Room Design	• Elevations • Key Elevation Details • Key Roofing Details • Initial Finish Schedules • Interior Construction Elements • Integration of Structural Framing • Key Interior Elevations • Outline Specification for Equipment Items
Mechanical HVAC Plumbing Fire Protection	• Basic Energy Concepts • Impact of Mechanical Concepts on Facility • Initial Systems Selection • Source Allocation • Performance Requirements for Plumbing, HVAC, Fire Protection	• Mechanical Systems Selection • Refinement of Service & Distribution Concepts • Input to Schematic Plans • Energy Conservation	• Detailed System Selection • Initial System Drawings & Key Details • Distribution & Riser Diagram • Outline Specifications for System Elements
Electrical Service & Distribution Lighting & Power	• Basic Power Supply • Approach to Use of Natural & Artificial Lighting • Performance Requirements for Lighting • Need for Special Electrical Systems	• Windows/Skylight Design & Sizing • Selection of Lighting & Electrical Systems • General Service, Power & Distribution Concepts	• Detailed Systems Selection • Distribution Diagrams • Key Space • Lighting Layouts • Outline Specification for Electrical Elements
Site Preparation Utilities Landscaping	• Site Selection • Site Development Criteria • Site Forms & Massing • Requirements for Access • Views to/from Facility • Utility Supply • Site Drainage	• Design Concept Elaboration • Initial Site Plan • Schematic Planting, Grading, Paving Plans	• Site Plan • Planting Plan • Typical Site Details • Outline Specifications for Site Materials

Figure 4.2

Approximate Level of Effort as a Function of the Number of VE Teams and Workshops

	Teams (5-Day Workshop)	VETC				Designer*				Total Labor-weeks
Level of Effort ~ Labor-weeks		Pre-workshop Prep	During Workshop	Report Preparation	Follow-up	Pre-workshop Prep	Consult to Teams	Draft Report Response	Coordinate w/Owner & Final Report	
1 - 1 Team Effort	5	1	1	1	–	0.5	0.5	0.5	0.5	10.0
1 - 2 Team Effort	10	2	1	2	0.5	1	1	1.5	1	20.0
1 - 3 Team Effort	15	2	1	2	1	1	1.5	2	1.5	27.0
1 - 4 Team Effort	20	3	1	2	1	1.5	2	2.5	2	35.0
1 - 5 Team Effort	25	4	1	3	1	2	2.5	3	2	43.5
2 - 2 Team Efforts	30	2	2	2	1	2	1	1	1	42.0
2 - 2 Team Efforts	35	4	2	3	1	2	2	2	2	53.0
2 - 3 Team Efforts	40	4	2	3	2	2	2	3	2	60.0
2 - 4 Team Efforts	45	6	2	3	2	3	2	5	3	71.0
2 - 5 Team Efforts	50	8	2	4	2	4	2	6	4	82.0

*Not including implementation of VE ideas

Figure 4.3

The costs for the two Level A studies are estimated at $35,000 for the 30%-50% stage and $20,000 for the early stage (0-15%), for a total of $55,000.

The cost for two Level B studies are estimated at $17,500 for the early stage and $30,000 for the 30%-50% stage, for a total of $47,500.

The cost for one Level C study applied at the 25%-50% stage is estimated at $22,500.

The program should be time phased, with an emphasis on training and familiarization during the first year. In the second year, less training and more application; and in the third year, full implementation with minimum training.

Target savings for this program would be:

$200,000,000 × 5% = $10,000,000 in initial costs

$200,000,000 × 0.5% = $1,000,000/yr. in annual costs

Present Worth of Annual Savings = Annual Savings × PWA (Present Worth of Annuity) = $1,000,000/yr. × Approx. 10.0 (PWA) = PW $10,000,000

Total present worth of savings is approximately:

$10,000,000 capital cost

$10,000,000 present worth of annual savings

$20,000,000

Return on Investment (ROI):

Savings/Program Cost = $20,000,000/$750,000 = 25:1

The above ROI reflects actual results attained in several agencies. Agencies with larger programs ($1 billion) have results in the 100:1 ROI range. (See Figure I.10, "Results of VE Programs.")

Case 2

Assuming the same construction program as in Case 1, if agency budget restrictions were critical, a minimum program would have to be considered. This could be achieved by adding VE provisions on selected design contracts and reducing the required number of studies. Again, by analyzing the 18 projects, some will have greater potential than others. By selecting the larger projects and those with the greatest potential, the proposed planning budget would be as follows:

Level	Projects	No. of Projects	Cost/Projects	Total
A	2 Studies Over $20,000,000	2	$55,000	$110,000
B	1 Study $10-20,000,000	4	30,000	120,000
C	1 Study $5-10,000,000	2	22,500	45,000
D	Project Mgmt. and Administration			75,000
Total Cost				$350,000

Targeted potential savings would be cut by approximately 50%, since expenditures are reduced by approximately $350,000/yr. ÷ $750,000/yr. = 47%.

Target savings for this program would be:

$5,000,000 in initial cost

$5,000,000 present worth of annual savings of approximately $500,000/yr.

$10,000,000 Total LCC savings

Return on Investment (ROI) = $10,000,000/$350,000 = 30:1

Team Selection

The VE team should have a qualified professional (preferably a Certified Value Specialist) as its coordinator. The Value Engineering Team Coordinator's (VETC) skills should be more creative, organizational, and motivational than technical.

The skills and expertise of VE team members must be tailored to the nature of the specific project. For example, VE for a major biological research laboratory should involve personnel with design experience using special mechanical systems with HEPA filters, architects with extensive lab design experience, and a specialist in laboratory equipment.

Regardless of the specific technical skills required for a project, there are some universal considerations for team members:

- The VETC should be a recognized leader in the application of VE procedures to similar projects as those being studied.
- Team members should be highly qualified, with equal (or more) experience as the design team members. If team members have more and better experience than the design team, then results are practically guaranteed. The technical competence of team individuals is more important than the team's precise composition.
- Disciplines on each team should be mixed. Too many members from the same discipline on a team tend to stifle creativity.
- Team members should have participated previously on VE study teams. Ideally, no more than one or two inexperienced members should be on a team.

Preference should be given to using people who have technical competence as well as the following traits:

- Sensitivity to the problems involved in gathering information.
- Ability to think quickly and write clearly.
- Open mindedness and enthusiasm.
- Perseverance in following through.
- Skill in selling and making presentations.

The VE Job Plan

A key point of the organized VE effort is the use of the Job Plan. The Job Plan is the organized problem-solving approach that separates VE from other cost-cutting exercises. The simplest Job Plan follows a five-step approach that is integral to VE methodology. Key questions are answered at each stage.

Steps in VE Job Plan

1. **Information Gathering Step**
   What functions are being provided?
   What do the functions cost?
   What are the functions worth?
   What functions must be accomplished?

2. **Creativity & Idea Generation**
   What else will perform the function?
   How else may the function be performed?

3. **Analyze Ideas/Evaluation & Selection**
   Will each idea perform the required functions?
   How might each idea be made to work?

4. **Development of Proposal**
   How will the new idea work?
   Will it meet all the requirements?
   How much will it cost?
   What is the LCC impact?

5. **Presentation/Implementation & Follow-up**
   Why is the new idea better?
   Who must be sold on the idea?
   What are the advantages/disadvantages and specific benefits?
   What is needed to implement the proposal?

Figure 4.4 is a flow chart of VE procedures. It outlines the Job Plan steps.

A work plan for the total VE effort incorporates the Job Plan in a comprehensive effort to deliver a finished product. The Work Plan serves as the framework for conducting the services.

Figure 4.5 outlines the tasks for the study. The VE Job Plan is blended into each phase.

Work Plan Study Phases

The VE Job Plan can be blended with the study Work Plan as follows:

Prestudy phase: Perform one-half of the VE Job Plan Information step.

Study phase: Perform the remaining one-half of the Information step; all of the Creative, Analysis, Development, and Presentation steps; and one-third of the Report step.

Poststudy phase: Perform the remaining two-thirds of the Report step.

Prestudy Phase

Prestudy activities should occur prior to conducting the study phase of the VE Work Plan.

The success of a VE study depends largely on proper preparation and coordination. Information and documents are furnished by the designer and distributed to the team to prepare them for their area of study. All participants are briefed on expectations for their roles and responsibilities expected during the study.

Thus, prestudy activity falls into two categories: Preparing for the Study and Beginning the Information Gathering Step.

Preparing for the Study: Preparing for the study generally involves the following:

- Prepare study plan and schedule.
- Establish study location.
- Arrange study facilities, equipment, etc.
- Set up owner/designer briefing for first day; for large projects, before first day.
- Set up client idea review for midweek.
- Set up presentation time.
- Advise team members.
- Arrange travel and accommodations.
- Distribute all project information to all team members for their review.
- Validate cost estimate and draft quality model (optional).

Beginning the Information Gathering Step: Whenever possible, sufficient lead time should be scheduled prior to the study phase to adequately perform several key areas of the Information Gathering step of the VE Job Plan. As much as possible should be completed before the Information Gathering step *except* for the three following activities. The VE team should begin these three activities on the first day of the study phase.

- Function analysis
- FAST Diagram development
- Assignment of cost/worth to function

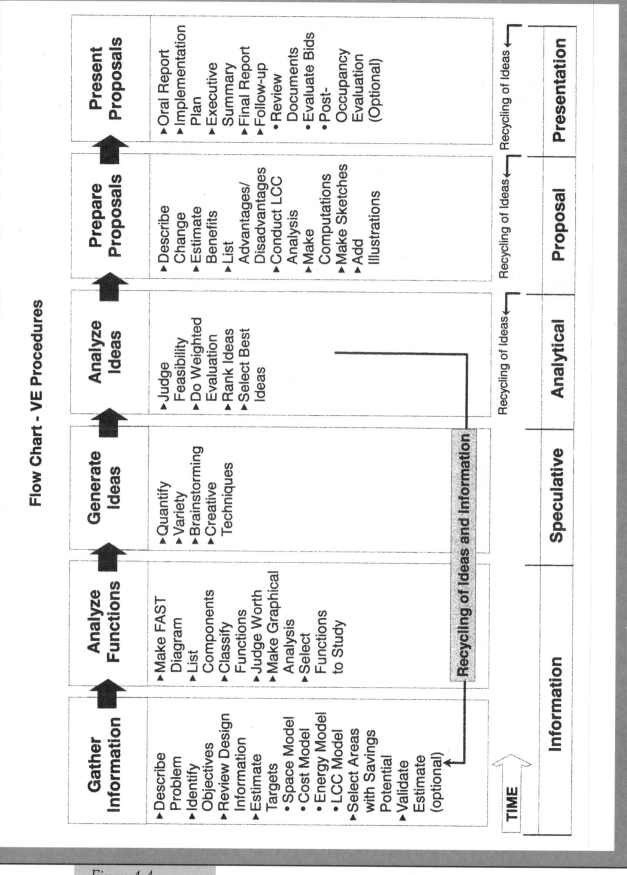

Flow Chart - VE Procedures

Gather Information	Analyze Functions	Generate Ideas	Analyze Ideas	Prepare Proposals	Present Proposals
▲ Describe Problem ▲ Identify Objectives ▲ Review Design Information ▲ Estimate Targets • Space Model • Cost Model • Energy Model • LCC Model ▲ Select Areas with Savings Potential ▲ Validate Estimate (optional)	▲ Make FAST Diagram ▲ List Components ▲ Classify Functions ▲ Judge Worth ▲ Make Graphical Analysis ▲ Select Functions to Study	▲ Quantify ▲ Variety ▲ Brainstorming ▲ Creative Techniques	▲ Judge Feasibility ▲ Do Weighted Evaluation ▲ Rank Ideas ▲ Select Best Ideas	▲ Describe Change ▲ Estimate Benefits ▲ List Advantages/ Disadvantages ▲ Conduct LCC Analysis ▲ Make Computations ▲ Make Sketches ▲ Add Illustrations	▲ Oral Report ▲ Implementation Plan ▲ Executive Summary ▲ Final Report ▲ Follow-up • Review Documents • Evaluate Bids • Post-Occupancy Evaluation (Optional)

Recycling of Ideas and Information

Recycling of Ideas

Information	Speculative	Analytical	Proposal	Presentation

TIME

Figure 4.4

Work Plan Phases

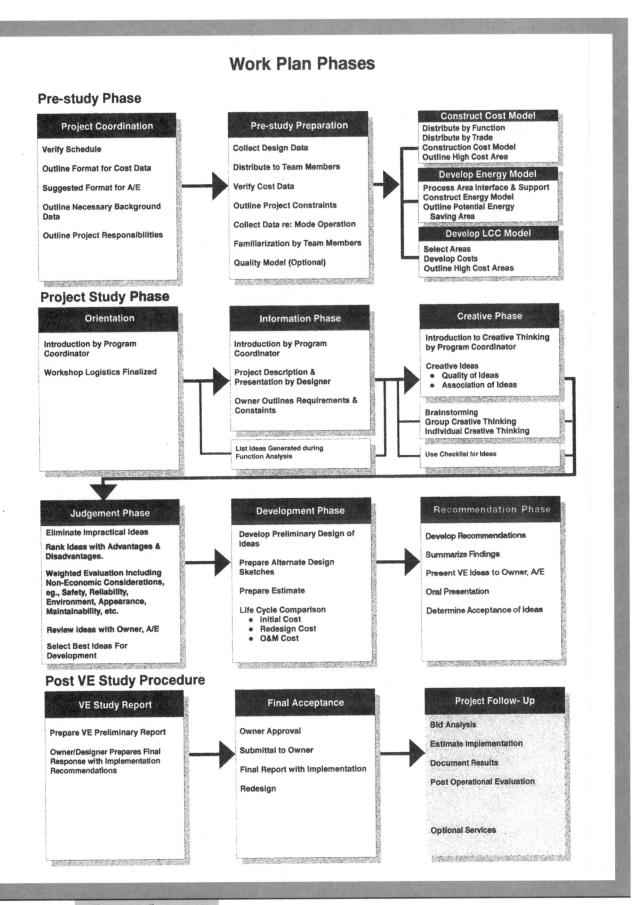

Pre-study Phase

Project Coordination

Verify Schedule

Outline Format for Cost Data

Suggested Format for A/E

Outline Necessary Background Data

Outline Project Responsibilities

Pre-study Preparation

Collect Design Data

Distribute to Team Members

Verify Cost Data

Outline Project Constraints

Collect Data re: Mode Operation

Familiarization by Team Members

Quality Model (Optional)

Construct Cost Model

Distribute by Function
Distribute by Trade
Construction Cost Model
Outline High Cost Area

Develop Energy Model

Process Area Interface & Support
Construct Energy Model
Outline Potential Energy
   Saving Area

Develop LCC Model

Select Areas
Develop Costs
Outline High Cost Areas

Project Study Phase

Orientation

Introduction by Program Coordinator

Workshop Logistics Finalized

Information Phase

Introduction by Program Coordinator

Project Description & Presentation by Designer

Owner Outlines Requirements & Constraints

List Ideas Generated during Function Analysis

Creative Phase

Introduction to Creative Thinking by Program Coordinator

Creative Ideas
  • Quality of Ideas
  • Association of Ideas

Brainstorming
Group Creative Thinking
Individual Creative Thinking

Use Checklist for Ideas

Judgement Phase

Eliminate Impractical Ideas

Rank Ideas with Advantages & Disadvantages.

Weighted Evaluation Including Non-Economic Considerations, eg., Safety, Reliability, Environment, Appearance, Maintainability, etc.

Review Ideas with Owner, A/E

Select Best Ideas For Development

Development Phase

Develop Preliminary Design of Ideas

Prepare Alternate Design Sketches

Prepare Estimate

Life Cycle Comparison
  • Initial Cost
  • Redesign Cost
  • O&M Cost

Recommendation Phase

Develop Recommendations

Summarize Findings

Present VE Ideas to Owner, A/E

Oral Presentation

Determine Acceptance of Ideas

Post VE Study Procedure

VE Study Report

Prepare VE Preliminary Report

Owner/Designer Prepares Final Response with Implementation Recommendations

Final Acceptance

Owner Approval

Submittal to Owner

Final Report with Implementation

Redesign

Project Follow- Up

Bid Analysis

Estimate Implementation

Document Results

Post Operational Evaluation

Optional Services

Figure 4.5

Information step activities to be completed during the prestudy phase include:

- Obtain the following project data, typical for buildings:
  - Program of requirements
  - Design criteria
  - Project constraints
  - Master plan (if available)
  - Environmental assessment
  - Pertinent building codes
  - Alternate designs considered
  - Drawings and outline specifications
  - Design calculations
  - Site utilities and soils data
  - Detailed construction cost estimate
- Obtain special data typical for buildings housing processes shown in Figure 4.6, "Process Data Requirements," if applicable.
- Prepare all models in advance. This ensures project familiarization.
- Read and review all information prior to the study. Make a list of all missing data or need-to-know data, and ask for it.
- Prepare a list of questions or clarifications to ask during the design briefing on the first day of the study.
- Validate cost estimate and draft quality model as required.

Study Phase

The Information Gathering step continues as both client and designer conduct presentations of the project on the first day of the study. They should be asked to leave telephone numbers of key points of contact for the VE study team to use during the study phase.

The Information step is concluded during the study phase by team preparation of the project FAST Diagram, function analysis, assignment of cost and worth to functions, completion of the worth models, calculation of the value index, and selection of specific areas for value improvement. If the major cost elements were not validated during the prestudy phase, the team quickly does so now, if authorized by owner.

The VE team then accomplishes the Creativity & Idea Generation step during the study phase. As many ideas as can be generated are listed.

The Analysis step involves the judgment of ideas. Whenever possible, the client/owner and A-E should be involved before ideas are selected for development. There are many advantages to client and A-E involvement during this step:

- The VE team has a forum in which to discuss advantages and disadvantages with the owner and A-E, from their points of view.
- The VE team can judge whether or not disadvantages to specific ideas can be mitigated or modified to be made acceptable.
- The VE team will not waste time developing proposals that have no chance of implementation. Pressing such proposals might have a detrimental effect on the acceptance of other study ideas.
- Client concerns regarding the study outcome are alleviated, and incubation time is provided for the ideas, permitting a better opportunity for acceptance.

During the Development step, specific recommendations for changes are prepared. Benefits are identified and estimated, impact on LCC is analyzed, sketches are prepared, and implementation costs are determined.

Process Data Requirements

Manufacturing Data

❏ Process flow chart

❏ Equipment list, each piece with:
- production capacity
- horsepower
- utilities required
- cost

❏ Production manpower plan
- shifts or schedule
- salaries/benefits

❏ Raw materials, each with:
- days of inventory needed
- rate used in production
- waste unit cost

❏ Items produced, each with:
- annual production volume
- acceptable reject rate

Warehouse/Shipping Data

❏ Equipment list, each piece with:
- production capacity
- horsepower
- cost

❏ Packaging/shipping methods
- cost

❏ Stock level
- maintain for each product
- shelf life for each product

Administration/Purchasing/Sales Data

❏ Manpower plan
- working hours
- salaries/benefits

❏ Organization chart

❏ Sales, each product
- expected volume
- market value

❏ Other vendor purchases
- volume and cost to support production

❏ Estimates of other annual expenses
- energy consumption
- maintenance/repair
- custodial
- security

Economic Data

❏ Desired return on investment (ROI)

❏ Financing period

❏ Interest rate for analysis purposes

❏ Escalation rates
- salaries
- energy
- raw materials

❏ Life span for analysis

❏ Overhead rate

Figure 4.6

The Presentation/Implementation step also begins during the study phase. On the last day of the study, the VE team makes an oral presentation of its proposals to both client and designer representatives. The purpose of the presentation is to explain the merits of each idea and the rationale for acceptance, and to estimate initial and follow-on cost impact. In addition, the VE team should listen to responses and questions after the presentation. These can often be addressed by modifying proposals to mitigate the concerns expressed.

Poststudy Phase

The balance of the Presentation/Implementation step is completed after the formal study time by the Value Engineering Team Coordinator (VETC), with or without selected team members. This phase normally consists of:

- The preparation of a preliminary draft VE Study Report for distribution to the client.
- An implementation meeting with the client and designer to discuss their responses.
- The preparation of a final report documenting the decisions of the implementation meeting.

Figure 4.7, "Typical VE Study Process," is a chart of the process, outlining the participants and milestones involved in a typical VE study. It indicates the interactions that occur among the study participants.

Note: As an aid for the VE engineer, a format for the VE report, including four sections that will quicken the assembly and preparation of the report, is included on the attached diskette.

Conclusion

VE is an organized approach to problem solving. Proper planning for VE services sets the stage for a successful study. Effective planning includes team selection, development of a Work Plan that incorporates the VE Job Plan, and careful attention to level of effort. A firm foundation for a study can be assured by the careful selection of a Value Engineering Team Coordinator (VETC) who has expertise in group dynamics, and team members whose skills reflect the technical needs of the study. Integration of the owner and designer into the process enhances study results. A Work Plan that incorporates the Job Plan serves as the framework for conducting services. The appropriate level of effort is a function of factors such as project size and complexity as well as constraints of cost versus time and degree of design completion. Level of effort for a given construction project should be reflective of the savings potential.

Typical VE Study Process

Participants and Milestones

I. Pre-study Phase

Owner	VE Consultant	Owner	Design Consultant	VE Consultant
1. Incorporate scope of service in VE contract 2. Advertise VE procurement	3. Identify team members 4. Submit team qualifications and cost proposal	5. Select VE consultant	6. Provide design data approved VE changes	8. Schedule VE study 9. Prepare models 10. Distribute data

II. Study Phase

Team Coordinator	Design Consultant	VE Team	Owner	Design Consultant
1. Assemble and lead VE study team	2. Brief VE team 3. Review VE ideas 4. Attend VE team briefing	5. Conduct VE study 6. Prepare VE proposals 7. Present VE proposals	8. Brief VE team 9. Review VE ideas 10. Attend VE study presentation	11. Comment on Team's Presentation

III. Post-Study Phase

Team Coordinator	Design Consultant	Owner	Design Consultant	Team Coordinator
1. Prepare draft report	2. Comment on each VE proposal	3. Review VE report 4. Review designer comments 5. Approve or disapprove each VE proposal	6. Implement approved VE changes	7. Prepare final report (optional)

Figure 4.7

Chapter Five

Function Analysis

Function analysis, the study of design performance, is the heart of value methodology. It is one of the few things that makes this technique different from all other cost reduction techniques.

The glossary accompanying this text provides definitions for 24 different types of functions that all value engineers need to study and understand. The key function of all those defined is the **basic function.**

Classifying Function

In an effort to make the classical methodology work better in the construction area (as opposed to the industrial area), the classifications of function were modified to include the following:

- Basic function(s)
- Required secondary functions (modification to industrial area)
- Secondary functions

These classifications are defined in the following paragraphs.

Basic Function

Basic function is:

- That which is essential to the performance of a user function, or
- The function describing the primary utilitarian characteristic of a product or design to fulfill a user requirement.

The determination of a basic function is made by asking, "Can the function be eliminated and still satisfy the user?" If the answer is no, the function is basic. All basic functions must be achieved as the result of VE. One cannot eliminate a basic function and satisfy the user. VE does not recommend changes that eliminate or compromise basic function. For example, the basic function of a match is to generate flame. The phosphorus tip is classified as a basic function. No flame can be generated without the tip.

Required Secondary Function

Since the construction field works according to many codes, standards, and safety requirements that must be met if a permit to construct is awarded, a new category—required secondary function—was developed by the author. A required secondary function is any function that must be achieved to meet codes, standards, or mandatory owner requirements. Without this innovation, the worth of the project function developed under the classical approach—either basic function with worth, or secondary function with no worth, resulted in a project worth so low that the value engineer appeared "foolish" to peers. In most cases, the impression it made on peers negated any value gained.

For example, under the classical approach, the basic function of a hospital is to treat patients. Using the classical approach, the fire protection system function is to control/extinguish fire—a secondary function worth zero. Patients can still realize treatment without this system. But, who would build a hospital without a fire protection system? Classifying the function as a required secondary function having worth is a more realistic approach. One can still challenge the extent and manner of performance, but the function is required by code.

Secondary Function

If secondary functions are removed from the design, both the basic and required secondary functions can be realized. As such, their worth is zero. Consider these examples:

- The label on a pencil that identifies product is a secondary function. The basic function of the pencil, making marks, can be achieved without the label.
- A secondary function would be a leveling slab under a slab on grade whose function is to prepare subgrade—a secondary function. The slab's basic function is to "support load." If the leveling slab were removed, you could still support load.

Defining Functions

Functions are defined by using a verb (active if possible) and a noun (measurable if possible). Everything that exists has a function(s) that can be defined in the two word, verb-noun form. Thus VE methodology can be applied to everything.

Functions can be defined at various levels of indenture. For example, the function of a store is to sell merchandise. The next higher-order function is to generate sales, and the next higher-order function would be to generate profits. At the project level, a value engineer asks, "What is the function of the building?" For a prison, the project function might be to confine convicts; for a hospital, to treat patients; for a school, to teach students.

Unless the VE is done at the early program phase, the probability of success for the value engineer working on the higher-order project function(s) of the project is relatively slim. However, this does not mean that the VE team should not challenge the project function(s) if there are strong feelings about it. Working at the lower level of indenture, however, provides greater opportunity for savings, because implementation does not depend on major project changes. For example, if a prison, hospital, or school project were to include a cafeteria, one might explore alternative ways to feed people and achieve implementation with a higher success rate than working on alternatives to teaching students.

Project Level Function Analysis System Technique (FAST) Diagram

Figure 5.1, "FAST Diagram Procedures," is the traditional FAST Diagram for taking project functions and arranging them in logical order.

In recent years, value engineers performing studies in the construction field have often omitted the preparation of a FAST Diagram. Their rationale involved the repetitiveness of redefining building functions that really never vary from project to project. The work and effort to prepare the FAST Diagram is not perceived as worth the benefits gained from project understanding. There are other ways to understand the details of a project, such as performing a cost estimate validation or a design review.

However, the value engineer may be missing out by skipping the FAST Diagram. Why not try to prepare one on the project as a whole, as well as a detailed FAST? When VE is scheduled early for a project, the project-level FAST Diagram helps to define the purpose(s) of the project from the owner's point of view. It brings out

FAST Diagram Procedures

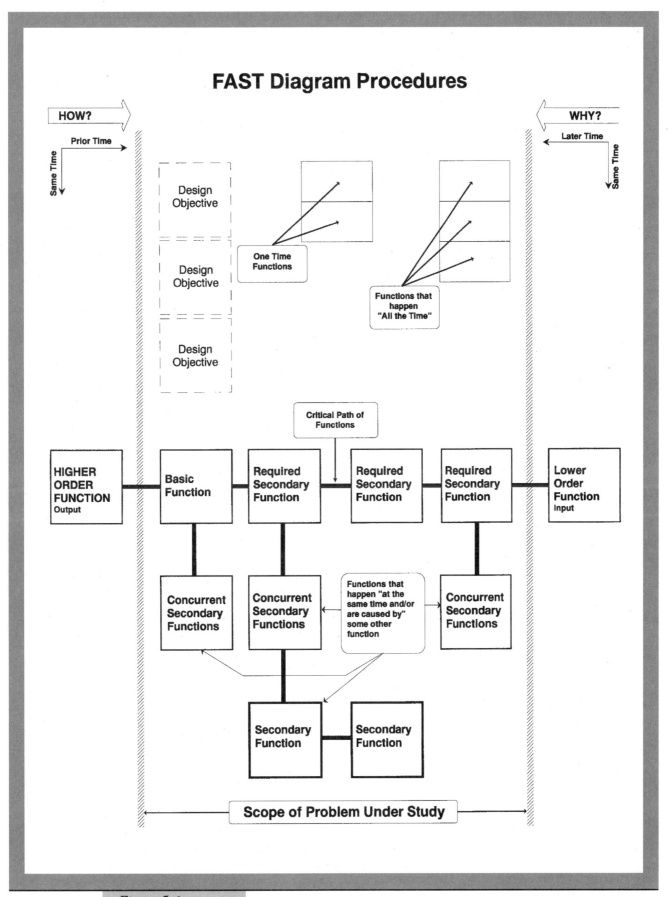

Figure 5.1

the owner's goals, objectives, and aspirations. Use of the FAST Diagram technique has proven to be of exceptional value (see example presented in Figures 5.2–5.11) when first-time VE applications on a project type are conducted. It provides a logical approach to get the team started on a solid basis.

Preparing a project-level FAST Diagram has the following benefits:

- It allows a quick function challenge to validate or question the proposed conceptual design decisions.
- It provides a valuable "mind setting" and "mind tuning" about the project in a short period of time.
- It facilitates presentation and discussion of the project's overall goals with the designer and owner for better communication.

Figure 5.2 illustrates a FAST Diagram prepared at the project level for a new 15,000 seat stadium on a military base. Preparing the diagram led the team to challenge (1) its size based on where it was located, and (2) how spectators and participants were invited to attend. The VE team thought the basic functions of the stadium were to conduct competition and ceremonies (e.g., graduation ceremonies) for the army. When these functions were presented to the commanding general (the user), however, he said it also would be used to parade tanks. Without preparing the FAST Diagram and discussing it with the user, this vital aspect of the VE study would not have been known. It surely influenced the type of ideas presented and the user's receptivity to those ideas.

Figures 5.3a and 5.3b are existing and proposed FAST Diagrams for a departmental contractor information system of a large federal government agency. It was necessary to do the FAST Diagram to find out what was happening and to develop labor-hour and cost elements for the functions being performed. This task consumed more than half of the 40-hour workshop. Idea generation had to be a concurrent effort to develop meaningful proposals within the workshop. The FAST Diagram focused on the high cost of sending tapes and correcting data. New equipment and methods were isolated that cut cost and time by 50%.

Failure to explore the function of a project leads the value engineer to overlook the obvious by assuming knowledge. One can assume that the function of a hospital is to treat patients, but consider the following case:

A request for $63 million was received by the Department of Health, Education, and Welfare (HEW) for a grant to build a hospital next to the beltway circling the city, even though existing city center hospitals were using only 50% of their bed capacity. It seems that traffic to get to them was unbearable and several patients had died in ambulances from beltway accidents.

In this case, the basic functions of the hospital were to save time and to treat patients. There was plenty of room to treat patients downtown, but the patients could not get there in time; so, the team looked at alternatives to save time. Instead of building a hospital, the team recommended using a helicopter service to save time. In this case, challenging the function of the project paid off.

Figure 5.4 illustrates a FAST Diagram developed for a dam project to be used for a water reservoir in Taiwan. The function analysis was costed out and isolated the high cost functions as being (1) to divert flow (temporary tunnel), and (2) to relieve pressure (spillway), both of which were required secondary functions. These costs appeared inordinately high when compared to the basic function of the dam (store water). The study resulted in using the temporary tunnel as part of the final design, thereby allowing the spillway to be reduced in scope.

Figure 5.5 is a FAST Diagram for a supporting service of automatic fare collection for a mass transit system. This FAST Diagram and the life cycle cost (LCC) model in Figure 5.6 focused the VE efforts on the LCC for the passenger agents and their

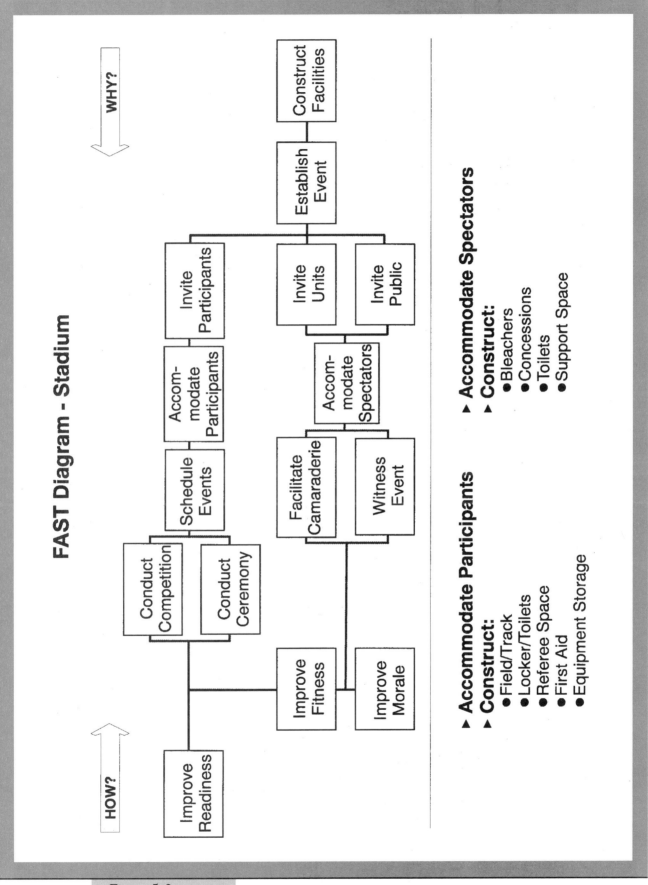

Figure 5.2

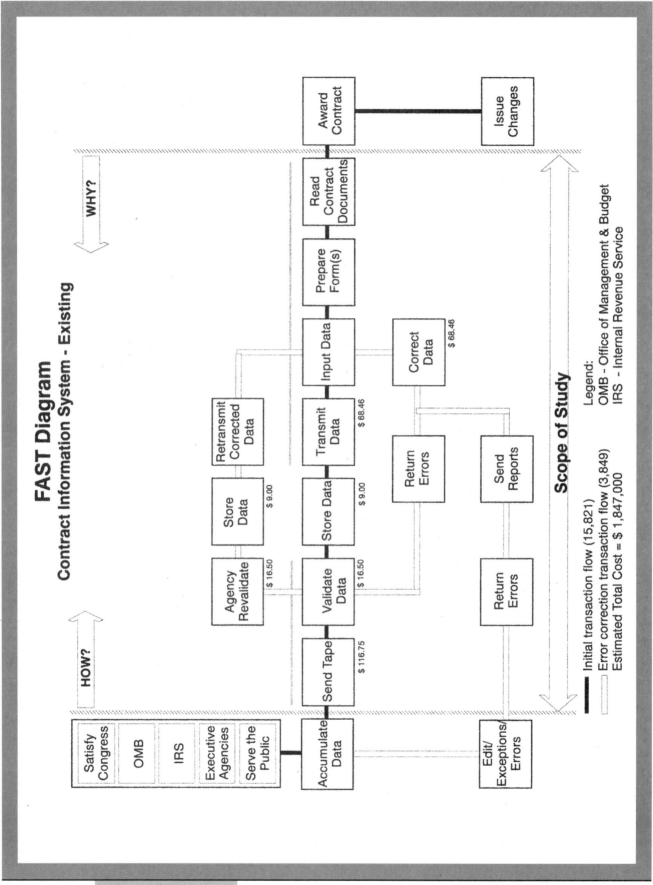

FAST Diagram
Contract Information System - Existing

HOW?
WHY?

Satisfy Congress
OMB
IRS
Executive Agencies
Serve the Public

Accumulate Data
Send Tape — $116.75
Validate Data — $16.50
Store Data — $9.00
Transmit Data — $68.46
Input Data
Prepare Form(s)
Read Contract Documents
Award Contract
Issue Changes

Agency Revalidate — $16.50
Store Data — $9.00
Retransmit Corrected Data

Correct Data — $68.46

Return Errors
Return Errors
Send Reports

Edit/ Exceptions/ Errors

Scope of Study

Legend:
OMB - Office of Management & Budget
IRS - Internal Revenue Service

Initial transaction flow (15,821)
Error correction transaction flow (3,849)
Estimated Total Cost = $ 1,847,000

Figure 5.3a

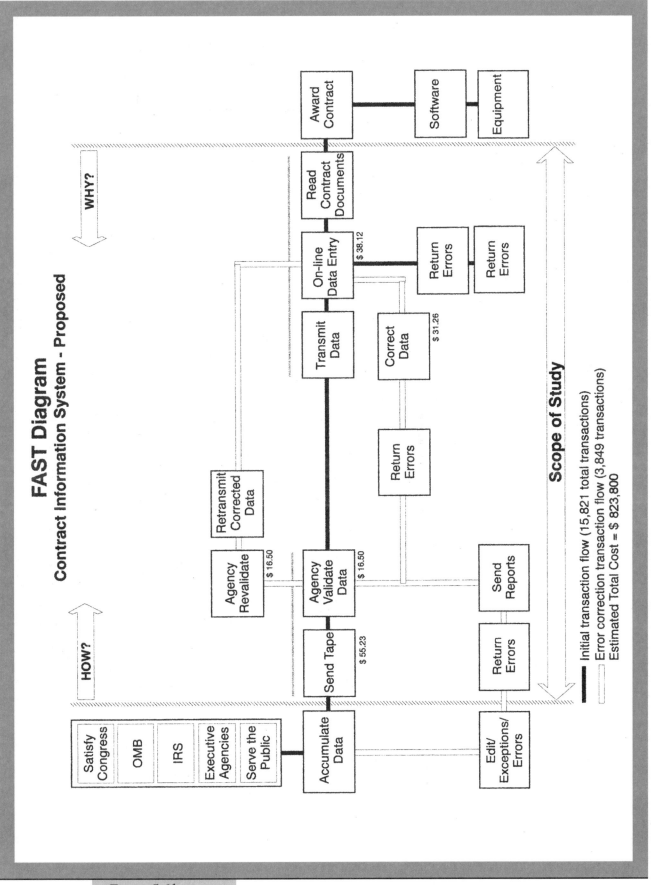

Figure 5.3b

FAST Diagram
Dam for
Large Water Reservoir

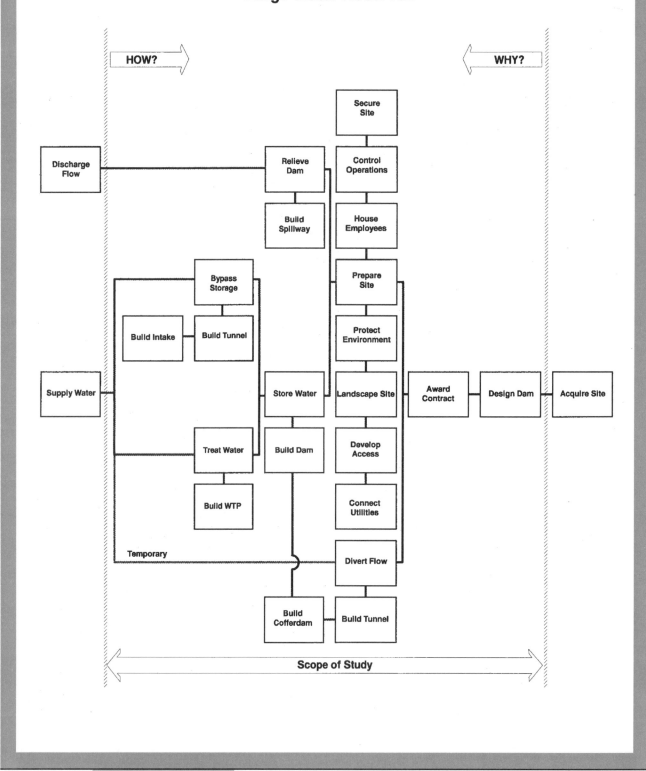

Figure 5.4

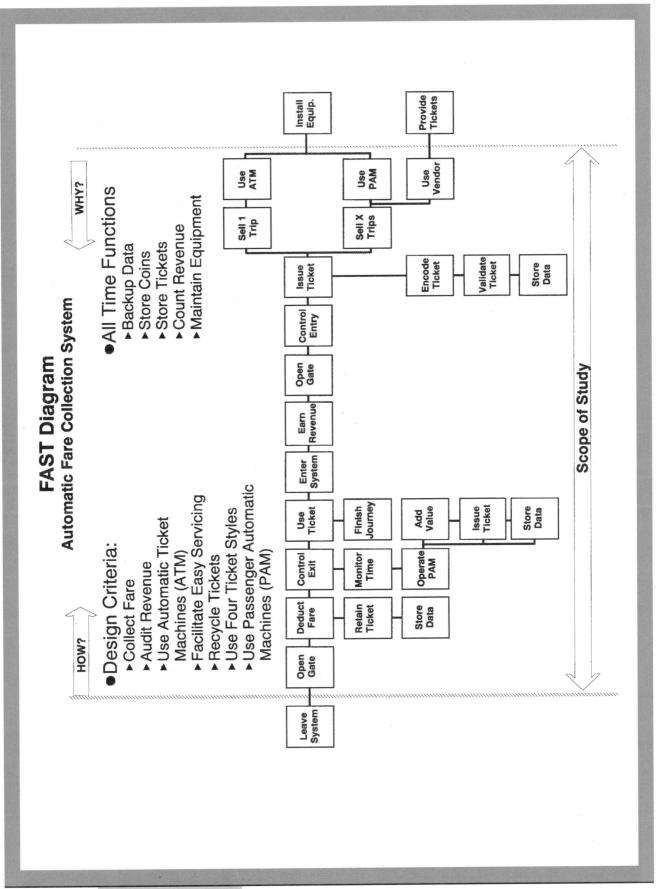

Figure 5.5

Life Cycle Cost Model
Value Engineering Study

Project: **Rapid Transit System**
Section: **Automatic Fare Collection**
Phase of Design:
Date:

AFC System	
848,968	
1,289,786	

Legend:
VE Target:
Actual/Estimated:

Component or System	
VE Target	X 1,000
Actual/Estimated	X 1,000

NOTES:
All costs in Present
Worth NT$ (Taiwan Dollars)
$1 US = 26 NT$

Equipment	Installation	Personnel	Support	Escalation
219,500	26,700	467,083	81,185	54,500
272,797	29,728	828,866	90,081	68,314
ATIN	**Erection**	**Pass. Agent**	**Consumable**	
84,100	25,000	317,935	30,785	
98,735	27,852	635,870	30,785	
PAM	**Cabling**	**Cash Counting**	**Documentation**	
11,500	1,300	16,516	3,200	
23,415	1,476	33,032	4,620	
Computer	**Testing**	**Trans./Recycle**	**Design/Software**	
6,500	400	33,032	34,000	
17,086	400	49,854	36,810	
Gates		**Maintenance**	**Training**	
115,000		99,600	10,000	
121,097		110,110	13,494	
Cash			**Prototype**	
2,400			3,200	
12,464			4,372	

Figure 5.6

required duties. A final study recommendation to use an upgraded automatic fare card (AFC) to issue larger value tickets, which reduced passenger agents' work, was approved.

Figure 5.7 illustrates a FAST Diagram of an air separation facility designed to produce oxygen. The FAST Diagram was converted into a functionally oriented cost model, illustrated in Figure 5.8. The exercise helped focus results on consolidating the design to reduce piping and electrical costs, combining and modifying equipment to reduce both initial costs and LCC. Initial savings of some 10% were implemented on a long-standing company product with a similar reduction in LCC. This study exemplifies the benefits that can accrue by using FAST and combining it with other techniques.

For typical building-oriented VE, a FAST Diagram for one office building is basically the same for all office buildings. This holds true for schools, police stations, hospitals, and so on. As a result, a standardized cost model broken into functional cost areas has been used over several hundred building projects. Figure 5.9 is the function analysis form used recently for a hospital study. The VE team first reviews the project documents, validates the cost estimate, and is briefed on project objectives and constraints. Then the function analysis is performed. The cost/worth model, Figure 5.10, is developed from data from the cost validation and from the function analysis (Figure 5.9). The cost model provides insight and guidance for future team action. In this case, the study focused on the equipment and architectural areas. Overall savings potential was also indicated.

The basis of the worth generated in the function analysis is:

- Historical costs from VE effort for those cost blocks.
- Ideas isolated during the reviews that would affect the cost for that block.
- Alternate system or material concepts to meet requirements, based on team experience.

For typical buildings, very few secondary functions exist. Most are required secondary functions because of codes, standards, and/or mandatory owner requirements.

For additional examples, see the case studies presented in Part Two.

Conclusion

As an aid to better understand the process, Figure 5.11 is a FAST Diagram outlining the steps of a typical VE study. Each task has been isolated and set forth using the "how-why" logic. This diagram, in one page, outlines the key functions performed in a VE study. Blank VE study forms are contained in the Value Engineering Workbook presented in Part Three. In practice, cost forms are linked to move data automatically.

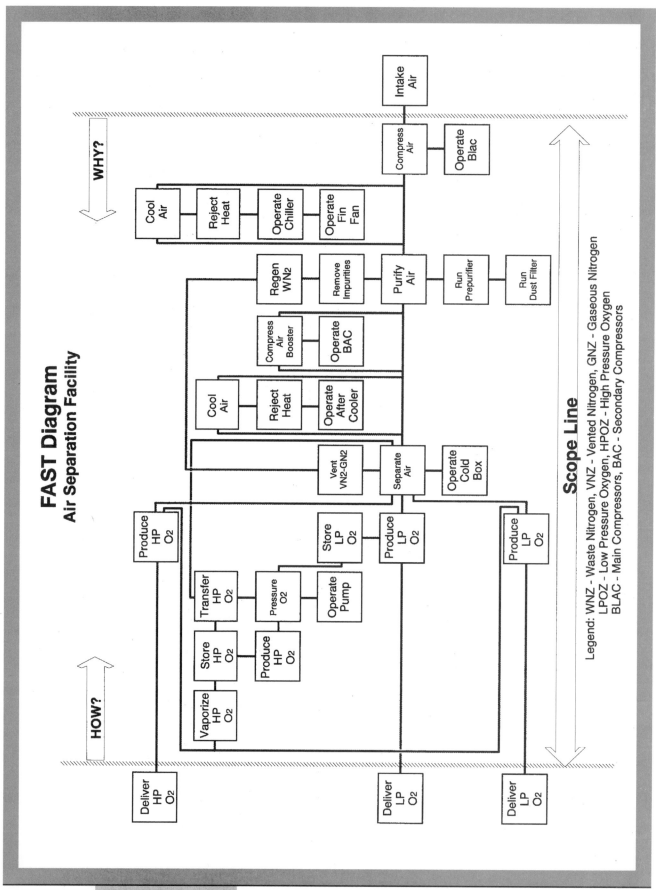

FAST Diagram
Air Separation Facility

Legend: WNZ - Waste Nitrogen, VNZ - Vented Nitrogen, GNZ - Gaseous Nitrogen
LPOZ - Low Pressure Oxygen, HPOZ - High Pressure Oxygen
BLAC - Main Compressors, BAC - Secondary Compressors

Figure 5.7

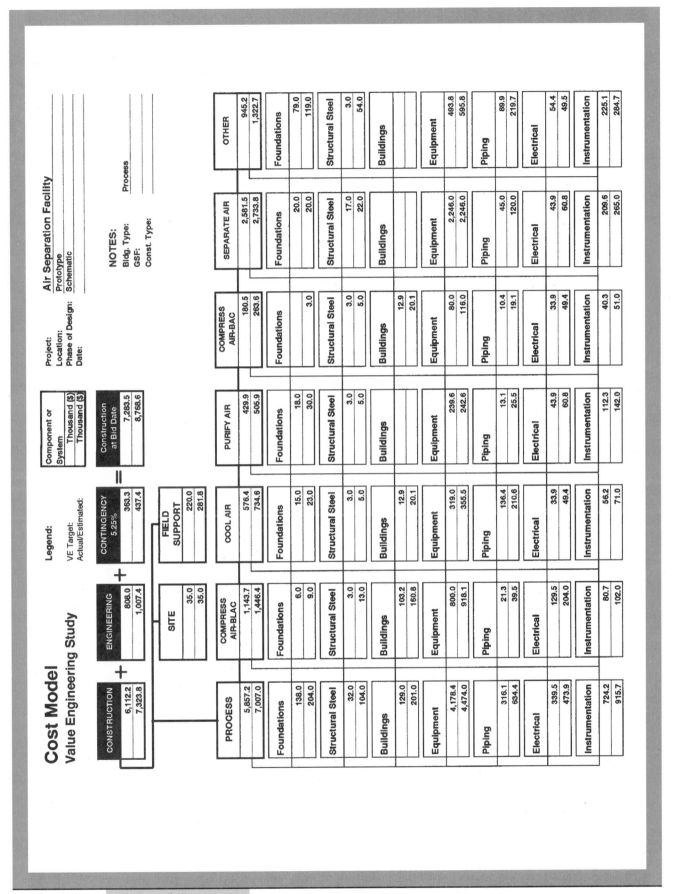

Figure 5.8

FUNCTION ANALYSIS WORKSHEET

PROJECT: Hospital
ITEM: COMPLETE LIST
BASIC FUNCTION: Treat Patients

COMPONENT DESCRIPTION	FUNCTION (VERB-NOUN)	KIND	COST	WORTH	COST/ WORTH	COMMENTS
B = Basic Function S = Secondary Function		RS = Required Secondary Function				
SITE WORK						
Overhead & Profit	Manage Work	RS	907,116	567,367	1.60	Reduce percentage
121 Site Preparation	Prepare Site	RS	62,667	50,133	1.25	
122 Site Improvement	Improve Site	RS	1,755,580	1,267,469	1.39	Relocate structures
123 Site Utilities	Supply Utilities	B	2,578,667	1,408,299	1.83	Revise layout
124 Off-Site Work	Supply Utilities	B	138,667	110,933	1.25	
TOTAL			**5,442,696**	**3,404,201**	**1.60**	
STRUCTURAL						
01 Foundation	Support Load	B	1,701,845	1,267,469	1.34	Eliminate water level
02 Substructure	Support Load	RS	960,557	704,149	1.36	Move substructure to grade level
03 Superstructure	Support Load	B	3,129,387	2,253,278	1.39	Simplify structural system
TOTAL			**5,791,789**	**4,224,896**	**1.37**	
ARCHITECTURAL						
04 Wall Closure	Enclose Space	B	1,816,320	985,809	1.84	Replace granite/marble with precast elements
05 Roofing	Protect Building	RS	408,787	281,660	1.45	Reduce space
06 Interior Const.	Finish and Divide Space	B	7,882,597	4,224,896	1.87	Change wall construction from gypsum to CMU
07 Conveying System	Transport Weight	B	1,123,200	1,126,639	1.00	
TOTAL			**11,230,904**	**6,619,004**	**1.70**	
MECHANICAL						
081 Plumbing	Service Building	B	2,225,867	1,780,693	1.25	Consolidate waste and soil line
082 HVAC	Condition Space	B	4,566,667	3,520,747	1.30	Use unitary cooling
083 Fire Protection	Protect Building and People	RS	800,787	492,905	1.62	Limit sprinklers at public areas
084 Special Mechanical	Control System	RS	933,333	633,734	1.47	
TOTAL			**8,526,653**	**6,428,079**	**1.33**	

Note: Cost in Construction Costs with no contingency or escalation

Figure 5.9

FUNCTION ANALYSIS WORKSHEET

PROJECT: Hospital
ITEM: COMPLETE LIST
BASIC FUNCTION: Treat Patients

COMPONENT DESCRIPTION	FUNCTION (VERB-NOUN)	KIND	COST	WORTH	COST/ WORTH	COMMENTS
B = Basic Function S = Secondary Function		RS = Required Secondary Function				
ELECTRICAL						
091 Service & Dist.	Distribute Power	B	862,667	690,133	1.25	Centralize load
092 Emergency & UPS	Backup Power	RS	2,093,333	1,408,299	1.49	
093 Lighting & Power	Light and Power Space	B	1,292,779	844,979	1.53	Improve light
094 Special Electrical	Support Systems	RS	3,013,333	1,760,373	1.71	
TOTAL			**7,262,112**	**4,703,785**	**1.54**	
EQUIPMENT						
111 Fixed & Mov. Equip.	Support Program	B	1,938,667	1,267,469	1.53	Use local market
112 Furnishing	Support Program	B	N/A	N/A		
113 Special Const. Medical Equipment	Support Program	B	15,733,333	9,153,941	1.72	Use local market & postpone expensive equip.
TOTAL			**17,672,000**	**10,421,410**	**1.70**	
GENERAL						
Mobilization 2%	Mobilize Site	RS	1,009,669	647,943	1.56	Reduce Percentage
Site Overhead 2.5%	Manage Work	RS	1,262,086	809,929	1.56	" "
Demobilization 0.5%	Demobilize Site	RS	252,417	161,986	1.56	" "
Office Expense & Profit 15%	Admin. Project Generate Profit	RS	7,572,519	4,859,576	1.56	" "
TOTAL			**10,096,692**	**6,479,435**	**1.56**	
OVERALL TOTAL			**66,022,846**	**42,280,809**	**1.56**	

Figure 5.9 (cont.)

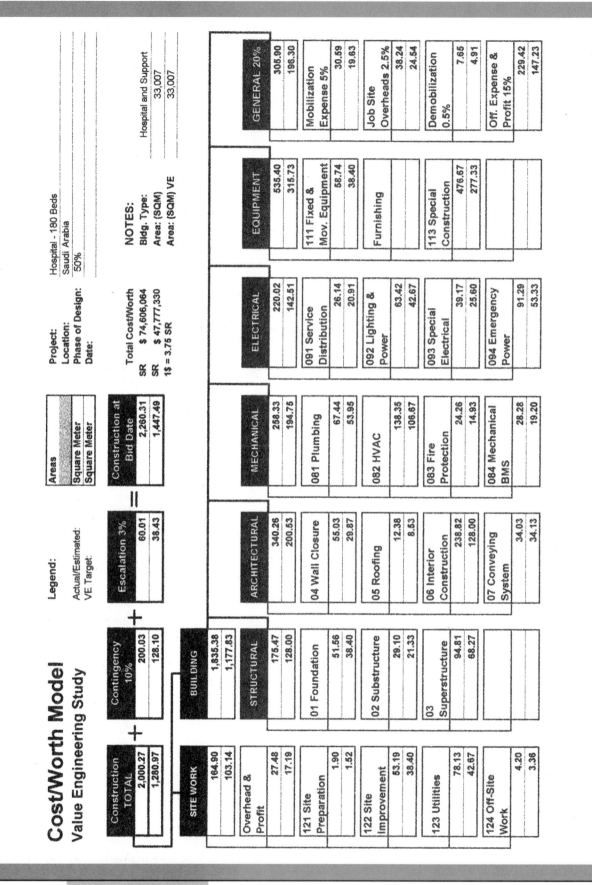

Figure 5.10

Fast Diagram
VE Study

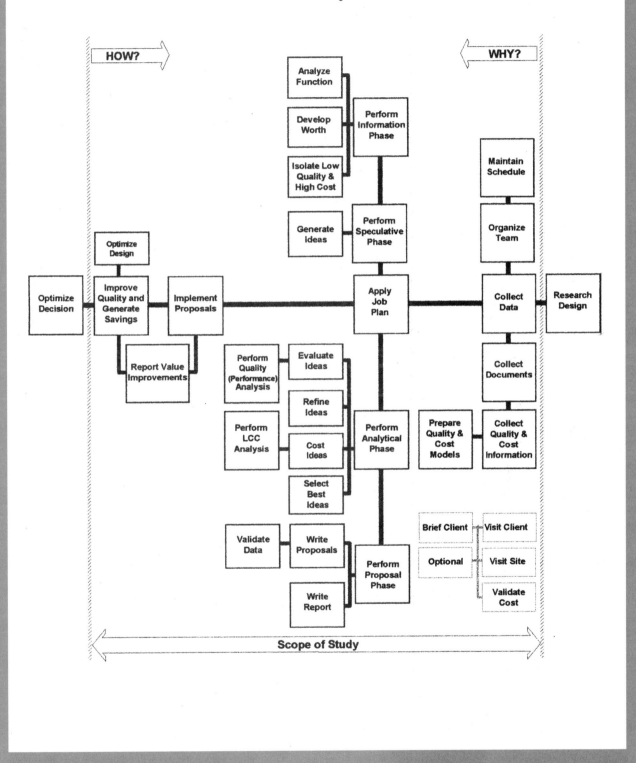

Figure 5.11

Chapter Six

Creativity and Interpersonal Skills

Creativity refers to behavior that uncovers a relationship where none previously existed; a relationship between people, objects, symbols, or any combination of these.

It is the author's belief that we are all born with creative ability and display creativity uninhibitedly as children. As time goes on, parents begin to restrain their children with rules, and formal education takes a toll on creativity. By the time the child grows older and arrives in the "real world," work experience ingrains into the mind what will work and what will not work. (See Figure 6.1, "Creative Ability Versus Age.")

There are many levels of creativity, ranging from discovering something that is new to oneself, to discovering something new to someone else, to patenting an invention.

Creativity and Fixation

When one addresses a problem, if a solution is not uncovered within a short period, fixation may occur. The longer one seeks a solution, the further away it may seem. The result of fixation is that the likelihood of solving a problem diminishes with the passage of time. Figure 6.2 illustrates this phenomenon.

For example, the nine-dot puzzle in Figure 6.2 is normally solved more quickly by homemakers than by engineers. This may be because engineers tend generally to be logical thinkers who may somewhat confine their thinking within preset limits. Homemakers, artists, and architects, on the other hand, may be inclined to reach out more often, establishing fewer boundaries in their problem solving. The example in Figure 6.2 demonstrates the need for a multidisciplinary team for optimizing results of a VE exercise. The solution to the problem—going outside the dots—is shown in Figure 6.3.

Fixation is addressed in the value engineering (VE) process because it can numb capacities to create, develop, and implement ideas. Fixation can force the use of traditional approaches over more creative ones.

Creative techniques are gimmicks (or exercises) to help one overcome fixation. Fortunately, with training and deliberate practice in creative techniques, everyone can regenerate and become highly creative. Because of the team element in the creative process, the rate at which you become creative can depend in large measure on your interpersonal skills.

Creative Ability Versus Age

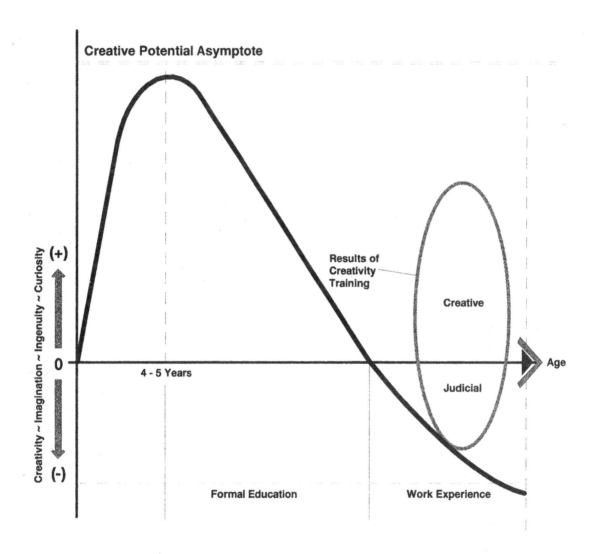

Figure 6.1

FIXATION

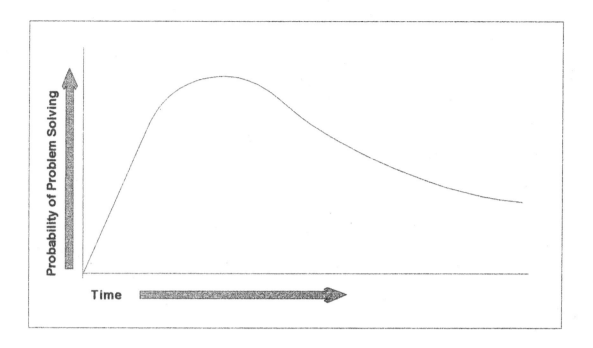

- **Basic solutions come early - the longer the time, the less the probability.**

- **Based on established patterns, fixation sets limits on creative thinking.**

- **Unless overcome, fixation stimulates mediocrity.**

EXAMPLE

Using a pencil, draw 4 straight lines without lifting the pencil off the paper. Connect all dots.

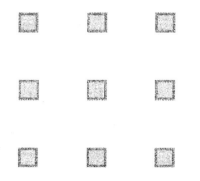

Figure 6.2

SOLUTION

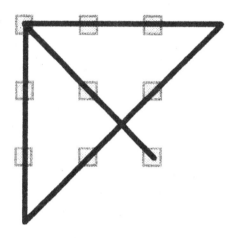

Logical thinkers (engineers, doctors and lawyers) tend to set artificial limits (codes, book solutions, formulas) to their thinking. Many times, the solution lies outside traditional problem solving. Eskimos, housewives, and children solve this problem much more easily than engineers do. This problem illustrates that creativity sometimes means moving beyond your fixed problem solving approaches, e.g., going outside the dots to solve the problem.

Figure 6.3

Interpersonal Skills

Dr. Richard E. Larew, a professor of civil engineering at Ohio State University, teaches engineers about interpersonal skills. His course explores the following six characteristics of an outstanding engineer.

Demonstrates technical ability.

Uses generally accepted and emerging technology.

Uses generally accepted and emerging industry practices.

Uses available resources (books, journals, films, files) to learn from others.

Knows own capabilities and does not exceed them.

Demonstrates analytical and problem-solving ability.

Distinguishes between relevant facts and extraneous information.

Identifies needed data.

Uses an organized plan for data collection, analysis, and presentation of results.

Completes assignments on time and within budget.

Demonstrates leadership skills.

Takes the initiative (proceeds without being told).

Develops effective interpersonal relationships.

Accepts the risks associated with initiative and responsibility.

Uses group resources.

Demonstrates communication skills.

Adapts to the reader or listener.

Presents relevant, logical, and timely summaries.

Listens, reads, and observes to understand the views of others.

Shares relevant information.

Demonstrates selling skills.

Supports proposals or suggestions for change with a convincing explanation or demonstration of

- the need for the project, effort, expenditure, etc.
- the practicality (workability) of the idea, plan, or device.
- the desirability (benefits exceed costs) of the effort.
- the preferability (better than alternatives) of the plan.

Defends the "sale" by answering questions, providing additional information, or refuting arguments.

Demonstrates personal attributes.

Integrity

Emotional stability

Enthusiasm

Self-confidence

Sense of responsibility

Empathy toward fellow workers

These factors closely relate to the professional development of a creative, outstanding value engineer. A review of contemporary building projects indicates that designs are satisfactory within discipline areas. However, poor value results from a failure to (1) develop a cost effective program to meet owner needs, and (2) to draw upon interpersonal skills to effectively integrate required building systems. Increases in cost and time are incurred for user/owner changes and compromises that are required to realize needed program and building system integration.

Human Factors

The leadership provided by the Value Engineering Team Coordinator (VETC) is a key component of the successful VE study. The VETC must orchestrate the study, using strong interpersonal skills to bring the owner and designers constructively into the process. For this reason, the VETC should have a basic understanding of the human factors that are aspects of any study.

Leadership

As indicated by Professor Carew, leadership skills are essential to success. Since VE deals more with people than the traditional approach does, we should overview the principal styles of leadership. Figure 6.4 illustrates these principal styles.

As noted in Figure 6.4, there are basically five styles of leadership. These styles vary in time and effectiveness. The "Tell" (dictatorial) style is the fastest way to implement a solution. However, the effectiveness of the solution leaves much to be desired. As we move from left to right, the styles of leadership take more time, but the effectiveness of solutions increases. The VE approach focuses on the "Join" type of leadership style. This style takes a bit more time, but the effectiveness of solutions is optimized. This is one of the principal reasons why the VE approach consistently can improve decision making over the traditional ("Non-Join") approach to design solutions.

Management

Since people make up the managers and problem solvers, a quick overview of the management matrix and people grid is appropriate. Figure 6.5 is a typical managerial grid. It indicates that there are basically three types of people:

- Strong achievers
- Friendly helpers
- Logical thinkers

By analyzing the people who are involved in a VE study and their reaction to various situations, a VE Team Coordinator has a much better chance of working with and motivating them towards acceptable solutions. Friendly helpers typically respond to requests for their assistance that let them know how well liked they are. Friendly helpers do not appreciate demands or yelling. The VETC who "kills them with kindness" will get their total support.

When working with strong achievers, make sure the environment is set up for quick results. You will hold their attention for only a short time. Also, if there are political or people problems, the strong achievers will become frustrated and unable to work well.

You must work with logical thinkers to overcome their frustration with group dynamics. They want to jump to developing proposals as soon as the information phase begins. They will focus on developing their own approach, rather than using the proven VE methodology. Logical thinkers are difficult to hold through the creative phase. However, when it comes to writing up proposals with technical documentation, this type is your best performer.

Know the personality types you have on the team, and learn to use them to your best advantage. In forming a team, try to select a balance of types. Get to know each team member and focus on each member's strong points.

Salesmanship

As indicated in Professor Carew's outline, selling skills are a basic requirement for success. This is especially important to value engineers, because without the owner/designer's acceptance of their proposals, there are no results.

The Adjustive-Reaction Model, an aid to help sell proposals, is illustrated in Figure 6.6. The key points this figure brings out are:

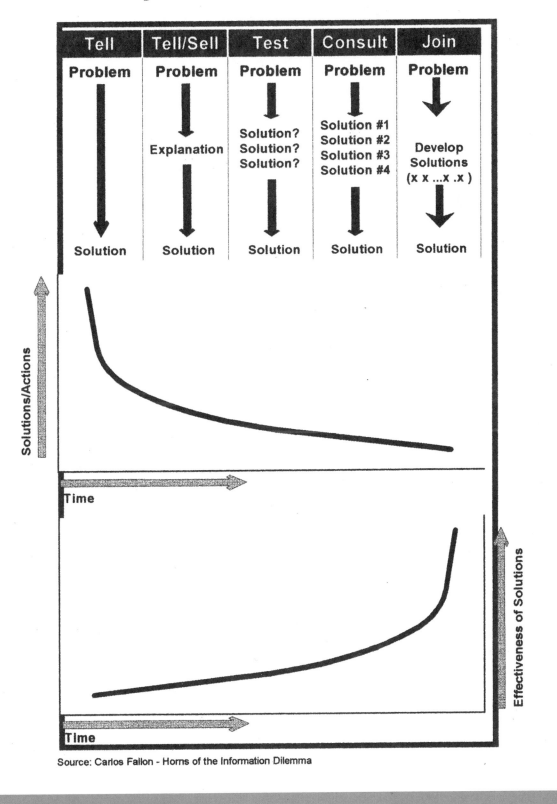

Styles of Leadership

Tell	Tell/Sell	Test	Consult	Join

Tell
Problem
↓
Solution

Tell/Sell
Problem
↓
Explanation
↓
Solution

Test
Problem
↓
Solution?
Solution?
Solution?
↓
Solution

Consult
Problem
↓
Solution #1
Solution #2
Solution #3
Solution #4
↓
Solution

Join
Problem
↓
**Develop Solutions
(x x ...x .x)**
↓
Solution

Solutions/Actions

Time

Effectiveness of Solutions

Time

Source: Carlos Fallon - Horns of the Information Dilemma

Figure 6.4

Managerial Grid

Types	Good With Group to:	Under Stress Would:	Tough Situation	Tender Situation	
STRONG ACHIEVER	Locomote, get decision; gatekeeper by command.	Rather **WIN** than solve problem.	COMFORTABLE	CAN'T HANDLE	Mover who gets decisions, anxious when frustrated.
FRIENDLY HELPER	Harmonize, compromise; gatekeeper out of concern.	Rather be **LIKED** than solve problem.	CAN'T HANDLE	COMFORTABLE	Harmonizes & compromises, supports, e.g., picker - upper.
LOGICAL THINKER	Order logic, information.	Rather be **RIGHT** than solve problem.	CAN'T HANDLE	CAN'T HANDLE	Establishes order, walks out when frustrated.

■ Strong Achiever~will win only when learns feelings are facts (tender feelings are facts).

■ Friendly Helper~has to learn that conflict is reality.

■ Logical Thinker ~must learn that feelings influence solutions; these are facts of life (feelings are facts).

Source: Wallen & Berry Oskdry - Managerial Grid

Figure 6.5

Adjustive - Reaction Model

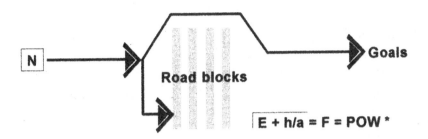

$$E + h/a = F = POW *$$

N = Set of Needs
E = Energy
h = hostility
a = anger
F = Frustration

* POW effect = Frustration, physical or
emotional suicide, to not
release frustration.

Model

Time →

Fight	Flight	Deny	Cope
▸ Agree ▸ Suppress ▸ Repress ▸ Project ▸ Displace ▸ Negativism	▸ Rationalization	▸ All or None	▸ Problem Solve ▸ Act

Motto: It is all right; expect negative reaction to change; however, allow time
to go though process of Fight - Flight - Deny and eventually Cope may
result.

Figure 6.6

- If one keeps pushing against a roadblock continually without relief, results could be catastrophic.
- One should seek the means to overcome or bypass roadblocks. If you are not initially successful, drop that particular effort.
- It is normal for people to resist change. Often, the initial reaction will be negative! Allow the original decision maker the time and space to go through the process and problem solve. Then that person can act constructively on the proposal. If you cannot get by the "fight" stage, it will be wise to drop that item and seek positive results in other areas.

Positive Attitude

An overview of VE study participants' attitudes in three separate studies is illustrated in Figure 6.7. The VE team leader should encourage a positive attitude in all participants throughout the study. However, the VE Job Plan application does result in some highs and lows. These should be recognized and dealt with in a positive manner. As long as the study concludes with positive reactions, the results will justify the means. The VE team leaders must maintain a positive attitude at all times. A positive attitude will lead to positive results, while a negative attitude will lead to negative results.

Creativity Throughout the Job Plan

Creativity and interpersonal skills seem to occupy one step in the VE Job Plan: the "Creativity & Idea Generation" step. Actually, the whole value process is creative and requires interpersonal skills, including the following:

- **The organization itself**. It must be open to and ready to accept change.
- **The project selection**. One must try to sense the best opportunities to make a difference in cost, performance, and/or schedule. Cost models, quality models, and techniques such as the Delphi Method will help to bring about a new sense of the possibilities. (See discussion of the Delphi Method later in this chapter.)
- **The team selection**. Try to assemble a group of strangers. Each person should come from a different discipline, bringing a point of view and premise not held by others. All must learn the value language to develop optimum solutions using the Job Plan. Results are gained from a creative climate, a new language, a stranger group, and an expectation that the project is larger than any one team member.
- **The information step**. Traditionally, the methodology urges us to gather more information, gather more exact information, place numbers on the key ideas, and build models for cost. All of these actions require new thinking.
- **Function analysis**. Building function/cost/worth analyses requires creativity in determining how to allocate cost and what alternatives are to be used to judge worth. It gives a new understanding of both the cost to perform a function and the amount of resources proposed to perform the function.
- **The creative step**. The application of creative methods should ensure that creative ideas are many, diverse, and respected for what they represent—the potential for an improved solution.
- **The analysis step**. This step involves creative application of the evaluation process—stimulating thought about advantages and disadvantages of all ideas, developing criteria for weighted evaluation, and ranking ideas. This step is an orderly approach to eliminating alternative solutions through a positive process.
- **The development step**. This step is creative in its insistence on bringing more facts to bear, including life cycle cost (LCC) and break-even analysis. It is creative in its effort to mitigate unfavorable features of ideas, in its analysis to anticipate potential roadblocks, and in its development of strategies to encourage implementation.

Participants' Attitudes During VE Study

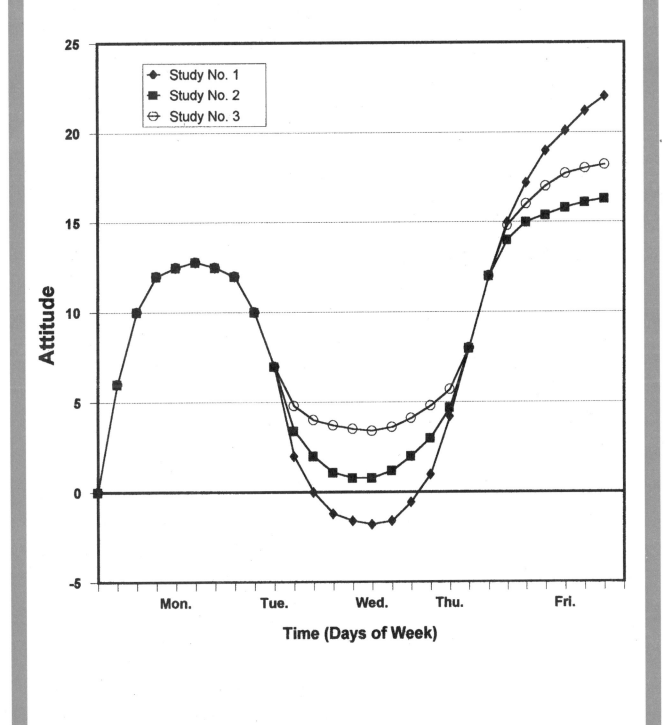

Figure 6.7

- **The presentation step**. This step can be either the most important or the least important of all the Job Plan steps. It is the most important step if the decision makers have not been active in the process. It is the least important, a pro forma, if the decision makers have taken an active part in creative activity from the project selection to proposal development.

Creativity goes further in anticipating, predicting, adapting to, and dealing with negativism and other forces that hinder implementation. If the entire process may be identified as creative, is there a real need to have a discrete step for creativity? If it is all creative—organization in attitudes and expectations; project selection; team selection; methods used to gather information; function analysis; and so on—what is left for the phase called "speculative" or "creative"?

The creative step is necessary to

- transform the team into a creative organization and process;
- produce and document alternative concepts;
- appreciate the accomplishment; and
- enable the team to use its results for the next steps in the Job Plan.

The Generation of Ideas

In VE, new ideas may occur at any stage, but there must be a step in which ideas are accumulated: the "Creativity & Idea Generation" step. To speculate is to ponder, to muse, to reach out. All have a serious tone. VE adds the notion that speculation may have a lighter tone. Techniques for generating ideas include brainstorming and checklisting, both of which are described in the following sections.

Brainstorming

Behavioral scientists know dozens of methods for speculation and generation of creative alternatives. In the general practice of VE in construction, brainstorming is most often used for the creative step. Figure 6.8 illustrates the generally accepted rules for brainstorming.

Brainstorming is a freewheeling type of creativity. A typical brainstorming session takes place when four to six people sit around a table and spontaneously generate ideas designed to solve a specific problem. During this session, no attempt is made to judge or evaluate the ideas. Evaluation takes place after the brainstorming session has ended. Normally, a group leader will open the session by posing a problem. A team leader records each idea offered by the group, sometimes with the assistance of a tape recorder. Before opening the session, the group leader might set the stage by reviewing the following group brainstorming guidelines:

1. Rule out criticism. Withhold adverse judgment of ideas until later. If nothing good can be said about an idea, nothing should be said.

2. Generate a large number of possible solutions; set a goal of multiplying the number of ideas produced in the first rush of thinking by five or ten.

3. Seek a wide variety of solutions that represent a broad spectrum of attacks on the problem.

4. Watch for opportunities to combine or improve ideas.

5. Before closing the session on possible solutions, allocate time for a subconscious operation on the problem while consciously performing other tasks.

The elimination of adverse judgment from the idea-producing stage allows for the maximum accumulation of ideas. It prevents the premature death of a potentially good idea. Also, it conserves time by preventing shifts from the creation of ideas to the evaluation of the ideas. Consideration of all ideas encourages everybody to

Rules of Brainstorming

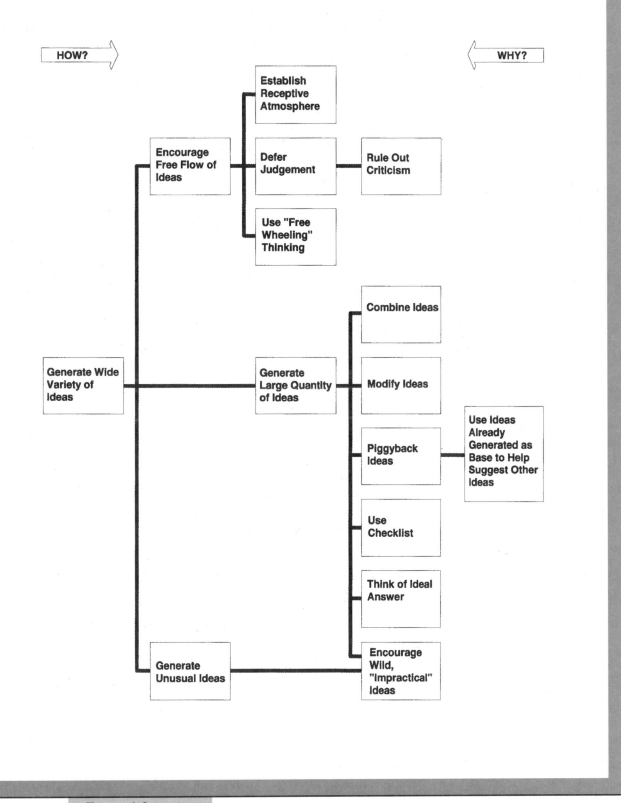

Figure 6.8

explore new areas, even those that seem impractical. This gives an opportunity to the innovator, who might be reluctant to voice thoughts under ordinary conditions for fear of ridicule.

In addition to contributing ideas of their own, participants should suggest how ideas of others might be expanded, or how two or more ideas can be joined into still another idea. Two or more people working together under these ground rules can generate more ideas than one person working alone. This is possible because ideas generated by various members of the group can be modified or improved, and the resulting ideas can be offered as possible solutions to the problem. The idea-generating efficiency of the group increases as its size increases, until it reaches the point where operation becomes so cumbersome as to discourage some members' participation. If this occurs, it may be time to split the group into smaller working groups.

The members of the group should be selected to represent different work backgrounds. However, a key member should have a working familiarity with the subject under study. Group members need not all know one another before the session, but they should not come from different levels within the organization. This will reduce the possibility of senior members exerting pressure or dominance on junior members.

The technique and philosophy of brainstorming may also be used by individuals to generate solutions to problems. However, this is not usually as productive as group brainstorming. Brainstorming does not always yield a final solution, but it does at least generate leads toward the final solution.

Checklisting

A checklist is an accumulation of points, areas, or possibilities that serve to provide ideas, clues, or leads concerning the problem or subject under consideration. The objective is to obtain a number of ideas for further follow-up and development. The checklist is one of the most commonly used aids in the search for new ideas. Checklists range from the specialized to the extremely generalized. For example, numerous publications assist the designer with energy conservation ideas, and they provide a checklist to simply remind the designer of key concepts that save energy. The author's experience indicates that from 20% to 40% of the ideas generated today are drawn from previous studies.

Using the Creative Problem-Solving Techniques

Creative problem-solving techniques are the tools used to expand the team's creative ability. The techniques eliminate habitual responses and force people to use innovative thinking. The human mind is greater than the most elaborate computer in that it can store an almost infinite amount of data; unfortunately, it can process and integrate only up to about seven bits of data simultaneously. Because of this limitation, the previous group brainstorming rules are helpful in applying the creative approach to problem solving.

However, these techniques can be modified for special situations. All people are not alike. People vary in education, importance, experience, and managerial level. VE studies also vary in size, complexity, and schedule. Thus it is difficult to always follow all the VE steps and brainstorming guidelines. However, there are two general rules that apply to all creative exercises:

- Withhold judgment about any idea(s).
- Treat all ideas with respect.

Following is a discussion of an idea-generating technique that is especially useful in construction situations.

Delphi Technique

The Delphi technique was born of a Rand Corporation response to the army's request for a way to overcome the dilemma of having to act on information provided by experts who give contradictory recommendations and by decision makers who are uninformed about the experts' specialties. It worked so well for the army that IBM picked it up. The Japanese government and industry adapted it to predict markets in dozens of countries and for hundreds of products. Now it is part of value engineering.

There are several Delphi patterns for various applications: construction, marketing, allocation of resources, and so forth. We will concentrate only on the pattern useful to construction.

The Delphi technique is particularly effective in the following situations:
- Short VE studies of one to three days.
- Studies made up of team members with no VE experience; i.e., the owner, designer, and other outside experts.
- Studies in which participants are high-caliber, high-salary employees who are not inclined to learn the "nitty gritty" about VE techniques.

The goal of Delphi is to pick the brains of experts quickly, treating them as contributors. Delphi identifies experts' central tendency regarding (1) where they feel VE potential lies in a project and (2) what they would do to change the design. Delphi was not originally intended to determine a consensus among experts on these matters; rather, when it is used in construction, the Delphi technique should foster constructive cooperation among participants who will agree not to disagree and to explore further.

Delphi works in phases or cycles, as illustrated by Figure 6.9. The following sequence applies:

1. **Group**: Each group of three to five experts is assigned a portion of the project relating to their area of expertise. This might be a team to study space, energy, or one of the building systems. In Delphi, the mechanical team might consist of all mechanical engineers. The team should not be multidisciplinary. Each group reviews and discusses its portion of the design, cost estimate, models, and specifications, and sets up a Delphi worksheet, as illustrated in Figure 6.10. In some cases, when time and funds are limited, the group may be assigned the total project and would be multidisciplinary.

2. **Individual**: Next, each individual in the group uses his or her expertise to write down ideas to improve value for the function(s) shown (see Figure 6.11). Once this is accomplished, the leader asks each individual to accept his or her own ideas and indicate what the effect would be on estimated cost if all of them were adopted. Target percentages of cost reduction are placed against each of the components. The new total of target cost is then recorded in the upper left corner of the format, and becomes an indication of system worth.

3. **Group**: Once the individuals are finished, all ideas are discussed in the group and individuals reveal cost targets to one another. It is important at this time that all members of the group listen to the individuals on either end of the central tendency of the group. Those who see savings opportunities and those who see spending opportunities should each explain the rationale for their thinking. The group should attempt to agree to report all of their ideas and their average target cost, as well as a minority report, as appropriate.

4. **Conference**: The conference is a meeting of all the groups—mechanical group, architectural group, etc. The purpose of the conference is for each group to reveal all ideas to the other groups for sharing, modifying, and "hitchhiking" (where one idea becomes an inspiration for another).

Delphi Phases & Cycles

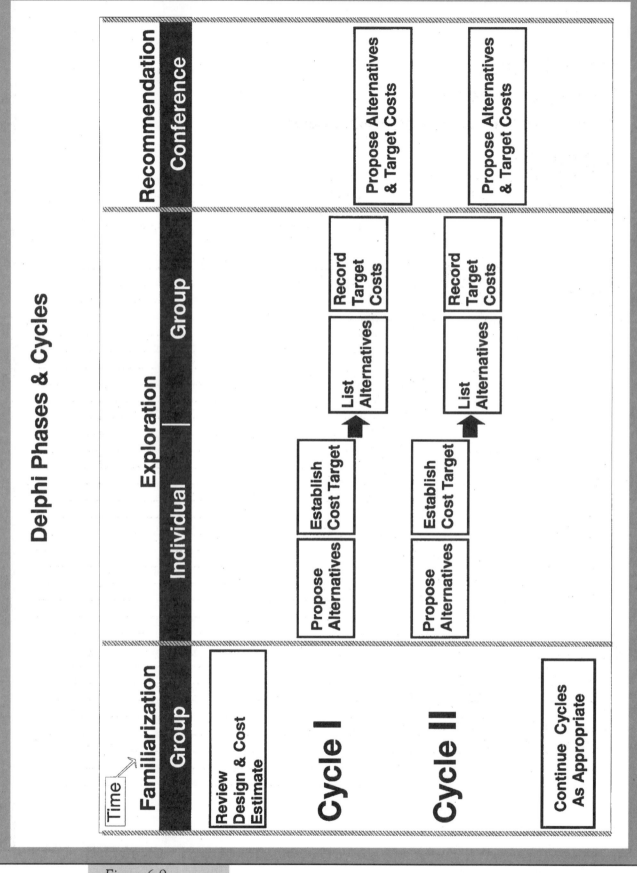

Figure 6.9

106

Chapter Six Creativity and Interpersonal Skills

Cost Control

The Delphi Method

Delphi Example of HVAC System Initial Setup

HVAC	
$850,00	

Element Description	Project:	GSA	Cycle	1
Target Cost	Location:		Sheet	1
Estimated Cost	Building Type:	Office	Date	
	Construction Type:		Phase	

Functions (Verb/Noun)

Control	Temperature
Reduce	Humidity
Supply	Air

Alternatives

Components — **Cost**

Components	Cost
Chiller	486,600
Cooling Tower	31,200
CW Connections	119,400
Pumps	23,300
CW Piping	10,000
Air Handling Units	81,400
Duct Work	70,900
VAV Boxes	20,200
Controls	7,500

Rational & Assumptions

110,000 GSF

VAV System, 440 tons, 250 SF/Ton

Rooftop Chiller with Cooling Tower

Design temperature 70 °F Summer, 72 °F Winter

Separate in-line electric duct heaters

Figure 6.10

Cost Control

The Delphi Method

Delphi Example of HVAC System Individual Worksheet

HVAC	
794,745	Target Cost
850,500	Estimated Cost

Element Description

Project: GSA   Cycle   1

Location: Sheet   1

Building Type: Office   Date

Construction Type: Phase

Functions (Verb/Noun)

Control	Temperature
Reduce	Humidity
Supply	Air

Components

Components	Cost	Targets
Chiller	486,600	-5%
Cooling Tower	31,200	-5%
CW Connections	119,400	
Pumps	23,300	-25%
CW Piping	10,000	
Air Handling Units	81,400	
Duct Work	70,900	-30%
VAV Boxes	20,200	-10%
Controls	7,500	-10%

Alternatives

Reduce Tonnage
Reorient Building
Water Cooled Chiller
FCU System
Reduce Outside Air
Fix Windows
Self Contained Packages
Return Air in Plenum
Increase VAV Spacing
Put Chiller on Grade
Air Cooled Condenser
78° F Summer Design
68° F Winter Design
Delete Return Air Insulation
Delete Standby Pumps
Split Chiller Loads
Reduce Lighting Loads
Energy Efficient Standards
Reduce Operating Hours

Rationale & Assumptions

110,000 GSF
VAV System, 440 Tons, 250 SF/Ton
Rooftop Chiller with Cooling Tower
Design Temperature, 70° F Summer, 72° F Winter
Separate In-line Electric Duct Heaters

Figure 6.11

The Delphi procedure is repeated for at least one more cycle to permit group discussion and accommodation of what they learned at the conference. From this effort comes a list of alternatives for further analysis and development into VE proposals.

Value Engineering—A Crafted Strategy

VE is crafted in its strategy and tactics to provide the designer and owner the time, the place, the staff—and conditions of dignity—to consider innovation to major improvements on the original design. The improvements can be made in total costs, performance, reliability, quality, producibility, serviceability, and use of resources.

This strategy is crafted from the very beginning to invite protected risk and the possibility to achieve design excellence. The tactics range from the project and team formation, to the problem-solving order of the Job Plan, to the offset of fixation. Throughout this process, the team leader should have a special sensitivity to human factors and exercise effective interpersonal skills as needed.

The creativity requirement in the VE program must answer these questions:
- What alternatives provide a lower total cost at no loss in performance of required functions?
- How can we adopt changes without violating fixed schedules?
- How can we be sure that the proposal will please the principals
  - for schedule?
  - for cost?
  - for performance?
  - for personal recognition?

Consider this example of a crafted strategy: A recent VE study was conducted on a corporate office building. The building consisted of two triangular-shaped, high-rise towers. The design concept was quite expensive but impressive. Looking at the design, the logical VE challenge was the twin tower design. However, experience indicated that any change would bring great resistance from the designer. In an effort to establish a positive environment, a trip to the architect's office was taken before the workshop. The opening statements from the VETC were, "Tell us what your essential design element is, and we will do all we can to preserve that element," and "Yet, we must achieve the owner's objective of meeting budget and schedule." The design architect expressed his firm desire to maintain the twin-tower concept. They discussed various other design elements over tea. The meeting established such a good relationship that the VE Team Coordinator invited the design architect to attend the workshop. The VETC also invited the general manager and chief engineer from the owner project real estate development firm.

At this workshop some 130 ideas were generated, from which 50 proposals were produced. A key contributor to these ideas was the design architect. At the end of the workshop the general manager approved all the proposals, and the design architect agreed to implement them with minor modifications. It was a grand success because of a bit of crafted strategy. See Case Study One in Part Two for more detail on the ideas that were implemented.

Note: An Excel spreadsheet is included in the VE tools on the diskette to collect and evaluate ideas generated.

Conclusion

Value engineering is crafted from the beginning to protect risk and to achieve design excellence. Creative VE strategies are included in project and team formation, the problem-solving order of the Job Plan, and in the offset of fixation, which results in an inability to solve a problem. Throughout the study process, the VE Team Coordinator (VETC) must encourage creativity, have a special sensitivity to human factors, and exercise effective interpersonal skills to bring the owner and the designers constructively into the process. For these reasons, the VETC's leadership is a key component of a successful VE study.

Value engineers should be cognizant of the variety of leadership styles and personality characteristics that might be displayed by people with whom they work. They must develop effective sales skills for promotion of proposals for owner/designer acceptance and for team motivation. They must become adept at brainstorming, checklisting, and creative problem-solving techniques—three methods for expanding the VE team's idea generation.

Often, it seems, a review of VE studies reveals a lack of creativity in the bulk of projects. An underlying cause appears to be the failure of curriculums to offer instruction in subjects such as creativity, group dynamics, interpersonal skills, and human factors. Technically satisfactory designs alone do not produce cost effective programs that meet owner needs and integrate required building systems. This type of poor value results in increased cost and time incurred for owner/designer changes and the compromises necessary to realize progam and building systems integration.

Chapter Seven

Life Cycle Costing

Life cycle costing (LCC) is the process of making an economic assessment of an item, area, system, or facility by considering significant costs of ownership over an economic life, expressed in terms of equivalent costs. The essence of LCC is the analysis of equivalent costs of various alternative proposals.[1] To ensure that costs are compared on an equivalent basis, the baseline used for initial costs must be the same as that used for all other costs associated with each proposal, including maintenance and operating costs.

LCC is used to compare proposals by identifying and assessing economic impacts over the design life of each alternative. In making decisions, both present and future costs are taken into account and related to one another. Today's dollar is not equal to tomorrow's dollar. Money invested in any form earns, or has the capacity to earn, interest. For example, $100 invested at 10% annual interest, compounded annually, will grow to $673 in 20 years. In other words, it can be said that $100 today is equivalent to $673 in twenty years' time if the money is invested at the rate of 10% per year. The exact amount depends on the investment rate (cost of money) and the length of time. A current dollar is worth more than the prospect of a dollar at some future time, as inflation changes the value of money over time. Total owning and operating costs of buildings have been rising steadily for many years. However, since LCC analysis involves cost at various times, constant dollars must be used for the analysis.

LCC techniques should also be used when undertaking cost-effectiveness studies and benefit-cost analyses. The lack of such formal procedures can lead to poor decisions.

LCC techniques were introduced as a direct consequence of the energy crisis. The Office of the President of the United States has issued directives to government agencies to reduce energy consumption and has encouraged everyone to reduce energy use. Since energy is an annual cost, LCC principles are required to equate its impact against initial costs.

A number of government agencies have already introduced mandatory LCC requirements. The Environmental Protection Agency (EPA) requires a cost-effectiveness analysis of alternative processes for the early planning and design of wastewater treatment plants. The U.S. Air Force was one of the first government agencies to use LCC for its housing schemes. The U.S. Naval

Facilities Engineering Command has published a guide,[2] and the Corps of Engineers has issued a manual.[3]

Several years ago, Alaska was the first state to pass mandatory LCC regulations. It was followed closely by Florida. By 1985, Colorado, Idaho, Maryland, Massachusetts, Missouri, Nebraska, New Mexico, North Carolina, Texas, Washington, Wisconsin, Wyoming, and New York had passed mandatory provisions, and Florida, Wyoming, Utah, and New York had issued formal guidance manuals for LCC requirements.

Decision Makers' Impact on LCC

Figure 7.1 illustrates the impact that design-stage decisions have on building costs. It portrays the design process as a team effort in which various disciplines make decisions in a discipline-oriented environment. Decisions made by one discipline will affect the cost of the work covered by the other disciplines.

One of the principal reasons for unnecessary costs is the uni-discipline approach used by most designers. Unnecessary costs occur especially where decision areas overlap. Traditionally, the design has been dictated by the architect; other disciplines merely respond to the architect's direction. However, a multi-disciplinary approach to building as a system can significantly reduce unnecessary costs. Unfortunately, the uni-disciplinary approach has expanded into LCC and discipline-oriented solutions to energy problems. In some cases, such as highly-automated office facilities and high-tech laboratories, the design of mechanical-electrical systems takes precedence over architectural design. It seems that the basic function of a facility—to house people—is superseded by energy conservation concerns. The multi-disciplinary approach shows that the best solutions are developed when all participants cooperate to solve the total problem.

Effective timing is also important. To take maximum advantage of LCC, the techniques should be applied at the earliest stages of the design concept, particularly during planning and budgeting, preliminary design, and design development phases. The cost of changing a design increases significantly with time. LCC exercises that are undertaken during the construction phase or owning and operating phases produce limited results, and they are beneficial only in providing data for future projects.

LCC and Total Building Costs

LCC is concerned with total building costs over the economic life of a facility. Figure 7.2 shows how the total costs of buildings are incurred. This model has been used as a basis for an automated approach; for example, a template is available for IBM-compatible equipment using Lotus 1-2-3 or Excel. The blocks are numbered C-1 through C-8.

Blocks C-1 (initial costs), C-2 (financing costs), C-3 (operating costs), and C-4 (maintenance costs) are self-explanatory.

Block C-5 (alteration and replacement costs) identifies costs involved with changing the function of a space. A replacement cost would be a one-time cost incurred at some time in the future to maintain the original function of the facility or item.

Block C-6 (tax elements) deals with the cost impact of the tax laws, and each case must be analyzed on an individual basis. These costs must be continually reviewed as tax laws change; for example, investment tax credits are given for energy conservation, different depreciation rates can be used, and different depreciation periods are allowed.

Block C-7 (associated costs) is concerned with costs such as insurance, denial of use, income, time impact, and staffing and personnel costs related to functional use. For example, suppose an LCC analysis is required for a branch bank. The function of the bank is to "service customers." Suppose two banks have exactly the same

Decision Makers' Impact on Total Building Costs

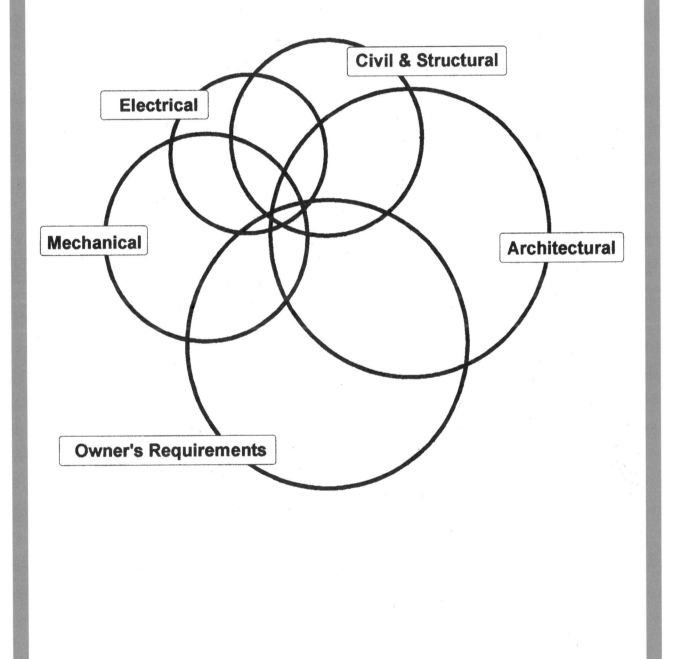

Figure 7.1

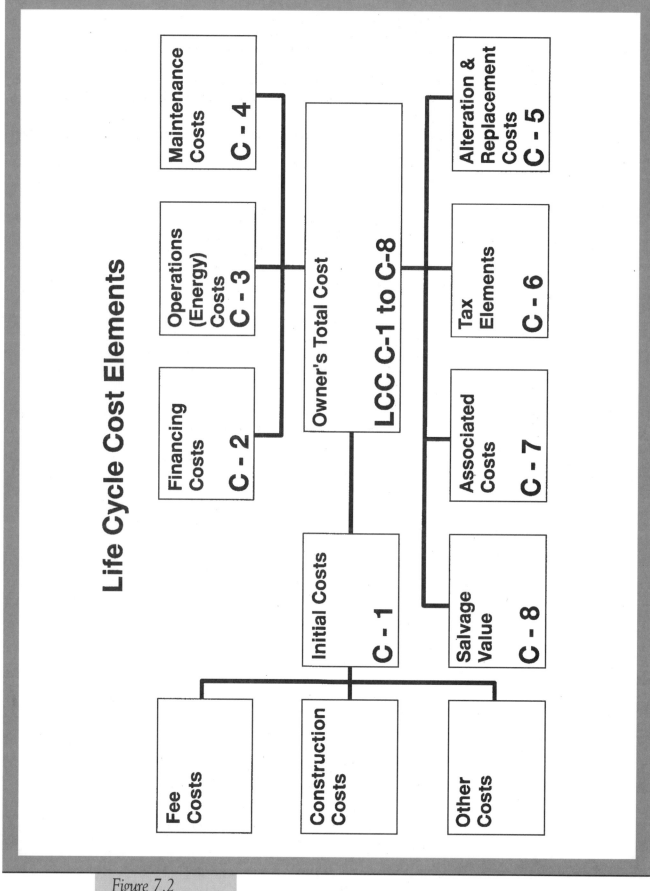

Life Cycle Cost Elements

Figure 7.2

initial costs. One bank can process 200 clients per day with a total staff of 10 people; the other bank requires a staff of 12 to process the same number of clients per day. Clearly, the one that uses less staff is more cost effective. This block of staffing-personnel costs represents the requirements related to the building function. Thus functional use costs for a branch bank would relate to servicing customers. In LCC analysis, a cost difference or some other comparison would have to be considered for the difference in staffing of these two banks to provide the basic function of the facility.

As another example of denial-of-use costs, suppose that there are two approaches to building alterations, the construction costs of which are the same. One alternative would require moving people out of a space for six months; the other alternative could be accomplished during non-working hours. In LCC, the cost of not being able to use the space would have to be considered.

The cost impact of insurance was illustrated by a recent study of a food-distribution warehouse. All costs were comparable, but one system had a lower annual insurance premium. In this case, the estimated cost equal to the present worth of the annual rates was used for each system in the LCC.

Block C-8 (salvage value) represents the economic value of competing alternates at the end of the life cycle period. The value is positive if it has residual economic value, and negative if additional costs, such as demolition, are required. Figure 7.3 indicates the difference in LCC for various building types. The differences in high and low initial costs are quite significant, as are annual costs. (See Chapter 3, "Preparation of Cost Models," for further information about life cycle costs.)

LCC Terminology and Examples

To compare design alternatives, both present and future costs for each alternative must be brought to a common point in time. One of two methods is used: Costs may be converted to today's cost by the present worth method, or they may be converted to an annual series of payments by the annualized method. Either method will properly allow comparison between design alternatives. Procedures, conversion tables, and examples for both methods are discussed in the following sections.

Present Worth Method

The present worth method requires conversion of all present and future expenditures to a baseline of today's cost. Initial (present) costs are automatically expressed in present worth. The following formulas are used to convert recurring and nonrecurring costs to present-day values. Recurring costs are as follows:

Equation 1

$$P = \frac{A(1 + i)^n - 1}{i(1 + i)^n} = PWA$$

Where:

i = interest rate per interest period (in decimals); minimum attractive rate of return

n = number of interest periods

P = present sum of money (present worth)

A = end-of-period payment or receipt in a uniform series continuing for the coming n periods, entire series equivalent to P at interest rate i

PWA = present worth of an annuity factor

Nonrecurring costs (when A = $1.00) are as follows:

Equation 2

$$P = F \times \frac{1}{(1+i)^n} = PW$$

Facility Types - Cost Per Building Gross Square Foot*

INITIAL COSTS:	Corp. Office $/GSF Low	High	Financial $/GSF Low	High	Medical $/GSF Low	High	University $/GSF Low	High	Research $/GSF Low	High	Industrial $/GSF Low	High
Initial Project Cost	**126.36**	**228.80**	**146.30**	**255.20**	**224.25**	**462.00**	**147.40**	**264.75**	**194.35**	**495.00**	**90.65**	**199.00**
Construction Cost (incl. Site)	95.00	130.00	110.00	145.00	150.00	210.00	110.00	150.00	130.00	225.00	70.00	100.00
Design Fees	4.28	7.80	4.95	8.70	10.50	21.00	6.05	9.75	9.10	22.50	2.45	5.00
Construction Administration	1.90	5.20	2.20	5.80	3.00	8.40	2.20	6.00	2.60	9.00	1.05	3.00
Site	4.75	19.50	5.50	21.75	7.50	31.50	5.50	22.50	6.50	33.75	2.10	10.00
Reservation Costs:												
Const. Contingency	4.28	7.80	4.95	8.70	6.75	12.60	4.95	9.00	5.85	13.50	3.15	6.00
Furnishings/Equip.	9.50	26.00	11.00	29.00	30.00	105.00	11.00	30.00	26.00	112.50	7.00	50.00
Interim Financing	5.70	19.50	6.60	21.75	9.00	31.50	6.60	22.50	7.80	33.75	4.20	15.00
Other	0.95	13.00	1.10	14.50	7.50	42.00	1.10	15.00	6.50	45.00	0.70	10.00
ANNUAL COSTS:	$/GSF/Year		$/GSF/Year		$/GSF/Year		$/GSF/Year		$/GSF/Year		$/GSF/Year	
Energy/Fuel Cost	**1.48**	**2.75**	**1.57**	**2.57**	**2.06**	**3.28**	**1.53**	**2.52**	**1.72**	**2.73**	**1.75**	**5.00**
Maintenance, Repair & Custodial	**2.24**	**5.23**	**1.94**	**3.92**	**2.65**	**5.53**	**1.66**	**3.48**	**2.40**	**5.28**	**1.85**	**4.15**
Cleaning (Custodial)	0.88	1.72	0.80	1.48	1.07	2.57	0.70	1.30	0.99	2.39	0.60	1.40
Repairs & Maintenance	1.07	2.65	0.96	1.90	1.20	2.18	0.80	1.70	1.12	2.03	1.05	2.00
Roads & Ground Maintenance	0.29	0.86	0.18	0.54	0.38	0.78	0.16	0.48	0.29	0.86	0.20	0.75
Alterations and Replacements	**2.85**	**6.50**	**3.30**	**7.25**	**4.50**	**18.90**	**3.30**	**7.50**	**3.90**	**20.25**	**2.10**	**9.00**
Alterations	0.95	2.60	1.10	2.90	1.50	10.50	1.10	3.00	1.30	11.25	0.70	5.00
Replacements	1.90	3.90	2.20	4.35	3.00	8.40	2.20	4.50	2.60	9.00	1.40	4.00
Associated Costs	**86.51**	**153.74**	**88.32**	**157.20**	**120.21**	**280.59**	**30.94**	**68.03**	**113.90**	**359.80**	**42.73**	**177.53**
Administrative (Bldg. Mgmt.)	0.44	1.04	0.37	0.92	0.48	0.98	0.30	0.70	0.45	1.10	0.40	0.90
Interest (Debt Service)	8.84	22.88	10.24	25.52	15.70	46.20	10.32	26.48	9.80	49.50	9.80	19.90
Staffing (Functional use)	75.00	125.00	75.00	125.00	100.00	225.00	20.00	40.00	100.00	300.00	30.00	150.00
Denial-of-Use Costs	(Lost Income)		(Lost Income)		(Lost Income)		(Lost Income)		(Lost Income)		(Lost Income)	
Other Costs:												
Security	0.07	0.22	0.23	0.68	0.19	0.39	0.04	0.12	0.23	0.68	0.20	0.70
Real Estate Taxes	1.90	3.90	2.20	4.35	3.00	6.30	N/A	N/A	2.60	6.75	1.40	3.00
Water & Sewer	0.16	0.31	0.17	0.29	0.69	1.09	0.17	0.28	0.69	1.09	0.86	2.73
Fire Insurance	0.10	0.39	0.11	0.44	0.15	0.63	0.11	0.45	0.13	0.68	0.07	0.30

*Excerpted from Life Cycle Costing for Design Professionals, Second Edition, McGraw-Hill, Inc., New York, 1995

Figure 7.3

Where:

F = sum of money at the end of n, from the present date that is equivalent to P, with interest rate i

PW = present worth factor

n = number of interest periods

To use these formulas, the owner or designer must determine the rate of return. This interest rate is discussed later. The federal government, through OMB Circular A-94, has established 10% as the interest rate to be used in studies of this type, excluding the lease or purchase of real property. The number of interest periods, n, or the life cycle period of the study is usually expressed in years. Normally, a life cycle between 25 and 40 years is considered adequate for estimating future expenses.

Escalation

Differential escalation (the rate of inflation above the general economy) is taken into account for recurring costs, such as energy, by the following formula:

Equation 3

$$P = A \frac{[(1 + e)/(1 + i)] \times [(1 + e)/(1 + i)^n - 1]}{[(1 + e)/(1 + i)] - 1} = PWA_e$$

Where:

e = escalation rate

A = $1.00

n = number of interest periods

i = interest rate per interest period (in decimals)

PWA_e = Present Worth of Annuity escalated

Where:

e = 1

P = An

Economic tables exist for the many combinations of interest rates, interest periods, and discount rates. However, escalation tables are not available. Some calculators, such as the Texas Instruments Business Analyst and the Hewlett-Packard HP-22 Business Management calculators, have economic equations built in for quick calculation, but they do not deal with escalation. Figure 7.4 is a table of escalating values at a base interest rate of 10%.[4]

Annualized Method

The annualized method converts initial, recurring, and nonrecurring costs to an annual series of payments. This method may be used to express all life cycle costs as an annual expenditure. Home mortgage payments are an example of this procedure; that is, a buyer opts to purchase a home for $349 per month (360 equal monthly payments at 10% yearly interest) rather than pay $50,000 all at once. Recurring costs, as previously discussed, are already expressed as annual costs; thus no adjustment is necessary. Initial and nonrecurring costs, however, require equivalent cost conversion. The following formulas are used for this conversion:

Initial costs:

Equation 4

$$A = P \frac{i (1 + i)^n}{(1 + i)^n - 1} = PP$$

Where:

A = annualized cost

P = $1.00

i = interest rate per interest period (in decimals)

n = number of interest periods

PP = period payment factor

Present Worth of an Escalating Annual Amount, 10% Discount Rate

Escalation Rate,%

Yrs.	0	1	2	3	4	5	6	7	8	9	10	11	12	13	14	Yrs.
1	0.909	0.918	0.927	0.936	0.945	0.965	1.636	1.973	0.982	0.991	1.000	1.009	1.018	1.027	1.036	1
2	1.736	1.761	1.787	1.813	1.839	1.866	1.892	1.919	1.946	1.973	2.000	2.027	2.055	2.083	2.110	2
3	2.487	2.535	2.584	2.634	2.684	2.735	2.787	2.839	2.892	2.946	3.000	3.055	3.110	3.167	3.224	3
4	3.170	3.246	3.324	3.403	3.483	3.566	3.649	3.735	3.821	3.910	4.000	4.092	4.185	4.280	4.377	4
5	3.791	3.899	4.009	4.123	4.239	4.358	4.480	4.605	4.734	4.865	5.000	5.138	5.279	5.424	5.573	5
6	4.355	4.498	4.645	4.797	4.953	5.115	5.281	5.453	5.630	5.812	6.000	6.194	6.394	6.599	6.812	6
7	4.868	5.048	5.234	5.428	5.628	5.837	6.053	6.277	6.509	6.750	7.000	7.259	7.528	7.807	8.096	7
8	5.335	5.553	5.781	6.019	6.267	6.526	6.796	7.078	7.372	7.680	8.000	8.334	8.683	9.047	9.426	8
9	5.759	6.017	6.288	6.572	6.871	7.184	7.513	7.858	8.220	8.601	9.000	9.419	9.859	10.321	10.806	9
10	6.145	6.443	6.758	7.090	7.441	7.812	8.203	8.616	9.053	9.513	10.000	10.514	11.057	11.630	12.235	10
11	6.495	6.834	7.194	7.575	7.981	8.411	8.868	9.354	9.870	10.418	11.000	11.619	12.276	12.974	13.716	11
12	6.814	7.193	7.598	8.030	8.491	8.963	9.510	10.072	10.672	11.314	12.000	12.733	13.517	14.355	15.251	12
13	7.103	7.523	7.972	8.455	8.973	9.530	10.127	10.770	11.460	12.202	13.000	13.858	14.781	15.774	16.842	13
14	7.367	7.825	8.320	8.853	9.429	10.051	10.723	11.449	12.233	13.082	14.000	14.993	16.068	17.231	18.491	14
15	7.606	8.103	8.642	9.226	9.860	10.549	11.296	12.109	12.993	13.954	15.000	16.139	17.378	18.729	20.200	15
16	7.824	8.358	8.941	9.576	10.268	11.024	11.849	12.752	13.739	14.818	16.000	17.294	18.713	20.267	21.971	16
17	8.022	8.593	9.218	9.903	10.653	11.477	12.382	13.377	14.470	15.674	17.000	18.461	20.071	21.847	23.806	17
18	8.201	8.808	9.475	10.209	11.018	11.910	12.895	13.985	15.189	16.523	18.000	19.638	21.454	23.470	25.708	18
19	8.365	9.005	9.713	10.496	11.362	12.323	13.390	14.576	15.895	17.363	19.000	20.825	22.862	25.137	27.679	19
20	8.514	9.187	9.934	10.764	11.688	12.718	13.867	15.151	16.588	18.196	20.000	22.024	24.296	26.850	29.722	20
21	8.649	9.353	10.139	11.015	11.996	13.094	14.326	15.711	17.268	19.022	21.000	23.233	25.756	28.610	31.839	21
22	8.772	9.506	10.329	11.251	12.287	13.454	14.769	16.255	17.936	19.840	22.000	24.453	27.243	30.417	34.033	22
23	8.883	9.647	10.505	11.471	12.562	13.797	15.196	16.784	18.591	20.650	23.000	25.685	28.756	32.274	36.307	23
24	8.985	9.776	10.668	11.678	12.822	14.124	15.607	17.299	19.235	21.454	24.000	26.927	30.297	34.181	38.664	24
25	9.077	9.894	10.819	11.871	13.069	14.437	16.003	17.800	19.867	22.250	25.000	28.181	31.866	36.141	41.106	25
26	9.161	10.003	10.960	12.052	13.301	14.735	16.384	18.287	20.488	23.038	26.000	29.446	33.464	38.154	43.638	26
27	9.237	10.102	11.090	12.221	13.521	15.020	16.752	18.761	21.097	23.820	27.000	30.723	35.090	40.222	46.261	27
28	9.307	10.194	11.211	12.380	13.729	15.291	17.107	19.222	21.695	24.594	28.000	32.012	36.746	42.346	48.979	28
29	9.370	10.278	11.323	12.528	13.926	15.551	17.448	19.671	22.283	25.361	29.000	33.312	38.433	44.528	51.797	29
30	9.427	10.355	11.426	12.667	14.112	15.799	17.777	20.107	22.859	26.122	30.000	34.624	40.150	46.770	54.717	30
31	9.479	10.426	11.523	12.798	14.287	16.035	18.095	20.532	23.426	26.875	31.000	35.947	41.898	49.073	57.743	31
32	9.526	10.491	11.612	12.920	14.453	16.261	18.400	20.944	23.982	27.622	32.000	37.283	43.678	51.438	60.879	32
33	9.569	10.551	11.695	13.034	14.610	16.476	18.695	21.346	24.527	28.362	33.000	38.631	45.490	53.868	64.129	33
34	9.609	10.606	11.771	13.141	14.759	16.682	18.979	21.736	25.063	29.095	34.000	39.992	47.335	56.365	67.497	34
35	9.644	10.657	11.843	13.241	14.899	16.878	19.252	22.116	25.589	29.821	35.000	41.364	49.214	58.929	70.988	35
36	9.677	10.703	11.909	13.335	15.032	17.065	19.516	22.486	26.106	30.541	36.000	42.749	51.127	61.564	74.606	36
37	9.706	10.745	11.970	13.423	15.158	17.244	19.770	22.845	26.613	31.254	37.000	44.147	53.075	64.270	78.355	37
38	9.733	10.784	12.027	13.505	15.276	17.415	20.014	23.195	27.111	31.961	38.000	45.558	55.058	67.050	82.241	38
39	9.757	10.820	12.079	13.582	15.389	17.578	20.250	23.535	27.600	32.661	39.000	46.981	57.077	69.906	86.268	39
40	9.779	10.853	12.128	13.654	15.495	17.733	20.478	23.866	28.080	33.355	40.000	48.417	59.133	72.840	90.441	40

$$P = A \left[(1 + e)/(1 + i)\right] \times \left[(1 + e)/(1 + i)^n - 1\right]/\left[(1 + e)/(1 + i)\right] - 1 = PWA_e$$

Figure 7.4

For nonrecurring costs, use Equation 2 to convert future expenditure to current cost (present worth), then use Equation 4 to convert today's cost (present worth) to an annual expenditure (annualized cost). Since all costs are expressed in equivalent dollars, for both the present worth and the annualized methods, the life cycle cost is the sum of the initial, recurring, and nonrecurring costs, all expressed in equivalent dollars.

Discount or Interest Rate

Calculation of present worth is often referred to as *discounting* by writers on economics, who frequently refer to an interest rate used in present worth calculations as a "discount rate." Any reference to the discount rate means either the minimum acceptable rate of return for the client for investment purposes, or the current prime or borrowing rate of interest. In establishing this rate, several factors must be considered, including the source of finance (borrowed money or capital assets), the client (government agency or private industry), and the rate of return for the industry (before or after income taxes).

At times the owner may establish the minimum attractive rate of return based only on the cost of borrowed money. Although this approach is particularly common in government projects and in personal economic studies, it may not be applicable to projects in a competitive industry.

Escalation

Escalation has a significant impact on LCC and is accommodated in LCC by expressing all costs in terms of constant dollars. For example, if the LCC is being conducted in 1997 dollars, then the purchasing power of a 1997 dollar should be used throughout the analysis. That is, in a comparative analysis it is not correct to mix 1997, 2000, 2010, and 2020 year dollars, as they will differ in terms of buying power.

When the comparative analysis includes items with equal escalation rates, the effect of escalation will be canceled out. However, when cost elements with varying escalation rates are included, the differences must be considered. For example, the rates of escalation for certain items such as energy have been increasing above the average devaluation of the dollar. To accommodate these differences, those elements that are differentially escalating or devaluating (at a different rate than the inflation of all other costs) need to be moderated. It is recommended that a differential escalation be applied. For example, say the life cycle for analysis is 20 years and energy is estimated to escalate at 5% per year. The devaluation of money is estimated at 4%. Therefore, the present worth of the energy cost should be differentially escalated at 1%. Equation 3 is the formula used to determine present worth of annuity factors having differential escalation. Figure 7.4 gives the present-day value of an escalating annual amount starting at $1.00 per year at a 10% interest rate. For the example above, the PWA equates to 9.187 versus an unescalated value of 8.514 if no differential escalation is applied. The disk supplied with this book contains the LCC program and all required values.

Depreciation Period

The depreciation period usually corresponds with the estimated useful life of an asset, during which time the capital cost of the asset is written off. This period becomes the basis for a deduction against income in calculating income taxes. There are several ways commonly used to distribute the initial cost over time; for example, straight line, sum of the year's digits, and double declining balance. The Internal Revenue Service has established and made available certain guidelines for various system components. Tax accountants have ready access to these changes in rates.

Amortization Period

The amortization period is the time over which periodic payments are made to discharge a debt. The period used is often arbitrary and is selected to meet the economic needs of the project. Financing costs are assessed during this period.

Salvage (Residual) Value

When evaluating alternatives with unequal useful lives during the economic life cycle period, a salvage or residual value must be established. The salvage value is the estimated value (constant baseline currency) of the system or component at the end of the economic life cycle or study period. The value of a system at the end of its useful life is normally equal to its salvage value less the cost incurred for its removal or disposal.

Time Frames

Several time frames are used in an LCC analysis. First is the economic or study period used in comparing design alternatives. The owner, not the designer, must establish this time frame. If the building life is considered as being forever, 25-40 years is long enough to predict future costs for economic purposes to capture the most significant costs. This is illustrated in Figure 7.5, where an annual cost for 100 years discounted to present worth at a 10% interest rate is plotted. The area under the curve is the cumulative total present-worth equivalent cost of the system. Note that 80% of the total equivalent cost is consumed in the first 25 years.

A time frame must also be used for each system under analysis. The useful life of each system, component, or item under study may be the physical, technological, or economic life. The useful life of any item depends on such things as the frequency with which it is used; its age when acquired; the policy for repairs and replacements; whether preventive maintenance procedures are followed as recommended by the manufacturer; the climate in which it is used; the state of the art; economic changes; inventions; and other developments within the industry.

Other Methods of Economic Analysis

Other methods of economic analysis can be used in a life cycle study, depending on the client's requirements and special needs. With additional rules and mechanics, it is possible to perform a sensitivity analysis; to determine the payback period; to establish a break-even point between alternatives; to determine rates of return, extra investment, and rate-of-return alternatives; to perform a cash flow analysis; and to review the benefits and costs.[5]

LCC Methodology

Figure 7.6 illustrates a flow chart for applying LCC to a project. The first requirement is the input data. With this data, alternatives can be generated, followed by LCC predictions. From these predictions, a noneconomic comparison is made to evaluate the assumptions about component costs balanced with the functional, technological, and aesthetic factors of the project. The resultant weighted choice is proposed as the lowest optimum alternative. That is the best alternative representing the best choice balancing costs and noneconomic criteria. Of the input data required, specific project information and site data are usually available, but it is unusual for facility components' data to be available, especially information regarding useful life, maintenance, and operations. Although such input is needed to calculate roughly 25% of total costs, few designers have access to comprehensive data in a format facilitating LCC analysis. There is no system retrieval format for LCC data readily available to designers. This presents a serious problem. The author has published two texts that attempt to publish such data.[6]

Consider this example of LCC methodology. A hospital staff and its design team are considering two alternative nursing-station designs for each bed wing. One will cost far more to construct than the other because it relies more heavily on

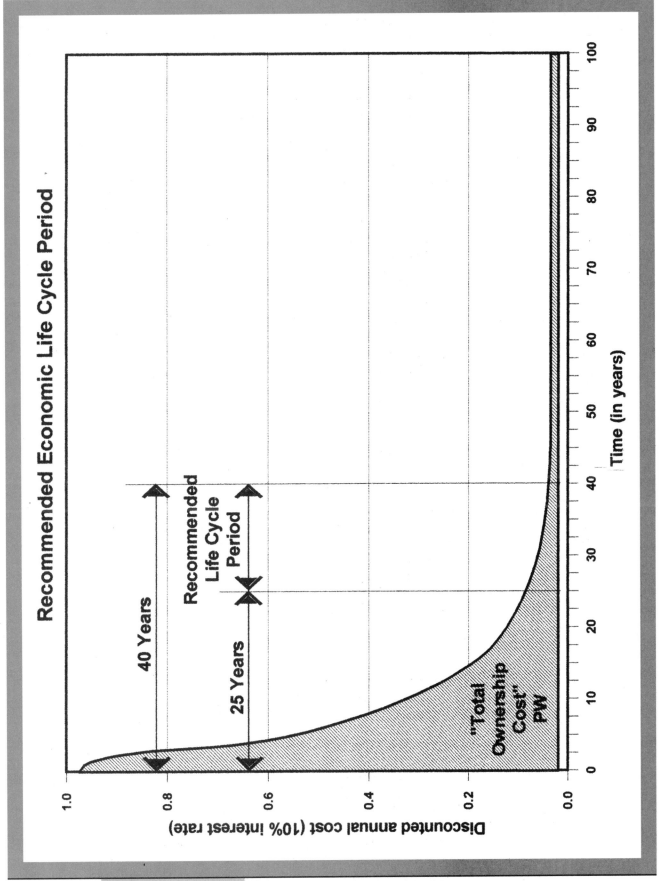

Figure 7.5

Life Cycle Costing Logic

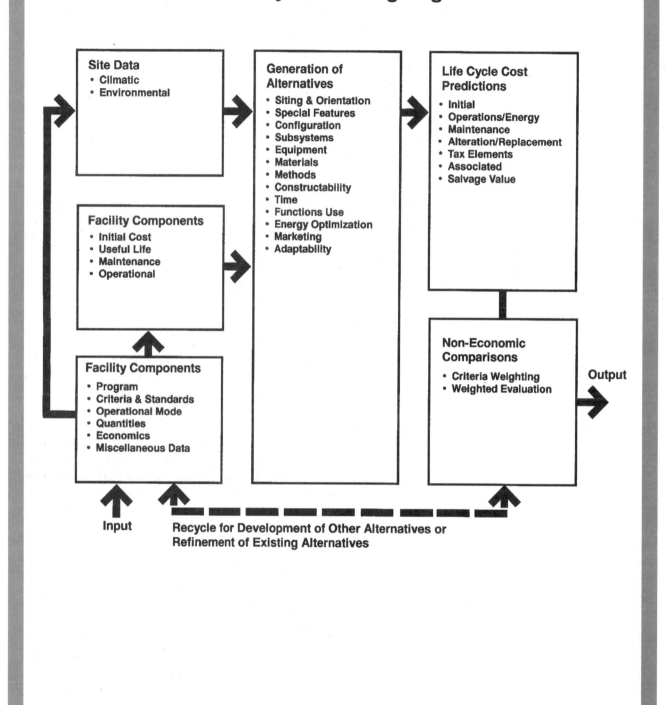

Figure 7.6

automated devices for patient monitoring and record keeping. Will the savings in nursing salaries justify the increased facility cost? Several steps using the LCC methodology are required to answer this question.

First, those facility elements that will be the same in any of the options being reviewed should be identified. Then, those elements should be fixed or removed from consideration to reduce the time and complexity of the comparative analysis. Next, the decision-making team isolates the significant varying costs associated with each alternative. The automated solution in this example has higher capital investment costs but lower functional use (nursing salary) costs. The costs isolated for each alternative must be grouped by year over the number of years equal to the economic life of the facility. If more appropriate, costs may be isolated by time spans equal to the mode of user operation. In either case, probable replacement and alteration costs should be considered. Salvage value, if relevant, is also considered for the end of the life cycle period.

All costs are converted to current dollar value by present worth techniques using a reasonable discount factor. A 10% interest rate is used by most federal agencies, but many private owners use a higher rate. Finally, the discounted costs are totaled and the lowest cost alternative is identified. It may be necessary to make a sensitivity analysis of each of the assumptions to see if a reasonable change in any of the cost assumptions would change the conclusions. If this happens, the probability of such an occurrence must be carefully weighed. If two or more events have roughly the same likelihood of occurrence, then the option selected must reflect this. The final selection of an option should be tempered with noneconomic factors. The impact on total cost of any noneconomic factors will be factored in by the decision maker using a weighted evaluation procedure. See the discussion of weighted evaluation later in the chapter for further details of the process.

LCC Formats

Formats for manual techniques and for computerized spreadsheets follow as examples. The short manual form procedure is used primarily to compare specific facility components such as the type of exterior siding, various roofing materials, piping, and so forth. The longer, more detailed procedure allows a more comprehensive total system or facility to be analyzed based on LCC. The manual procedures provide LCC information from which improved decisions can be made.

When the annualized method of LCC is being used, the equivalent cost baseline is annual costs. Initial cost and present worth of future costs are reduced to annual series. For example, assume that the mortgage payment on a house is a monthly series that can be converted to an annualized series. Annual costs of operations, maintenance, taxes, and so forth, are added to yield the total annual costs.

For the present worth method, the equivalent cost baseline is present-day values. All initial capital expenditures are in present-day values and require no conversion. All follow-on costs are recalculated to present-day values (discounted for the cost of money).

Both procedures will result in the same economic recommendation. The present worth method allows easier consideration of differential escalation; therefore, it is more commonly used. Referenced economic tables are contained in Figures 7.4 and 7.7 through 7.9, and blank worksheets are available in Part Three, "Value Engineering Workbook." The disk that is part of this book package contains a parameter-based cost-estimating system that is tied to the Cost Model and to a life cycle costing system.

Present Worth (PW)

What $1.00 Due in the Future is Worth Today (Present Worth) Single Payment

Yrs.	6% PW	7% PW	8% PW	9% PW	10% PW	12% PW	14% PW	16% PW	18% PW	20% PW	Yrs.
1	0.943396	0.934579	0.925926	0.917431	0.909091	0.892857	0.877193	0.862069	0.847446	0.833333	1
2	0.889996	0.873439	0.857339	0.841680	0.826446	0.797194	0.769468	0.743163	0.718184	0.694444	2
3	0.839169	0.816298	0.793832	0.772183	0.751315	0.711780	0.674972	0.640658	0.608631	0.578704	3
4	0.792094	0.762895	0.735030	0.708425	0.683013	0.635518	0.592080	0.552291	0.515789	0.482253	4
5	0.747258	0.712986	0.680583	0.649931	0.620921	0.567427	0.519369	0.476113	0.437109	0.401878	5
6	0.704961	0.666342	0.630170	0.596267	0.564474	0.506631	0.455587	0.410442	0.370432	0.334898	6
7	0.665057	0.622750	0.583490	0.547034	0.513158	0.452349	0.399637	0.353830	0.316925	0.279082	7
8	0.627412	0.582009	0.540269	0.501866	0.466507	0.403883	0.350559	0.305025	0.266038	0.232568	8
9	0.591898	0.543934	0.500249	0.460428	0.424098	0.360610	0.307508	0.262953	0.225456	0.193807	9
10	0.558395	0.508349	0.463193	0.422411	0.385543	0.321973	0.269744	0.226684	0.191064	0.161506	10
11	0.526788	0.475093	0.428883	0.387533	0.350494	0.287476	0.236617	0.195417	0.161919	0.134588	11
12	0.496969	0.444012	0.397114	0.355535	0.319631	0.256675	0.207559	0.168463	0.137220	0.112157	12
13	0.468839	0.414964	0.367698	0.326170	0.289664	0.229174	0.182069	0.145227	0.116288	0.093464	13
14	0.442301	0.387817	0.340461	0.299246	0.263331	0.204620	0.159710	0.125195	0.098549	0.077887	14
15	0.417265	0.362446	0.315242	0.274538	0.239392	0.182696	0.140096	0.107927	0.083516	0.064905	15
16	0.396343	0.338735	0.291890	0.251870	0.217629	0.163122	0.122892				16
17	0.371364	0.316574	0.270269	0.231073	0.197845	0.145644	0.107800				17
18	0.350344	0.295864	0.252490	0.211994	0.179858	0.130040	0.084561				18
19	0.330513	0.276508	0.231712	0.194490	0.163508	0.116107	0.082948				19
20	0.311805	0.258419	0.214548	0.178431	0.148644	0.103667	0.072762	0.051385	0.036506	0.026084	20
21	0.294155	0.241513	0.198656	0.163698	0.135132	0.092560	0.063826				21
22	0.277505	0.225713	0.183941	0.150182	0.122846	0.082643	0.055988				22
23	0.261797	0.210947	0.170315	0.137781	0.111678	0.073788	0.049112				23
24	0.246979	0.197147	0.157699	0.126405	0.101526	0.065882	0.043081				24
25	0.232999	0.184249	0.146018	0.115968	0.092296	0.058823	0.037790	0.024465	0.015957	0.010482	25
26	0.210810	0.172195	0.135202	0.106393	0.083905	0.052521	0.033149				26
27	0.207368	0.160930	0.125187	0.097608	0.076278	0.046894	0.029078				27
28	0.195630	0.150102	0.115914	0.089548	0.069343	0.041869	0.025507				28
29	0.184557	0.140563	0.107328	0.082155	0.063039	0.037383	0.022375				29
30	0.174110	0.131367	0.099377	0.075371	0.057309	0.033378	0.019627	0.011648	0.006975	0.004212	30
31	0.164255	0.122773	0.092016	0.069148	0.052090	0.029802	0.017217				31
32	0.154957	0.114741	0.085200	0.063438	0.047362	0.026609	0.015102				32
33	0.146186	0.107235	0.078889	0.058200	0.043057	0.023758	0.013248				33
34	0.137912	0.100219	0.073045	0.053395	0.039143	0.021212	0.011621				34
35	0.130105	0.093663	0.067635	0.048986	0.035584	0.018940	0.010194	0.005546	0.003049	0.001693	35
36	0.122741	0.087535	0.062625	0.044941	0.032349	0.016910	0.008942				36
37	0.115793	0.081809	0.057986	0.041231	0.029408	0.015098	0.007844				37
38	0.109129	0.076457	0.053690	0.037826	0.026735	0.013481	0.006880				38
39	0.103056	0.071455	0.049713	0.034703	0.024304	0.012036	0.006035				39
40	0.097222	0.066780	0.046031	0.031838	0.022095	0.010747	0.005294	0.002640	0.001333	0.000680	40

*Formula $PW = (1/(1+i)^n)$

Where: i represents an interest rate per interest period

n represents a number of interest periods

PW represents the present worth of $1 due in the future

Figure 7.7

Compound Interest Factors (PWA)

Present Worth of Annuity (PWA): What $1.00 Payable Periodically is Worth Today*

Yrs.	6% PW	7% PW	8% PW	9% PW	10% PW	12% PW	14% PW	16% PW	18% PW	20% PW	Yrs.
1	0.943396	0.934579	0.925926	0.917431	0.909001	0.892857	0.877193	0.862069	0.847446	0.833333	1
2	1.833393	1.808018	1.783265	1.759111	1.735537	1.690050	1.646661	1.605232	1.565642	1.527778	2
3	2.673012	2.624316	2.577097	2.531295	2.486852	2.401830	2.321632	2.245890	2.174273	2.106481	3
4	3.465106	3.387211	3.312127	3.329720	3.169865	3.037350	2.913712	2.798181	2.690062	2.588735	4
5	4.212364	4.100197	3.992710	3.889651	3.790787	3.604470	3.433081	3.274294	3.127171	2.990612	5
6	4.917624	4.766540	4.622880	4.485919	4.355261	4.111400	3.888668	3.684736	3.497603	3.325510	6
7	5.582381	5.389289	5.206370	5.032953	4.868419	4.563750	4.288305	4.038565	3.811528	3.604592	7
8	6.209794	5.971299	5.746639	5.534819	5.334926	4.967640	4.638864	4.343591	4.077566	3.837160	8
9	6.801602	6.515232	6.246888	5.995247	5.759024	5.328250	4.946372	4.606544	4.303022	4.030967	9
10	7.360087	7.023582	6.710081	6.417658	6.144567	5.650230	5.216116	4.833227	4.494086	4.192472	10
11	7.886875	7.498674	7.138964	6.805191	6.495061	5.937710	5.452733	5.028644	4.656005	4.317060	11
12	8.383844	7.942686	7.536078	7.160725	6.813692	6.194370	5.660292	5.197104	4.793225	4.439217	12
13	8.852683	8.357651	7.903776	7.486904	7.103356	6.423560	5.842362	5.342334	4.909513	4.532681	13
14	9.294984	8.745468	8.244237	7.786150	7.366687	6.628180	6.002072	5.467529	5.008062	4.610567	14
15	10.712279	9.107914	8.559479	8.060688	7.606080	6.810880	6.142168	5.575456	5.091578	4.675473	15
16	10.105895	9.446649	8.851369	8.312558	7.823709	6.973990	6.265060				16
17	10.347726	9.763223	9.121638	8.543631	8.021553	7.119620	6.372859				17
18	10.827603	10.059087	9.371887	8.755625	8.201412	7.249690	6.467420				18
19	11.158116	10.335595	9.603599	8.950115	8.364920	7.365780	6.550369				19
20	11.409921	10.594014	9.818147	9.128546	8.513564	7.469730	6.623131	5.928844	5.352744	4.869580	20
21	11.764077	10.835527	10.016803	9.292244	8.648694	7.562010	6.686957				21
22	12.041582	11.061240	10.200744	9.442425	8.771540	7.644620	6.742944				22
23	12.303379	11.272187	10.371059	9.580207	8.883218	7.718430	6.792056				23
24	12.550358	11.469334	10.528758	9.706612	8.981744	7.784340	6.835137				24
25	12.783356	11.653583	10.674776	9.822580	9.077040	7.843140	6.872927	6.097094	5.466905	4.947590	25
26	13.003186	11.825779	10.809978	9.928797	9.160945	7.895650	6.906077				26
27	13.210536	11.986709	10.935165	10.026580	9.237223	7.942560	6.935155				27
28	13.406166	12.137111	11.051078	10.116128	9.306567	7.984410	6.960662				28
29	13.590721	12.277674	11.158406	10.198283	9.369606	8.021820	6.983037				29
30	13.764831	12.409041	11.257783	10.273654	9.426914	8.055160	7.002664	6.177200	5.516805	4.978940	30
31	13.929086	12.531814	11.349799	10.342802	9.479013	8.084990	7.019881				31
32	14.084013	12.656555	11.434999	10.406240	9.526376	8.111620	7.034983				32
33	14.230230	12.753790	11.513888	10.464441	9.569432	8.135370	7.048231				33
34	14.368141	12.854009	11.586934	10.517835	9.608575	8.156540	7.059852				34
35	14.498246	12.947672	11.654568	10.566821	9.644159	8.175480	7.070045	6.215337	5.538618	4.991535	35
36	14.620987	13.035208	11.717193	10.611763	9.676508	8.192420	7.078987				36
37	14.73678	13.117017	11.775179	10.652993	9.705917	8.207490	7.086831				37
38	14.846019	13.193473	11.828869	10.690820	9.732651	8.220980	7.093711				38
39	14.949073	13.264958	11.878582	10.722523	9.756956	8.233030	7.099747				39
40	15.046297	13.331700	11.924613	10.757360	9.779051	8.243750	7.105041	6.233500	5.548150	4.996600	40

*Formula $P = A \left((1+I)^n - 1/i (1+i)^n \right)$

Where: A represents the end-of-period payment or receipt in a uniform series continuing for the coming n periods, the entire equivalent to P at interest rate i.

Figure 7.8

Compound Interest Factors (Periodic Payment)

Periodic Payment (PP): Periodic Payment Necessary to Pay Off Loan of $1.00
(Capital Recovery) Annuities (Uniform Series Payments)*

Yrs.	6% PW	7% PW	8% PW	9% PW	10% PW	12% PW	14% PW	16% PW	18% PW	20% PW	Yrs.
1	1.060000	1.070000	1.080000	1.090000	1.100000	1.120000	1.14000000	1.16000000	1.18000000	1.20000000	1
2	0.545437	0.553092	0.560769	0.568469	0.576190	0.591698	0.60728972	0.62296296	0.63871560	0.65454545	2
3	0.374110	0.381052	0.388034	0.395055	0.402115	0.416349	0.43073148	0.44525787	0.45992386	0.47472527	3
4	0.288591	0.295228	0.301921	0.308669	0.315471	0.329234	0.34320478	0.35737507	0.37173867	0.38628912	4
5	0.237396	0.243891	0.250156	0.257092	0.263797	0.277409	0.29128355	0.30540938	0.31977784	0.33437970	5
6	0.203363	0.209796	0.216315	0.222920	0.229607	0.243226	0.25715750	0.27138987	0.28591013	0.30070575	6
7	0.179135	0.185553	0.192072	0.198691	0.205405	0.219118	0.23319238	0.24761268	0.26236200	0.27742393	7
8	0.161036	0.167468	0.174015	0.180674	0.187444	0.201303	0.21557002	0.23022426	0.24524436	0.26060942	8
9	0.147022	0.153486	0.160080	0.166799	0.173641	0.187679	0.20216838	0.21708249	0.23239482	0.24807946	9
10	0.135868	0.142378	0.149029	0.155820	0.162745	0.176984	0.19171354	0.20690108	0.22252464	0.23852276	10
11	0.126793	0.133357	0.140076	0.146947	0.153963	0.168415	0.18339427	0.19886075	0.21477639	0.23110379	11
12	0.119277	0.125902	0.132695	0.139651	0.146763	0.161437	0.17666933	0.19241473	0.20862781	0.22526496	12
13	0.112960	0.119651	0.126522	0.133357	0.140779	0.155677	0.17116366	0.18718411	0.20368621	0.22062000	13
14	0.107585	0.114345	0.121297	0.128433	0.135746	0.150871	0.16660914	0.18289797	0.19967806	0.21689306	14
15	0.102963	0.109795	0.116830	0.124059	0.131474	0.146824	0.16280896	0.17935752	0.19640278	0.21388212	15
16	0.098952	0.105858	0.112977	0.120300	0.127817	0.143390	0.15961540				16
17	0.095445	0.102425	0.109629	0.117046	0.124664	0.140457	0.15691544				17
18	0.092357	0.099413	0.106702	0.114212	0.121930	0.137937	0.15462115				18
19	0.089621	0.096753	0.104128	0.111730	0.119547	0.135763	0.15266316				19
20	0.087185	0.094393	0.101852	0.109546	0.117460	0.133879	0.15098600	0.16866700	0.18682000	0.20535600	20
21	0.085005	0.092289	0.099832	0.107617	0.115624	0.132240	0.14954486				21
22	0.083016	0.090106	0.098032	0.105905	0.114005	0.130811	0.14830317				22
23	0.081278	0.088714	0.096722	0.104382	0.112572	0.129560	0.14723081				23
24	0.079679	0.087189	0.094978	0.103023	0.111300	0.128463	0.14630284				24
25	0.078227	0.085811	0.093679	0.101806	0.110168	0.127500	0.14549841	0.16401200	0.18291900	0.20211900	25
26	0.076904	0.084561	0.092507	0.100715	0.109159	0.126652	0.14480001				26
27	0.075697	0.083426	0.091448	0.099735	0.108258	0.125904	0.14419288				27
28	0.074593	0.082392	0.090489	0.098852	0.107451	0.125244	0.14366449				28
29	0.073580	0.081449	0.089619	0.098056	0.106728	0.124660	0.14320417				29
30	0.072649	0.080586	0.088827	0.097336	0.106079	0.124144	0.14280279	0.16188600	0.18126400	0.20084600	30
31	0.071792	0.079797	0.088107	0.096686	0.105496	0.123686	0.14245256				31
32	0.071002	0.079073	0.087451	0.096096	0.104972	0.123280	0.14214675				32
33	0.070273	0.078408	0.086852	0.095562	0.104499	0.122920	0.14187958				33
34	0.069598	0.077797	0.086304	0.095077	0.104074	0.122601	0.14164604				34
35	0.068974	0.077234	0.085803	0.094636	0.103690	0.122317	0.14144181	0.16089200	0.18055000	0.20033900	35
36	0.068395	0.076715	0.085345	0.094235	0.103343	0.122064	0.14126315				36
37	0.067857	0.076237	0.084924	0.093870	0.103030	0.121840	0.14110680				37
38	0.067358	0.075795	0.084539	0.093538	0.102747	0.121640	0.14096993				38
39	0.066894	0.075387	0.084185	0.093236	0.102491	0.121462	0.14085010				39
40	0.066462	0.075009	0.083860	0.092960	0.102259	0.121304	0.14074514	0.16042300	0.18024000	0.20013600	40

*Formula $PP = i(1+i)^n / (1+i)^n - 1$

Figure 7.9

Format Using the Annualized Method

Figure 7.10 shows a model form for predicting annualized LCC. The form is divided into three parts as follows:

1. Initial project costs or other capital investment costs.

2. All major single future costs of replacement expenditures and salvage values, taken back to present worth (discounted), using data in Figure 7.7.

3. The output data that takes all present worth equivalent costs and equates them to a common baseline of annual costs using the capital recovery factor or period payment (PP) necessary to pay off a loan of $1 from Figure 7.9.

These costs are totaled, all annual costs are added, and the annual differences are calculated. These can then be converted to present worth costs by using the correct factor Present Worth of Annuity (PWA), as illustrated in Figure 7.8.

The following is an example of a LCC study for a proposed car purchase (see Figure 7.11). A consulting engineer needs to purchase a new car. It will be a company car and as such will be eligible for investment tax credits and depreciation allowances. The engineer has selected three cars for an in-depth LCC analysis; Car A is a moderately priced import; Car B is a larger size American model; and Car C is a luxury model. The input data collected is shown in Figure 7.12.

First, the initial costs of getting the car on the road are calculated. The intended purchaser has friends in the local dealerships and can purchase the car slightly above dealer cost with the first year's license and insurance. The investment tax credit is calculated at 10% of each car's base cost. For example, Car A's credit is 10% of $16,500, or $1,650. The next step is to calculate the present worth of replacement-salvage costs. The replacement costs are listed and the present worth factor for each year determined. The present worth of the future costs are then calculated. All costs should be in constant dollars; that is, the LCC analysis baseline is normally current dollar so all costs listed should be the equivalent to the purchasing power of the current dollar. It is only when there is differential escalation that the use of differentially escalated dollars should be considered. For example, assume that tires are replaced in two and four years. For Car A, the cost is estimated at $225 each cycle. In terms of constant dollars, the costs of the tires in terms of current dollars is constant. The present worth factors for two and four years are 0.826 and 0.683, respectively, so the present worth of the tire replacement at two years is $186 ($225 × 0.826) and at four years is $154 ($225 × 0.683). (See Figure 7.11.)

The salvage value should be taken into account. When dollars are realized from the trade-in, a credit results: the salvage or residual value. For example, the trade-in of Car A equates to a credit of $3,900 × 0.62, or $2,418.

Part Three of Figure 7.11 summarizes the annual owning and operating costs. The periodic payment (PP) necessary to pay off a loan of $1 at 10% interest over five years is PP = 0.2638, or for Car A $15,675 × PP equals $4,135/year for five years. The same calculation is made for salvage and replacement costs. The present worth of each cost is amortized using the periodic payment (PP) factor. For example, for the salvage of Car A, the equivalent annual cost at 10% interest for a salvage value of $3,900 over five years would be a credit of $2,418 (present worth of salvage) × 0.2638 (PP), or $638/year for five years.

In terms of equivalent costs, $3,900 five years from now has the same buying power as $2,418 today, as has $638/year for five years. They all are equivalent costs assuming a 10% rate for interest.

After determining the annualized equivalent cost for the initial and replacement costs, the annual costs are entered. Car A has $2,200/year for maintenance and operation cost, $750/year for licenses and insurance, and a depreciation credit of $990/year. The depreciation credit is calculated as follows:

Life Cycle Costing (Annualized)

Item: _____

☐ Others ☐ Process ☐ Mechanical ☐ Electrical

Economic Life: _____ Years   Discount Rate: _____ %

Date: _____
Sheet No.: _____

Item	Description	Original	Alternate No. 1	Alternate No. 2
Collateral & Instant Contract Costs	**Base Costs**			
	Interface Costs			
	a. _____			
	b. _____			
	c. _____			
	Other Initial Costs			
	a. _____			
	b. _____			
	c. _____			
	Total Initial Cost Impact (IC)			
	Initial Cost Savings			
Salvage & Replacement Cost	**Single Expenditures @ Interest**			
	Present Worth			
	1. Year _____ Amount			
	PW = Amount x PW factor _____			
	2. Year _____ Amount			
	PW = Amount x PW factor _____			
	3. Year _____ Amount			
	PW = Amount x PW factor _____			
	4. Year _____ Amount			
	PW = Amount x PW factor _____			
	5. Year _____ Amount			
	PW = Amount x PW factor _____			
	Salvage Amount x (PW Factor _____) =			
Life Cycle Costs (Annualized)	**Annual Owning & Operating Costs**			
	1. Capital IC x PP			
	Recovery _____ Years @ _____ %			
	Replacement Cost: PP x PW _____			
	a. Year _____			
	b. Year _____			
	c. Year _____			
	d. Year _____			
	e. Year _____			
	Salvage			
	2. Annual Cost			
	a. Maintenance			
	b. Operations			
	c. _____			
	d. _____			
	e. _____			
	3. Total Annual Cost			
	Annual Difference (AD)			
	4. Present Worth of Annual Difference			
	(PWA Factor _____) x AD			

(left margin: Input Data → Output)

PP = Periodic Payment to pay off loan of $1
PWA = Present Worth of Annuity (what $1 payable periodically is worth today)
PW = Present Worth (what $1 due in the future is worth today)

Figure 7.10

Life Cycle Costing (Annualized)

Item: **CAR PURCHASE**

☐ Others ☐ Process ☐ Mechanical ☐ Electrical

Date: _N/A_

Sheet No.: _1 of 1_

Economic Life: 5 Years   Discount Rate: 10%

Item	Description		Original	Alternate No. 1	Alternate No. 2
Collateral & Instant Contract Costs	**Base Costs**		16,500	15,000	30,000
	Interface Costs				
	a. *Sales Tax*		825	750	1,500
	b.				
	c.				
	Other Initial Costs				
	a. *Investment Tax Credit*		(1,650)	(1,500)	(3,000)
	b.				
	c.				
	Total Initial Cost Impact (IC)		15,675	14,250	28,500
	Initial Cost Savings				
Salvage & Replacement Cost	**Single Expenditures 10.00% Interest**				
	Present Worth				
	1. Year _2 (Tires)_	Amount	225	300	350
	PW = Amount x PW factor	0.826	186	248	289
	2. Year _2.5 (Major Replac.)_	Amount	500	750	400
	PW = Amount x PW factor	0.789	395	592	316
	3. Year _4(Tires)_	Amount	225	300	350
	PW = Amount x PW factor	0.683	154	205	239
	4. Year _5 Trade-In_	Amount	(3,900)	(3,500)	(15,000)
	PW = Amount x PW factor	0.620	(2,418)	(2,170)	(9,300)
	5. Year	Amount			
	PW = Amount x PW factor				
	Salvage Amount x (PW Factor ____) =				
Life Cycle Costs (/Annualized)	**Annual Owning & Operating Costs**				
	1. Capital IC x PP	0.2638	4,135	3,759	7,518
	Recovery ___ Years @ ___ %				
	Replacement Cost: PP x PW				
	a. Year _2 -Tires_		49	65	76
	b. Year _2.5 -Major rpt_		104	156	83
	c. Year _4 -Tires_		41	54	63
	d. Year				
	e. Salvage, Year 5		(638)	(572)	(2,453)
	2. Annual Cost				
	a. *Maintenance & Operation*		2,200	2,800	2,000
	b. *Licenses & Insurance*		750	1,000	1,500
	c. *Depreciation Credits**		(990)	(900)	(1,800)
	d.				
	e.				
	3. Total Annual Cost (TAC)		5,651	6,362	6,987
	Annual Difference (AD)		(1,336)	(625)	
	4. PW of Annual Costs (PWA x TAC)		21,423	24,118	26,488
	5. PW of Annual Diff.(AD x PW 3.971 = PWA		5,065	2,370	

PP = Periodic Payment (periodic payment necessary to pay off loan of $1)

PWA = Present Worth of Annuity (what $1 payable periodically is worth today)

PW= Present Worth (what $1 due in the future is worth today)

*Investment tax credit assumes a 30% tax bracket, five-year straight-line depreciation.

Figure 7.11

Car Purchase Input Data ($)

Cost Element	Car A	Car B	Car C
Initial cost	$ 16,500	$ 15,000	$ 30,000
Sales tax	5%	5%	5%
Trade-in value (5 years)	3,900	3,500	15,000
License and insurance cost/yr.	750	1,000	1,500
Maintenance and operating cost/yr.	2,200	2,800	2,000
Tire costs at 2 and 4 years	225	300	350
Major replacement at 2-1/2 years	500	750	400
Depreciation 5 years straight line			
Investment tax credit 10%			
Tax bracket of consultant 30% tax rate			

Figure 7.12

$16,500 (initial cost) / five years (straight line depreciation) = $3,300/yr. × 30% tax bracket or $990/year credit.

Format Using the Present Worth Method

The same result is obtained when the present worth concept is used, as demonstrated in Figure 7.13. In Part One, the initial costs are listed and are already in present worth terms. Next, the present worth of the replacement-salvage costs are calculated. Again, salvage values are negative.

For example, the present worth of salvage of Car A is $3,900 × 0.62, or a credit of $2,418.

Finally, the annual costs are converted to present worth. For example, the annual operating cost of Car A is $ 2,200/yr., equivalent to $2,200/yr. × (present worth of annuity in Figure 7.8) 3.791, or $8,340 present worth (see Figure 7.13). The present worth amounts are then totaled and differences calculated.

Weighted Evaluation

As a final action, the economic data of costs have to be tempered with the human factors such as comfort, appearance, performance, safety, and costs (initial, operation and maintenance, replacement, and salvage). A weighted evaluation is used to more formally organize the process. Weighted evaluation ensures optimum decisions. Good decisions are made by placing the proper emphasis on all criteria. During evaluation it is important to discuss and weigh the following areas:

- Needs versus desires
- Important versus unimportant
- Design tradeoffs versus required functions

Note: An Excel weighted evaluation worksheet is included in the VE tools section of the diskette.

Procedure

The recommended procedure for weighted evaluation has been broken down into two processes, the criteria-weighted process and the analysis matrix. The criteria-weighted process is designed to isolate important criteria and establish their weights or relative importance.

On the criteria scoring matrix, all criteria important in the selection of the alternatives are listed. Criteria are compared, one against another. This series of comparisons is the simplest way to achieve the evaluation.

In comparing two criteria, preference for one over the other is scored according to its strength. (That is, 4–major preference, 3–above average preference, 2–average preference, 1–light preference). When criteria are deemed equal, each criterion is assigned a score of 1. Scores are then tallied, the raw scores brought to a common base (10 is used for a normal evaluation), and the criteria and weights transferred to the analysis matrix.

In the analysis matrix, each alternative is listed and ranked against each criterion, and the rank and weight of each constraint are multiplied and totaled. The alternatives are then scored for recommended implementation. No alternatives are considered that do not meet minimum criteria. For example, if a car does not meet minimum safety requirements, it is dropped from the evaluation.

Results

From Figure 7.14, the purchaser developed the criteria weights shown and selected Car A. Even though it was not the lowest initial cost, its follow-on costs were the lowest; and the owner benefits in the other criteria made it the optimum choice.

Life Cycle Costing Example (PW)

Item: _Car Purchase_

❑ Process ❑ Electrical ❑ Mechanical ❑ Others

Date: _N/A_

Sheet No.: _1 of 1_

Economic Life: 5 Years   Discount Rate: 10%

Description			Original		Alternate No. 1		Alternate No. 2	
			Estimated Cost	Present Worth	Estimated Cost	Present Worth	Estimated Cost	Present Worth
1. Initial/Collateral Costs								
A. Base Costs on Road			16,500	16,500	15,000	15,000	30,000	30,000
B. Sales Tax			825	825	750	750	1,500	1,500
C. Investment Tax Credits			(1,650)	(1,650)	(1,500)	(1,500)	(3,000)	(3,000)
D. _____								
E. _____								
F. _____								
G. _____								
Total Initial/Collateral Cost (PW)				15,675		14,250		28,500
Total Initial/Collateral Cost Savings								
2. Replacement/Salvage Costs								
	Year	PW						
A. _Tires_	2	0.826	225	186	300	248	350	289
B. _Major Replace._	2.5	0.789	500	395	750	592	400	316
C. _Tires_	4	0.683	225	154	300	205	350	239
D. _____								
E. _Salvage_	5	0.620	(3,900)	(2,418)	(3,500)	(2,170)	(15,000)	(9,300)
F. _____								
G. _____								
H. _____								
Total Replacement/Salvage Costs (PW)				(1,683)		(1,125)		(8,456)
3. Annual Costs								
	Dif. Escal.	PWA$_e$						
A. _Operating Cost_	0	3.791	2,200	8,340	2,800	10,615	2,000	7,582
B. _License & Insur._	0	3.791	750	2,843	1,000	3,791	1,500	5,687
C. _Dep. Credits_	0	3.791	(990)	(3,753)	(900)	(3,412)	(1,800)	(6,824)
D. _____								
E. _____								
F. _____								
G. _____								
H. _____								
Total Annual Cost								
Total Annual Cost (PW)				7,430		10,994		6,445
Grand Total Present Worth Costs				21,422		24,119		26,489
Life Cycle Present Worth Savings				5,067		2,370		
Savings %				23.65%		9.83%		

PW = Present Worth Factor (what $1 due in the future is worth today)

PWA = Present Worth of Annuity Factor (what $1 payable periodically is worth today)

PWA$_e$ = Present Worth of Annuity Escalating (what $1 payable periodically that is
        differentially escalating is worth today)

The depreciation credits column is based on 30% tax rate, straight-line five-year depreciation.

Figure 7.13

Weighted Evaluation

Project: Car Purchase

☐ Architectural ☐ Structural ☐ Mechanical ☐ Others

Date:

Sheet No.: 1 of 1

How Important:

4 - Major Preference
3 - Above Average Preference
2 - Average Preference
1 - Slight Preference
1 - Letter/Letter
   No Preference
   Each Scored One Point

Criteria
Criteria Scoring Matrix

A. **Cost (LCC)**

B. **Appearance**

C. **Comfort**

D. **Performance**

E. **Safety**

F.

G.

A - 2
A - 2
B / C   A - 1
D - 1   A - 1
D - 1   B / E
C / E
D - 1

Analysis Matrix
Alternatives

	G	F	E	D	C	B	A	Total
Raw Score			2	3	2	2	6	
Weight of Importance (0 - 10)			3	5	3	3	10	
1. **Car A (Original)**			9 / 3	15 / 3	6 / 2	6 / 2	50 / 5	86*
2. **Car B (Alternative No. 1)**			9 / 3	10 / 2	12 / 4	9 / 3	40 / 4	80
3. **Car C (Alternative No. 2)**			12 / 4	25 / 5	15 / 5	15 / 5	10 / 1	77
4.								
5.								
6.								
7.								

* Selected based on weighted evaluation

5 -Excellent   4 -Very Good   3 -Good   2 -Fair   1 -Poor

Figure 7.14

Application of LCC to Buildings

The application of the LCC concept to buildings is graphically illustrated by Figure 7.15, which shows hypothetical ownership costs of an office building using present worth concepts. The figure indicates that for the building type and data used, approximately 40% of the total cost of ownership is in initial cost, 28% of the cost of ownership is in financing (cost of money), and 22.5% is in annual maintenance and operation charges. The remaining amounts are for design, indirect costs, and alterations and replacement costs.

The data on which the figure is based are as follows:

Initial cost of building	$80/ft.^{2} ($861/m^2)
Building size	100,000 ft.^{2} (9,290m^2)
Cost of real estate (not included)	
Interest rate	12%
Life cycle	20 years
Cost of maintenance, operations, etc.	Average $6.00/ft.^{2} ($64.58/m^2)
Design	4.5%
Indirect construction costs	10%
Alteration and replacement costs	$1,500,000 every ten years

Cost of Ownership Calculations:

1. Present worth of initial costs equals cost per unit area times building size.

    Initial Costs = $80/ft.^{2} × 100,000 ft.^{2} = $8,000,000 ($861/m^2 × 9290 m^2 = approximately $8,000,000).

2. Present worth of annual costs equals the area times the annual cost times the present worth of $1.00 payable periodically (PWA) 12% interest rate from Figure 7.8.

    Annual cost = 100,000 ft.^{2} × $6.00 × 7.47 (PWA) or approximately $4,482,000 (9290 m^2 × $64.58 × 7.47 PWA).

3. Present worth of financing costs equals present worth of financing for estimated initial costs and annual costs.
    Present worth of the interest costs for the estimated costs equals the present worth of annual difference of payoff with interest, less the payoff without interest. Annual charges with interest equals initial costs times periodic payment necessary to pay off a loan of $1.00 (see Figure 7.9).

    $8,000,000 × 0.134 = $1,072,000/year.

    Annual charge without interest equals initial costs divided by number of years:

    $8,000,000/20 = $400,000/year.

    Difference = $1,072,000 − $400,000/year = $672,000/year, which is the annual value of interest.

    Present worth of annuity, interest = $672,000 × (PWA) 7.47 = $5,019,840, approx. $5,020,000 (see Figure 7.8).

    Present worth of interest (financing) of annual costs equals annual financing costs times present worth of $1.00 payable periodically (Figure 7.8).

    Annual financing charge = 12% × $600,000 = $120,000.

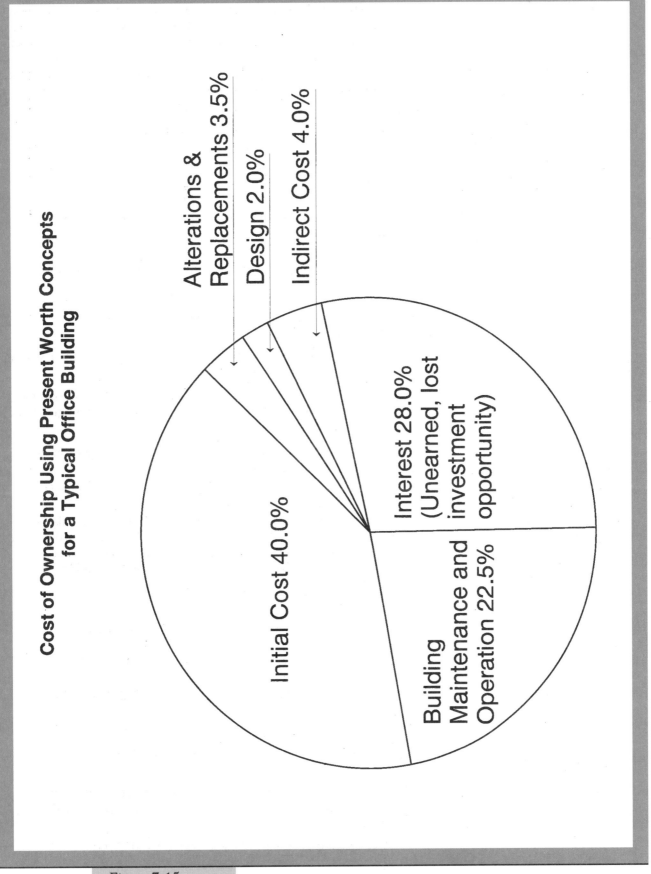

Cost of Ownership Using Present Worth Concepts for a Typical Office Building

Alterations & Replacements 3.5%

Design 2.0%

Indirect Cost 4.0%

Interest 28.0% (Unearned, lost investment opportunity)

Initial Cost 40.0%

Building Maintenance and Operation 22.5%

Figure 7.15

Present worth = $120,000 × (PWA) 7.47 = $537,840 (approximately $540,000).
Total present worth of financing costs = $540,000 + $5,020,000 = $5,560,000.

4. Other Costs

Design costs = design percentage times initial costs = 4.5% × $8,000,000 = $360,000

Indirect cost = indirect cost percentage times initial costs = 10% × $8,000,000 = $800,000.

Present worth of alteration and replacement costs = cost in future year(s) times present worth of $1.00 due in the future (Figure 7.7).

Present worth of alteration and replacement costs = $1,500,000 × 0.322 (PW for tenth year) = $483,000.
$1,500,000 × 0.104 (twentieth year) = $156,000
Total PW Alterations and Replacement = $483,000 + $156,000 = $639,000.

Summary of Costs:

	Present Worth	Approximate Percent of Total
Initial Costs	$8,000,000	40.0
Annual Costs	4,482,000	22.5
Financing Costs:		
Initial	5,020,000	
Annual	540,000	28.0
Other Costs:		
Design	360,000	2.0
Indirect	800,000	4.0
Alteration and Replacement	639,000	3.5
Total		100.0%
Present Worth—Total Cost of Ownership	$19,841,000	

If we take the above concept and add to the life cycle costs of the office workers' salaries, another viewpoint is achieved. Figure 7.16 illustrates a commercial office operations expenses on an annual cost basis (1990 prices). For example, it cites where a renovation/upgrade in office space was paid back in productivity gains in less than one year. The figure is taken from an article in *Consulting Specifying Engineer* (January 1997) entitled, "Giving Productivity an Energy-Efficient Boost." The article states, "Because of the importance of salaries in operating budgets, payback calculations should include potential performance improvements and absenteeism reductions, as well as efficiency savings." This statement should be the ultimate goal of the VE efforts—savings in total costs. A similar situation was recently experienced when additional initial costs added to a five-star hotel complex was more than justified through projected increase in occupancy.

Figure 7.17 illustrates the total cost for the total present worth for capital expense, staff, operation and maintenance for a hospital. It is interesting to note the percentage of initial costs to the total cost, which is about 6%, while staffing is 50%. Yet, decisions made during design significantly influence the bulk of the total costs.

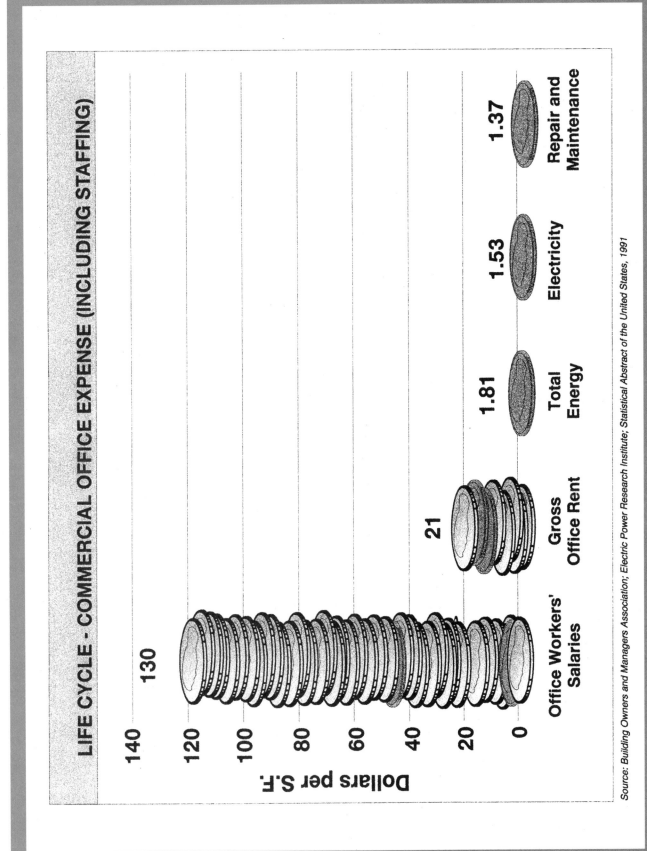

LIFE CYCLE - COMMERCIAL OFFICE EXPENSE (INCLUDING STAFFING)

Dollars per S.F.

130	Office Workers' Salaries
21	Gross Office Rent
1.81	Total Energy
1.53	Electricity
1.37	Repair and Maintenance

Source: Building Owners and Managers Association; Electric Power Research Institute; Statistical Abstract of the United States, 1991

Figure 7.16

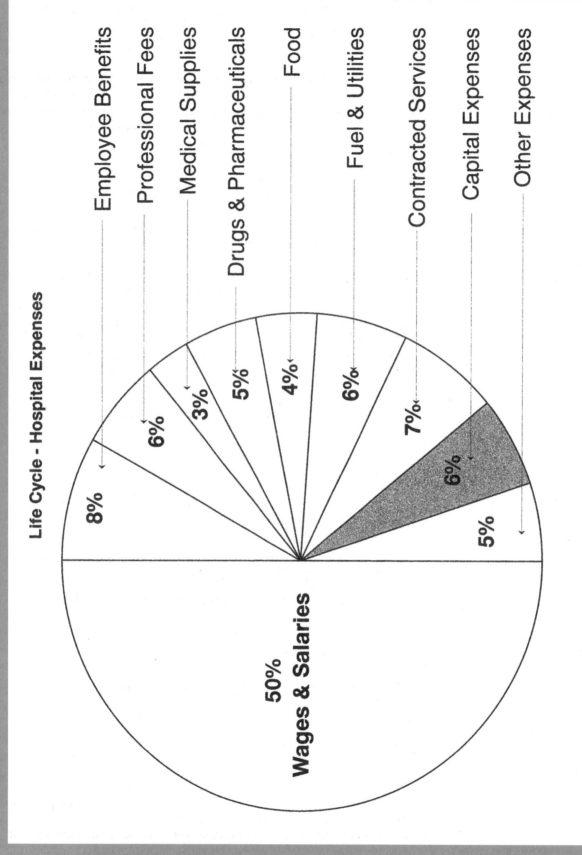

Life Cycle - Hospital Expenses

Employee Benefits

Professional Fees

Medical Supplies

Drugs & Pharmaceuticals

Food

Fuel & Utilities

Contracted Services

Capital Expenses

Other Expenses

8%

6%

3%

5%

4%

6%

7%

6%

5%

50%
Wages & Salaries

Excerpted from Life Cycle Costing for Design Professionals, Second Edition, McGraw-Hill, Inc., New York, 1995

Figure 7.17

Application of LCC to HVAC Systems

Following is an example of the use of LCC for selection of a heating, ventilation, air conditioning system (HVAC) system. It is assumed that the study group considered the original design and developed two alternatives for comparison. Figure 7.18 shows the LCC analysis of this example using the annualized method.

The original design initial base bid cost is estimated at $49,150, alternative system No. 1 is estimated at $70,000, and alternative system No. 2 is estimated at $62,000. These figures are shown under "Base Costs." The interface costs for electrical total $10,000 for the original design, $4,835 for alternative No. 1, and $7,200 for alternative No. 2. Owner-supplied equipment costs $48,450 for the original design, $25,000 for alternative No. 1, and $27,000 for alternative No. 2.

Next, replacement and salvage costs are considered. The original design results in substantial replacement costs of $35,000 at the tenth and twentieth year. For alternative No. 1, replacement costs of $30,000 will be incurred in the twentieth year. For alternative No. 2, costs of $35,000 are estimated for the twentieth year. Finally, the salvage value of each alternative at the end of the life cycle period is estimated. These amounts are then discounted to determine the present worth using Figure 7.7. For example, the present worth of $35,000 due 10 years in the future is 0.3855 × $35,000, or $13,494. Replacement costs used must be those costs (using current dollars) estimated for the year indicated. In some cases, this will require using present-day costs escalated for future price increases. However, the escalation should be limited to only the amounts of differential escalation over and above dollar devaluation. This must be done to keep all amounts in terms of a constant present-day dollar purchasing power. For example, replacement of a chiller was estimated to occur at 20 years. A market study indicated that the cost of that particular type of chiller was estimated to escalate at 12% per year and dollar devaluation was averaging 10% per year. A 2% differential escalation would be applied to the 20-year cost estimate. The formula for calculating escalation is $F = (1+i)^y$, where F is the factor to be used, i is the differential interest rate in decimals, and y is the number of years. In this instance, $F = (1 + .02)^{20} = 1.49$. For example, the chiller to be replaced costs $23,500 today. Twenty years from now in terms of constant dollars, it is estimated to cost $23,500 × 1.49(F) or $35,000.

Next, the annualized costs are determined. The initial cost must be amortized by determining the annual payment costs necessary to pay off a loan equaling the total initial cost impact. For the exercise, a span of 25 years at 10% interest is used. Information from the table in Figure 7.9 is entered under the interest rate across the 25-years line to find the periodic payment necessary to pay off a loan of $1; in this case $0.1102 per year. Each total initial cost is multiplied by this factor to determine the annual capital recovery costs. For example, the annual cost required to recover the original cost of $107,600 over 25 years at 10% would be $107,600 × 0.1102, or $11,858 per year.

The next step is to convert the replacement and salvage costs to a uniform series of payments. To do this, the present worth (discounted future costs) is amortized over the projected life. In the case of salvage value, the costs are negative, as indicated by the parentheses. For example, the original design has replacement costs of $35,000 at year 10, which has a present worth of $13,494. The periodic payment necessary to pay off a loan of this amount is $13,494 × 0.1102, or $1,487 per year.

After determining the annual amount of initial and replacement costs, other annual costs—such as operation, maintenance, and taxes—are added. The total represents a uniform baseline comparison for the alternatives over a projected life at a selected interest rate. The annual differences are then determined and used for

Life Cycle Costing (Annualized)

Item: *Enlisted Men's Quarters, HVAC System*

☐ Others ☐ Structural ☐ Mechanical ☐ Electrical

Economic Life: 25 Years   Discount Rate: 10%

Life Cycle Period _____

Date: N/A

Sheet No.: 1 of 1

Item	Description	Original	Alternate No. 1	Alternate No. 2
Collateral & Instant Contract Costs	**Base Costs**	49,150	70,000	62,000
	Interface Costs			
	a. *Electrical Installation*	10,000	4,835	7,200
	b.			
	c.			
	Other Initial Costs			
	a. *Owner Supplied Equipment*	48,450	25,000	27,000
	b.			
	c.			
	Total Initial Cost Impact (IC)	107,600	99,835	96,200
	Initial Cost Savings		7,765	11,400
Salvage & Replacement Cost	**Single Expenditures 10.00% Interest**			
	Present Worth			
	1. Year *10 Equip. Replace.* Amount	35,000		
	PW = Amount x PW factor 0.3855	13,494		
	2. Year *20 Equip. Replace.* Amount	35,000	30,000	35,000
	PW = Amount x PW factor 0.1486	5,203	4,459	5,203
	3. Year ____ Amount			
	PW = Amount x PW factor			
	4. Year ____ Amount			
	PW = Amount x PW factor			
	5. Year *25* Amount	(18,000)	(22,500)	(26,250)
	PW = Amount x PW factor 0.0923	(1,661)	(2,077)	(2,423)
	Salvage			
Life Cycle Costs (Annualized)	**Annual Owning & Operating Costs**			
	1. Capital IC x PP 0.1102	11,858	10,914	10,601
	Recovery 25 Years @ 10.00%			
	Replacement Cost: PP x PW			
	a. Year *10*	1,487		
	b. Year *20*	573	491	573
	c. Year ____			
	d. Year ____			
	e. Year *25*	(183)	(229)	(267)
	Salvage			
	2. Annual Cost			
	a. *Maintenance*	2,900	2,200	2,000
	b. *Operations*			
	c. *Cooling Energy*	13,650	13,950	16,025
	d. *Heating Energy*	1,060	2,425	2,425
	e. *Domestic HW Energy*	7,500	3,667	3,667
	3. Total Annual Cost	38,845	33,418	35,024
	Annual Difference (AD)		5,427	3,821
	4. Present Worth of Annual Difference			
	PWA Factor x AD 9.077 = PWA Factor		49,261	34,683

PP = Periodic Payment to pay off loan of $1

PWA = Present Worth of Annuity (what $1 payable periodically is worth today)

PW = Present Worth (what $1 due in the future is worth today)

Figure 7.18

recommendations. In this example, alternative No. 1, which has the lowest annual owning and operating costs savings (annual differences)—$5,427/year—would be recommended.

The present worth of the annual difference (PWA from Figure 7.8 × the annual difference) can also be determined. In this example, the present worth of the annual difference indicated for alternative No. 1 is the annual difference of $5,427 × the present worth of $1.00 payable annually for 25 year, or $5,427 × 9.077, which equals $49,261.

As previously stated, LCC analysis can be accomplished using either the annualized method or the present worth method. In the case of the present worth method, the baseline of comparison is the present-day value. Figure 7.19 shows the application of the present worth method and uses the information from the previous example. In using the present worth concept, collateral and initial costs are in present-day values and are entered directly. Single costs in the future (salvage and replacement) are discounted using present worth factors from Figure 7.7.

Annual costs are entered and multiplied by present worth of annuity (PWA) factors from Figure 7.8. For example, for the original design the present worth of the annual costs for maintenance equals $2,900/yr × 9.077 (PWA), or $26,323.

All present worth amounts are added and the comparison is made for recommendations. The results validate conclusions developed using the annualized cost baseline.

Figure 7.20 shows the same example but uses differentially escalating rates using a discount rate of 10% for operation and maintenance costs. As previously explained, these escalating rates were calculated as the differential between the escalation rate and the rate of inflation. Operation costs are differentially escalated annually at 5% per year while maintenance costs are differentially escalated at 2% per year. The example points out the impact of considering escalation and shows that alternative No. 1 is still the recommended alternative.

If the annualized method is used, the annual sum for operations and maintenance may also be increased by a factor to account for differential escalation. Figure 7.4 provides the required data. For example, the factor for 2% differentially escalating maintenance cost would be 10.82/9.077, or 1.19. The operation cost factor for 5% would be 14.44/9.077, or 1.59. These factors would be used to adjust the annual costs per year accordingly. For example, the adjustment for the annual maintenance costs of the original design would be $2,900/yr. × 1.19, or $3,541/yr.

General Purpose Worksheet

Figure 7.21 shows a general purpose LCC worksheet that can be used for a more detailed system analysis using present worth. This form is also useful as a summary sheet for individual items or component analysis.

Figure 7.22 shows an LCC analysis using this worksheet for the selection of emergency power systems of a large computer complex. The original concept was validated as the optimum choice.

LCC Analysis—Equipment Procurement

Figure 7.23 outlines a formal procedure for LCC of an equipment procurement (freezer). For this procurement, bidder D was awarded the contract even though his initial unit cost was $309.50, versus $231.53 for bidder B. The impact of recurring costs, $357.42 for D versus $464.91 for B, more than offset the difference in initial cost (on the basis of present worth analysis).

Life Cycle Costing Example (PW)

Item: _____ HVAC System _____

Date: N/A

☐ Transportation ☐ Electrical ☐ Mechanical ☐ Others

Sheet No.: 1 of 1

Economic Life: 25 Years   Discount Rate: 10%

Description	Closed Loop Heat Pump System — Original		4-Pipe System with Water Cooled Chiller & Heat Recovery — Alternate No. 1		4-Pipe System with Air Cooled Chiller & Heat Recovery — Alternate No. 2	
	Estimated Cost	Present Worth	Estimated Cost	Present Worth	Estimated Cost	Present Worth
1. Initial/Collateral Costs						
A. *Refrigeration Equipment*	48,450	48,450	25,000	25,000	27,000	27,000
B. *Piping, Ductwork & Support Equip.*	49,150	49,150	70,000	70,000	62,000	62,000
C. *Electrical Installation*	10,000	10,000	4,835	4,835	7,200	7,200
D.						
E.						
F.						
G.						
Other Initial Cost						
A.						
B.						
C.						
Total Initial Impact (IC)		107,600		99,835		96,200
Initial Cost Savings (PW)				7,765		11,400
2. Replacement/Salvage Costs						
	Year	PW				
A. *Equip. Replac.* 10 0.3855	35,000	13,493				
B. *Equip. Replac.* 20 0.1486	35,000	5,202	30,000	4,459	35,000	5,205
C.						
D.						
E.						
F.						
G.						
Salvage 25 0.0923	(18,000)	(1,661)	(22,500)	(2,076)	(26,250)	(2,422)
Total Replacement/Salvage Costs (PW)		17,034		2,383		2,783
3. Annual Costs						
Escl. % PWA						
A. *Maintenance* 9.077	2,900	26,323	2,200	19,969	2,000	18,154
B. *Cooling Energy* 9.077	13,650	123,902	13,950	126,625	16,025	145,460
C. *Heating Energy* 9.077	1,060	9,622	2,425	22,012	2,425	22,012
D. *Domestic HW* 9.077	7,500	68,078	3,667	33,286	3,667	33,286
E.						
F.						
G.						
H.						
Total Operation/Maintenance Costs (PW)		227,925		201,892		218,912
Grand Total Present Worth Costs		352,559		304,110		317,895
Life Cycle Present Worth Savings				48,449		34,664
Savings %		0.00%		13.74%		9.83%

PW = Present Worth   PWA = Present Worth of Annuity

Figure 7.19

Life Cycle Costing Example (Present Worth Escalated)

Item: _____HVAC System_____   Date: _N/A_____

☐ Transportation ☐ Electrical ☐ Mechanical ☐ Others   Sheet No.: _1 of 1_

Economic Life: 25 Years   Discount Rate: 10%

Description			Closed Loop Heat Pump System		4-Pipe System with Water Cooled Chillers & Heat Recovery		4-Pipe System with Air Cooled Chillers & Heat Recovery	
			Original		Alternate No. 1		Alternate No. 2	
			Estimated Cost	Present Worth	Estimated Cost	Present Worth	Estimated Cost	Present Worth
1. Initial/Collateral Costs								
A. Refrigeration Equipment			48,450	48,450	25,000	25,000	27,000	27,000
B. Piping, Ductwork & Support Equip.			49,150	49,150	70,000	70,000	62,000	62,000
C. Electrical Installation			10,000	10,000	4,835	4,835	7,200	7,200
D.								
E.								
F.								
G.								
Other Initial Cost								
A.								
B.								
C.								
Total Initial/Collateral Cost (PW)				107,600		99,835		96,200
Total Initial/Collateral Cost Savings						7,765		11,400
2. Replacement/Salvage Costs								
	Year	PW						
A. Equip. Replac.	10	0.386	35,000	13,493				
B. Equip. Replac.	20	0.149	35,000	5,201	30,000	4,458	35,000	5,205
C.								
D.								
E.								
F.								
G.								
Salvage	25	0.0923	(18,000)	(1,661)	(22,500)	(2,076)	(26,250)	(2,422)
Total Replacement/Salvage Costs (PW)				17,033		2,382		2,783
3. Annual Costs								
	Escl. %	PWA						
A. Maintenance	2.0%	10.8190	2,900	31,375	2,200	23,802	2,000	21,638
B. Cooling Energy	5.0%	14.4370	13,650	197,065	13,950	201,396	16,025	231,353
C. Heating Energy	5.0%	14.4370	1,060	15,303	2,425	35,010	2,425	35,010
D. Domestic HW	5.0%	14.4370	7,500	108,278	3,667	52,940	3,667	52,939
E.								
F.								
G.								
H.								
Total Annual Cost								
Total Annual Cost (PW)				352,021		313,148		340,940
Grand Total Present Worth Costs				476,653		415,365		439,923
Life Cycle Present Worth Savings						61,288		36,731
Savings %				0.00%		12.86%		7.71%

PW = Present Worth   PWA = Present Worth of Annuity

Figure 7.20

Life Cycle Costing Estimate (PW)
General Purpose Work Sheet

Study Title: _____   Date: _____

☐ Transportation ☐ Electrical ☐ Mechanical ☐ Others   Sheet No.: _____

Economic Life: ___ Years   Discounted Rate: ___%

	Description	Original		Alternate No. 1		Alternate No. 2		Alternate No. 3	
		Estimated Cost	Present Worth	Estimated Cost	Present Worth	Estimated Cost	Present Worth	Estimated Cost	Present Worth
Initial Cost	**Initial/Collateral Costs**								
	A.								
	B.								
	C.								
	D.								
	E.								
	F.								
	G. Contingencies %								
	H. Escalation %								
	Total Initial Costs								
Owning Cost	**Operations (Annual)** Diff. Escal. Rate PW w/Escal.								
	A.								
	B.								
	C.								
	D.								
	E.								
	F.								
	Total Annual Operation Costs								
	Maintenance (Annual) Diff. Escal. Rate PW w/Escal.								
	A.								
	B.								
	C.								
	D.								
	E.								
	F.								
	Total Annual Maintenance Costs								
	Replacement/Alterations (Single Expenditure) Year PW Factor								
	A.								
	B.								
	C.								
	D.								
	E.								
	F.								
	Total Replacement/Alterations Costs								
	Tax Elements Diff. Escal. Rate PW w/Escal.								
	A.								
	B.								
	C.								
	D.								
	Total Tax Elements								
	Associated (Annual) Diff. Escal. Rate PW w/Escal.								
	A.								
	B.								
	C.								
	D.								
	Total Annual Associated Costs								
	Total Owning Present Worth Costs								
Salvage	**Salvage at End of Economic Life @ 10%** Year PW Factor								
	A.								
	B.								
	C.								
	Total Salvage								
LCC	**Total Present Worth Life Cycle Costs**								
	Life Cycle Present Worth Dollar Savings								

PW = Present Worth   PWA = Present Worth of Annuity

Figure 7.21

Life Cycle Costing Estimate (PW)
General Purpose Work Sheet

Study Title: **Standby Generators**

☐ Transportation ☐ Electrical ☐ Mechanical ☐ Others

Date: _____

Sheet No.: **1 of 1**

Economic Life: 40 Years   Discount Rate: 10%

Description		Original 8 - 1000 KW Recip. Diesel Engines		Alternate No. 1 4 - 2000 KW Recip. Diesel Engines		Alternate No. 2 8 - 1000 KW Gas Turbines		Alternate No. 3 4 - 2000 KW Gas Turbines	
		Estimated Cost	Present Worth	Estimated Cost	Present Worth	Estimated Cost	Present Worth	Estimated Cost	Present Worth
Initial/Collateral Costs									
A. *Generators*			1,400,000		1,800,000		2,000,000		2,000,000
B. *Switchgear*			128,000		126,000		128,000		126,000
C. *Mechanical*			157,000		175,000		151,000		175,000
D.									
E.									
F.									
G *Contingencies*	%								
H *Escalation*	%								
Total Initial Costs			1,685,000		2,101,000		2,279,000		2,301,000
Operations (Annual)	Diff. Escal. Rate / PW w/Escal.								
A. *1 MW Recip. 70 gal/hr x 8*	0% / 9.779	89,600	876,200						
B. *2 MW Recip. 140 gal/hr x 4*	0% / 9.779			89,600	876,200				
C. *1 MW Turbine 161 gal/hr x 8*	0% / 9.779					154,600	1,511,800		
D. *2 MW Turbine 268 gal/hr x 4*	0% / 9.779							128,600	1,258,000
E.									
F.									
Total Annual Operation Costs			876,200		876,200		1,511,800		1,258,000
Maintenance (Annual)	Diff. Escal. Rate / PW w/Escal.								
A. *Lubricate, change filters*	0% / 9.779	10,200	99,700	9,000	88,000	10,200	99,700	9,000	88,000
B. *Check & adjust ignition*									
C. *Inspect winding rings*									
D. *Belts, etc., check fuel*									
E. *Coolant, electrolyte, etc.*	0% / 9.779								
F. *Replace failed components as required*	0% / 9.779	800	7,800	400	3,900	2,000	19,600	1,000	9,800
Total Annual Maintenance Costs			107,500		91,900		119,300		97,800
Replacement/Alterations (Single Expenditure)	Year / PW Factor								
A. *1 MW Turbine*						500,000	46,100		
B. *2 MW Turbine*								500,000	46,100
C. *1 MW Diesel*		350,000	32,300						
D. *2 MW Diesel*				450,000	41,500				
E.									
F. *(Failure rate one in four)*									
Total Replacement/Alterations Costs			32,300		41,500		46,100		46,100
Tax Elements	Diff. Escal. Rate / PW w/Escal.								
A.									
B.									
C.									
D.									
Total Tax Elements									
Associated (Annual)	Diff. Escal. Rate / PW w/Escal.								
A. *Denial of use space*	- / -	6,000	270,000	3,500	157,500	1,000	45,000		
B. *Cost $45.00/SF*									
C.									
D.									
Total Annual Associated Costs			270,000		157,500		45,000		
Total Owning Present Worth Costs			1,286,000		1,167,100		1,722,200		1,401,900
Salvage at End of Economic Life @ 10%	Year / PW Factor								
A. *Building (Struc.,Arch.,ME&P)*	40 / 0.022	(140,000)	(3,100)	(180,000)	(4,000)	(224,000)	(4,900)	(200,000)	(4,400)
B. *Other*									
C. *Site Work*									
Total Salvage			(3,100)		(4,000)		(4,900)		(4,400)
Total Present Worth Life Cycle Costs			2,967,900		3,264,100		3,996,300		3,698,500
Life Cycle Present Worth Dollar Savings			-		(296,200)		(1,028,400)		(730,600)

PW = Present Worth   PWA = Present Worth of Annuity

Figure 7.22

Summary of Life Cycle Costs for Top Mounted Freezer[a]

Zone	Type Cost	A	B	C	D	E	F
1	A[b]	242.21	231.53	263.45	309.50	252.90	248.36
	R[c]	518.01	464.91	431.24	357.42	486.96	493.40
	LCC[d]	760.22	696.44	694.69	666.92	739.86	741.76
2	A[b]	243.33	230.37	263.45	309.50	244.95	248.38
	R[c]	518.01	464.91	431.24	357.42	486.96	493.40
	LCC[d]	761.34	695.28	694.69	666.92	731.91	741.76
3	A[b]	250.84	232.98	263.45	309.50	251.69	248.36
	R[c]	518.01	464.91	431.24	357.42	486.96	493.40
	LCC[d]	768.85	697.89	694.69	666.92	738.65	741.76
4	A[b]	272.09	245.04	257.45	309.50	267.25	248.36
	R[c]	518.01	464.91	431.24	357.42	486.96	493.40
	LCC[d]	790.10	709.95	688.69	666.92	754.21	741.76

[a] See reference procurement discussion in text.

A[b] = Acquisition costs

R[c] = Recurring.

LCC[d] = Life Cycle Cost - Present Worth

Figure 7.23

The procurement in Figure 7.23, based on anticipated demand quantities, provided a projected cost savings over the useful life (15 years) of some $260,000. The LCC formula used in this procurement is:

$$LCC = A + R$$

Where:

LCC = life cycle cost in present value dollars

A = acquisition cost (bid price)

R = present value sum of the cost of the electrical energy required by the refrigerator freezer during its useful life.

$$R = P \times T \times D \times C$$

Where:

P = computed electrical energy

T = annual operating time in days

D = total discount factor, which will convert the stream of operating costs over the life of the equipment to present worth form (Figure 7.8).

C = cost of one kilowatt hour of electricity

The discounted cash flow or present value methodology was used as a decision-making tool to allow direct comparison between different expenditure patterns of alternative investment opportunities. The present value sum represents the amount of money that would be required to be invested today, at a given rate of interest, to pay the expected future costs associated with a particular investment alternative. For purposes of this procurement, a discount rate of 8% and a product life of 15 years were used, resulting in a total discount factor, D, of 8.56 (Figure 7.8). Also, an energy cost of $0.04 per kilowatt hour was used.

The value for P in the energy cost equation is a function of the net refrigerated volume, V, of the product being offered and the energy factor, EF, which relates refrigerated volume and the electrical energy consumed to maintain the refrigerated volume. Stated in mathematical notation, the value of P is determined as P = V/EF, where:

$$EF = \frac{(\text{Vol froz. food compartments}) \times (\text{correction factor}) \times (\text{food compartments})}{\text{kWh of elec. energy consumed in 24 hrs. of operation}}$$

The correction factor is a constant of 1.63. Thus the LCC evaluation formula, $LCC = A + R = A + (P \times C \times T \times D)$, can be written as follows:

$$LCC = V + V \times \$.04 \times 365 \times 8.56$$
$$EF = A + V/EF \times 124.976.$$

Overall Note

Certain liberties have been taken in the above discussion to simplify the LCC process. One such liberty was assuming all initial and collateral costs were at the same baseline. In some cases, these costs could vary a few years in a construction project, but the complications involved did not warrant incorporation of additional refinement. Also, follow-on costs—annual, replacement, etc.—would vary from the beginning of the year to the end of the year. Tables for annuity factors and so forth have been developed for beginning of the year and end of the year values. In this chapter, all costs were end of the year values; the tables reflect that assumption. The examples were prepared in an Excel spreadsheet that referred to more detailed data than is indicated on the spreadsheets. Therefore, the extensions are more complete than they would be if a hand calculator had been used.

Conclusion

With the advent of increasing interest rates and escalating energy and labor rates, the concept of LCC for decision making has become increasingly important. No major decision regarding buildings that involve large follow-on costs should be made without using the LCC technique. This technique must be based on bringing all costs to a common baseline—the concept of equivalent costs for comparison before selection.

Escalation factors based on differential factors should be applied if the evaluation group feels they are appropriate. When the evaluation group feels the available data are too variable, a sensitivity analysis should be conducted using the best available estimated escalation factors. Where savings are augmented by escalation, a stronger recommendation can be made. Where savings are compromised by escalation, a conditional recommendation should be made. LCC analysis techniques using the equivalent cost concept provide vital tools that should be used by all designers.

References

1. A.J. Dell'Isola and S.J. Kirk, *Life Cycle Costing for Design Professionals, Second Edition,* (New York: McGraw Hill, Inc., 1995).

2. U.S. Naval Facilities Engineering Command, *Economic Analysis Handbook, P-442.* (Washington, D.C., July, 1980).

3. U.S. Army Corps of Engineers, *Economic Studies for Military Construction Design Applications, TM-5-802-1.*

4. See *Life Cycle Costing for Design Professionals, Second Edition* for more complete tables.

5. See *Life Cycle Costing for Design Professionals, Second Edition* for further details.

6. A.J. Dell'Isola and S.J. Kirk, *Life Cycle Costing for Design Professionals, Second Edition,* (New York: McGraw Hill, Inc., 1995).
   A.J. Dell'Isola and S.J. Kirk, *Life Cycle Cost Data* (New York: McGraw-Hill, Inc., 1983).

Chapter Eight

Integrating VE into the Construction Industry

Value engineering is effective in many areas of the construction industry, and it can be utilized at different stages in the life of a building. The greatest potential for the integration of VE exists in three major areas:

1. Planning and design
2. Construction
3. Maintenance and operations

Planning and Design

Of these three construction areas, the greatest potential for integrating value engineering lies in planning and design. Early in the development of value engineering, architects and engineers were resistant to the implementation of VE. The typical approach to planning and design was to (1) proceed with design until an established time—for example, schematic or design development, or (2) wait until a cost overrun surfaced. In time, it became apparent that more savings were being lost than realized. Eventually, the U.S. government and owners, who recognized continual cost overruns and poor value results, encouraged the design community to embrace VE. As a result, the application of value engineering moved to earlier design phases and was integrated into the design process.

The experiences of the A/E firm of Smith, Hinchman & Grylls (SH&G) offer an illustration of this evolution. In the early 1970s, the firm realized the importance of VE and established one of the first consulting VE offices. This VE consulting office continues to thrive, offering the classical approach to VE applied during design to owners and design consultants, both nationally and internationally. Billions of dollars in savings have resulted from these efforts.

However, when the firm used the same classical approach for its own in-house design, difficulty arose. At first, an analysis of the problem suggested that the VE specialists were located too far from where the design was prepared. However, the classical approach is always remote. Further study of the problem indicated that the real issue was the need for value consultation throughout the design process. This realization was critical to improved decision making for the design team.

Figure 8.1 represents a typical solicitation from a government agency for VE services. As the text indicates, the recent trend has moved from requests for individual studies to a more comprehensive task order approach. This strategy has reduced the time and effort required for contracts and administration.

Solicitation for VE Services

COMMERCE BUSINESS DAILY
Issue No. PSA-1788
Publication Date: 02/24/97
Services
Architect and Engineering Services -- Construction

Synopsis# SN033843-0029
NOTICE TYPE: Solicitation
NOTICE DATED: 021997
OFFICE ADDRESS: Commanding Officer, Southern Division, Naval Facilities Engineering
Command, 2155 Eagle Drive (29406), PO Box 190010, North Charleston, SC
ZIP CODE: 29419-9010
SUBJECT: C - Indefinite Delivery Requirements (IDR) for Value Engineering (VE) Studies and
Reports in the Southern Division AOR
SOLICITATION NO.: SOL N62467-97-R-0883
RESPONSE DEADLINE: DUE 032597
CONTACT: POC Admin Questions: Ms. Frances J. Mitchell, (803) 820-5749

NOTICE TEXT: Two firms will be selected for this solicitation, one for each contract. No firm
will be awarded more than one (1) contract. A separate submittal is required to be considered for
each contract covered by this solicitation. Firms shall indicate in Block 1 of their SF 255 the
contract number for which they wish to be considered. The two contracts shall be for value
engineering (V-E) studies and reports on all types of facility design projects and the ability to
provide a 40-hour Society of American Value Engineers certified training workshop. The first
contract, N62467-97-R-0883, will encompass the following states: NC, SC, GA, FL, AL, MS,
TN, and KY. The second contract, N62467-97-R-0884, will encompass the following states:
LA, TX, OK, AR, MO, KS, CO, WY, SD, ND, NE, IA, IL, MN, WI, IN, MI, and OH. The
contractors may also, on occasion, be asked to provide the services described herein at
government activities outside the geographical area encompassed by these contracts. These
actions will be decided on a case-by-case basis as approved by the contracting officer. In the
event that a selected A-E firm cannot perform their duties under the terms of the contract due to
quality, workload, negotiations or any other problems, a different A-E firm (backup) will be
employed to perform the work. The A-E firm selected for contract number 97-R-0883 will be
the backup for contract number 97-R-0884 and the A-E firm selected for contract number
97-R-0884 will be the backup for contract number 97-R-0883. The contract period shall be one
year with four (4) one-year options for the complete services listed above. This contract may use
negotiated fee schedules. Contract award is contingent upon availability of funds. The
anticipated value of this contract is between $100,000.00 to $500,000.00 per year.

The following criteria (listed in descending order of importance) will be used for the basis of
selection. The format for responding to each criteria shall be indicated in lieu of completing
Blocks 7, 8, 9 and 10 in the SF 255.

Figure 8.1

1. PROFESSIONAL QUALIFICATIONS: Technical qualifications of the firm's proposed team to a) Provide Value Engineering (VE) studies and reports; b) Conduct Value Engineering training; and c) Professional registration and Certified Value Specialist (CVS) certification of the proposed team members. SUBMISSION FORMAT: Submit a matrix for proposed team(s), including alternates, that contains the following data about the member's assignment: Team member's name, firm name, office location, proposed team assignment, % time to be spent on this team, highest education level/discipline (example: BS, mechanical engineering), states of professional registration, number of years of professional experience and number of years with the firm. Also, for project managers and team leaders, identify the number of teams (planning/design, consultants and joint venture partners) they have managed over the past three years.

2. SPECIALIZED EXPERIENCE: Recent experience (within the past 5 years) of the individuals assigned to the proposed team in a) Organizing and leading VE study/review; b) Conducting Value Engineering training; and c) Designing various types of facilities. SUBMISSION FORMAT: Provide a description of at least 3 projects with client references (point of contact and phone number) for which team members provided a significant technical contribution. Work on these projects must have been done in the last 5 years. Indicate how each project is relevant to the work described herein. In matrix form, identify which team members worked on the projects described above. Projects shall be in the left column and team members' names shall be across the top row of the matrix.

3. PERFORMANCE: Past performance ratings by Government agencies and private industry in terms of value engineering studies/reviews and value engineering training. SUBMISSION FORMAT: Provide a tabular listing of all excellent performance ratings and letters of commendation from both private and DOD clients (designate your role: prime, consultant or joint venture partner). These ratings should be dated 1992 or later and should include those for joint venture partners and consultants. Provide a list of projects of various sizes, managed by proposed project managers(s), that started since January 1992 and include the following data: client's contact, client's need date, project completion date and final cost estimate compared to the contract award amount (note whether bid or negotiated).

4. CAPACITY: a) Capacity of firm and proposed teams to accomplish the work; b) Ability of the firm to conduct several studies concurrently and sustain the loss of key personnel while accomplishing work within required time limits. SUBMISSION FORMAT: Submit an organizational chart with the following information: Principal point of contact, project manager, team leaders, the name of each planning team member, all team members' assignments, and the name of at least one alternate for each key person.

5. LOCATION: a) Knowledge of probable site conditions over the Southern Division geographic area of responsibility; b) Knowledge of regulatory requirements; and c) Geographic location of the firm to ensure timely response to requests for on-site support. SUBMISSION FORMAT: Provide a list of recent projects performed by the firm or joint venture partners and appropriate consultants in the enumerated 26 state area.

Figure 8.1 (cont.)

6. VOLUME OF DOD WORK: Firms will be evaluated in terms of work previously awarded to the firm by DOD within the past twelve months with the objective of effecting an equitable distribution of contracts among qualified A-E firms including small and small disadvantaged business firms and firms that have not had prior DOD A-E contracts.

7. JOINT VENTURE, TEAMING OR SUBCONTRACTOR UTILIZATION: Firms will be evaluated on the extent to which they commit to using small businesses, small disadvantaged businesses, historically black colleges and universities or minority institutions in performance of the contract, whether as a joint venture, teaming arrangement, or consultant. If the successful firm is a large business, they will be asked to provide a formal subcontracting plan in accordance with FAR 52.219-9, Small Business and Small Disadvantaged Business Subcontracting Plan, prior to award. SELECTION INTERVIEW REQUIREMENTS: Prior to the selection interview, A-E firms slated must submit their Design Quality Assurance Plan (DQAP). This shall include an explanation of their management approach and commitment to accomplishing numerous small projects (less than $1M) as well as large projects (more than $1M), their commitment to a quality philosophy, specific quality control process, a portfolio of VE engineering studies (both new construction and upgrades to existing facilities), a listing of present business commitments with their required completion schedules, financial and credit references (include name and telephone numbers of officers at their financial institutions), and performance references other than Southern Division, Naval Facilities Engineering Command (include 3 or more with names and telephone numbers of the contract administrators).

For consideration, provide one original SF 255 and SF 254 for the prime and an SF 254 for each consultant proposed. The SF 255 with attachments shall be limited to 25 pages (8.5 x 11 one side), with print size not smaller than 12 pitch font. The submittal package must be received in this office not later than 4:00 P.M. EASTERN TIME on TUESDAY, 25 MARCH 1997. Submittals received after this date and time will not be considered. If additional firms are needed for consideration, SF 254s already on file will be used. Include telefax numbers in Block 3a and Contractor Establishment Code (formerly the DUNS number), Commercial and Government Entity (CAGE) Codes, if known, and Taxpayer Identification Number (TIN) in Block 3. The DUNS, CAGE and TIN are discussed in the DOD FAR Supplement, Part 204 Subpart 204.671-5. For each contract, label lower right corner of outside mailing envelope with "A-E Services, 97-R-0883 or 97-R-0884."

This is not a request for proposal. Site visits will not be arranged during advertisement period. Address all responses to ATTN: Code 0213FM.

Source: Federal Information & New Dispatch, Inc. (Find), http://www.find-inc.com. e-mail: find@find-inc.com, 202-544-4800

Figure 8.1 (cont.)

Differences Between the Old and New Approaches

Until value consultation through the design process became an accepted practice, actual application of individual VE studies for a project were on a case-by-case basis. The classical approach separated VE application from the remainder of the A/E activities. The design team prepared each stage of design with little or no coordinating input from the value engineer, as illustrated in Figure 8.2. Architect/engineers did not have much say in this approach. They simply agreed to keep this application separate.

The VE consultants (as independent evaluators) performed their duties at the end of each stage—at the "nodes" shown in Figure 8.2. They believed that the overall project schedule would not be affected, since the study coincided with the normal review and approval process of most owners. Unfortunately, many good VE ideas came too late to be incorporated into the design. And still, the consulting value engineers did not oppose. It was easier to maintain a discrete set of work activities requiring little coordination with the variety of A/E design decision-making activities that occur between the nodes. Little or no integration with the design team resulted in fewer management headaches for the VE consultant. Unfortunately, many good VE proposals were not accepted by the design team because of lack of integration within the design decision-making process. Poor timing of an otherwise good idea, or pressure from design project management "to forget the VE idea" to maintain the design schedule, negated many good ideas. This "review and revise" approach is not particularly appealing to an A/E firm that ideally prefers a "review and approve" approach, within the nodes.

The Need for VE "Between the Nodes"

In 1987, SH&G embarked on a pilot program to integrate VE into the design process (between the nodes) for all large design projects. To do this effectively, the firm assigned a value specialist to its main design office. So that VE might succeed, top management committed to a revised organization that placed VE in a prominent position, provided active participation in the early planning, and monitored results. The first several months were devoted to the study of how best to incorporate the principles of VE into the routine activities of the A/E office. Figure 8.3 illustrates the resulting group, called "Facility Economics," and the cost, quality, and value engineering responsibilities. The cost staff is a team of architectural, structural, mechanical, and electrical estimators and schedulers. Elevator specialists, hospital equipment specialists, mechanical controls specialists, and so on, also provide input into the preparation of a cost estimate. The quality (value) teams are selected and organized specifically for the needs of each project from those architects and engineers who have no prior input to the design being reviewed. This objectivity is further assured by the team coordinator, who has no direct management reporting responsibility to the design team. Once assembled, the VE team participates throughout the progression of design following the project design work plan schedule.

Project Work Plan

Before every design begins, a project schedule is prepared to graphically portray the stages of design, discipline responsibilities, coordinating relationships, and design products. This set of information is referred to as the **Project Work Plan.** The Work Plan is updated throughout the design process. In Figure 8.4, key information from a typical project has been abstracted to graphically illustrate how VE is integrated into the design process.

In Figure 8.4, VE is defined broadly as the balancing of cost, quality, and time to meet required owner functions. As such, the controlling elements of cost and quality place a "bounds" to the design Work Plan and are shown above and below the normal design activities. Both cost and quality are further subdivided into modeling,

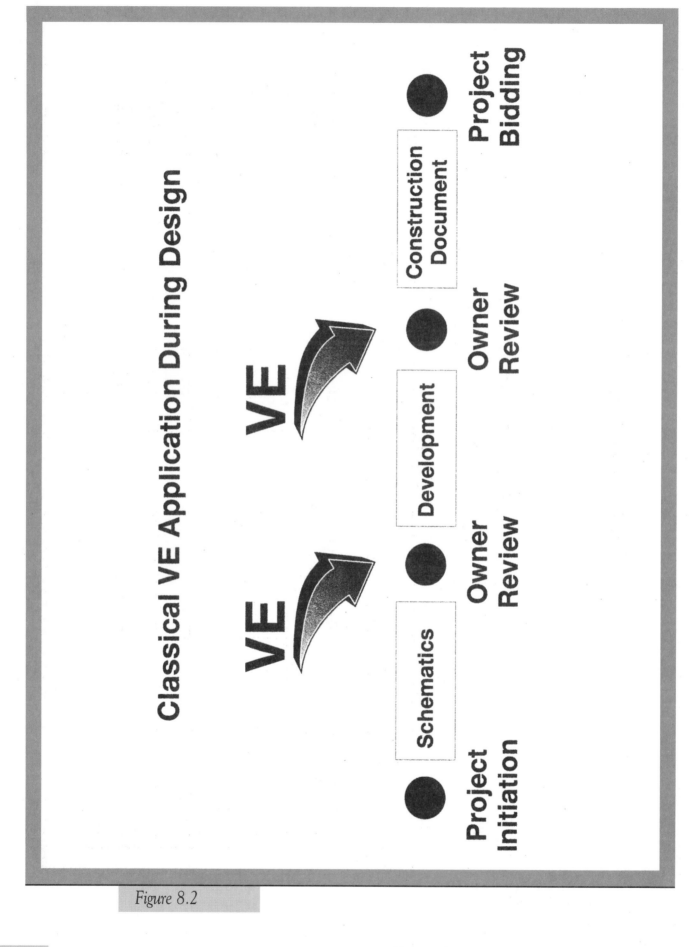

Figure 8.2

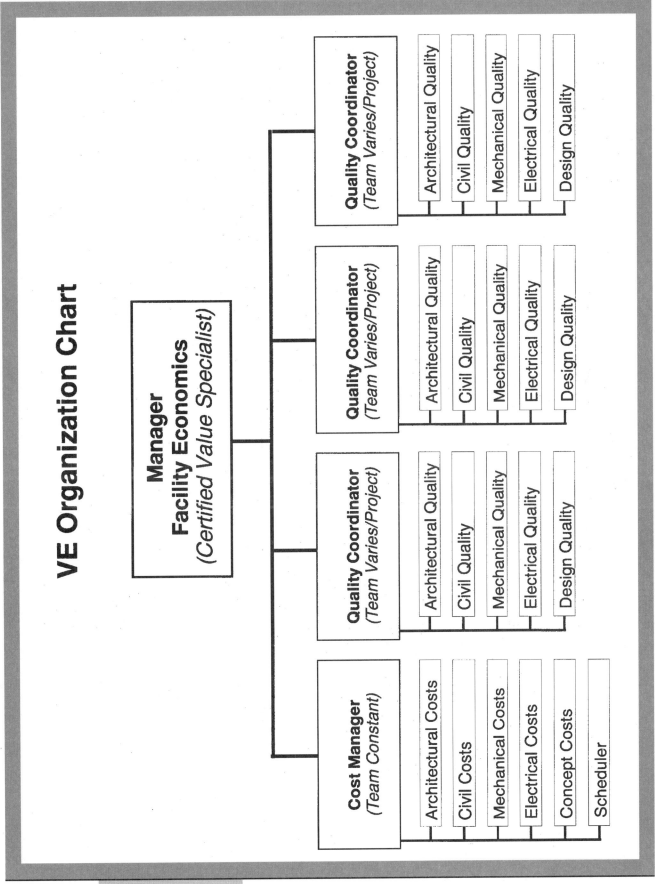

Figure 8.3

Integrated Cost/Quality Value Management
Project Approach

Quality - Program - Cost

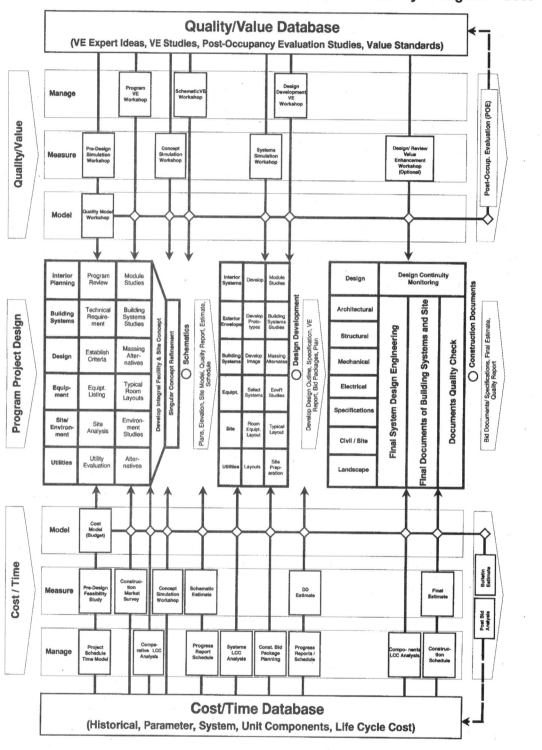

Figure 8.4

measuring, and managing. **Modeling** is the initial budgeting of both cost and quality requirements by the owner. **Measurements** (or estimates) of cost and quality are taken at various times during the design progression. **Management** of cost and quality occurs only when management takes specific corrective design actions to deal with the variations between the budget model and the actual design measurement. As the diagram shows, these activities occur throughout the design decision-making process. They may be performed by an independent team of value engineers (as in the classical approach); but they are also performed by the original design team, a group that was not involved with the previous decision. However, the classical VE reviews still occur at the completion of each major stage of design. These reviews are augmented by other less-formalized, value-related studies "between the nodes." These studies are scheduled by the VE manager to coincide with key cost-driver decisions. The diagram also isolates the design and cost information needed to conduct workshops and when they should be held.

Databases have been created to support both cost and quality VE activities. The cost database includes historical, parameter, systems, unit component, and life cycle cost (LCC) information. A specially designed, automated cost-estimating system has been developed to integrate these efforts into the VE process. The database includes information such as ideas from previous VE studies, findings from post-occupancy evaluations, and design standards regarding space and engineering functions. These databases continue to be improved through experience and formalized feedback from post-bid analyses and post-occupancy evaluations at the completion of projects.

Each VE activity is coded in the Project Work Plan to describe the task in greater detail to the project manager, the design team, and the VE team. For example, Quality Task 204: Schematic VE Workshop is described in a one-page narrative covering the topics of:

- Purpose
- Participants
- Data required
- Activity
- Product

The narrative for this particular activity is included in Figure 8.5. Explaining each of the tasks helps both the project manager and the design team better understand what the duties of the value engineer are, as well as when they will be done and how. Also, this documentation provides guidance for others in the integration of work assignments and data requirements, so the value engineer can in turn complete needed assignments.

Changes from Classical VE

This new approach in design has resulted in several fundamental changes to the classical way of conceptualizing VE. One significant change is that VE can be practiced on both a formal and an informal basis, by both an independent team (to maintain objectivity) and, as a convenience, by the design team. The independent VE team is structured based on the needs of the specific value study, but it always consists of other design team members who have not participated in the original design of the project. The principles of VE—including following the Job Plan, function analysis, separation of creativity and evaluation, LCC analysis and recommendations—are still a fundamental part of every study.

Another difference is that the VE team's job does not end when the VE recommendations are given to the original designers. The VE team, being part of the same organization, must assist in the implementation of each idea. If further research is required, this team may be called upon to complete the work.

Facility Economics Activities
Schematic Design

204: Schematic VE Workshop

Purpose	Review the schematic submittal to optimize decisions, for technical adequacy, compliance with required standards, desired quality and cost.
Participants	The basic work is performed by an independent VE team under the leadership of a Certified Value Specialist, who serves as the quality coordinator. The owner/user representatives and the construction manager also participate. The design team provides information and is available throughout the VE workshop to answer questions.

Data Required	Prior to the VE workshop, the project manager should obtain the following data:
	  - Site Analysis, Soils Report
	  - Plans, Elevations, Sections
	  - Building Description Forms
	  - Schematic Estimate, Project Schedule
	
	Once this information is complete, it should be given to the quality coordinator for review prior to the schematic VE workshop.

Activity	The quality coordinator prepares a VE work session agenda and recommends the independent team members. The project manager is requested to arrange a VE session. (The actual length of the VE session depends on the size/complexity of the project and the results to be achieved. The quality coordinator will recommend the proper length of the VE workshop to achieve the objectives of the project manager).
	
	Once the team is assembled, a project briefing is presented by the design team. The team then reviews the documentation, cost and quality models, and begins to isolate areas for in-depth value improvements. The following phases are followed:
	  Information Phase (including function analysis)
	  Idea Phase
	  Analytical Phase
	  Recommendation Phase
	
	Upon completion of the above, the team gives an oral presentation of VE recommendations to the design team and senior owner/user representatives. A draft VE report is presented at this time documenting the recommendations.

Product	A final report, prepared by the VE coordinator, documents the VE process and recommendations.

Figure 8.5

Benefits of Integration

Since integration of VE with the design process in 1987, every major project has followed similar Work Plans. Because VE has been applied from project initiation through completion, it is difficult to isolate all the value improvements resulting from this new approach. The owner, project manager, and design team have all benefited from the organized methods of VE. Clients and designers alike agree that greater value results from the integration of VE into the design process. Other improvements include:

- Greater team interaction.
- Greater knowledge of costs and the resulting economic impact of various design decisions.
- Easier and more economical implementation of VE recommendations.
- Increased monitoring and management of quality and cost throughout design.

On a more personal basis, the value engineer on one project becomes the designer on the next. This results in the informal incorporation of VE ideas and attitude into the mainstream of design for the next project. Since each VE team member knows that the next project he or she designs might be value-analyzed by the same people now being evaluated, interpersonal relationships within the organization are improved.

The Cost of Integrated VE

The classical approach to VE application segregated the labor involved in a study by the VE consultants. This cost was paid by the owner directly. With integration of VE into the design decision-making process, the added cost has a lesser impact on the overall fees for designing a project. At the same time, it improves the effect on project value and design production efficiency. In fact, VE began as an essential part of a larger overall production/manufacturing organization where the benefits outweigh the added design management responsibilities for the designer and its clients.

Another successful integration of VE has occurred in project/construction management. When used for fast track, bid packaging, or just plain increased project management application, the use of VE as a part of the managers' scope of work is an innovative tool to increase the effectiveness of their services. The scope of services within the framework of PM/CM responsibilities differs from those offered by a VE consultant and/or an in-house designer or owner. In all instances, experience on over 50 large PM/CM projects has shown a resultant VE savings that far exceeds fees.

A typical scope of work for value engineering services for PM/CM is provided in the Appendix of this book. These guidelines result in greater objectivity in the VE process than the in-house designer efforts can offer. When a PM/CM approach is used, the contract for these services is the preferred placement for the VE provisions. Since the PM/CM is responsible for cost, schedule, and quality control, VE belongs in this professional's tool kit.

Construction

Initially, VE was applied during the construction cycle. In 1968 the Armed Services Procurement Regulations began to write construction contracts that included Value Engineering Incentive Contracts. Since then, all Department of Defense Construction Contracts (unless specifically exempted with good reason and in writing) have included the VE Incentive Clause. This clause is part of the Standard General Conditions, and it becomes effective after award of the contract. The basis of bid is not changed. However, contractors are invited to submit Value Engineering Change Proposals (VECPs) on contract changes that reduce costs. They share in any approved VECPs, as set forth in the clauses (normally about 50%). Figure 8.6, "Value Engineering—Construction," is an excerpt from the *VE Program Guide for Design and Construction*.

52.248-3 Value Engineering--Construction

As prescribed in 48.202, insert the following clause:
Value Engineering -- Construction
(March 1989)

(a) *General.* The Contractor is encouraged to develop, prepare, and submit value engineering change proposals (VECPs) voluntarily. The Contractor shall share in any instant contract savings realized from accepted VECPs, in accordance with paragraph (f) below.

(b) *Definitions.* "Collateral costs," as used in this clause, means agency costs of operation, maintenance, logistic support, or Government-furnished property.

"Collateral savings," as used in this clause, means those measurable net reductions resulting from a VECP in the agency's overall projected collateral costs, exclusive of acquisition savings, whether or not the acquisition cost changes.

"Contractor's development and implementation costs," as used in this clause, means those costs the Contractor incurs on a VECP specifically in developing, testing, preparing, and submitting the VECP, as well as those costs the Contractor incurs to make the contractual changes required by Governmental acceptance of a VECP.

"Government costs," as used in this clause, means those agency costs that result directly from developing and implementing the VECP, such as any net increases in the cost of testing, operations, maintenance, and logistical support. The term does not include the normal administrative costs of processing the VECP.

"Instant contract savings," as used in this clause, means the estimated reduction in Contract cost of performance resulting from acceptance of the VECP, minus the allowable Contractor's development and implementation costs, including subcontractors' development and implementation costs (see paragraph (h) below).

"Value engineering change proposal (VECP)" means a proposal that --

(1) Requires a change to this, the instant contract, to implement; and

(2) Results in reducing the contract price or estimated cost without impairing essential functions or characteristics; *provided*, that it does not involve a change --

    (i) In deliverable end item quantities only; or

    (ii) To the contract type only.

(c) *VECP preparation.* As a minimum, the Contractor shall include in each VECP the information described in subparagraphs (1) through (7) below. If the proposed change is affected by contractually required configuration management or similar procedures, the instructions in those procedures relating to format, identification, and priority assignment shall govern VECP preparation. The VECP shall include the following:

(1) A description of the difference between the existing contract requirement and that proposed, the comparative advantages and disadvantages of each, a justification when an item's function or characteristics are being altered, and the effects of the change on the end item's performance.

(2) A list and analysis of the contract requirements that must be changed if the VECP is accepted, including any suggested specification revision.

(3) A separate, detailed cost estimate for (i) the affected portions of the existing contract requirements and (ii) the VECP. The cost reduction associated with the VECP shall take into account the Contractor's allowable development and implementation costs, including any amount attributable to subcontracts under paragraph (h) below.

(4) A description and estimate of costs the Government may incur implementing the VECP, such as test and evaluation and operating and support costs.

(5) A prediction of any effects the proposed change would have on collateral costs to the agency.

(6) A statement of the time by which a contract modification accepting the VECP must be issued in order to achieve the maximum cost reduction, noting any effect on the contract completion time or delivery schedule.

(7) Identification of any previous submissions of the VECP, including the dates submitted, the agencies and contract numbers involved, and previous Government actions, if known.

(d) *Submission.* The Contractor shall submit VECPs to the Resident Engineer at the worksite, with a copy to the Contracting Officer.

(e) *Government Action.*

(1) The Contracting Officer shall notify the Contractor of the status of the VECP within 45 calendar days after the contracting office receives it. If additional time is required, the Contracting Officer shall notify the Contractor within the 45-day period and provide the reason for the delay and the expected

52.248-3 Value Engineering--Construction

date of the decision. The Government will process VECPs expeditiously; however, it shall not be liable for any delay in acting upon a VECP.

(2) If the VECP is not accepted, the Contracting Officer shall notify the Contractor in writing, explaining the reasons for rejection. The Contractor may withdraw any VECP in whole or in part, at any time before it is accepted by the Government. The Contracting Officer may require that the Contractor provide written notification before undertaking significant expenditures for VECP effort.

(3) Any VECP may be accepted, in whole or in part, by the Contracting Officer's award of a modification to this contract citing this clause. The Contracting Officer may accept the VECP, even though an agreement on price reduction has not been reached, by issuing the Contractor a notice to proceed with the change. Until a notice to proceed is issued or a contract modification applies a VECP to this contract, the Contractor shall perform in accordance with the existing contract. The Contracting Officer's decision to accept or reject all or any part of any VECP shall be final and not subject to the Disputes clause or otherwise subject to litigation under the Contract Disputes Act of 1978 (41U.S.C.601-613).

(f) *Sharing.*

  (1) *Rates.* The Government's share of savings is determined by subtracting Government costs from instant contract savings and multiplying the result by

    (i) 45 percent for fixed-price contracts or

    (ii) 75 percent for cost-reimbursement contracts.

  (2) *Payment.* Payment of any share due the Contractor for use of a VECP on this contract shall be authorized by a modification to this contract to--

    (i) Accept the VECP

    (ii) Reduce the contract price or estimated cost by the amount of instant contract savings; and

    (iii) Provide the Contractor's share of savings by adding the amount calculated to the contract price or fee.

(g) *Collateral savings.* If a VECP is accepted, the instant contract amount shall be increased by 20 percent of any projected collateral savings determined to be realized in a typical year of use after subtracting any Government costs not previously offset. However, the Contractor's share of collateral savings shall not exceed (1) the

contract's firm-fixed-price or estimated cost, at the time the VECP is accepted, or (2)$100,000, whichever is greater. The Contracting Officer shall be the sole determiner of the amount of collateral savings, and that amount shall not be subject to the Disputes clause or otherwise subject to litigation under 41U.S.C.601-613.

(h) *Subcontracts.* The Contractor shall include an appropriate value engineering clause in any subcontract of $50,000 or more and may include one in subcontracts of lesser value. In computing any adjustment in this contract's price under paragraph (f) above, the Contractor's allowable development and implementation costs shall include any subcontractor's allowable development and implementation costs clearly resulting from a VECP accepted by the Government under this contract, but shall exclude any value engineering incentive payments; *provided,* that these payments shall not reduce the Government's share of the savings resulting from the VECP.

(i) *Data.* The Contractor may restrict the Government's right to use any part of a VECP or the supporting data by marking the following legend on the affected parts:

"These data, furnished under the Value Engineering--Construction clause of contract........., shall not be disclosed outside the Government or duplicated, used, or disclosed, in whole or in part, for any purpose other than to evaluate a value engineering change proposal submitted under the clause. This restriction does not limit the Government's right to use information contained in these data if it has been obtained or is otherwise available from the Contractor or from another source without limitations."

If a VECP is accepted, the Contractor hereby grants the Government unlimited rights in the VECP and supporting data, except that, with respect to data qualifying and submitted as limited rights technical data, the Government shall have the rights specified in the contract modification implementing the VECP and shall appropriately mark the data. (The terms "unlimited rights" and "limited rights" are defined in Part 27 of the Federal Acquisition Regulation.)

(End of clause)

Alternate I (APR 1984). When the head of contracting activity determines that the cost of calculating and tracking collateral savings will exceed the benefits to be derived in a construction contract, delete paragraph (g) from the basic clause and redesignate the remaining paragraphs accordingly.

Source: *Value Engineering Program Guide for Design and Construction,* PBS-PQ251, May 10, 1993, Vol. 2, p. 4-7.

Figure 8.6 (cont.)

In addition, some contractors who have bid Guaranteed Maximum Contracts have used VE. They have developed a trained staff that performs a "mini" VE study. These contractors offer owners a reduced cost, if their proposals are accepted.

Maintenance and Operations (M&O)

This is the area where VE has least penetrated. It is difficult because of the current budgeting practices that independently budget M & O and capital expenditures. As a result, adding extra costs to reduce M & O are not normally considered. However, what has been done in a number of occasions is to add an M & O team to the VE studies scheduled during design. These teams have resulted in adding creativity and sensitivity to the process not previously realized. In a few rare instances, VE has been conducted solely for M & O projects. Results have been quite significant, but the opportunities have been very limited. However, the VE Incentive Clauses have been included in many U.S. government contracts for M & O services.

Conclusion

The real goal of a value engineer should be to integrate the VE process into standard operating procedures. The effort would be integrated with the normal cost, schedule, and design review procedures, but these would be augmented with the VE techniques. The owner, design team project/construction managers, and contractors will discover that this approach has little impact on their overall fees; yet, it will maximize the effect on project value and owner satisfaction. As a result, sales and profit should increase significantly when VE is sold as part of their services.

Chapter Nine

VE Applications to Risk Assessment and Analysis

In 1993, there was an opportunity with a large, city port authority to apply VE methodology in conjunction with formal risk assessment and analysis. The client owned a large, 30-year-old office complex that was in the process of an extensive upgrade and modernization. Several recent projects had large cost and schedule overruns with adverse occupancy effects. Therefore, the owner required a VE effort that would be augmented with an application of risk assessment and analysis for future projects. The marriage of the two concepts would give additional assurance that more accurate project budgets and schedules, along with improved total project objectives, would be realized. Quickly, it became obvious that the combination was a very powerful tool. The VE team worked with a risk analyst to provide more comprehensive feedback regarding potential risk areas and a broader evaluation basis for establishing cost ranges. The development of mitigating actions using the VE methodology proved more powerful than was initially imagined. This chapter describes a simplified example outlining the techniques used in this study.

Risk Assessment

A VE study was scheduled during early schematics, using 15 professionals covering the major aspects of the project. The team was broken into several groups, one of which would cover risk assessment and analysis. Team members conducted a formal VE study along with an initial assessment of project-related risk. After presentations of the project by the owner's staff and a review of available information, the risk assessment team discussed the phases and scheduling of the project and identified with the other VE teams the following categories of risk to be included in the assessment:

I. Design

II. Administration and Contractual Issues

III. Construction

IV. Tenant Relations and Public Image

During the information phases, a wide range of possible risks was identified, along with levels of severity or risk exposure. The risks were isolated by all teams and consolidated by the risk team. Risks were categorized as "medium" or "high." Random or extraordinary risks were not included. During the creative phase, ideas were solicited from all teams for possible mitigation of the identified risks.

Identification of Risks

The assessment effort identified five risks as most important:

Tenant Risks: There was a serious risk that tenants would not renew leases if they believed the modernization program ignored their needs or if improvements took excessive time. In addition, owner response to tenant complaints needed to be improved.

Design Risks: The perception of how design decisions for necessary technology upgrades affect cost and rental revenues was isolated as a risk item.

Contractor Risks: The submittal of competitive contracting bids was evaluated as "uncertain," with a potential adverse effect on costs and schedule.

Environmental Risks: The presence of asbestos affected costs and had a significant impact on scheduling.

Administrative Risks: The complexity of the modernization program required a dedicated owner/management team. The absence of such a team could adversely affect the upgrade results, including revenues.

Following is a more detailed outline of the categories.

   I. Design

      A. The key design risk factors identified:

         1. Level of information in bid documents (high risk)

         2. Design uncertainties (medium risk)

         3. Environmental/asbestos issues (high risk)

      B. Mitigation

      The following were general recommendations to mitigate design risk:

         1. Improve documentation of existing conditions of equipment and systems prior to development of bid documents, with some risk-sharing by owner on any changes identified.

         2. Improve detail of any performance specifications and provisions of information to bidders.

         3. Provide bidders with more detail and available documents on existing conditions and owner, local authority guidance on life safety, asbestos, and indoor environmental issues.

         4. Schedule technical review by VE team to focus on ability of design to accomplish objectives without significant adverse impact on costs and revenue.

   II. Administration and Contractual Risk Issues

      A. The key administration and contractual risk factors identified:

         1. Interest and availability of qualified modernization and maintenance contractors (high risk).

         2. Dedicated owner/management coordination (high risk).

         3. Union participation and work claims (medium risk).

         4. Owner biases of general conditions (medium risk).

         5. Advantage of contractors currently doing work (medium risk).

      B. Mitigation

      The following were general recommendations to mitigate administration and contractual risk:

         1. Indicate a dedicated owner/management team to communicate to top management all aspects (including contractual) of modernization program. Team would also be responsible for tenant/ public/contractor communications. Key target: Plan work so that only clean, asbestos-free areas are subject to new construction. Owner to assume more risk in asbestos cleanup efforts (see environmental and design risk issues).

2. Review owner general conditions for possible changes of more onerous requirements.

3. Expand and improve technical specifications by requiring consultants to retain specification consultant(s) for concurrent development of specifications.

4. Assign responsibility to seek out additional qualified contractors and conduct interviews to indicate objectivity in bid award and selection process.

III. Construction Risk Issues and Mitigation

A. The general recommendations to mitigate construction risk:

1. Develop more detailed information provision to prospective bidders and risk-sharing by owner.

2. Establish dedicated management team for the modernization program to include responsibility for developing detailed construction inspection program and improved level of detailed specifications.

3. Establish and enforce detailed equipment acceptance testing procedures.

IV. Tenant Relations and Public Impact Risk Issues

A. The key tenant relations and public impact risk factors:

1. Reduction of value of office space as perceived by current and prospective tenants (high risk).

2. Length of time for modernization and upgrade (medium risk).

B. Mitigation

The following were general recommendations to mitigate tenant relations and public impact risk:

1. Under the guidance of the dedicated management team, implement an increased tenant public relations program during construction to communicate project status. Explain benefits of modernization program to tenants.

2. As technology advances, owner must keep abreast of changes and implement those considered cost effective. After project completion, reevaluate system upgrades for cost effectiveness.

3. Anticipate prospective tenant elevator demands and identify service options to ensure marketing success.

4. Minimize adverse tenant impact through fast track schedule, with scheduling of operations and shut-downs during off hours as much as possible. Management team will be responsible for maintaining communications with facility tenants to promote and enhance public relations during the project.

Risk Analysis

This section presents the methods and findings of the risk analysis performed by the VE team. After the risk areas and possible mitigation are identified, the risk team—with added cost expertise from the VE team—performed a number of project cost estimate adjustments. These included the project estimate runs, which are listed in Figure 9.1 in columns 1 and 2.

Tracking the Estimate and Risk Analysis

Column 1: Original (Designer/Owner) Estimate

The designer's estimate submitted for the project by the owner's project manager includes the hard costs (construction = $46,000,000) for this project. To this estimate was added the designer's concept of standard owner markups, to arrive at the total project cost estimate of $82.5 million. Column 1 (Submitted Designer Budget Estimate) was the starting point for the VE team evaluation.

Office Modernization Program
Cost Estimates Summary (Millions)

	Column 1	Column 2	Column 3
	Submitted Designer Budget Estimate	Designer/Owner Budget Estimate Adjusted @ Risk	Approved VE Team Estimate @ Risk
Total Construction Contract Cost	**46.8**	**93.8**	**101.5**
Project Cost Before Contingency	75.0	143.7	144.3
Project Contingency	7.5	10.8	13.2
Total Project Cost	**82.5**	**154.5**	**157.5**
Risk Analysis Adjustment	-	14.3	Incl.
Adjusted Total Project Cost	**82.5**	**168.8**	**157.5**
Potential Project Savings			11.3
Additional Savings (PW) Reduced Maintenance			0.9
Total Potential Savings			**12.2**

Figure 9.1

Column 2: Estimates Adjusted to all Applicable Owner Standards, Approved Add-ons, and VE Team Estimate Revisions Adjusted for At-Risk

Adjustments included the following:

1. The estimate was adjusted to include the Standard Owner Guidelines not included by the designer for add-on allowances (e.g., planning and engineering, construction contingency, extra work allowances).

2. Items were added to the estimate to reconcile it with components identified as essential by the VE team to meet owner initial objectives (e.g., other elevator costs, tenant construction costs, temporary construction costs). Note: These costs were reviewed with owner/design personnel and accepted as valid costs.

3. The VE team made further adjustments to the original estimate to allow for comparison of equal projects. This is the risk-adjusted estimate. The team estimated the normal level of construction uncertainty and then reviewed the various risk factors affecting the project as proposed. The appropriate levels of uncertainty (potential viability) were identified for the primary project components. The following factors resulted:

Construction Costs	Low	Mid	High
Architectural	.95	1.00	1.35
Mechanical	.95	1.00	1.35
Elevators	.95	1.00	1.35
Other	.95	1.00	1.35
Modular overlays, electrical	.95	1.00	1.35
Structural	.80	1.00	1.10
Other Costs			
Security	.90	1.00	2.00
Tenant construction	.90	1.00	2.00
Soft Costs			
Escalation, contingency, etc.	1.00	1.10	1.30

In the above chart, the "low" factor represents an estimate of cost with a 10% probability of being too high. The "high" factor represents an estimate of cost with a 10% probability of being too low. This column shows the results of the risk analysis for the original project proposal as adjusted. The construction and project contingency and risk adjustment were estimated after a simulation analysis was performed for the adjusted base estimate. The VE team identified major project components as ranges of cost (rather than single estimates), and a simulation analysis was used to identify the 80th percentile (80% level of confidence) that was deemed appropriate by team and owner for the construction cost. The simulation was performed using a microcomputer spreadsheet program (Lotus 1-2-3) and a simulation program (@ Risk). For this simulation, 1,000 samples (using a Monte Carlo sampling technique) were taken within the ranges of data identified and the distribution of outcomes identified.

The 80th percentile was then identified from the results of the simulation. (See Figure 9.2.) The figure illustrates results of risk analysis for an estimate having an 80% probability, with a baseline estimate of $143.7 million, a project contingency of $10.8 million and a risk adjustment of $14.3 million, for a total project cost of $168.8 million.

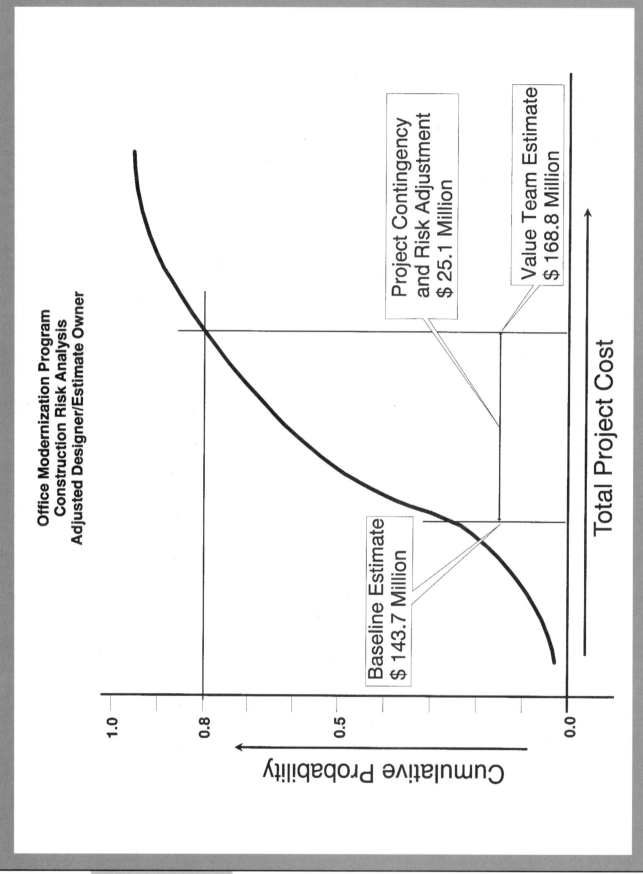

Office Modernization Program
Construction Risk Analysis
Adjusted Designer/Estimate Owner

Project Contingency
and Risk Adjustment
$ 25.1 Million

Value Team Estimate
$ 168.8 Million

Baseline Estimate
$ 143.7 Million

Total Project Cost

Cumulative Probability

1.0

0.8

0.5

0.0

Figure 9.2

Column 3: Approved VE Team Estimate Adjusted for At-Risk

Adjustments included the following:

1. The VE team estimate was adjusted to include the accepted VE proposals. These involved the typical VE ideas plus the risk mitigation ideas approved by the group during the risk assessment and study. Note that initial costs were slightly increased due to the extra initial costs incurred for mitigation.

2. The risk analysis simulation was performed on the data. The appropriate levels of uncertainty were identified for the project components. The following factors resulted:

Construction Costs	Low	Mid	High
Architectural	.95	1.00	1.20
Mechanical	.95	1.00	1.20
Elevators	.95	1.00	1.20
Other	1.00	1.15	1.20
Modular overlays, electrical	.95	1.00	1.20
Structural	.80	1.00	1.10
Other Costs			
Security	.90	1.00	2.00
Tenant construction	.90	1.00	2.00
Soft Costs			
Escalation, contingency, etc.	.95	1.00	1.10

Using the above input, another computer run using the Risk software was conducted. Figure 9.3 portrays the results. The plot shows a baseline estimate of $144.3 million that, when adjusted for contingency and risk ($13.2 million), equates to $157.5 million.

Conclusion

The immediate factor recognized by all personnel involved in the study was this: Validation of the baseline estimate by a project- rather than design-oriented team is mandatory. It follows that the risk analysis identifies the specific levels of risk or uncertainty facing the program and quantifies the risk wherever possible. The method used in this analysis identifies overall levels of cost uncertainty and then varies the percentages based on additional risk factors (such as availability of a dedicated management team). Costs were also included for particular risk elements such as net cost work (security), general conditions, and tenant interface impact.

The level of project contingency and risk adjustments based on the uncertainties isolated for the adjusted designer/owner estimate is 17.5%. For the accepted VE team proposal, an overall additional markup of 9.2% is recommended.

The recommended project proposal budget is estimated to be $168.8 million (as shown in Figure 9.2).

The recommended and approved VE team proposal budget is estimated to be $157.5 million (as shown in Figure 9.3), which is $11.3 million less than the project proposal because of several VE recommendations and reduced risk. Also, the VE team budget indicates additional follow-on savings of $0.9 million in maintenance and operations.

In summary, the key differences between a typical VE study and a study with a risk assessment and analysis (RAA) requirement are:

- RAA requires a greater emphasis on initial cost efforts. A team effort is required to set realistic ranges and isolate risk areas as well as to estimate mitigation actions. Also, RAA requires a clear idea of total project costs. Most project

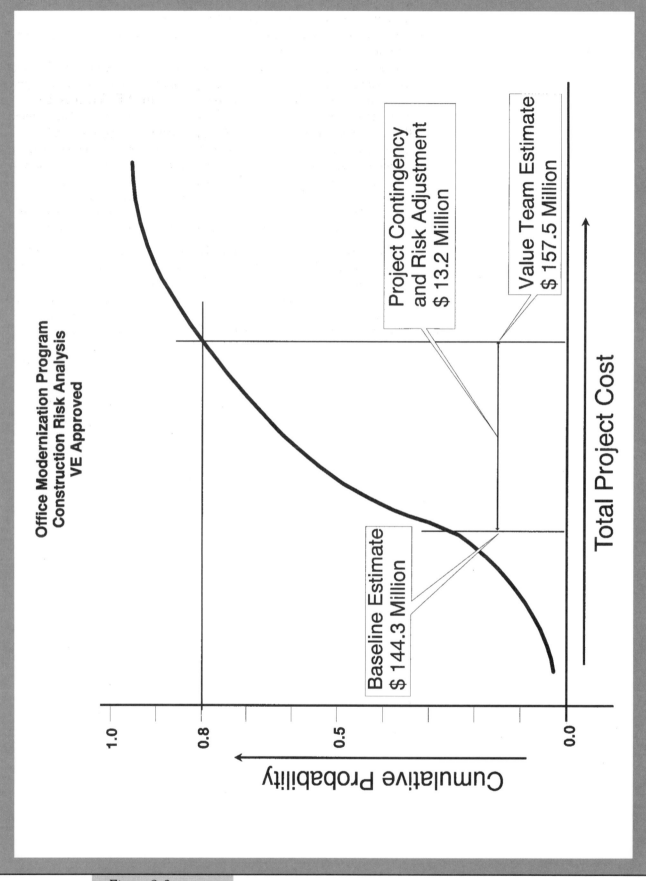

Figure 9.3

design and development teams consider only construction costs, which do not represent an accurate picture of total owner costs.

- RAA requires additional creative efforts (such as brainstorming) to develop mitigation ideas for isolated risks.
- The agenda and time schedule of a typical study will not work well. The final risk analysis requires the results of the approved VE actions to be meaningful. Before they can fix the ultimate project budget, the VE ideas must be implemented. As a result, the post-VE study efforts are longer and augmented.
- RAA requires enlightened owners (highly structured, compartmentalized owners do not respond) with easy access to total budget thinking. This requires owners who are responsive to initial startup, sales and marketing, operations and maintenance, insurance, financial expense, security and user costs. A principal reason for this is that risk mitigation frequently requires adding initial cost to reduce soft (contingencies) costs. Too few owner/managers of facility projects have the ability, or are organizationally structured, to respond.

From the discussion in this chapter, it would appear that owners would be most responsive to using a VE study with RAA. However, the real world is not so logical. Owners who are not sophisticated in budgeting and project cost control may be inclined to base decisions on known pathways and familiar products. This book and this chapter will, hopefully, provide information and methodology enabling owners to choose VE studies that combine risk assessment and analysis.

Part Two

Case Studies

- Corporate Office Building
- Hospital and Staff Housing Complex
- Refinery Facility
- Master Planning Competition
- Application to Design Review Govt. Headquarters/Complex
- Highway Project: South Interchange
- Wastewater Treatment Plant

Corporate Office Building

I n 1994, four teams—architectural, structural, mechanical, and electrical—studied a large commercial office headquarters facility[1] consisting of the following:

800,000 square feet   3 basement levels of parking

3 levels of shops   1 mezzanine level for a restaurant

2 17-story office towers

Principal study constraint: Maintain the architectural image of the building.

On the final implementation, approximately $10,000,000, or 15% of the initial cost, was saved. In addition, $350,000/year in follow-on savings resulted in increased utilization of space, and reduced costs for operations and maintenance.

Case Study Elements   The items listed below and shown in this case study have been excerpted from an actual VE report. (The Table of Contents on page 177 is one of the excerpts and refers to some documents not listed here or shown in the section.)

[1]Acknowledgment is made to the National Company for Cooperative Insurance/(NCCI), with special thanks to Sulliman S. Al Medeiheem, Project Manager of Cooperative Real Estate Investment Company, and Basem Al Shihabi, Principal Designer of Omarania & Associates. Their input was critical to the success of this study.

VALUE ENGINEERING REPORT

Corporate Office Building

Table of Contents

This is the Table of Contents from the actual VE report. Selected excerpts appear in this case study.

Value Engineering Report

Corporate Office Building

Executive Summary

This document is a report of a value engineering (VE) workshop conducted in 1994 at the request of a real estate investment company.

This commercial office headquarters facility consisted of approximately 800,000 square feet of space with three basement levels of parking, three levels of shops, a mezzanine level for a restaurant, and two 17-story office towers. The design was at the Design Development Phase (60%) stage; the estimated construction cost was approximately $71,000,000. A principal constraint of the project study was to maintain the architectural image of the building.

Four teams conducted the study: Architectural, Structural, Mechanical, and Electrical. Team members were drawn from the offices of the VE consultant, the designer, and the owner.

SUMMARY OF RESULTS

The teams generated 130 ideas to improve the value of the project. From these ideas, 50 proposals (including alternates) were written, recommending initial cost savings of $14.5 million. If all these proposals were implemented, they would result in an additional annual savings in facility operations and maintenance of $500,000/year.

In addition, this report includes 30 design suggestions for overall project enhancement that were documented for consideration during continuing development of the design.

SUMMARY OF PRINCIPAL RECOMMENDATIONS

Following is a summary of the major recommendations made during the workshop. The Summary of Results in this report contains detailed proposals for each recommendation.

ARCHITECTURAL

Sixteen proposals were generated with the constraint that no major architectural feature or concept would be touched. The major areas isolated were as follows:

- Stop elevators at the upper ground floor, add hydraulic elevators for the basement, and stop one bank of elevators on each tower at the 16th floor. This would result in $1.33

million in savings and improve elevator service over the present scheme, which is marginal.

- Delete escalators and stairs on the north side up to newly proposed office areas. About $750,000 would be saved, since traffic flow and separation of traffic negated the value of escalator service.

Note: Significant savings in maintenance and operation would also be realized from implementing the above items.

- Use less expensive, yet adequate penthouse walls and interior wall modifications ($500,000).

- Relocate and delete one set of outside stairs to the basement not required by code ($130,000).

- Use a lower category of finish material that will still meet owner requirements, to bring costs closer to budget ($800,000).

- Since the net to gross space could be improved, reduce proposed lobby space on each floor. By changing space to useable (rentable), a large increase in revenue of $70,000/year was forecasted.

STRUCTURAL

Nine basic and optional structural proposals were developed. The major items were as follows:

- Consider precast hollow-core floor planks for either or both basement and tower floors (savings: up to $1.44 million).

- Delete 4th and 5th basement levels used for storage tanks and relocate tanks and spaces (savings: up to $530,000).

- Modify floor slab design using two-way slab and beam (savings: up to $800,000 but not in addition to using precast).

MECHANICAL

Seventeen basic and optional mechanical proposals were developed. The major items were as follows:

- Eliminate 2nd-level penthouse by relocating water tanks at roof and in conjunction with deletion of 4th- and 5th-level basement (savings: up to $1,000,000).

- Modify thermal energy storage (TES) systems by relocating tanks at basement levels 1-3 and relocating pump rooms to level 1 basement (savings: $450,000 in initial cost and $54,000/year). Project value would also be improved significantly by increasing rentable space with this relocation.

  Note: A detailed economic analysis was conducted on deleting the TES system. The results indicated that although the life cycle costs of the TES system were estimated as less expensive, the order of magnitude was disappointing. Therefore, the team focused on modifying the proposed design to optimize usage.

- Increase coverage of variable air volume (VAV) boxes. Present coverage of 270 S.F. per box appears too costly and should be reviewed in light of potential savings of $370,000 plus maintenance savings of $25,000/year.

- Use light troffers for distribution in lieu of linear diffusers, which would result in a more flexible ceiling system for tenant layout and save $265,000.

There were three additional suggestions that were rather controversial but should be reviewed for project value improvement:

- Delete metering and use proportional charges to tenants.
- Use ASHRAE inside temperature design criteria of 78°F for summer and 68°F for winter.
- Consider "shelling" space to reduce capital expenditures, postponing fitup cost until tenant desires are known or leasing the space is certain.

ELECTRICAL

Nine electrical proposals were developed. The major ideas were as follows:

- Reconfigure electrical distribution using a high voltage bus to the penthouse and relocating transformers to the various floors ($1.73 million in potential savings).

- In conjunction with the above proposal, reconfigure HVAC electrical distribution using 380V equipment rather than 240V equipment. Also, use demand and load factors usual for similar buildings ($1.3 million in savings).

- Reduce loads on emergency power by using diesel-driven fire pumps, backup battery-operated emergency lighting fixtures, and reducing the number of emergency receptacles. Decrease the number of generators from two each per tower at 900 KVA to one per tower. The generator will be sized at approximately 1,000 KVA to meet power company requirements (savings: $650,000).

· Make a number of lighting changes: Delete emphasis lighting for inside of exterior wall in office areas where control is questionable, change from use of parabolic to less expensive, satisfactory office fixtures, and selected system reconfiguration (savings: up to $350,000 in initial costs and $20,000/year in annual costs).

COST

During the initial phase of the workshop, the A-E estimate was reviewed by the VE team and a number of cost questions were generated. The VE team and A-E representative sat down and agreed to a new baseline estimate of $70,634,000 for the building. The only point in question was the area of the building; approximately 35,000 S.F. of extra gross area was calculated by the VE team. It was deemed by the A-E team not to be of significance at this phase of design.

CONCLUSION

All of the above recommendations and design suggestions are contained in the Summary of Results of this report.

In summary, about 50 ideas, if implemented, would mean savings of up to $12.5 million. Normally, it is unlikely that all ideas will be accepted. However, the results of this workshop should prove to not only reduce initial cost but to favorably influence follow-on costs of ownership in the range of $265,000 per year.

We appreciate the splendid cooperation of the designer and owner, in particular, the president of the design firm, for their participation in this workshop. Without their cooperation and input, the potential to improve the value of this project would not have been as significant.

Note: At the final presentation the owner directed the designer to make all the changes immediately. Only those in which choices were indicated were left open to future selection.

Construction Cost Summary

Corporate Office Building
60% Design Stage

DIV. NO.	SYSTEM	TOTAL COST PER SYSTEM		Sub System	UOM-Unit of Measure	Quant.	Total Cost Per UOM	Total Cost $ US	Cost Per SQF
	DEMOLITION			Demolition					
01	FOUNDATION	1,657,949	011	Std. Foundations	MPA	80,054	20.71	1,657,949	2.07
			012	Special Foundations	MPA				
02	SUB STRUCTURE	3,772,695	021	Slab on Grade	MPA				
			022	Basement Excavation	BCF	525,413	7.18	3,772,695	4.71
			023	Basement Walls	BWA				
03	SUPER STRUCTURE	5,388,481	031	Floor Construction	UFA	520,913	7.80	4,060,669	5.07
			032	Roof Construction	SQF	80,054	16.59	1,327,812	1.66
			033	Stair Construction	FLT				
04	EXTERIOR CLOSURE	11,956,119	041	Exterior Walls	XWA	311,868	31.16	9,718,992	12.13
			042	Ext. Doors & Windows	XDA	9,361	238.98	2,237,127	2.79
05	ROOFING	1,000,234	05	Roofing	SQF	80,054	12.49	1,000,234	1.25
06	INTERIOR CONSTRUCTION	9,663,400	061	Partitions	PSM				
			062	Interior Finishes	TFA	318,980	30.29	9,663,400	12.06
			063	Specialties	GSF				
07	CONVEYING SYSTEM	7,413,333	071	Elevators	LO	276	19,323.67	5,333,333	6.65
			072	Escalators & Others	LS	12	173,333.33	2,080,000	2.60
08	MECHANICAL	12,331,068	081	Plumbing	FXT	640	1,698.23	1,086,867	1.36
			082	HVAC	TON	1,440	5,809.05	8,365,037	10.44
			083	Fire Protection	AP	761,076	2.98	2,266,631	2.83
			064	Special Mech. Systems	LS	616	994.37	612,534	0.76
09	ELECTRICAL	8,757,334	091	Service & Distribution	KVA	8,000	600.00	4,800,000	5.99
			092	Emergency Power & UPS	KVA	1,800	237.04	426,667	0.53
			093	Lighting & Power	GSF	761,076	5.07	3,861,401	4.82
				Bldg. Mgmt. System	SQF	761,076	1.24	946,677	1.18
				Security System	EA	30	8,888.89	266,667	0.33
				CCTV System	Riser	2	33,333.33	66,667	0.08
				Underfloor System	SQF	519,407	1.74	901,335	1.12
				Fire Alarm Syst./ Paging	STA	92	8,521.74	784,000	0.98
				PABX System	Port	680	1,098.04	746,667	0.93
								65,963,362	82.32
10	GEN. COND. & PROFIT	1,863,677	101	Site Overhead	MOS				
			102	Preliminaries	PCT	2.71%	68,770,371.79	1,863,677	2.33
11	EQUIPMENT	1,441,036	111	Fixed Equipment	LS	1	561,035.73	561,036	0.70
			112&113	Kitchen	LS	1	16,000.00	16,000	0.02
			112	Window hoist	EA	4	213,333.33	853,333	1.06
			113	Dock levellers	EA	2	13,333.33	26,667	0.03
12	SITE WORK	1,329,974	121	Site Preparation	SQF				
			122	Site Improvements	SQF	80,054	16.61	1,329,974	1.66
			123	Site Utilities	SQF				
			124	Off-Sitework	LS				
				Cost Including Office Overhead & Profit					
				Escalation					
				Total Estimated Construction Cost				**70,634,049**	**88.12**

Abbreviations

AP	Area protected	LF	Linear Foot	PSF	Partition Square Foot		
BCF	Basement Cubic Foot	LO	Landing Opening	TFA	Total Finishes Area		
BWA	Basement Wall Area	LS	Lump Sum	TON	12000Btuh		
FLT	Flight	MOS	Months	UFA	Upper Floor Area		
FXT	Fixture Count	PA	Print Area	XDA	Exterior Doors & Window Area		
GSF	Gross Square Foot	SQF	Square Foot	XWA	Exterior Wall Area		
KW	Kilowatts Connected	PCT	Percent				

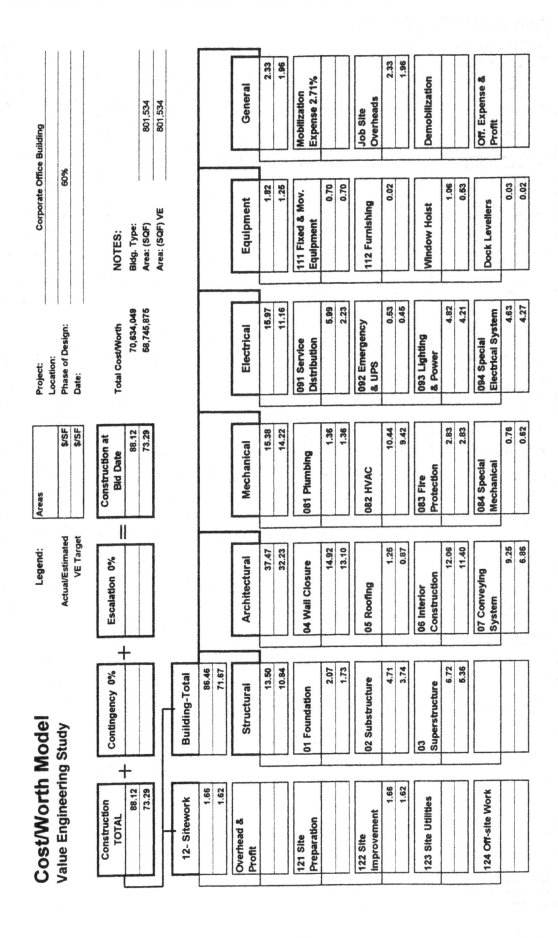

Cost/Worth Model
Value Engineering Study

Legend:
Actual/Estimated _____ $/SF
VE Target _____ $/SF

Project: Corporate Office Building
Location:
Phase of Design: 60%
Date:

NOTES:
Bldg. Type:
Area: (SQF) 801,534
Area: (SQF) VE 801,534

Total Cost/Worth
70,634,049
58,745,875

Construction TOTAL		Contingency 0%		Escalation 0%		Construction at Bid Date
88.12	+		+		=	88.12
73.29						73.29

Building-Total
86.46
71.67

Structural		Architectural		Mechanical		Electrical		Equipment		General
13.50		37.47		15.38		15.97		1.82		2.33
10.84		32.23		14.22		11.16		1.25		1.96

Structural
01 Foundation	2.07 / 1.73
02 Substructure	4.71 / 3.74
03 Superstructure	6.72 / 5.36

Architectural
04 Wall Closure	14.92 / 13.10
05 Roofing	1.25 / 0.87
06 Interior Construction	12.06 / 11.40
07 Conveying System	9.25 / 6.86

Mechanical
081 Plumbing	1.36 / 1.36
082 HVAC	10.44 / 9.42
083 Fire Protection	2.83 / 2.83
084 Special Mechanical	0.76 / 0.62

Electrical
091 Service Distribution	5.99 / 2.23
092 Emergency & UPS	0.63 / 0.45
093 Lighting & Power	4.82 / 4.21
094 Special Electrical System	4.63 / 4.27

Equipment
111 Fixed & Mov. Equipment	0.70 / 0.70
112 Furnishing	0.02
Window Hoist	1.06 / 0.53
Dock Levellers	0.03 / 0.02

General
Mobilization Expense 2.71%	
Job Site Overheads	2.33 / 1.96
Demobilization	
Off. Expense & Profit	

12- Sitework
1.66
1.62

Overhead & Profit	
121 Site Preparation	1.66 / 1.62
122 Site Improvement	
123 Site Utilities	
124 Off-site Work	

Areas

FUNCTION ANALYSIS WORKSHEET

PROJECT: Corporate Office Building
LOCATION:

BASIC FUNCTION: Offices

COMPONENT	FUNCTION (VERB-NOUN)	KIND	COST	WORTH	COST/ WORTH	COMMENTS
B = Basic Function	S = Secondary Function	RS = Required Secondary Function				
SITE WORK						
Overhead & Profit					0.00	
121 Site Preparation			0		0.00	
122 Site Improvement			1,329,974	1,300,000	1.02	No comment
123 Site Utilties			0		0.00	
124 Off-Site Work			0		0.00	
TOTAL			**1,329,974**	**1,300,000**	**1.02**	
STRUCTURAL						
01 Foundation	Support load	B	1,657,949	1,390,517	1.19	Relocate 4th & 5th level tanks.
02 Substructure	Services	B	3,772,695	3,000,000	1.26	Relocate 4th & 5th level tanks.
03 Superstructure	Support load and house staff	B	5,388,481	4,300,000	1.25	Consider hollow precast planks for floor and masonry core walls. Delete outside stairs.
TOTAL			**10,819,126**	**8,690,517**	**1.24**	
ARCHITECTURAL						
04 Wall Closure	Enclose space	B	11,956,119	10,500,000	1.14	Combine triangular buildings.
05 Roofing	Protect building	RS	1,000,234	695,259	1.44	Reduce skylights. Reduce planters & granite.
06 Interior Construction	Finish and beautify	B	9,663,400	9,137,685	1.06	Re-evaluate finishes. Re-evaluate door selection.
07 Conveying System	Transport people	B	7,413,333	5,500,000	1.35	Reduce basement stops; use hydraulics. Reduce escalators.
TOTAL			**30,033,087**	**25,832,944**	**1.16**	

FUNCTION ANALYSIS WORKSHEET

PROJECT: Corporate Office Building
LOCATION:

BASIC FUNCTION: Offices

COMPONENT	FUNCTION (VERB-NOUN)	KIND	COST	WORTH	COST/WORTH	COMMENTS
B = Basic Function	S = Secondary Function	RS = Required Secondary Function				
MECHANICAL						
081 Plumbing	Service building	B	1,086,867	1,086,789	1.00	
082 HVAC	Condition space	B	8,365,037	7,548,523	1.11	Reduce AHU's Reduce VAV boxes Simplify diffusers Simplify lobby supplies Delete A/C of garage lift lobbies
083 Fire Protection	Protect building & people		2,266,631	2,266,543	1.00	
084 Special Mechanical	Control system		612,534	496,613	1.23	
TOTAL			**12,331,068**	**11,398,468**	1.08	
ELECTRICAL						
091 Service & Dist.	Distribute power	B	4,800,000	1,787,808	2.68	Extend 13.8 KV system through building. Locate transformers in basement. Delete bus ducts.
092 Emergency & UPS	Backup power		426,667	357,000	0.12	Reduce generator capacity; use diesel backup pumps.
093 Lighting & Power	Light space	B	3,861,401	3,376,971	1.14	Reduce lighting fixtures. Reduce cable sizes.
094 Special Electrical	Support systems		3,712,012	3,422,550	1.09	Reduce telephone risers. Reduce exchange capacity. Optimize floor outlets.
TOTAL			**12,800,081**	**8,944,329**	1.43	
EQUIPMENT						
111 Fixed & Mov. Equip.	Support building		561,036	560,974	1.00	
112 Furnishing	Provide services		16,000	0	0.00	Re-evaluate furnishings.
113 Special Const.			880,000	439,999	2.00	Re-evaluate special construction.
TOTAL			**1,457,036**	**1,000,974**	1.46	

FUNCTION ANALYSIS WORKSHEET

PROJECT: **Corporate Office Building**

LOCATION:

BASIC FUNCTION: Offices

COMPONENT	FUNCTION (VERB-NOUN)	KIND	COST	WORTH	COST/ WORTH	COMMENTS
B = Basic Function S = Secondary Function RS = Required Secondary Function						
GENERAL						
Mobilization Exp.				0	0.00	
Site Overheads			1,863,677	1,574,000	1.18	Reduce percentage.
Demobilization				0	0.00	
Off. Exp. & Profit				0	0.00	
TOTAL			1,863,677	1,574,000	1.18	
OVERALL TOTAL			70,634,049	58,741,230	1.20	

VALUE ENGINEERING REPORT

Corporate Office Building

Section 4 - Summary of Results

GENERAL

This section of the report summarizes the results and recommendations for the study. Ideas that were developed are submitted here as recommendations for acceptance.

When reviewing the results of the VE study, it is important to review each part of a recommendation based on its own merits. Often, there is a tendency to disregard a recommendation because of concern about one portion of it. When reviewing this report, consider the areas within a recommendation that are acceptable, and apply those parts to the final design.

VALUE ENGINEERING RECOMMENDATIONS

The VE teams developed 45 proposals for change, representing $14.5 million in potential initial cost savings and $19.4 million in life cycle (PW) cost savings that represents follow-on annual savings of $500,000/year. Not included in this total are two optional mechanical proposals ("Shell construction" and "Delete TES system"). The proposal to delete the TES system was dropped. The shell space is presented for consideration, as well as four alternate structural proposals. In addition, 30 ideas are provided as Design Suggestions that clarify design, improve design, or affect cost. For clarity, proposals have been separated into groups as shown below:

Recommendation Category	No. of Proposals	Initial Savings	Life Cycle Savings
Architectural	16	4,025,197	6,353,287
Structural	5	2,248,280	2,248,220
Mechanical	15	3,672,580	5,434,720
Electrical	9	4,703,730	5,391,390
TOTAL	45	14,649,727	19,430,617

Savings Summary
(All Costs in U.S. Dollars)

Cost is a primary basis on which to compare alternate designs. To assure continuity of cost among the recommendations proposed by the VE team, we have used the project cost estimate developed by the VE team in cooperation with the A/E as the basis of cost. Where this was not possible, the VE team used R.S. Means cost data, adjusted for local conditions for comparative purposes, and data provided by Saudi Projacs estimators.

All life cycle costs were based on the economic factors listed in Section 3 of this report. Where appropriate, the impact of energy costs and replacement costs, and the effect on operations and maintenance, are shown within each recommendation.

A summary of potential cost savings for each VE recommendation follows.

SUMMARY OF
POTENTIAL COST SAVINGS FROM VE PROPOSALS

PROPOSAL	INITIAL SAVINGS	LIFE CYCLE SAVINGS
ARCHITECTURAL		
A-3 Relocate basement stairs.	139,630	139,630
A-4 Stop elevators at upper ground floor.	1,058,017	1,159,297
A-9 Delete escalators & stairs.	741,350	816,530
A-13 Delete terrace planters.	13,160	13,160
A-14 Delete one bank of elevators at floors 7-18.	232,275	232,275
A-15 Plant level curtain wall glazing and interior modifications.	556,800	556,800
A-16 Change roof of bridges.	8,000	8,000
A-17 Change granite at prayer roof.	7,500	7,500
A-18 Reduce lobby for 2-tenant floors.	71,400	2,162,000
A-19 Delete skylights over stairs 5 & 6.	2,800	2,800
A-20 Redesign cove at triangular offices.	32,270	32,270
A-27 Increase granite wall at triangle offices.	466,670	466,670
A-32 Modify granite usage between towers.	607,400	607,400
A-34 Revise floor paving at colonnade.	46,825	46,825
A-35 Delete tents at second floor.	41,100	102,130
A-36 Eliminate 4th & 5th level and relocate spaces.	See S-3	
ARCHITECTURAL TOTAL	**$4,025,197**	**$6,353,287**

PROPOSAL	INITIAL SAVINGS	LIFE CYCLE SAVINGS
STRUCTURAL		
S-3 Full hollow-core plank floor construction.	1,441,600	1,441,600
S-4 Delete 4th & 5th basement levels.	535,200	535,200
S-6 In core areas use 20 cm masonry for cross walls in lieu of CIP for top 30 m of walls.	129,350	129,350
S-9 Use steel stairs in lieu of CIP.	121,350	121,350
S-10 Reduce basement wall thickness from 30 cm to 20 cm at first level.	20,720	20,720
STRUCTURAL TOTAL	**$ 2,248,220**	**$ 2,248,220**

Optional Ideas

S-1a Use two-way beam and slab design for all structural floors in lieu of rib slab and beam design.	849,600
S-1b Similar to S-1a above, but exclude basement parking floors.	643,730
S-2 Use precast prestressed concrete hollow-core planks spanning between CIP beams for basement levels 1 and 2.	349,100
S-7 Similar to S-6 but also use masonry for E-W core walls on grid lines 8.5 and 11.5. S-7 can be used only if S-1 is used.	10,100

Note: Optional ideas are not included in totals. The combination of ideas totaled above is recommended as it provides the maximum savings. The other optional ideas may be used only in one of the following two combinations:

- S-1b, S-2, S-4, S-6, S-7, S-9, S-10 = $ 1,900,000

- S-1a, S-4, S-6, S-7, S-9, S-10   = $ 1,757,000

Case Study One   Corporate Office Building

PROPOSAL	INITIAL SAVINGS	LIFE CYCLE SAVINGS
MECHANICAL		
M-1 Simplify air conditioning in core of basement level.	43,500	8,530
M-2a Modify TES design.	454,700	975,000
M-3 Simplify air conditioning in core of basement level 5.	5,500	10,130
M-5 Delete air conditioning in car park lift lobbies.	16,300	25,280
M-8 Revise air conditioning at east entrance of ground and mezzanine.	6,200	11,200
M-9 Revise air conditioning at common spaces of ground and mezzanine.	1,050	49,100
M-16 Simplify stair pressurization with 2 small wall-mounted propeller fans.	9,550	16,600
M-22 Revise air conditioning at common spaces of 1st floor.	65,630	80,800
M-23 Simplify air distribution in lift lobbies.	8,750	8,750
M-26 Increase coverage of VAV boxes.	382,400	631,500
M-29 Modify HVAC for 3-tenant suites.	39,600	127,730
M-30 Modify office supply air device.	260,800	260,800
M-36 Delete level 2 penthouse.	1,077,300	1,439,200
M-38 Use ASHRAE recommended criteria.*	1,141,300	1,590,100
M-39 Delete BTU metering.	200,000	200,000
MECHANICAL TOTAL	**$ 3,672,580**	**$ 5,434,720**

* Needs further review by client.

PROPOSAL	INITIAL SAVINGS	LIFE CYCLE SAVINGS
Optional Ideas		
M-2 Delete TES system.	Dropped	
Bid alternate option.		
M-24 Shell construction	$3,450,000	

Note: Optional ideas are not included in totals.

Case Study One   Corporate Office Building

PROPOSAL	INITIAL SAVINGS	LIFE CYCLE SAVINGS
ELECTRICAL		
E-1 Reconfigure electrical distribution.	1,735,000	1,898,130
E-4 Reconfigure HVAC system electric.	1,324,130	1,449,100
E-7 Reconfigure lighting systems.	133,630	200,800
E-18 Reconfigure emergency power.	653,730	716,530
E-29 Reconfigure telephone exchange & system.	336,000	367,700
E-35 Delete lobby cove lighting in rental tower.	16,370	27,200
E-37 Replace parabolic lighting fixtures in offices.	166,700	182,400
E-38a Delete glazing cove lighting.	249,800	457,000
E-39 Reconfigure electrical connections for for VAV boxes.	88,370	95,530
ELECTRICAL TOTAL	**$ 4,703,730**	**$ 5,394,390**
GRAND TOTAL	**$14,649,927**	**$19,430,617**

VALUE ENGINEERING RECOMMENDATION   No. A-4

PROJECT: Corporate Office Building
ITEM: Stop elevators at upper ground floor

ORIGINAL DESIGN

In each tower, six elevators serve the 3rd basement level for garage parking. These same elevators serve podium shopping and the 18-story office towers.

PROPOSED DESIGN

Stop office tower elevators at the upper ground floor. Add two 2,500-pound hydraulic elevators in the basement at each tower, one on each side of the end of each elevator bank, to serve garage parking only between basement level 3 and the upper ground floor.

DISCUSSION

Attached to this proposal is an elevator consultant's report (not included in this case study), which indicates that the present design does not meet minimum requirements for good elevator service. The proposed separation of elevator function improves service to office tower users and to car park and shop users. It improves privacy for office tower use, because shoppers cannot go past the upper ground-floor level as they might do in the original design.

This proposal improves handicap accessibility in the basement by ensuring that all elevators serving the basement levels will be accessible, which is not the case in the present design. Space savings is gained on basement levels 1 through 3. The space saved is approximately 100 square meters per floor. The space currently occupied by the elevators on the lower ground floor becomes the elevator pit for the towers. This proposal also eliminates service to B4 and B5 levels (three stops). However, it is unsafe to combine people and water tanks in these lower levels. It is assumed that these functions will be relocated elsewhere, as suggested in other proposals. As a result of this proposal, the space saved herein could be used for the relocated small dormitory, water storage, engineering office, and other support functions. Maintenance on elevator landing openings will be reduced. This is estimated to be worth $300 per opening per year.

Life Cycle Cost Summary	Capital	Replacement	Annual O&M	
Original	1,558,017	0	16,800	
Proposed	499,295	0	6,130	
Savings	1,058,722	0	10,670	
TOTAL LIFE CYCLE (PW) SAVINGS:				**$1,159,257**

PROJECT: Corporate Office Building
ITEM: Stop elevators at upper ground floor

Proposed Elevators at Upper Ground Floor

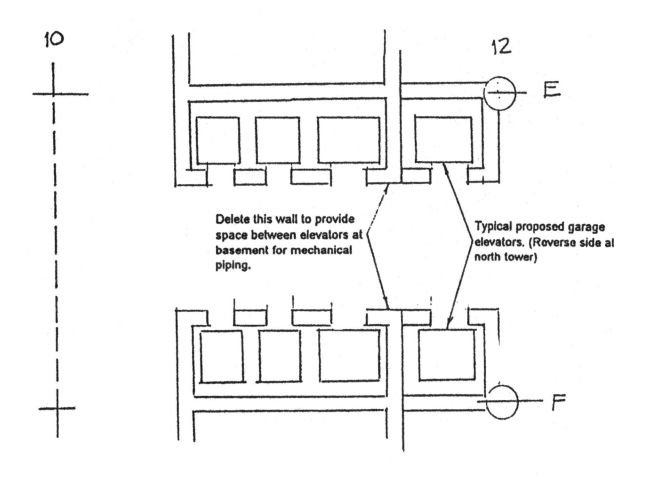

Delete this wall to provide space between elevators at basement for mechanical piping.

Typical proposed garage elevators. (Reverse side at north tower)

**South Tower
DRW FD A-15**

COST WORKSHEET RECOMMENDATION

No. A-4

PROJECT: Corporate Office Building
ITEM: Stop elevators at upper ground floor

ITEM	UNIT	QUANTITY	UNIT COST	TOTAL
ORIGINAL DESIGN				
Tower elevators (UG to B3)	LO	60	19,323	1,153,380
Tower elevators (B4/B5)	LO	3	19,323	57,969
Shaft walls (27 1m x 20m high per shaft)	m²	2,160	74	159,840
Lobby finishes	m²	864	106	91,584
Lobby doors	EA	6	13,330	79,980
Lobby services	m²	144	106	15,264
Total				$US 1,558,017
PROPOSED DESIGN				
Tower elevators	LO	3	19,325	57,975
Basement hydraulics	LO	20	17,330	346,600
Garage elevator shaft walls	m²	960	74	71,040
Tower shaft walls	m²	320	74	23,680
Total				$US 499,295
SAVINGS				**$US 1,058,722**

VALUE ENGINEERING RECOMMENDATION

PROJECT: Corporate Office Building
ITEM: Use precast hollow-core plank floor construction

ORIGINAL DESIGN

The typical floor construction for all floors above level 1 basement is cast-in-place (CIP) concrete rib/slab spanning between CIP concrete beams. A 7 cm topping slab is placed over the floor.

PROPOSED DESIGN

Use precast, prestressed concrete hollow-core planks. The construction is proposed in all floor areas where rib/slab design is presently shown. The precast planks will be 25 cm thick, with 7 cm topping slab. The topping is also provided in the original design. The hollow-core planks would span 10 m (9 m clear span) between CIP concrete beams running in N-S direction.

DISCUSSION

The proposed design generates significant savings in construction cost and time.

A new 21-story hotel is being designed locally using hollow-core planks. We have also conferred with the director of the local precast plant regarding the use and availability of precast hollow-core planks. In addition, a specialist in the use of structural precast products highly recommends the use of hollow-core plank as both economical and available.

LIFE CYCLE COST SUMMARY	Capital	Replacement	Annual O&M
Original	4,248,700	0	0
Proposed	2,806,900	0	0
Savings	1,441,800	0	0

TOTAL LIFE CYCLE
(PW) SAVINGS: **$US 1,441,800**

Life Cycle Cost Savings
(in U.S. dollars)

COST WORKSHEET RECOMMENDATION

No. S-3

PROJECT: Corporate Office Building
ITEM: Use precast hollow-core plank floor construction

ITEM	UNIT	QUANTITY	UNIT COST	TOTAL
ORIGINAL DESIGN				
CIP rib/slab	m^2	56,900	74.67	4,248,700
Total				$4,248,700
PROPOSED DESIGN				
Hollow-core plank	m^2	56,900	49.33	2,806,900
Total				$2,806,900
SAVINGS				$1,441,800

VALUE ENGINEERING RECOMMENDATION   No. M-2a

PROJECT: Corporate Office Building
ITEM: Modify Thermal Energy Storage (TES) design

ORIGINAL DESIGN

Present design calls for a thermal energy storage system (TES) consisting of four 690 m^3 tanks attached to two 214-ton chillers. The chillers run at approximately 100% during off-peak hours and store energy that is used (cold water) for peak periods and for emergency usage.

PROPOSED DESIGN

The VE team proposes to eliminate the 4th & 5th basement levels and relocate the pump room to basement level 1. This proposal can be implemented only if the elevators are stopped at the ground floor. See No. A-4. The mat slab must be dropped 2 meters and provisions made for a lift room under the elevators that stop at the upper ground level. Also, only one riser per tower is proposed for the new TES system.

DISCUSSION

This alternate will require approximately $124,000 of tank construction and a reduced rental impact because of relocation of the pump rooms from the 1st floor to the basement.

> Tank area involved = 7 m x 36 m x 3 floors = 756 m^2
> Rental cost lost per yr. = $30,150/tank area x 2 tank area = $60,300/yr.

This proposal now shows an improved return on investment of 48.4% over the original design of 21.3%.

Note: This proposal must be evaluated for tank depth of 10.6 m vs. 12.0 m ideal, relocation of TES pump rooms, and use of one riser per tower.

The original costs are included M-2.

LIFE CYCLE COST SUMMARY	CAPITAL	REPLACEMENT	ANNUAL O&M
Original	2,466,700	0	237,860
Proposed	2,012,030	0	182,660
Savings	454,670	0	55,200
LIFE CYCLE (PW) SAVINGS			**$US 975,000**

Life Cycle Cost Savings
(in U.S. dollars)

LIFE CYCLE COST WORKSHEET VE RECOMMENDATION NO. M-2a

PROJECT: Corporate Headquarters Building
ITEM: Modify TES System

Discount rate: 10% Economic Life: 30 years
(All costs in $US x 1,000)

	Factor	ORIGINAL Est. Costs	ORIGINAL PW Costs	PROPOSED Est. Costs	PROPOSED PW Costs
INITIAL COSTS					
Chillers	1	1,728,000	1,728,000	1,728,000	1,728,000
Other costs					
TES equipment	1	200,000	200,000	186,700	186,700
Tank cost 4&5	1	600,000	600,000		
Tank support	1	66,700	66,700	66,700	67,700
Transfer beam	1			13,300	13,300
Elev walls 1-3	1	3,200	3,200		
Pump rm mods	1			53,300	53,300
Extra tank cost	1			124,000	124,000
Other savings	1	(160,000)	(160,000)	(160,000)	(160,000)
Total Initial Cost		**2,466,700**	**2,466,700**	**2,012,030**	**2,012,030**
REPLACEMENT COSTS					
20 years	0.1486	1,728,000	256,800	1,728,000	256,800
Total Replacement Costs			**256,800**		**256,800**
ANNUAL COSTS					
energy	9.426	93,330	879,760	93,300	879,760
maintenance	9.426	28,000	263,930	28,000	263,930
value - rental	9.426	116,530	1,098,440	61,330	578,100
Total Annual Costs (PW)			**2,242,130**		**1,721,790**
TOTAL PW COSTS			**4,965,630**		**3,990,620**
LIFE CYCLE PRESENT WORTH SAVINGS			**975,010**		
RETURN ON INITIAL INVESTMENT			975,010/2,012,030 = 48.4%		

VALUE ENGINEERING RECOMMENDATION   VE Rec. No. M-2a

Project: Corporate Headquarters Building
Item: Modify TES design

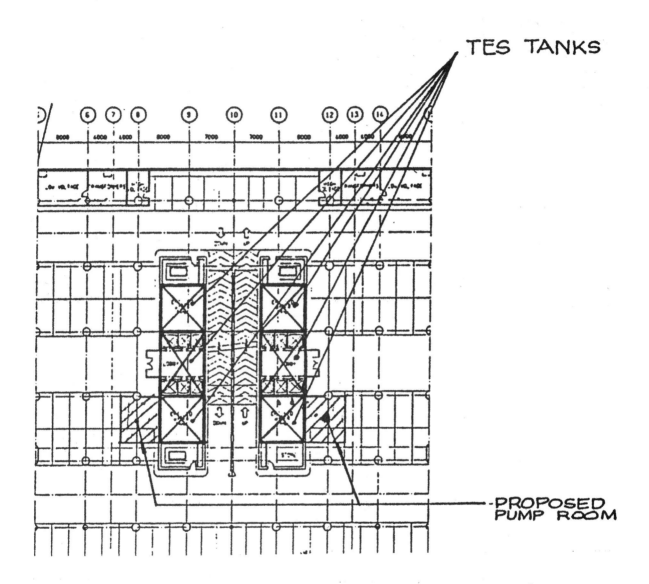

Elevation top ground floor (upper) = 2.950 m
Proposed elevation top of tanks 0.0 m - water level - 2.3 m
Proposed elevation bottom of bottom tanks = 12.9 m
Volume of tanks = 6.5 m x 10.6 m x 23.4 m x (2 sides) = 3,224 m^3
Required volume = 690 x 4 = 2,760 m^3
Note:

   Tank depth of 10.6 is marginal - if not satisfactory, additional tank depth will be required.

VALUE ENGINEERING RECOMMENDATION

No. E-1

PROJECT: Corporate Office Building
ITEM: Reconfigure electrical distribution

ORIGINAL DESIGN

Existing system uses 13.8 KV feeder from the local power company room connected to owner's 13.8 KV switchgear with four 2000 KVA transformers to step voltage down to 220V. Each transformer is connected to a main switchboard (MSB) for HVAC loads and general power. From each MSB, a set of bus ducts distributes load to building floor panels and distribution boards. Basement boards are connected by cables and each transformer is considered a separate unit and cannot support another in case of failure. General power MSBs are connected through automatic transfer switches (ATS) to separate emergency generators for each tower and no bus coupling exists between towers for emergency use.

The bus duct system set consists of two 2500 Amp. connected to each MSB for general power, four 4000 Amp. connected to HVAC MSBs, and a 3000 Amp. connected from each MSB for general power to each emergency switchboard. Every panel is metered, a total of 418 panels.

All lighting panels have 48 poles. The load assumed for future shop spaces results in having some 70 mm^2 cable. No demand or diversity factor was used for riser design. The main circuit breaker (MCB) for each MSB is 5000 Amp., which is a rare size, and it is connected by a specially manufactured 5000 Amp. bus duct.

PROPOSED DESIGN

Delete the bus duct system. Relocate transformers on building floors. Reduce the size of equipment by using 380V for HVAC, using more than 2 transformers for general power distribution with 220V secondary. Connect all transformers by a looped 13.8 KV cable. Loop can be achieved across the 17th floor bridge. Transformers should be as follows:

    2 ea. 2000 KVA for HVAC located at roof plant rooms
    1 ea. 1000 KVA for emergency power
    2 ea. 500 KVA for floors basement 5 through floor 2 at 220V
    2 ea. 300 KVA at 6th floors
    2 ea. 300 KVA at 14th floors at 220V
    2 ea. 300 KVA for elevators at 380V

Use 3 x 150 mm^2 13.8 KV cable for the loop. Reconfigure 13.8 KV switchgear to include 1 incoming and 2 outgoing for the looped 13.8 KV cable.

LIFE CYCLE COST SUMMARY	CAPITAL	REPLACEMENT	ANNUAL O&M
Original	$US 2,515,380	0	$US 25,154
Proposed	$US 781,041	0	$US 7,810
Savings	$US 1,734,339	0	$US 17,360
LIFE CYCLE (PW) SAVINGS			**$US 1,897,974**

Life Cycle Cost Savings (in U.S. dollars)

VALUE ENGINEERING RECOMMENDATION

PROJECT: Corporate Office Building
ITEM: Reconfigure electrical distribution

PROPOSED DESIGN (continued)

Refer to attached sketch for additional details of the proposed system. Use cables in conduits from transformer board to each panel. Reconfigure all panels for anticipated loads and the required number of poles.

DISCUSSION

The system as designed is very expensive, without any flexibility to transfer power from one tower to the other. Use of bus duct requires much more maintenance cost than does cable. The proposed system achieves both flexibility and lower initial cost.

This proposal requires space for the transformers on the recommended floors. With 2 plant rooms in each tower on each floor, this can be accomplished without extra cost except for a shaft for the high voltage cables. Transformers located at floors will also improve system performance.

The proposed system should use standard materials to maximize competition and eliminate the use of specialized manufacturers for designed equipment. This proposal minimizes the use of expensive draw-out circuit breakers.

Annual maintenance and operation costs are estimated to be 1% of initial cost.

PROJECT: Corporate Office Building
ITEM: Reconfigure electrical distribution

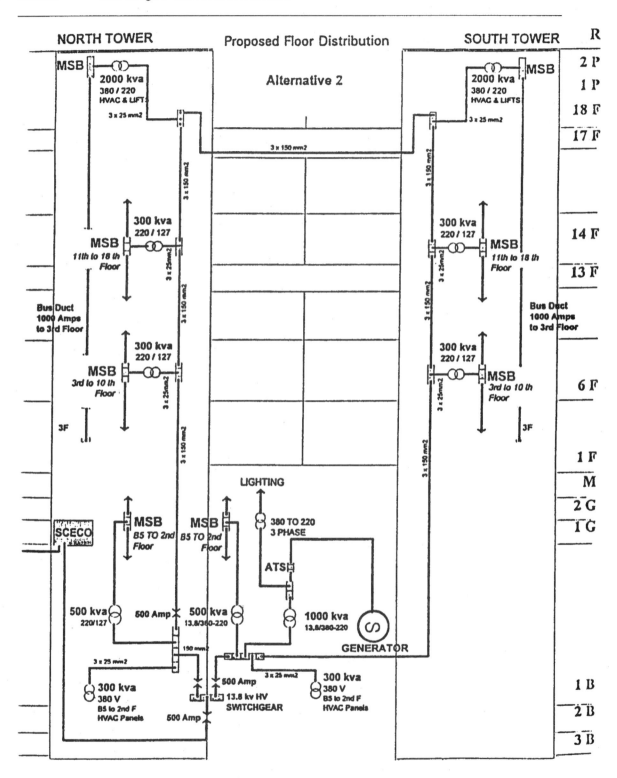

VALUE ENGINEERING RECOMMENDATION   VE Rec. No. E-1

PROJECT: Corporate Office Building
ITEM: Reconfigure electrical distribution

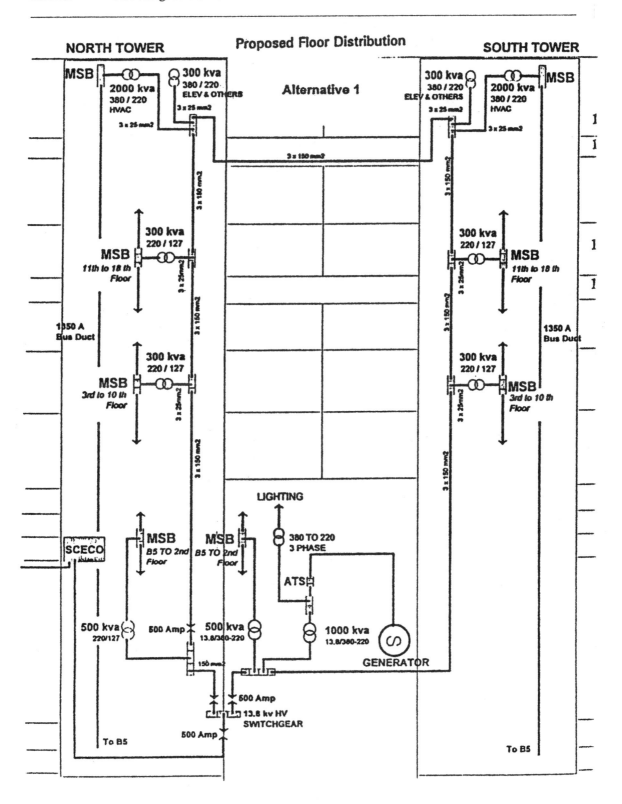

COST WORKSHEET

PROJECT: Corporate Office Building
ITEM: Reconfigure electrical distribution

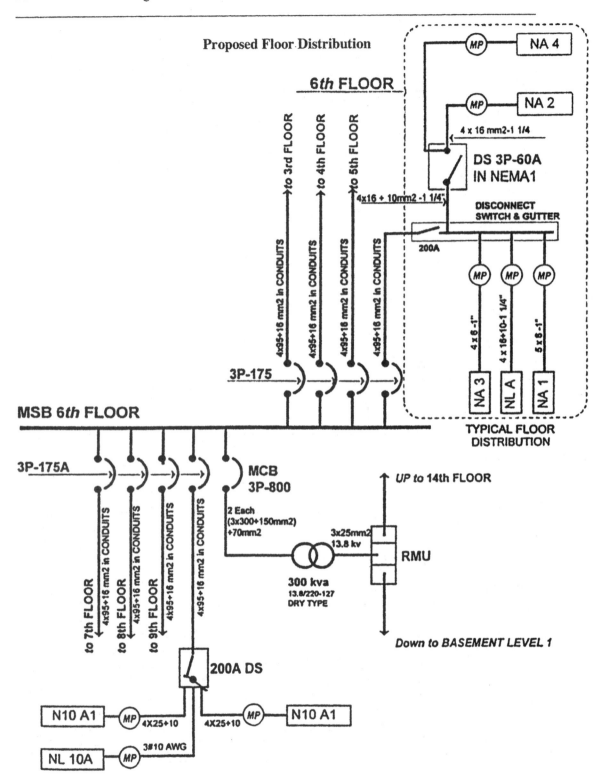

COST WORKSHEET

Recommendation No. E-

PROJECT: Corporate Office Building
ITEM: Reconfigure electrical distribution

Cost of Original Design

ITEM	UOM	QTY	Unit Cost	Total $US
ELECTRICAL POWER DISTRIBUTION				
Transformer 13.8/220-127, 2000 KVA	EA	4	45,333	181,333
High Voltage Switchgear	Lot	1	160,000	160,000
HV Cable 3 x 150 SqMM	LF	262	18	4,800
MSB N1	EA	1	57,333	57,333
MSB N2	EA	1	57,333	57,333
BUS DUCT SYSTEM				
Busway, Copper 5000 Amps	LF	177	658	116,640
5000 Amps Service Head - Trade Unit	EA	4	3,400	13,600
Switchboard Stub Unit 5000 A	EA	4	1,540	6,160
Bus Duct Supports & Hangers	EA	25	120	3,000
Elbow	EA	12	2,500	30,000
Ground Bus 2000 Amps	LF	210	32	6,707
Busway, Copper 3000 Amps	LF	2,139	415	886,720
Switchboard Stub Unit 3000 A	EA	12	900	10,800
Elbow 3000 Amps	EA	54	1,560	84,240
Plug in C.B. Rating 3000 Amps	EA	4	1,240	4,960
Bus Duct Supports	EA	75	40	3,000
Ground Bus 1600 Amps	LF	2,139	21	44,858
Busway, Copper 2500 Amps	LF	7	323	2,120
Switchboard Stub Unit 2000 A	EA	4	800	3,200
Elbow 2000 Amps	EA	4	1,300	5,200
Ground Bus 1600 Amps	LF	7	21	138
Bus Duct Supports	EA	2	67	133
Busway, Copper 2000 Amps	LF	2,198	265	583,168
Switchboard Stub Unit 2000 A	EA	4	650	2,598
Elbow 2000 Amps	EA	32	1,000	32,000
End Box 2000 Amps	EA	4	85	339
Plug in C.B. Rating 800 Amps	EA	4	2,269	9,075
Plug in C.B. Rating 600 Amps	EA	3	1,800	5,400
Plug in C.B. Rating 300 Amps	EA	4	1,240	4,960
Plug in C.B. Rating 150 Amps	EA	1	640	640
Plug in C.B. Rating 100 Amps	EA	59	280	16,520
Plug in C.B. Rating 60 Amps	EA	8	260	2,080
Plug in C.B. Rating 30 Amps	EA	58	260	15,080
Bus Duct Supports	EA	70	33	2,333
Ground Bus 800 A	LF	2,198	16	34,840
Cables From Plug-in C.Bs to Floor Boards in MC Conduits				
To SB/GA, MA & SB/GB, MB; Size 120 SqMM	LF	131	15	1,920
To SB/1A & SB/1B, N2P, Size 240 SqMM	LF	197	23	4,608
Size: 95 SqMM to BD/X1: In Conduit	LF	10	14	136
Size: 50 SqMM to Floor Panels: in Conduit	LF	656	8	5,067
Size: 25 SqMM to Floor Panels	LF	82	6	467
Size: 5 x 6 SqMM in Conduit	LF	525	4	2,048

PROJECT: Corporate Office Building
ITEM: Reconfigure electrical distribution

Cost of Original Design

ITEM	UOM	QTY	Unit Cost	Total $US
Reconfigure Floor Lighting Floor Panels				
PNL, NLGA & NLGB	EA	2	907	1,813
PNL NUGA	EA	1	773	773
PNL NMA	EA	1	800	800
PNL NMB	EA	1	800	800
PNL NL1A	EA	1	887	887
PNL NL1B	EA	1	947	947
PNLS: PFA1 & PFB1	EA	2	847	1,693
PNLS: PFA2 & PFB2	EA	2	773	1,547
PNLS: PFA3 & PFB3	EA	2	967	1,933
PNLS: PFA4 & PFB4	EA	2	860	1,720
PNLS: NA3 & NA4 Floors 3 to 9	EA	14	607	8,493
PNLS: NA1 & NA2 Floors 3 to 9	EA	14	647	9,053
PNLS: NLA Floor 3 to 9	EA	7	833	5,833
PNLS: NA1 & NA2,NB1,NB2: Floors 10-18	EA	18	833	15,000
PNLS: NLA Floors to 18	EA	14	607	8,493
PNLS: SMA & SMB	EA	2	3,413	6,827
SM PANELS	EA	2	3,333	6,667
Cable Tray 450 mm	LF	34	9	304
Cable Tray 300 mm	LF	138	8	1,064
Cable Tray 225 mm	LF	499	7	3,243
Cable Tray 150 mm	LF	440	6	2,501
Cable Tray 100 mm	LF	223	5	1,088
Cable 4 x 70 + 16 SqMM	LF	2,008	5	10,608
Cable 4 x 50 + 10 SqMM	LF	2,087	4	7,632
Cable 4 x 35 + 10 SqMM	LF	39	2	83
Cable 4 x 25 + 10 SqMM	LF	2,330	2	4,355
Reconfigure SB1A & SB1B	EA	2	2,833	5,667
Totals				2,515,380

PROJECT: Corporate Office Building
ITEM: Reconfigure electrical distribution

Cost of Proposed Design

ITEM	UOM	QTY	Unit Cost	Total USD
ELECTRICAL POWER DISTRIBUTION				
Transformer 13.8/220-127, 2000 KVA	EA	2	45,333	90,667
Transformer 13.8/220-127, 500 KVA	EA	1	21,333	21,333
Transformer 13.8/220-127, 1000 KVA	EA	1	37,333	37,333
Transformer 13.8/220-127, 300 KVA	EA	6	19,200	115,200
High Voltage Switchgear	Lot	1	93,333	93,333
HV Cable 3 x 150 SqMM	LF	984	18	18,000
Ring Main Unit 2 Feed	EA	3	17,333	52,000
Ring Main Unit 1 Feed	EA	5	13,333	66,667
MSB N1 for Floor B5 to 2nd Floor	EA	1	17,333	17,333
MSB S1 for Floors B5 to 2nd Floor	EA	1	17,333	17,333
CABLES FROM MN1 & MS1 Up to GF Thru 2nd Floor Switchboards in Conduits				
3x300+150+70 SqMM in IMC Conduit	LF	492	27	13,200
3x240+120+70 SqMM in IMC Conduit	LF	2,133	23	49,920
4x35+10 SqMM in IMC Conduit	LF	525	6	3,285
MSB 14th Floor	EA	2	9,600	19,200
MSB 6th Floor	EA	2	9,600	19,200
Disconnect 3P-200 & Gutter	EA	14	960	13,440
Disconnect 3P-200 Amps	EA	18	293	5,280
CB 3P-50A in NEMA 1 Enclosure	EA	14	253	3,547
CABLES FROM 6th & 14 Floors MSBs				
3x300+150+70 SqMM in Conduit	LF	131	27	3,520
4x95+25 SqMM in Conduit	LF	1,641	14	22,667
4x25+10 SqMM - 1 1/2" Conduit	LF	2,051	6	11,667
4x16+10 SqMM - 1 1/4" Conduit	LF	1,641	5	7,600
5x6 SqMM - 1" Conduit	LF	230	4	896
4x6 SqMM - 1" Conduit	LF	525	4	1,920
FLOOR PANELS RECONFIGURED				
PNL NLGA & NLGB	EA	2	667	1,333
PNL NUGA	EA	1	587	587
PNL NMA	EA	1	587	587
PNL NMB	EA	1	587	587
PNL NL1A	EA	1	773	773
PNL NL1B	EA	1	827	827
PNLS PFA1 & PFB1	EA	2	740	1,480
PNLS PFA2 & PFB2	EA	2	587	1,173
PNLS PFA3 & PFB3	EA	2	813	1,627
PNLS PFA4 & PFB4	EA	2	747	1,493
PNLS NA3 & NA4 Floors 3 to 9	EA	14	339	4,741
PNLS NA1 & NA2 Floors 3 to 9	EA	14	433	6,067
PNLS NAL Floors 3 to 9	EA	7	740	5,180
PNLS NA1 & NA2,NB1, NB2: Floors 10 to 18	EA	18	740	13,320
PNLS NLA Floors 10 to 18	EA	14	364	5,096
PNLS SMA & SMB	EA	2	2,800	5,600
PNLS SB	EA	2	2,800	5,600

COST WORKSHEET

PROJECT: Corporate Office Building
ITEM: Reconfigure electrical distribution

Cost of Proposed Design

ITEM	UOM	QTY	Unit Cost	Total USD
Cable Tray 300 mm	LF	98	8	760
Cable Tray 225 mm	LF	656	7	4,267
Cable Tray 150 mm	LF	262	6	1,493
Cable Tray 100 mm	LF	394	5	1,920
Cable 4x35+10 SqMM	LF	2,008	2	4,243
Cable 4x25+10 SqMM	LF	0	2	0
Cable 4x16+10 SqMM	LF	2,087	1	3,053
Cable 4x10+10 SqMM	LF	0	4	0
Reconfigure SB1A & SB1B	EA	2	2,347	4,693
Totals				781,041

Hospital and Staff Housing Complex

A value engineering study was conducted on the proposed design development, Phase 3 (50% working drawings), for a hospital and staff housing complex. The VE team studied the project from four viewpoints: architectural, structural, mechanical, and electrical. Separately, the medical equipment specialist documented three areas that would generate additional income.

Study objective: Review the design documents to optimize the cost impact of design decisions.

Based on several reviews with the owner and A/E, approximately 35 proposals were implemented. Initial cost savings of $10,000,000 to $12,000,000 will result, depending on progression of the design and future estimates. Follow-on cost savings vary up to $1,000,000/year, depending on the final design alternative.

Case Study Elements

The items listed below and shown in this case study have been excerpted from an actual VE report. (The Table of Contents on page 213 is one of the excerpts and refers to some documents not listed here or shown in the section.)

VALUE ENGINEERING REPORT
Hospital

> *This is the Table of Contents from the actual VE report.*
> *Selected excerpts appear in this case study.*

VALUE ENGINEERING REPORT

Hospital

EXECUTIVE SUMMARY

A Value Engineering study was conducted on the design development, Phase 3, 50% working drawings proposed for the hospital. The study was conducted at the Architect's and Engineer's office in November 1996. The objective of the study was to review the design documents to optimize the cost impact of design decisions. The project involved a hospital of some 350,000 S.F. and a housing complex of five buildings of some 195,000 S.F. The costs validated by the VE team and agreed to by the A/E amounted to approximately $93,000,000.

Some 127 ideas were generated during the initial review phase, from which 56 ideas were developed. In addition, some 22 design suggestions representing VE team design review type comments were generated; these are located in Section 4, Figure 4-2. A marked-up set (one copy) of drawings indicating these and additional comments are attached. These proposals represent potential initial savings of over $16,000,000 and additional follow-on potential savings in operation, maintenance, and increased revenue of about $265,000/year. Also, suggested recommendations of potential deferred construction costs for supporting and medical equipment are included amounting to some $5,000,000.

As a separate input, the medical equipment specialist documented three areas to generate additional income of some $100,000 /year by: adding three beds to hemodialysis, one mobile ultra sound, and two mobile radiographic X-ray machines.

SUMMARY OF PRINCIPAL RECOMMENDATIONS

General

The team suggests that the Owner considers two options to defer initial cost outlays:

- Delete nurses' house and rent space. A rough cash flow analysis indicates Owner will be some $200,000 /yr ahead using an equivalent cash flow analysis avoiding a $3,500,000 capital expenditure.
- Consider design build, lease-back for 20 years. By doing this Owner will defer some $15,000,000 in capital outlay and own the facilities after 20 years. He incurs some additional annual leasing costs that would be less than amortizing his capital investment over 20 years.

  Note: The above savings are not additive.

Architectural - 16 Items totalling approximately $3,500,000

The principal items are:

- Review design of interior partitions for housing and hospital.
- For housing, delete doctors' unit balconies, less expressive canopies, eliminate basement in water table and use less expensive exterior wall panels.
- Revise design of hospital and housing exterior pre-cast panels from 7" to 5" thick or consider using masonry and local stone.
- Raise hospital basement level by one meter to reduce hydrostatic uplift on slab.
- Revise finishes of ground floor (granite) and use less expensive, more practical floor finish for operating rooms.

Structural - 2 Items totalling approximately $130,000

- Revise structural system to flat slab and increase floor-to-floor height to 14'-3". Note: Original design of 13 feet would not accommodate economically the required utilities. An increase in cost would be incurred in trying to fit utilities in the proposed ceiling space.
- Simplify ground and basement slab levels to reduce changes in grade.

Mechanical - 14 Items totalling about $1,000,000 in initial and $110,000/yr. in annual savings

The major items being:

- Consolidate the sanitary waste and sewer lines within the building.
- Consider eliminating the sewage treatment plant. Alternate solutions: a) Consider a less expensive plant yielding $320,000 initial cost savings, or b) provide a septic tank system resulting in $375,000 initial cost savings. Hookup to municipal would occur when new line is installed.
- Consider providing a chilled water thermal energy storage system as a means of electrical load shedding during peak hours. This recommendation was not analyzed in great detail; however, it could be developed should the electrical building load grow beyond electric company standard substation size or ability to deliver peak power.
- Consider increasing chilled water temperature rise from 42°F to 46°F across the cooling coils. This results in an overall chilled water flow reduction leading to lower piping costs, reduced pumping energy and an overall efficiency increase of the chiller operation.
- Design general patient bedrooms for 75°F rather than 65°F inside design temperature during the cooling season. This results in overall initial and life cycle cost savings without compromising the required environmental patient comfort.
- Use a central variable air volume system approach rather than fan coils in the general patient rooms. The central system improves indoor environmental conditions for patients by providing higher filtration levels in the space, eliminates intrusive maintenance, and lowers operating costs.

Electrical - 11 Items totalling approximately $3,800,000 in initial savings and $100,000/yr. in annual costs.

The principal items are:

- Re-configure site electrical distribution system to optimize use of high voltage distribution.
- Replace parabolic with prismatic lens fixtures and electronic ballasts with high power factor. Energy savings do not offset initial costs.
- Re-configure outdoor lighting reducing number of poles, etc.
- Centralize the Uninterruptable Power Supply (UPS) system.
- Relocate switchgear nearer to load center.
- Change chiller voltage from 280 volts to 380 volts.

Medical Equipment - 9 Items totalling approximately $7,500,000 in initial costs plus $650,000/yr. in additional income.

There are several significant proposals presented:

- Consider deferring several items to postpone costs until patient load increases to create break-even conditions, e.g., MRI, cardiac catheter lab, nuclear and gamma cameras. Deferred capital cost of some $5,300,000 not included above.

- Consider adding select equipment to generate additional revenue such as:
  - Add one additional ultra sound scanner.
  - Add three additional beds in hemodialysis for pediatric patients presently not covered.
  - Add 2 mobile radiographic X-ray machines.

The above equipment will add some $675,000/year in additional income.

- The largest area of potential savings was isolated by a critical look at the medical equipment and recommending the following:

  - Eliminate items redundant with building (construction) equipment estimate.

  - Procure local equipment wherever available at less cost.

  - Reduce quantities that appear excessive and buy alternate equipment (other manufacturers) that produce equipment (non-proprietary) adequate for the hospital functions.

  - Add equipment needed to meet overall hospital requirements (added costs).

SECTION 2 - Project Description

1. ## Requirements of the Hospital

   a. Number of Beds = 180

   b. Area of land = 500,000 S.F.

   c. Parking one car per bed plus staff and out-patient

   d. Site plan is provided.

   e. Housing:
   It is required to accommodate all doctors and a total of 130 nurses;
   a recreational area is to be provided.

2. ## Civil Structural Engineering

   a. Site

   On-site wastewater treatment, effluent recycled for irrigation. Utility building housing chillers, O_2, incinerator.

   b. Structure

   Pre-cast hollow-core slabs with a reinforced concrete frame.

3. ## Architectural

   a. Walls

   Interior: Drywall partitions with two (2) 1/2" sheets each side.
   Exterior: Pre-cast concrete panels with upper 20% window area.

   b. Floor

   Heavy-duty vinyl flooring, in general, with lobbies and ground-floor granite specified in selected areas.

   c. Finishing Material of Facia

   Pre-cast concrete panels

   d. Partition Wall Finishes

   Enamel paint.

   e. Ceilings

   Armstrong-type painted tiles and waterproofed gypsum board for wet areas. Selected area in basement calls for linear metallic ceilings.

4. Mechanical Systems

The mechanical works include the following systems:

a. Domestic hot and cold water system.

b. Reverse osmosis/ionized water system.

c. Drainage system.

d. Rainwater drainage system.

e. Oxygen, vacuum and other medical gases network system.

f. Heating, ventilation and air-conditioning system, consisting of:
   - Four (4) air-cooled chillers (size not noted in outside equipment area)
   - Fan coil units with fresh-air ventilation in general patient rooms
   - Fan coil units in general out-patient areas
   - VAV in administration areas
   - Single-zone constant volume, 100% outside air with heat recovery in critical areas.

g. Steam boiler for laundry, sterilizing and washer/decontaminators units.

h. Fire fighting system: Wet pipe, combined sprinkler standpipe system with combination electric and diesel fire pumps.

i. Waste disposal and incinerator system.

j. Low-pressure gas (LPG) services.

k. Irrigation system.

l. Automatic temperature control system.

5. Electrical

Building load is estimated at 6000 KVA. The following systems are proposed:

a. Standing Generator System: 2 - 700 KVA units.

b. UPS Systems: Central plus 2 floor units for selected areas. A minimum of 30 minutes backup used.

c. Power Distribution: Vertically via XLPE cable in shafts.

d. Lighting: Primary lighting recessed parabolic fluorescent fixtures and energy-saving lamps. Fixtures to have electronic ballasts and deo starters.

e. Telecommunication: Distribution will be by horizontal and vertical ladder-type cable trays. Telephone company to provide backup lines. Standard equipment to be specified.

f. Radio Communication: Masts and power to be provided on roof.

g. Fire Alarm System: System to be microprocessor-based automatic, analog addressable system alarm, to be displayed on a digital readout screen, and CRT shall display graphics of system under activated alarm.

h. Security System: Four sub-systems to be provided:

    a) Key management system for low-risk public areas

    b) Card access control for high-risk areas

    c) Closed-circuit TV

i. Lightning Protection: System to consist of air terminal, electric device, arrestor, lightning conductors, earthing rods and pits.

j. Earthing (Grounding) System: System to consist of Power Co. transformer grounding, equipment grounds, foundation earthing, and special systems, e.g., OR, UPS, medical equipment, low-current systems.

k. Special Call Systems:

    1) Staff automatic system

    2) Nurse call and hospital communications system

    3) Radio paging system

6. Cost Estimate

The estimate was developed by the Project Manager and adjusted and validated by the designers' estimator (see Section 3 - Value Engineering Procedures for Estimates).

The project estimate at bid and area analysis follows:

- Main Hospital and supporting areas (356,000 S.F.)
    = $ 74,000,000
Unit Cost = $ 210/S.F.

- Housing and Dormitories plus supporting areas (197,000 S.F.)
    = $ 18,000,000.
Unit Cost = $ 93/S.F.

Total Estimated Costs $ 93,000,000

SECTION 3 - VALUE ENGINEERING PROCEDURE

GENERAL

Value engineering is a creative, organized approach, whose objective is to optimize the life cycle cost and/or performance of a facility. To present a clear description of our assessment of the project in terms of cost and life cycle usage, and the approach that we applied to the study, we have outlined the procedure followed for the study.

A multidisciplinary team was formed to analyze the project design utilizing applicable value engineering techniques. It was the objective of each team member to analyze the project, find high-cost areas, recommend alternatives and estimate initial and life cycle costs whenever significant for the original system and for each proposed alternative. Also, other criteria were used to assure the proposed recommendations did not sacrifice essential functions and timely completion of the project. The actual recommendations derived from the analysis are identified in Section 4 of this report.

PRE-STUDY

Upon receipt of the project documents-- namely, selected plans and design documents (Design development) -- selected members of the VE team reviewed them. At this time the estimate did not reflect the level of details of the documents. Also, a list of questions and ideas to be reviewed during the first day of the formal workshop was generated.

The project documents were also reviewed by a medical equipment layout specialist for basic comments. The comments received from the medical equipment specialist, from a large A/E firm specializing in hospitals, were given to the client and design team. These comments were reviewed with the consultants by the team and incorporated, as applicable, into the ideas generated during the formal workshop.

VE JOB PLAN

The VE team analyzed the project documents submitted by the design team. These were the design documents, including plans, cost estimate, and design report.

The VE study was organized into six distinct parts comprising the VE Job Plan: (1) Information phase, (2) Creative phase, (3) Judgment phase, (4) Development phase, (5) Presentation phase, (6) Report phase.

In accordance with the agenda, the design team and owner made an initial presentation on the design constraints and development. At that time, additional drawings were submitted to the team. A VE budget level estimate using the UniFormat system was prepared at the start of the workshop. This estimate was resolved with the design team estimator and the resolved estimate was used for cost modeling and proposals.

Information Phase

Following a study of the latest engineered documents, the VE team performed function analyses of the different components of the project. The functions of any system are the controlling elements in the overall VE approach. This procedure forces the participants to think in terms of function, and the cost associated with that function. Preparing the function analysis helped to generate many of the ideas that eventually resulted in recommendations. Included in this report are the function analysis worksheets (Figures 3.1a and 3.1b).

Next, based on the resolved cost estimate, cost/worth models were developed for hospital (Figure 3-2a) and housing units (Figure 3-2b) to assist in isolating areas for value improvement. Cost is in the form of unit cost ($/SF) for the project, as taken from the resolved cost estimate for the project. Backup cost data is furnished with the model.

The teams assigned worth to the cost model based upon the function analysis performed, their experience, and historical data for similar systems. This model indicated that the greatest potential for value improvement exists in medical equipment, architectural, and, to a lesser extent, the electrical and mechanical. Additional site savings in electrical utilities were isolated, based on the differences in the cost/worth estimates. Actual savings implemented will depend on time required to implement, stage of design, and owner preferences.

Creative Phase

This step in the value engineering study involves the listing of creative ideas. During this time, the value engineering team thinks of as many ways as possible to provide the necessary functions at a lower initial and/or life cycle cost and design enhancements to improve required functions. During the creative phase, judgment of the ideas is restricted. The value engineering team looks for quantity and association of ideas, which will be screened in the next phase of the study. This list may include ideas that can be further evaluated and used in the design. The creative idea listing is presented in the last part of this report as Figure 3-3.

Judgment Phase

In this phase of the project, the value engineering teams judged and ranked the ideas generated from the creative session. The remainder of the creative idea listing worksheet was used for this phase, and the results are included on the right side of the worksheet. Ideas found to be impractical or not worthy of additional study are disregarded, and those ideas that represent the greatest potential for cost savings are developed further.

Factors used in evaluating the ideas included: the state-of-the-art of the idea, cost to develop, probability of implementation, the time necessary to implement, the magnitude of its potential benefit, and its impact on aesthetics. The ideas were ranked from 1 to 10, with 10 being the best idea. Ideas with a ranking of 8 or more were developed or combined into proposals.

To assist in preliminary judging of ideas and to gain additional knowledge regarding them, all ideas were reviewed with the designer and owner team to hear any objections, problems or agreement.

Development Phase

During the development phase of the value engineering study, selected ideas were expanded into workable solutions. Development consisted of the recommended design, life cycle cost comparisons, and a descriptive evaluation of the advantages and disadvantages of the proposed recommendations. It was important that the value engineering team convey the concept of their recommendation to the Designer. Therefore, each recommendation has a brief narrative to compare the original design method to the proposed change.

Sketches and design calculations, where appropriate, are included with the recommendations. The VE recommendations are included in Section 4 - Summary of Results.

Presentation and Report Phase

The last phase of the value engineering effort was the presentation and preparation of recommendations. The VE recommendations were further screened by the VE team before the oral presentation of results. On the final day of the VE study workshop, a presentation of recommendations contained in this report was made to the same team who attended the first day.

At the conclusion of the workshop, VE proposals were reviewed, edited for clarity, and re-evaluated for computation of cost savings. Recommendations and the rationale that went into the development of each proposal are described in the proposals presented in Section 4.

ECONOMIC FACTORS

During the value engineering study, construction cost and life cycle cost summaries are prepared for each element of the project. Economic data and assumptions made for the life cycle cost comparisons were as follows:

Discount Rate	10% (compounded annually)
Analysis Period	30 years
Equivalence Approach	Present Worth converted to Annualized Method
Inflation Approach	Constant Dollars
Present Worth Annuity Factor	9.42

Operating Costs

Energy Cost	0.03 cents/KWhr (average)
Maintenance Cost	1 to 5% of capital cost depending on element

FUNCTION ANALYSIS WORKSHEET

PROJECT: Hospital
ITEM: **Hospital and Supporting Facilities**
BASIC FUNCTION: House and treat patients

COMPONENT DESCRIPTION	FUNCTION (VERB-NOUN)	KIND	COST	WORTH	COST/ WORTH	COMMENTS
B = Basic Function S = Secondary Function RS = Required Secondary Function						
SITE WORK						
Overhead & Profit			907,116	567,367	1.60	
121 Site Preparation			62,667	50,133	1.25	
122 Site Improvement			1,755,580	1,267,469	1.39	
123 Site Utilties			2,578,667	1,408,299	1.83	
124 Off-Site Work			138,667	110,933	1.25	
TOTAL			5,442,696	3,404,201	1.60	
STRUCTURAL						
01 Foundation	Support load	B	1,701,845	1,267,469	1.34	Eliminate water level problem.
02 Substructure	Services	B	960,557	704,149	1.36	Move substructure to grade level.
03 Superstructure	Support load and house patients	B	3,129,387	2,253,278	1.39	Simplify structural system.
TOTAL			5,791,789	4,224,896	1.37	
ARCHITECTURAL						
04 Wall Closure	Enclose space	B	1,816,320	985,809	1.84	Replace granite/marble with precast element.
05 Roofing	Protect building	RS	408,787	281,660	1.45	Reduce space.
06 Interior Construction	Finish and beautify space	B	7,882,597	4,224,896	1.87	Change wall construction from gypsum board to CMU.
07 Conveying System	Transport people	B	1,123,200	1,126,639	1.00	
TOTAL			11,230,904	6,619,004	1.70	
MECHANICAL						
081 Plumbing	Service building	B	2,225,867	1,780,693	1.25	Consolidate waste and soil line.
082 HVAC	Condition space	B	4,566,667	3,520,747	1.30	Use unitary cooling.
083 Fire Protection	Protect space & people	RS	800,787	492,905	1.62	
084 Special Mechanical	Control systems	RS	933,333	633,734	1.47	
TOTAL			8,526,653	6,428,079	1.33	

FUNCTION ANALYSIS WORKSHEET

PROJECT: Hospital
ITEM: Hospital and Supporting Facilities
BASIC FUNCTION: House and treat patients

COMPONENT DESCRIPTION	FUNCTION (VERB-NOUN)	KIND	COST	WORTH	COST/ WORTH	COMMENTS
B = Basic Function S = Secondary Function RS = Required Secondary Function						
ELECTRICAL						
091 Service & Dist.	Distribute power	B	862,667	690,133	1.25	Centralize load.
092 Emergency & UPS	Backup power	RS	2,093,333	1,408,299	1.49	
093 Lighting & Power	Light space	B	1,292,779	844,979	1.53	Improve light distribution.
094 Special Electrical	Support systems	RS	3,013,333	1,760,373	1.71	
TOTAL			7,262,112	4,703,785	1.54	
EQUIPMENT						
111 Fixed & Mov. Equip.	Support building	B	1,938,667	1,267,469	1.53	
112 Furnishing	Provide services	RS	0	0	0.00	Use local market.
113 Special Const.	Support building (Medical equipment)	B	15,733,333	9,153,941	1.72	
TOTAL			17,672,000	10,421,410	1.70	
GENERAL 20%						
Mobilization Exp. 2%			1,009,669	647,943	1.56	
Site Overheads 2.5%			1,262,086	809,929	1.56	
Demobilization 0.5%			252,417	161,986	1.56	
Off. Exp. & Profit 15%			7,572,519	4,859,576	1.56	
TOTAL			10,096,692	6,479,435	1.56	

FUNCTION ANALYSIS WORKSHEET

PROJECT: Hospital
ITEM: **Housing and Dormitories**
BASIC FUNCTION: House doctors and hospital staff

COMPONENT DESCRIPTION	FUNCTION (VERB-NOUN)	KIND	COST	WORTH	COST/ WORTH	COMMENTS
B = Basic Function S = Secondary Function RS = Required Secondary Function						

FUNCTION ANALYSIS WORKSHEET

PROJECT: Hospital
ITEM: **Housing and Dormitories**
BASIC FUNCTION: House doctors and hospital staff

COMPONENT DESCRIPTION	FUNCTION (VERB-NOUN)	KIND	COST	WORTH	COST/ WORTH	COMMENTS
B = Basic Function S = Secondary Function RS = Required Secondary Function						

COMPONENT DESCRIPTION	FUNCTION (VERB-NOUN)	KIND	COST	WORTH	COST/ WORTH	COMMENTS
SITE WORK						
Overhead & Profit			0	0	0.00	
121 Site Preparation			0	0	0.00	Included in Hospital
122 Site Improvement			0	0	0.00	Included in Hospital
123 Site Utilties			0	0	0.00	Included in Hospital
124 Off-Site Work			0	0	0.00	Included in Hospital
TOTAL			**0**	**0**	0.00	
STRUCTURAL						
01 Foundation	Support load	B	210,477	168,382	1.25	Eliminate water level problem.
02 Substructure	Services	B	93,832	75,066	1.25	Move substructure to grade level.
03 Superstructure	Support load and house staff	B	1,904,773	1,358,933	1.40	Simplify structural system.
TOTAL			**2,209,083**	**1,602,381**	1.38	
ARCHITECTURAL						
04 Wall Closure	Enclose space	B	1,979,200	1,358,933	1.46	Change granite/marble with precast.
05 Roofing	Protect building	RS	94,777	58,240	1.63	Reduce space occupant.
06 Interior Construction	Finish and beautify space	B	3,450,144	2,329,600	1.48	Change wall construction from gypsum board to CMU.
07 Conveying System	Transport people	B	912,000	729,600	1.25	
TOTAL			**6,436,121**	**4,476,373**	1.44	
MECHANICAL						
081 Plumbing	Service building	B	787,200	582,400	1.35	Consolidate waste and soil line.
082 HVAC	Condition space	B	1,950,667	1,358,933	1.44	Use unitary cooling.
083 Fire Protection	Protect building & people			0	0.00	None
084 Special Mechanical	Control system		0	0	0.00	None
TOTAL			**2,737,867**	**1,941,333**	1.41	

FUNCTION ANALYSIS WORKSHEET

PROJECT: Hospital
ITEM: **Housing and Dormitories**
BASIC FUNCTION: House doctors and hospital staff

COMPONENT DESCRIPTION	FUNCTION (VERB-NOUN)	KIND	COST	WORTH	COST/ WORTH	COMMENTS
B = Basic Function S = Secondary Function RS = Required Secondary Function						
ELECTRICAL						
091 Service & Dist.	Distribute power	B	230,667	174,720	1.32	Centralize load.
092 Emergency & UPS			0	0	0.00	
093 Lighting & Power	Light space	B	630,933	388,267	1.63	Improve light distribution.
094 Special Electrical	Support systems		146,667	97,067	1.51	
TOTAL			**1,008,267**	**660,053**	1.53	
EQUIPMENT						
111 Fixed & Mov. Equip.	Support building		224,000	155,307	1.44	
112 Furnishing	Provide services		920,000	582,400	1.58	Use local market.
113 Special Const.			0	0	0.00	
TOTAL			**1,144,000**	**737,707**	1.55	
GENERAL 20%						
Mobilization Exp. 2%			270,707	188,357	1.44	
Site Overheads 2.5%			338,383	235,446	1.44	
Demobilization 0.5%			67,677	47,089	1.44	
Off. Exp. & Profit 15%			2,030,301	1,412,677	1.44	
TOTAL			**2,707,067**	**1,883,569**	1.44	
OVERALL TOTAL			**16,242,405**	**11,301,417**	1.44	

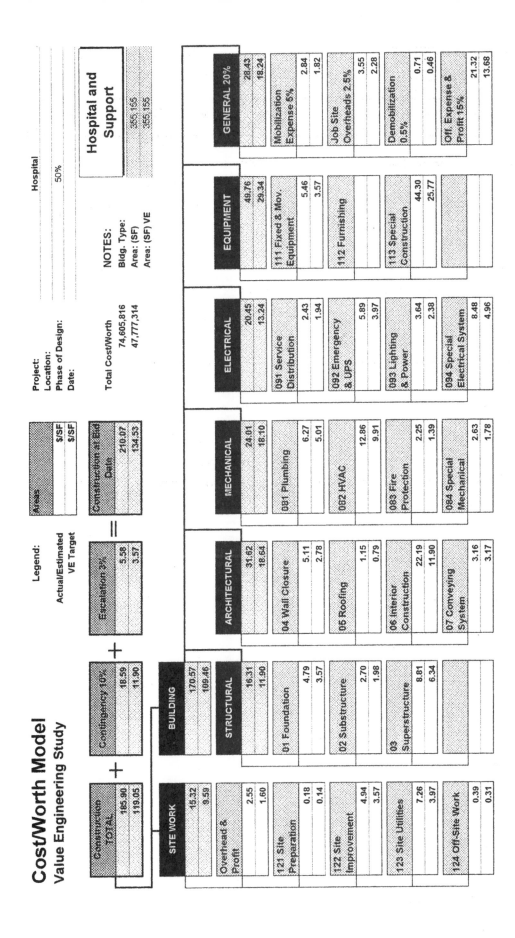

Cost/Worth Model
Value Engineering Study

Hospital and Support

Hospital 50%

355,155
355,155

NOTES:
Project:
Location:
Phase of Design:
Date:

Bldg. Type:
Area: (SF)
Area: (SF) VE

Total Cost/Worth
74,605,816
47,777,314

Legend:

Areas $/SF $/SF

Actual/Estimated
VE Target

Construction at Bid
Date   210.07   134.53

Escalation 3%   5.58   3.57

Contingency 10%   18.59   11.90

Construction TOTAL   185.90   119.05

SITE WORK   15.32   9.59

Overhead & Profit   2.55 / 1.60
121 Site Preparation   0.18 / 0.14
122 Site Improvement   4.94 / 3.57
123 Site Utilities   7.26 / 3.97
124 Off-Site Work   0.39 / 0.31

BUILDING   170.57   109.46

STRUCTURAL   16.31   11.90
01 Foundation   4.79 / 3.57
02 Substructure   2.70 / 1.98
03 Superstructure   8.81 / 6.34

ARCHITECTURAL   31.62   18.64
04 Wall Closure   5.11 / 2.78
05 Roofing   1.15 / 0.79
06 Interior Construction   22.19 / 11.90
07 Conveying System   3.16 / 3.17

MECHANICAL   24.01   18.10
081 Plumbing   6.27 / 5.01
082 HVAC   12.86 / 9.91
083 Fire Protection   2.25 / 1.39
084 Special Mechanical   2.63 / 1.78

ELECTRICAL   20.45   13.24
091 Service Distribution   2.43 / 1.94
092 Emergency & UPS   5.89 / 3.97
093 Lighting & Power   3.64 / 2.38
094 Special Electrical System   8.48 / 4.96

EQUIPMENT   49.76   29.34
111 Fixed & Mov. Equipment   5.46 / 3.57
112 Furnishing
113 Special Construction   44.30 / 25.77

GENERAL 20%   28.43   18.24
Mobilization Expense 5%   2.84 / 1.82
Job Site Overheads 2.5%   3.55 / 2.28
Demobilization 0.5%   0.71 / 0.46
Off. Expense & Profit 15%   21.32 / 13.68

Cost/Worth Model
Value Engineering Study

Project: Hospital
Location:
Phase of Design: 50%

Housing and Dormitories
195,832
195,832

NOTES:
Bldg. Type:
Area: (SF)
Area: (SF) VE

Total Cost/Worth	
18,353,917	
12,770,601	

Legend:
Actual/Estimated
VE Target

Areas	
$/SF	
$/SF	

Construction at Bid Date	
93.72	
65.21	

Escalation 3%	
2.49	
1.73	

Contingency 10%	
8.29	
5.77	

Construction TOTAL	
82.94	
57.71	

BUILDING	
82.94	
57.71	

GENERAL 20% — 13.82 / 9.62
Item	Actual/Est.	VE Target
Mobilization Expense 2%	1.38	0.96
Job Site Overheads 2.5%	1.73	1.20
Demobilization 0.5%	0.35	0.24
Off. Expense & Profit 15%	10.37	7.21

EQUIPMENT — 5.84 / 3.77
Item	Actual/Est.	VE Target
111 Fixed & Mov. Equipment	1.14	0.79
112 Furnishing	4.70	2.97
113 Special Construction		

ELECTRICAL — 5.15 / 3.37
Item	Actual/Est.	VE Target
091 Service Distribution	1.18	0.89
092 Emergency & UPS		
093 Lighting & Power	3.22	1.98
094 Special Electrical System	0.75	0.50

MECHANICAL — 13.98 / 9.91
Item	Actual/Est.	VE Target
081 Plumbing	4.02	2.97
082 HVAC	9.96	6.94
083 Fire Protection		
084 Special Mechanical		

ARCHITECTURAL — 32.87 / 22.86
Item	Actual/Est.	VE Target
04 Wall Closure	10.11	6.94
05 Roofing	0.48	0.30
06 Interior Construction	17.62	11.90
07 Conveying System	4.66	3.73

STRUCTURAL — 11.28 / 8.18
Item	Actual/Est.	VE Target
01 Foundation	1.07	0.86
02 Substructure	0.48	0.38
03 Superstructure	9.73	6.94

SITE WORK
Overhead & Profit
121 Site Preparation
122 Site Improvement
123 Site Utilities
124 Off-Site Work

Case Study Two   Hospital and Staff Housing Complex

VALUE ENGINEERING REPORT
Hospital
SECTION 4 - SUMMARY OF RESULTS

GENERAL

This section of the report summarizes the results and recommendations for the study. Ideas that were developed are submitted here as recommendations for acceptance. It is important when reviewing the results of the VE study to review each part of a recommendation on its own merits. Often there is a tendency to disregard a recommendation because of concern about one portion of it. When reviewing this report, consideration should be given to areas within a recommendation that are acceptable and apply those parts to the final design.

VALUE ENGINEERING RECOMMENDATIONS

The value engineering team developed fifty-six (56) proposals for change. They represent approximately sixteen million dollars ($16,000,000) in potential initial cost savings and over $265,000/year in present worth of annual O & M cost savings, plus over $500,000/year in additional income. In addition, 22 design suggestions are provided to clarify design, improve design, or increase cost. For Owner consideration, some recommendations for deferred cost reduction of $19,000,000 are presented. For clarity, proposals have been separated into groups, as shown below.

Recommendation Category	No. of Proposals	Deferred Cost Reductions	PW of Add'l Income	Initial Savings	Life Cycle Savings
GENERAL	2	16,000,000			
ARCHITECTURAL	17			3,359,143	3,359,143
STRUCTURAL	3			128,784	128,784
MECHANICAL	14			1,242,477	2,146,809
ELECTRICAL	11			3,783,086	4,566,725
MEDICAL EQUIPMENT	8	3,919,345	4,947,427	7,494,228	7,494,228
Total of Proposals	55				
TOTALS		**19,919,345**	**4,947,427**	**16,007,718**	**17,695,690**

Savings Summary Legend
(All Costs in $US)

To assure continuity of cost between the recommendations proposed by the VE team, we have used the project cost estimate developed by the VE team in cooperation with the Designer as the basis of cost. Where this was not possible, the VE team used data provided by PM estimators. All life cycle costs were based on using the economic factors listed in Section 3 of this report.

A summary of potential cost savings for each VE recommendation follows.
Value engineering recommendations are presented in Section 4.

Summary of Potential Cost Savings from VE Proposals

Hospital

PROPOSALS		Deferred Reductions	Life Cycle Savings (PW)
GENERAL, SITE			
G 9	Delete Male housing and rent space. (Not additive to G-10)	2,661,333	2,661,333
G 10	Bid housing using design, build, lease back	16,000,000	
	General Total	**16,000,000**	

PROPOSALS		Initial Savings	Life Cycle Savings
ARCHITECTURAL			
A 3	Relocation of medical gases PMG	5,273	5,273
A 5	Revise layout of outpatient area waiting room.		
A 7	Clinical Labs / Hemodialysis Department	-95,191	-95,191
A 8	Exterior precast panels, Hospital. (See A 24 & A 25)	1,890,264	1,890,264
A 9a	Interior partitons - Housing (See A 24 & A 25, not included in total)	162,720	162,720
A 9b	Interior partitions - Hospital	298,320	298,320
A 10	Change canopies on Housing units (See A 25, not included in total)	142,380	142,380
A 11	Eliminate balconies on doctors' housing units. (See A 24 & A 25, not included in total)	239,327	239,327
A 12	Relocate basement of housing units to above grade. grade. (See A 24 & A 25; savings not included in total.)	105,561	105,561
A 13	Courtyard re-evaluation	178,088	178,088
A 17	Raise hospital & building grade by 1 meter.	478,216	478,216
A 22	Raise partition size from 10 cm to 20 cm minimum in basement.	(28,627)	(28,627)
A 24	Combine nurses' dormitories and optimize design. Note: If G 10 implemented, savings are redundant. (Savings not included in total.)	2,485,815	3,668,118
A 25	Combine doctors' housing and optimize design. Note: If G 10 not implemented, these savings can be implemented. (Savings not included in total.)	4,467,605	7,206,288

Summary of Potential Cost Savings from VE Proposals

Hospital

A 27	Consider masonry exterior walls.	1,064,336	1,064,336
	Note: If G 10 or A 8 not implemented, these savings can be implemented. (Savings not included in total.)		
A 28	Internal floor finish - change granite to perlato sicilian.	271,200	271,200
A 29	Change OR floor finish to less expensive material.	361,600	361,600
	Architectural Total	**3,359,143**	**3,359,143**

PROPOSALS		Initial Savings	Life Cycle Savings
STRUCTURAL			
S 1,2,3,4	Reduce slab on grade thickness and use vapor barrier membrane.	156,808	156,808
S 7&8	Re-evaluate the use of hollow-core slabs & change floor-to-floor height (4.4)	(506,240)	(506,240)
S 14	Simplify ground-level heights.	478,216	478,216
	Structural Total	**128,784**	**128,784**
MECHANICAL			
M 2	Consider point use water coolers vs. central.	28,055	51,233
M 5	Consolidate sewage and waste lines.	205,333	205,333
M 6	Connect to Balada sewer; eliminates STP.	320,000	621,760
M 10	Consider using water-cooled chillers vs. air.	349,600	135,335
M 12	Use de-coupled loop piping.	35,467	55,648
M 14	Shade air-cooled chillers.	(20,000)	93,160
M 15	Increase CHW temperature rise.	85,500	116,417
M 19	Modify summer inside design conditions.	56,800	88,937
M 20	Reduction of OR airflow when not used.		36,196
M 21	Provide for HEPA filtered re-circulation of operating-room air.	28,576	24,379
M 22	Use central AHUs vs. fan coil units in patient rooms.	83,413	566,246
M 26	Cool computer rooms with AC units w/Econocoil.	27,333	34,877
M 28	Delete diesel fire pump and provide emerg. power.	28,000	53,147
M 29	Use CHW cooled units for substation/UPS cooling.	14,400	64,140
	Mechanical Total	**1,242,477**	**2,146,809**

Summary of Potential Cost Savings from VE Proposals

Hospital

PROPOSALS		Initial Savings	Life Cycle Savings
ELECTRICAL			
E 1,2&4	Reconfigure electrical distribution system.	1,659,473	1,831,818
E 1a	Consider alternate configuration.	1,272,621	1,424,745
E 5	Replace parabolic fixtures w/select prismatic lens.	205,316	395,344
E 6	Replace electronic ballast with high-power factor ballast.	262,865	403,272
E 10	Use GFI to control 1 circuit receptacles.	4,014	4,014
E 11	Reconfigure outdoor lighting.	93,413	184,512
E 14	Delete plumbing fixtures sensor.	15,730	33,733
E 15	Delete clocks in patient rooms.	26,035	45,668
E 16	Centralize UPS.	80,000	80,000
E 17	Change chillers supply voltage to 380 V.	56,952	56,952
E 20	Relocate switchgear room in basement.	106,667	106,667
	Electrical Total	**3,783,086**	**4,566,725**

PROPOSALS		Deferred Initial Cost	Initial Cost	Life Cycle Savings
MEDICAL EQUIPMENT				
ME 1	Consider leasing equipment for clinical labs.			
ME 2	Defer cardiac equipment.			
	Deferred Initial Cost	**1,250,000**		
ME 3	Defer MRI equipment			
	Deferred Initial Cost	**2,250,000**		
ME 4	Defer procurement of Nuclear Medicine/Gamma.			
	Deferred Initial Cost	**419,345**		
ME5	Add one additional ultrasound unit.		(28,500)	606,621
ME 6	Add 3 additional beds to hemodialysis (see A7 for new layout).			1,617,606
ME8	Optimize procurement of medical equipment / furniture / kitchen / laundry.		7,613,395	
ME9	Add mobile radiographic units.		(90,667)	2,723,200
	Deferred Initial Cost	**3,919,345**		
	Initial Savings		**7,494,228**	
	Present Worth of Additional Income			**4,947,427**
	Life Cycle Savings			**7,494,228**

Value Engineering Recommendation

Project: Hospital

Item: Revise Layout of Clinical Labs / Hemodialysis Department

VE Rec. No.

A 7

Original Design

The clinical labs and hemodialysis department are located between axis 10, 15 and A, F. They are divided into separate areas for blood donation, clinical lab and for hemodialysis.
See attached plan.

Proposed Design

Consider rearrangement of the clinical labs and blood donation as per Sketch No. A-7. The change allows for an improved separation between the donation area and clinical labs, and accessibility of outpatients to donation area. In addition, switching the donation area and hemodialysis area will allow an increase of 3 additional beds for hemodialysis patients.

Note: See ME 6 for overall savings generated.

Discussion, Advantages and Disadvantages

The rearranged layout improves the flow of outpatients to the labs and the blood donator to the donation area, keeping the required privacy of the clinical labs. It will allow the addition of hemodialysis beds that will increase the revenue of the hospital. Also, the present design does not accommodate pediatric patients. Additional beds will be designated for this purpose.

Original Design

	Unit	Quantity	Unit Cost	Total
Not applicable				
			Total Cost	**N.A.**

Proposed Design

	Unit	Quantity	Unit Cost	Total
Curtains		3	53	160
Chart dressing		3	400	1,200
Chair dialysis		3	1,333	4,000
Hemodialysis unit		3	24,000	72,000
Oxygen outlet		3	2,000	6,000
Medical air outlet		3	160	480
Medical vacuum outlet		3	133	400
Markup	%	0.13	84,240	10,951
			Total Cost	**$95,191**

Life Cycle Cost Summary

	Initial		Annual O&M
Original	N.A.		
Proposed	95,191		
Savings	-95,191		
PW Annual Savings at (Factor)		**9.43**	
TOTAL SAVINGS (Initial + PW Annual)			**($95,191)**

Sketch No. A7

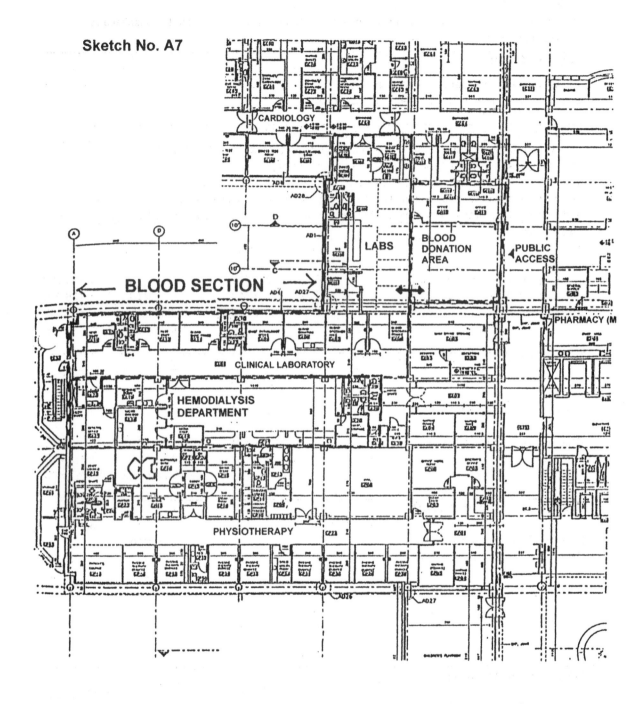

Value Engineering Recommendation

Project: Hospital

Item: Revise exterior precast panels for hospital and housing.

Original Design

Present design calls for 7" exterior precast concrete exterior wall panels for both the hospital and housing (see AD-1).

Proposed Design

1. Use 5" precast wall panels for hospital only.
2. Use CMU, plaster and texture paint for housing units.

Discussion, Advantages and Disadvantages

The team discussed panels with a local manufacturer, who indicated that a 5" panel would suffice. This change will result in considerable weight and cost savings.

The recommendation to use CMU, plaster and paint for the housing is based on budgetary resrictions. Maintenance costs should be slightly higher for the housing exteriors requiring painting and for the thinner precast wall panels. These costs should not exceed the value of $3,000/yr.

Original Cost

	Unit	Quantity	Unit Cost	Total
7" thick precast panels, hospital	SF	213,156	9.91	2,113,067
7" thick precast panels, housing	SF	114,594	9.91	1,136,000
Mark up	%	0.13	3,249,067	422,379
			Total Cost	3,671,445

Proposed Cost

	Unit	Quantity	Unit Cost	Total
5" thick precast panels for hospital building only	SF	213,156	6.20	1,320,667
CMU, plaster and paint, housing	SF	114,594	2.23	255,600
Mark up	%	0.13	1,576,267	204,915
			Total Cost	1,781,181

Operation Maintenance Savings

				Savings
Exterior Wall Maintenance - Original	LS	1	Based	
Exterior Wall Maintenance - Proposed	LS	1	3,000.00	3,000
			Savings	3,000

Life Cycle Cost Summary

	Initial		Annual O&M
Original	3,671,445		
Proposed	1,781,181		3,000
Savings	1,890,264		-3,000
PW Annual Savings at (Factor)		9.43	-28,278
TOTAL SAVINGS (Initial + PW Annual)			1,861,986

Value Engineering Recommendation

VE Rec. No. A 8

PROJECT: Hospital

ITEM: Revise exterior precast panels for hospital and housing

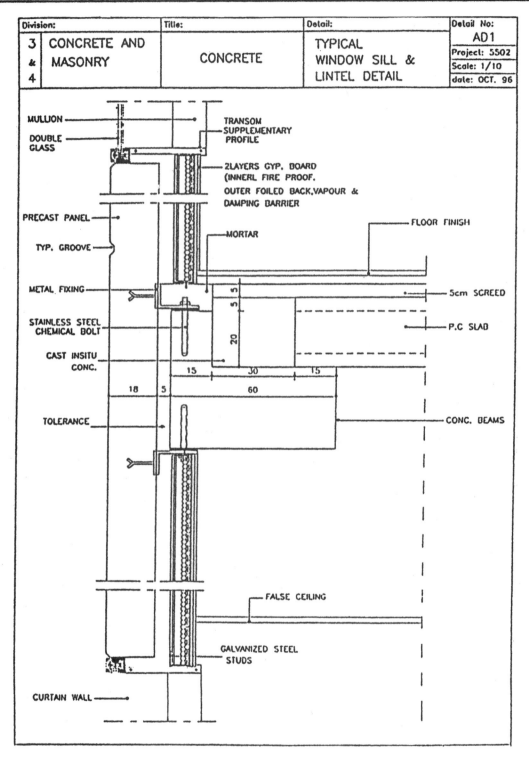

Division:	Title:	Detail:	Detail No: AD1
3 & 4 CONCRETE AND MASONRY	CONCRETE	TYPICAL WINDOW SILL & LINTEL DETAIL	Project: 5502 Scale: 1/10 date: OCT. 96

Value Engineering Recommendation

Project: Hospital	**VE Rec. No.**
Item: Reconfigure electrical distribution system.	**E 1,2&4**

Original Design

The design document shows a substation building of about 9,500 SF to house 6 transformers for both housing and hospital. After revising the loads to all facilities, the required transformers capacity will be 9000 KVA. From the substation, it is required to run about 59,000 LF of 3 x 300 plus 150 mm^2 low voltage cables complete with manholes and all supporting items to feed electrical loads in all buildings and chiller compound.

Proposed Design

The VE team recommends the use of high voltage distribution utilizing 13.8 KV network to different facilities and using oil-type transformer, outdoor mounted near load concentration. Pad mounted transformers of the loop feed type are recommended.

Discussion, Advantages and Disadvantages

The VE team feels that proposed design will result both in initial and LCC cost savings. In addition, better power distribution performance and improvement of service is achieved.

The only disadvantage is that the owner has to maintain the transformers. Maint. should not exceed 2 hours/yr. for each unit. Replacement costs are minimal when transformers are designed as they are at 80% of their capacity. Their life expectancy should not be less than 25 years. High voltage cables once properly installed needs no more maintenance time than low voltage cables.

Life Cycle Cost Summary

	Initial		Annual O&M
Original	2,449,594		32,464
Proposed	792,126		13,492
Savings	1,657,469		18,972
	PW Annual Savings at (Factor)	**9.43**	178,834
	TOTAL SAVINGS (Initial + PW Annual)		1,836,302

Cost Worksheet

Project: Hospital

Item: Reconfigure electrical distribution system

Original Design

	Unit	Quantity	Unit Cost	Total
Transformer type 1000 KVA	ea	9	33,333	300,000
High voltage switchgear 11 CBS, tie break.	ea	1	333,333	333,333
LV cables to 2 doctors' housing	LF	31,104	23	706,548
3 x 3000 + 150 mm^2 3%VD				
Cable to recreation building	LF	869	19	16,929
3 x 240 + 120 mm^2 2.73% UD				
Cable to main building	LF	5,906	23	134,155
3 x 300 + 150 mm^2 2.5%VD				
Cables to female dormitories	LF	2,789	23	63,351
3 x 300 + 150 mm^2 at 2.9%VD				
Cable to mosque	LF	279	15	4,073
3 x 185 + 95 mm^2 at 1.55%VD				
Cables to Hospital	LF	3,937	23	89,436
3 x 300 + 150 mm^2 at 1.25%VD				
Cables to chillers, MCC only	LF	13,780	23	313,028
3 x 300 + 150 mm^2				
Manholes	ea	7	1,200	8,400
Substation building	SF	3,385	55	184,556
HV cables 300 mm^2	LF	492	28	13,974
Markup (Contingencies)	%	0.13	2,167,783	281,812
			Total Cost	**2,449,594**

Operation and Maintenance Cost - Original

	Unit	Quantity	Unit Cost	Total
Maintenance cost	%	0.01	2,449,594	24,496
Operation cost / Power loss	KWhrs/yr	0.03	265,601	7,968
			Total Cost	**32,464**

Value Engineering Recommendation

Hospital

Reconfigure electrical distribution system

VE Rec. No.

E 1,2&4

Proposed Design

	Unit	Quantity	Unit Cost	Total
For Housing: Transformer pad-mount oil type 1500 KVA	ea	2	30,667	61,333
For Hospital: Transformer pad-mount oil type 1000 KVA	ea	2	25,333	50,667
For Chillers: Transformer pad-mounte oil type 2000 KVA	ea	2	44,000	88,000
HV switchgear incld. CBS for 1 incom outgoing, 4 for loop feed	ea	1	173,333	173,333
13.8 KV loop feed 300 mm^2	LF	3,281	28	93,163
Cables:				
For hospital: 3 x 300 + 150 mm^2	LF	1,312	23	29,812
For chiller: 3 x 300 + 150 mm^2	LF	2,297	23	52,171
For Doctors housing: 3 x 300 + 150 n	LF	2,625	23	59,624
Dorm: 3 x 95 + 150mm^2	LF	2,297	23	52,171
For Mosque: 3 x 95 + 50 mm^2	LF	328	8	2,662
For Recreation: 3 x 95 + 50 mm^2	LF	328	8	2,662
Building for switchgear & SCECo switchgear	SF	646	55	35,397
Mark up (Contingencies)	%	13%	700,996	91,130
			Total Cost	**792,126**

Operation and Maintenance Cost - Original

	Unit	Quantity	Unit Cost	Total
Maintenance cost	%	0.015	792,126	11,882
Operation cost / Power loss	KWhrs/yr	0.03	53,655	1,610
			Total Cost	**13,492**

Value Engineering Recommendation

Project: Hospital

Item: Add 3 Additional Beds to Hemodialysis Dept. (see A 7 for new layout)

VE Rec. No.

ME 6

Original Design

Present design call for 4 beds in hemodialysis.

Proposed Design

Revise design to add 3 additional beds to cover needs for pediatric patients & the prenatal units. Relocate the unit to a larger space (see A-7).

Discussion, Advantages and Disadvantages

This area is in demand. Hemodialysis is a needed service with long waiting lists at existing hospitals. The local market should be more than able to supply the need for the additional beds. The projected income will easily offset initial costs and help defray other expenses. At present, pediatric patients cannot be properly serviced.

See income projection and costs attached. Break-even is less than one year.

Life Cycle Cost Summary

	Initial	Annual O&M
Original		See present worth of additional annual income
Proposed	105,000	
Savings	-105,000	
PW Annual Savings at (Factor)		
TOTAL SAVINGS (Initial + PW Annual)		$1,617,600

Cost Worksheet

Project: Hospital

Item: Add 3 Beds to Hemodialysis Dept. (See A-7 for new layout)

VE Rec. No.

ME 6

Investment Analysis @ 20years @ 10%

	Unit	Quantity	Unit Cost	Total
Initial Cost				
Beds at $35,000	bed	3	35,000	105,000
			Subtotal	**105,000**
Replacement @ 8 years and 16 years				
PW @ 8 years		0.47		
PW @ 16 years		0.22		
	Total	0.69	105,000	**72,450**
Annual Cost				
Maintenance				
Main equipment	%	0.05	105,000	5,250
Operation supplies	$/yr	1	2,667	2,667
			Subtotal	**7,917**
Staffing				
Specialist	Staff	1.3	40,000	52,000
Technologist	Staff	1.3	21,333	27,733
			Subtotal	**79,733**

Income Projections (outlays in equivalent annual dollars)

	Unit	Quantity	Unit Cost	Total
Revenue			$/yr	**299,040**
Average case per wash	$	267		
Case per day (3 hrs per wash)	Case	4		
Days of operation per year	Day	280		

Break-even analysis -- Equivalent Annual Cost

(Initial + Replacement Cost) x PP				20,850
Initial		177,450		
PP		0.1175		
Maintenance and Operation				8,000
Staffing				79,733
			Total $/yr	**108,584**

Break-even in $/yr = Equivalent annual cost of expenditures / annual income

       = $108,584/yr / $298,667/yr = 0.36years or less than 5 months

PW = Annual Income x PWA   = 190,083 x 8,561 =   **$1,617,600**

     Annual Income = Income - Expense = 298,667 - 108,583 = $ 190,083

     PWA   8.51

Refinery Facility

I n 1993 a value engineering study was performed as one component of a training program at a refinery facility in California. Three teams, studied the facility from the following points of view: layout, process, and electrical/mechanical/piping.

On final implementation, 60%—or approximately $35,000,000—in savings were realized, representing an 11% reduction. Follow-on annual savings were $500,000/year.

Case Study Elements

The items below and shown in this case study have been excerpted from an actual VE report. (The Table of Contents on page 245 is one of the excerpts and refers to some documents not listed here or shown in the section.)

VALUE ENGINEERING REPORT

Refinery Project

TABLE OF CONTENTS

This is the Table of Contents from the actual VE report.
Selected excerpts appear in this case study.

Value Engineering Report

Refinery Project

EXECUTIVE SUMMARY

This report presents the results of a 1993 value engineering (VE) study as part of a training effort for the proposed subject facility. There were three study teams for the refinery facilities located overseas: layout, process, and mechanical/piping/electrical. These teams comprised some 15 professionals from the oil company and their consultants. This Executive Summary describes their efforts.

Team 1: Project Layout

The team conducted a component function analysis and developed a Function Analysis System Technique (FAST) Diagram as an aid to understanding the present design. The team generated 64 ideas, from which four were selected for development. In addition, the team developed 12 design suggestions.

The principal proposals were to consolidate the site to reduce interface cost, reduce the size, and consolidate buildings to reflect required rather than desired future requirements. The team isolated potential savings of some $8.5 million in initial costs.

Team 2: Process

The team reviewed the process flow for the project and developed a component function analysis and FAST Diagram. The team generated 44 ideas, from which four proposals and five design suggestions were generated. These would result in $38 million in VE recommendations. An additional $1 million in annual cost savings would also be achieved.

The principal proposals were to combine or delete excessively redundant type tanks, use seawater for process cooling, reduce the number of seawater pumps, and eliminate pipeline scrapers.

Team 3: Electrical/Mechanical/Piping

The team reviewed a myriad of functional areas from their function and FAST analyses. The team focused on the piping as well as the electrical comments generated by the electrical team. The team generated 32 ideas and developed five proposals with estimated savings of $7.6 million, and 24 mechanical and electrical design suggestions estimated at $2.2 million in additional savings.

The principal proposals were to eliminate one product loading arm at the port facility because of its poor value; eliminate some of the excessive fill requirement in the off-plot tank area; install the main electrical distribution line above ground; and reduce the size of the main transformers closer to actual needs. Some key design suggestions were to eliminate the 15% overdesign for tanks, use earthen berms for the site, reduce pump spares, and delete one of the pipe launchers and receivers.

Total Impact

The total impact of this workshop was to identify potential savings in initial costs of about $55 million. This represents approximately 17% of the planned investment for the project areas studied.

Another $1 million in annual operations and maintenance savings could be accomplished if all of the ideas were implemented.

Careful follow-on study should be given to the design suggestions that have a potential additional savings in excess of $2 million.

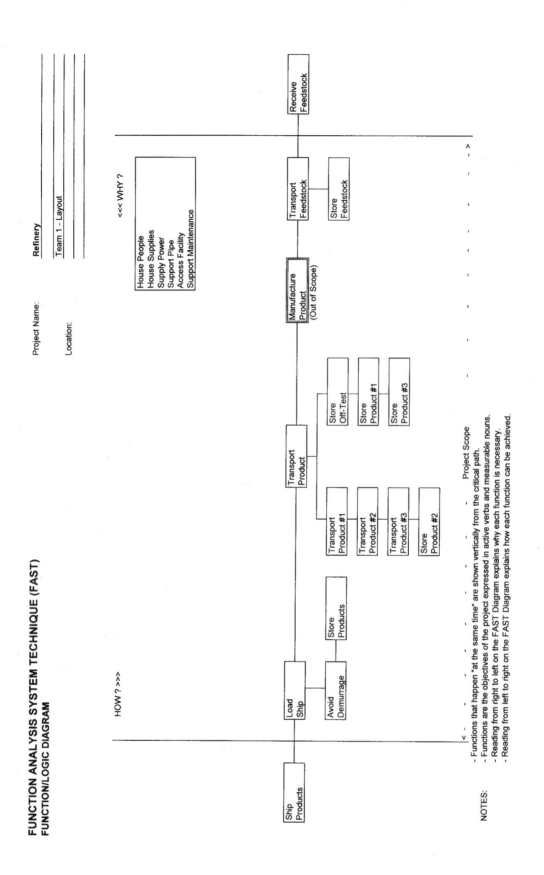

FUNCTION ANALYSIS SYSTEM TECHNIQUE (FAST)
FUNCTION/LOGIC DIAGRAM

Project Name: **Refinery**

Location: Team 1 - Layout

<<< WHY ?

HOW ? >>>

House People
House Supplies
Supply Power
Support Pipe
Access Facility
Support Maintenance

Receive Feedstock

Transport Feedstock

Store Feedstock

Manufacture Product
(Out of Scope)

Transport Product

Store Off-Test

Store Product #1

Store Product #3

Transport Product #1

Transport Product #2

Transport Product #3

Store Product #2

Load Ship

Store Products

Avoid Demurrage

Ship Products

— | — Project Scope

NOTES:
- Functions that happen "at the same time" are shown vertically from the critical path.
- Functions are the objectives of the project expressed in active verbs and measurable nouns.
- Reading from right to left on the FAST Diagram explains why each function is necessary.
- Reading from left to right on the FAST Diagram explains how each function can be achieved.

FUNCTION ANALYSIS SYSTEM TECHNIQUE (FAST)
FUNCTION/LOGIC DIAGRAM

Project Name: **Refinery**

Location: Team 2 - Process

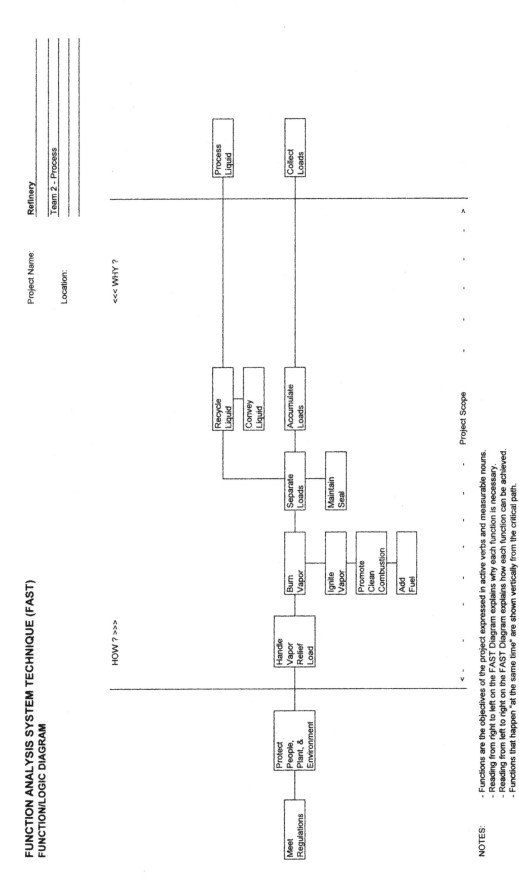

HOW ? >>>

<<< WHY ?

Project Scope

NOTES:
- Functions are the objectives of the project expressed in active verbs and measurable nouns.
- Reading from right to left on the FAST Diagram explains why each function is necessary.
- Reading from left to right on the FAST Diagram explains how each function can be achieved.
- Functions that happen "at the same time" are shown vertically from the critical path.

FUNCTION ANALYSIS SYSTEM TECHNIQUE (FAST)

Project Name: **Refinery**
Electrical Distribution
Team 3a

Location:

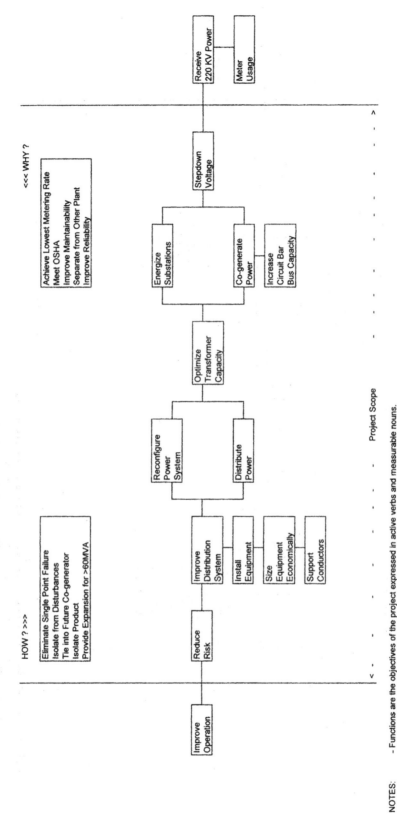

HOW ? >>>

<<< WHY ?

Eliminate Single Point Failure
Isolate from Disturbances
Tie into Future Co-generator
Isolate Product
Provide Expansion for >60MVA

Achieve Lowest Metering Rate
Meet OSHA
Improve Maintainability
Separate from Other Plant
Improve Reliability

Improve Operation

Reduce Risk

Improve Distribution System

Install Equipment

Size Equipment Economically

Support Conductors

Reconfigure Power System

Distribute Power

Optimize Transformer Capacity

Energize Substations

Co-generate Power

Increase Circuit Bar Bus Capacity

Stepdown Voltage

Receive 220 KV Power

Meter Usage

Project Scope

NOTES:

- Functions are the objectives of the project expressed in active verbs and measurable nouns.
- Reading from left to right on the FAST Diagram explains why each function is necessary.
- Reading from right to left on the FAST Diagram explains how each function can be achieved.
- Functions that happen "at the same time" are shown vertically from the critical path.

FUNCTION ANALYSIS SYSTEM TECHNIQUE (FAST)
FUNCTION/LOGIC DIAGRAM

HOW ? >>>   <<< WHY ?

```
Ship          Load          Store         Transfer      Store         Test          Recycle       Produce
Product       Product       Off-Site      Product       Off-Plot      Product       Off-Test      Product
                                                                                     Product

              Operate       Burn          Operate       Transfer      Transfer
              Loading       Vapor         Pipelines     Product       Product
              Arms

              Burn          Meter         Operate       Operate       Operate
              Vapor         Product       Pumps         Pipelines     Pipelines

                                          Operate       Burn          Operate
                                          Pumps         Vapor         Pumps
```

v   Project Scope   ^

NOTES: - Functions are the objectives of the project expressed in active verbs and measurable nouns.
        - Reading from right to left on the FAST Diagram explains why each function is necessary.
        - Reading from left to right on the FAST Diagram explains how each function can be achieved.
        - Functions that happen "at the same time" are shown vertically from the critical path.

COST/WORTH MODEL

VALUE ENGINEERING STUDY

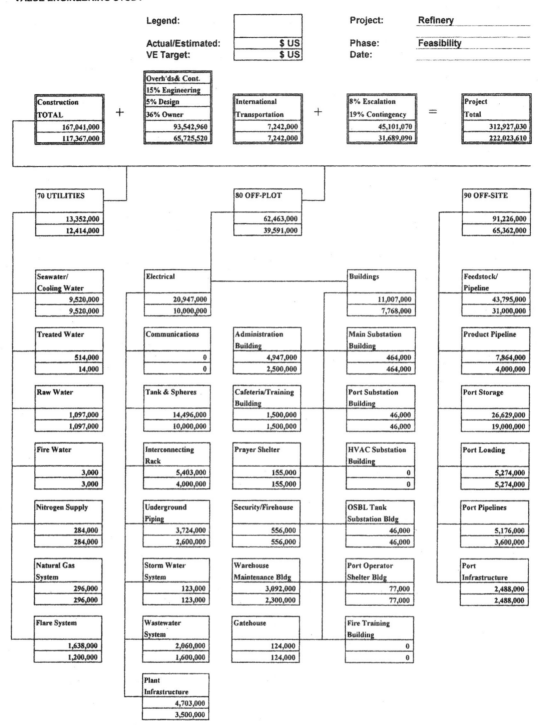

Legend:		
Actual/Estimated:	$ US	
VE Target:	$ US	

Project: **Refinery**

Phase: **Feasibility**

Date:

Construction TOTAL
167,041,000
117,367,000

+

Overh'ds& Cont.
15% Engineering
5% Design
36% Owner
93,542,960
65,725,520

International Transportation
7,242,000
7,242,000

+

8% Escalation
19% Contingency
45,101,070
31,689,090

=

Project Total
312,927,030
222,023,610

70 UTILITIES
13,352,000
12,414,000

80 OFF-PLOT
62,463,000
39,591,000

90 OFF-SITE
91,226,000
65,362,000

Seawater/ Cooling Water	Electrical		Buildings	Feedstock/ Pipeline
9,520,000	20,947,000		11,007,000	43,795,000
9,520,000	10,000,000		7,768,000	31,000,000

Treated Water	Communications	Administration Building	Main Substation Building	Product Pipeline
514,000	0	4,947,000	464,000	7,864,000
14,000	0	2,500,000	464,000	4,000,000

Raw Water	Tank & Spheres	Cafeteria/Training Building	Port Substation Building	Port Storage
1,097,000	14,496,000	1,500,000	46,000	26,629,000
1,097,000	10,000,000	1,500,000	46,000	19,000,000

Fire Water	Interconnecting Rack	Prayer Shelter	HVAC Substation Building	Port Loading
3,000	5,403,000	155,000	0	5,274,000
3,000	4,000,000	155,000	0	5,274,000

Nitrogen Supply	Underground Piping	Security/Firehouse	OSBL Tank Substation Bldg	Port Pipelines
284,000	3,724,000	556,000	46,000	5,176,000
284,000	2,600,000	556,000	46,000	3,600,000

Natural Gas System	Storm Water System	Warehouse Maintenance Bldg	Port Operator Shelter Bldg	Port Infrastructure
296,000	123,000	3,092,000	77,000	2,488,000
296,000	123,000	2,300,000	77,000	2,488,000

Flare System	Wastewater System	Gatehouse	Fire Training Building	
1,638,000	2,060,000	124,000	0	
1,200,000	1,600,000	124,000	0	

Plant Infrastructure
4,703,000
3,500,000

VALUE ENGINEERING REPORT

REFINERY PROJECT

SECTION 4 - SUMMARY OF RESULTS

GENERAL

This section of the value engineering study summarizes the results and recommendations for the study. Ideas that were developed are submitted here as recommendations for acceptance.

It is important when reviewing the results of the VE study to review each part of a recommendation on its own merits. Often there is a tendency to disregard a recommendation because of concern about one portion of it. When reviewing this report, consideration should be given to the areas within a recommendation that are acceptable and apply those parts to the final design.

VALUE ENGINEERING RECOMMENDATIONS

The value engineering teams developed 13 VE proposals for change based on the current design and 41 design suggestions having a potential initial cost savings of some $60 million and present worth life cycle cost savings of $68 million. One additional proposal (P-44) is not included in the above totals because it is an alternate which was not fully developed and affects ROI. The table below provides a summary of proposals.

Recommendation Category	Ref. Code	No. Proposal	Initial Cost Savings	Total PW Cost Savings
VE Proposals				
Layout	L	4	8,540,000	8,422,000
Process	P	4	38,700,000	47,177,000
Mechanical	M	5	7,662,000	7,874,500
TOTALS		13	54,902,000	63,473,500
Design Suggestions				
Layout	L	12	2,900,000	2,900,000
Process	P	5	25,000	45,000
Mech/Elec	M/E	24	2,180,000	2,180,000
TOTALS		41	5,105,000	5,125,000
GRAND TOTALS		54	$60,007,000	$68,598,500

SUMMARY OF POTENTIAL COST SAVINGS FROM VE RECOMMENDATIONS

NO.	DESCRIPTION	INITIAL COST SAVINGS	ANNUAL O&M COST SAVINGS	TOTAL PW COST SAVINGS
LAYOUT TEAM				
L-2	Reduce Size of Admin. Building	4,590,000	(21,000)	4,010,000
L-3	Combine Buildings	990,000	11,000	1,118,000
L-10	Revise Layout of Site	2,660,000	26,000	2,940,000
L-27	Combine MCC and Control Room	300,000	5,000	354,000
L-DS	Design Suggestions	2,900,000		2,900,000
	Layout Totals	$11,440,000	$21,000	$11,322,000
PROCESS TEAM				
P-14	Use Seawater for Process Cooling	3,100,000	257,000	6,432,000
P-17	Eliminate/Reduce Seawater Pumps	1,500,000	(60,000)	987,000
P-25	Product Pipeline Scrapers	300,000	(17,000)	158,300
P-36	Combine/Reduce Size of Storage/Port Tanks	33,800,000	685,000	39,600,000
P-44	Reconfigure Plant to Make no Benzene[1]	123,000,000[1]	3,500,000[1]	153,000,000[1]
P-DS	Design Suggestions	25,000	2,000	45,000
	Process Totals	$38,725,000	$867,000	$47,222,300

Note: [1] Idea is not fully evaluated, needs further study, and is not included in totals.

SUMMARY OF POTENTIAL COST SAVINGS FROM VE RECOMMENDATIONS

NO.	DESCRIPTION	INITIAL COST SAVINGS	ANNUAL O&M COST SAVINGS	TOTAL PW COST SAVINGS
MECHANICAL/PIPING TEAM				
M-10	Eliminate One Loading Arm	1,980,000	(50,000)	1,555,000
M-17	Combine Wastewater & Off-Plot Tankfeed	118,000	80,000	798,000
M-21	Eliminate Tank Area Fill	400,000	(5,000)	357,500
E-2	Reevaluate Substation	864,000		864,000
E-3	Revise 115 KV Plant Feed	4,300,000		4,300,000
M-DS	Design Suggestions	2,180,000		2,180,000
E-DS	Electrical Design Suggestions	TBD	TBD	TBD
	Mechanical/Piping Totals	$9,842,000	$25,000	$10,054,500
	Grand Total	**$60,007,000**	**$913,000**	**$68,598,800**

VALUE ENGINEERING RECOMMENDATION   NO. L-10

PROJECT: Refinery Projects
ITEM: Revise Layout of Site

ORIGINAL DESIGN

Layout and flow sequences are shown on Attachment I. Refinery and product store tanks run along the north side of the site. Feed enters at (1), goes to tank at (2) and back to Refinery at (3). Products flow from (3) to (4) C_6 (benz), (4) four other product types (mixed parts). Then all products flow from tanks to point (5).

PROPOSED DESIGN

Various rearrangements were considered as a means to reduce pipe costs. They are briefly described and comparatively ranked on the attached Weighted Evaluation sheet.

As shown, the highest ranked alternate was based on moving the tanks to the south of Refinery and moving all hydrocarbon products facilities to the east. Most personnel and utility facilites move to the west near the site center. All the future siting is moved to the far west. The rearrangement is shown on the attached sketch. Lengths were scaled from the drawings.

DISCUSSION

The primary driver for this proposal was to minimize the piping to carry the back and forth flow sequences. The result was a reduction in on-site piping from 7,847 meters to 4,499 meters.

Added costs of moving building further from water and power supplies are assumed balanced by cost reduction in moving wastewater treatment and surge ponds closer to the wastewater pumping station.

LIFE CYCLE COST SUMMARY	Capital	Annual O&M
Original	$ 6,028,000	$60,000
Proposed	$ 3,368,000	$34,000
Savings	$ 2,660,000	$26,000

LIFE CYCLE (PW) SAVINGS	$ 2,940,000

VALUE ENGINEERING RECOMMENDATION   NO. L-10

PROJECT: Refinery Projects
ITEM: Revise Layout of Site

Piping Unit Cost Determination

Extension of off-site pipeline to feed storage tanks:

> Line cost $43,795,000 for 67.5 km length; this is $649/m.
> Information is from area/unit 90-90 from cost estimate.

On-site hydrocarbon piping, except cyclohexanes:

> Cost from estimate is $5,332,000, and length from layout drawing is 6,030 m. Thus, unit cost is $884/m.

Cyclohexane pipe is 852 meters long and costs $71,000. Unit cost is then $83.30/m.

PROJECT: Refinery Projects
ITEM: Revise Layout of Site

Original Layout

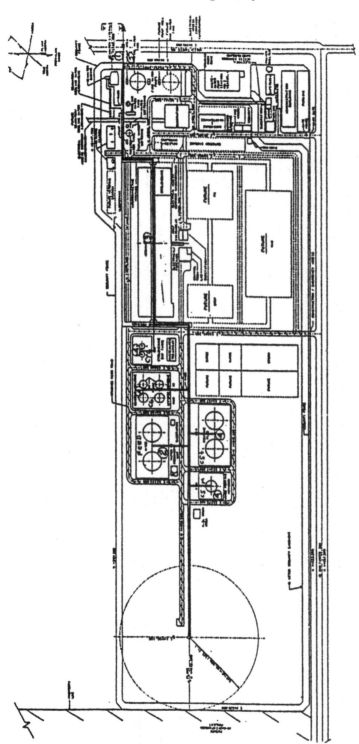
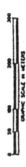

PROJECT: Refinery Projects
ITEM: Revise Layout of Site

Proposed Layout

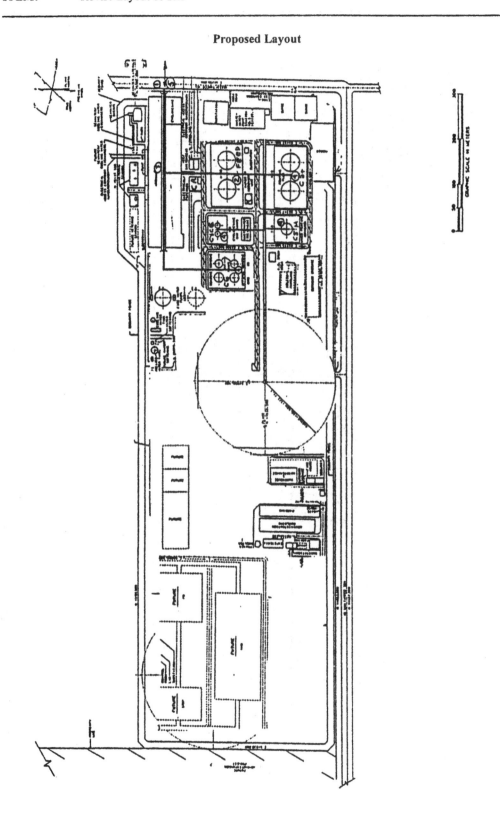

Weighted Evaluation
Project: Refinery Facility

Revise Layout of Site

Criteria
Criteria Scoring Matrix

How Important:

4- Major Preference
3 -Above Average Preference
2 -Average Preference
1-Slight Preference
 -Letter / Letter
 -No Preference
 -Each Scored One Point

A. *Safety on/off Site*

A-2

B. *Operations & Maintenance*

A-1/C-1

C-1   A-1

C. *Environmental Impact*

C-D

D-1

D. *Initial Costs*

E.

F.

G.

Analysis Matrix
Alternatives

		G	F	E	D	C	B	A	
Raw Score					2	3	1*	4	
Weight of Importance (0 - 10)					5	8	3	10	**Total**
1. *Existing Design*					10 / 2	40 / 5	12 / 4	40 / 4	102
2. *Move tanks south*					20 / 4	40 / 5	15 / 5	30 / 3	105
3. *Move all HC to SE Support Fac. N&W*					15 / 3	40 / 5	12 / 4	50 / 5	117*
4. *Switch tank sites*					10 / 2	40 / 5	6 / 2	40 / 4	96
5.									
6.									
7.									

*Arbitrarily assigned score of 1 to keep in evalutation.
5 -Excellent   4 -Very Good   3 -Good   2 -Fair   1 -Poor

COST WORKSHEET RECOMMENDATION   NO. L-10

PROJECT: Refinery Projects
ITEM: Revise Layout of Site

Item	Quan.	Meas.	Unit Cost	Total
ORIGINAL DESIGN				
Pipeline extension to feed tank	965	m	649.00	626,285
Feed tank to Refinery	630	m	884.00	556,920
Refinery to 1st storage to site edge	1374	m	884.00	1,214,616
Refinery to 2nd storage to site edge	1435	m	884.00	1,268,540
Refinery to 3rd storage to site edge	1643	m	884.00	1,452,412
Refinery to 4th storage to site edge	852	m	83.30	70,972
Refinery to flare	948	m	884.00	838,032
Total				$6,027,777
PROPOSED DESIGN				
Pipeline extension to feed tank	326	m	649.00	211,574
Feed tank to Refinery	139	m	884.00	122,876
Refinery to 1st storage to site edge	917	m	884.00	810,628
Refinery to 2nd storage to site edge	752	m	884.00	664,768
Refinery to 3rd storage to site edge	1022	m	884.00	903,448
Refinery to 4th storage to site edge	665	m	83.30	55,395
Refinery to flare	678	m	884.00	599,352
Total				$-3,368,041
SAVINGS				**$ 2,659,736**

LIFE CYCLE COST WORKSHEET RECOMMENDATION   NO. L-10

PROJECT: Refinery Projects
ITEM: Revise Layout of Site

Discount Rate: 10%
Economic Life: 20 years

PRESENT WORTH ANALYSIS

| | | (Costs all $ x 1,000) | | | |
| | | Original | | Proposed | |
	Factor	Estim. Costs	PW Costs	Estim. Costs	PW Costs
INITIAL COSTS					
Pipelines	1	6,028	6,028	3,368	3,368
Total initial cost	1	6,028	6,028	3,368	3,368
REPLACEMENT COSTS					
Not applicable					
Total repl. cost		0		0	
ANNUAL COSTS					
Assume maintenance equals 1% of investment					
Maintenance	10.7	60	642	34	364
Total Annual Costs		60		34	
Total Annual Costs (PW)			642		364
TOTAL PW COSTS			6,670		3,732
					-3,732
LIFE CYCLE PRESENT WORTH SAVINGS					**$2,938**

VALUE ENGINEERING RECOMMENDATION   NO. P-36

PROJECT: Refinery Projects
ITEM: Combine/Reduce Size Storage/Port Tanks

ORIGINAL DESIGN

Feed: Feed arrives from source to one of two stock tanks. While one is filling, the other feeds the process.

Interim Product Storage: Benzene and cyclohexane run down to day tanks for checking product quality prior to shipment to the port. If off-spec, they are re-run via an off-spec tank. On-spec Benzene goes to a product tank for either shipment to port or for local sale.

By-product Storage: The two by-products run down to day storage prior to batch shipment down a common line.

PROPOSED DESIGN

Feed: Feed directly to process. A feed stock tank is provided to, a) keep the plant on-line during a feed line interruption, b) provide surge in case plant is off-line and c) catch off-spec product for rerun.

Interim Product Storage: None is provided on-site. All products run down directly to the port. Product quality is continuously monitored by line sampling. If a product is off-spec it is routed directly to the process or to the feed stock tank.

By-product Storage: All by-products are shipped directly to the port in dedicated lines.

DISCUSSION

The excess tankage and associated large volume pumps and large diameter piping represent a textbook "cost of quality." Changing paradigms involving break tanks will result in significant cost savings of $25.25 million without sacrificing/compromising the operation. The perceived improved reliability of the original system is just that, at a very high cost of initial capital outlay, greater maintenance (more/larger pumps, more instrumentation, more monitoring wells, etc.) and permanent cash tied up of $11.5 million in the hydrocarbon inventory of these tanks.

LIFE CYCLE COST SUMMARY	Capital	Annual O&M
Original	$ 60,900,000	$ 830,000
Proposed	$ 27,100,000	$ 145,000
Savings	$ 33,800,000	$ 685,000

LIFE CYCLE (PW) SAVINGS		$ 39,600,000

VALUE ENGINEERING RECOMMENDATION

PROJECT: Refinery Projects
ITEM: Combine/Reduce Size Storage/Port Tanks

DISCUSSION (Continued)

Feed: The feed from the field must be approximately equal to the process feed at any given time. So why not feed the plant directly? A booster pump may need to be run to do this, but the charge pump can remain off. Only one charge pump is required as it is in intermittent service. A spare can be warehoused. The feed stock tank is available to catch off-spec, to catch feed if the process is down, or to feed the plant if the pipeline is down.

Interim Product Storage: It is not possible to get a representative sample of an 8,000 - 14,000 bbl tank as the contents are not well mixed. If the tank is off-spec, then 8,000 - 14,000 bbl of material must be reprocessed. Not only is the cost to process this material lost the first time, but an equivalent amount of new feed will never be processed - a permanent revenue loss. Instead, check product quality continuously, if a reliable on-line analyzer exists and/or through frequent sampling. Operator intervention should occur as soon as the problem shows up instead of risking an 8,000 - 14,000 bbl batch to be spoiled. Local sales can be taken right off the run-down line. If the rate isn't sufficient, flow can be reversed in the off-plot line by shipping back from the port. Off-spec products are routed back to the front end (or into the process immediately). This will be similar to product handling during start-up as the process becomes lined-out.

By-products: Send these directly to the port. There does not seem to be a good reason for on-site storage.

Savings in Associated Facilities:
       Reduce quantity of monitoring wells
       Smaller VRS required (only one tank vs. four)
       Eliminate N2 pad for 6 tanks
       Eliminate N6 pad for 3 tanks
       Eliminate 14 pumps
       Replace 5 miles of 10", 12", and 14" line with
              1 - 4", 2 - 6" and 1 - 8" line
       Reduction in energy costs for extra pumping
       Increase reliability (less pumping & VRS equipment in chain)

Basis for Savings:

o   Ability to frequently sample, analyze, and take action (must be able to operate a chromatograph 24 hours/day).

o   Process has sufficient stability to allow normal operation under spec.

o   Any required blending can be done at the port.

PROJECT: Refinery Projects
ITEM: Combine/Reduce Size Storage/Port Tanks

Original Layout

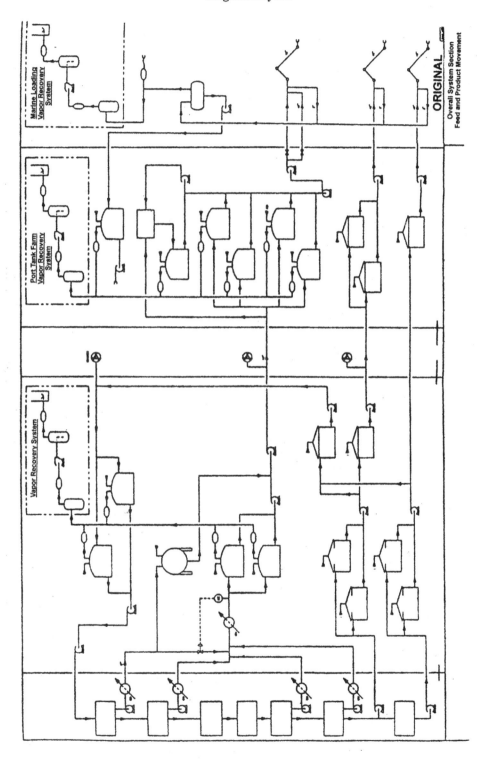

VALUE ENGINEERING RECOMMENDATION

NO. P-36

PROJECT: Refinery Projects
ITEM: Combine/Reduce Size Storage/Port Tanks

Proposed Layout

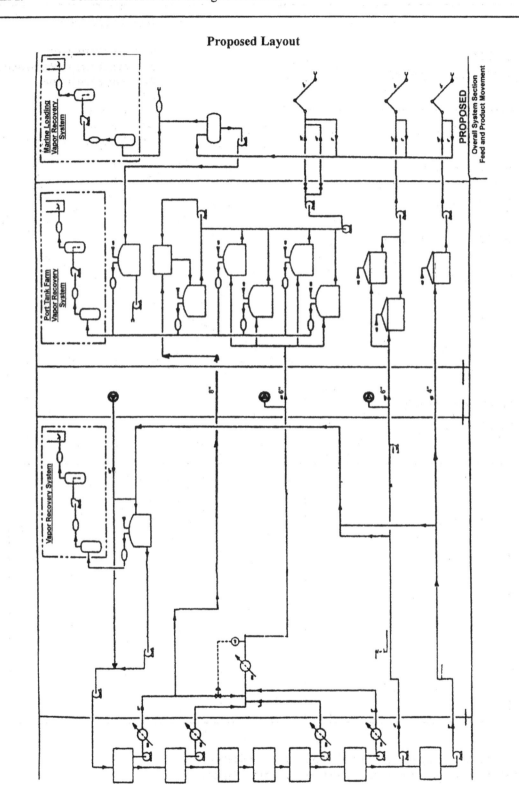

Weighted Evaluation

Project: Refinery Facility

Combine / Reduce Size Storage / Port Tanks

VE: *P - 36*

Criteria
Criteria Scoring Matrix

How Important:

4 - Major Preference
3 - Above Average Preference
2 - Average Preference
1 - Slight Preference
 - Letter / Letter
 - No Preference
 - Each Scored One Point

A. *Initial Costs*

A-4

B. *Energy Costs*

A-2

C-2   A-3

C. *Operability*

D-1   A-2

C-2   E-2

D. *Maintainability*

E-2

E-2

E. *Reliability*

F.

G.

	G	F	E	D	C	B	A	Total
Raw Score			6	1	4	0	11	
Weight of Importance (0 - 10)			6	2	5	1*	10	

Analysis Matrix
Alternatives

	G	F	E	D	C	B	A	Total
1. *Original*			24 / 4	6 / 3	20 / 4	3 / 3	20 / 2	73
2. *Proposed*			30 / 5	10 / 5	2 / 4	5 / 5	50 / 5	115*
3.								
4.								
5.								
6.								
7.								

* Arbitrarily assigned a score of 1 to keep in evaluation.
5 - Excellent   4 - Very Good   3 - Good   2 - Fair   1 - Poor

COST WORKSHEET

VE RECOMMENDATION NO. P-36

PROJECT: Refinery Projects
ITEM: Combine/Reduce Size Storage/Port Tanks

Item	Quan.	Meas.	Unit Cost	Total ($ x 1,000)
ORIGINAL DESIGN				
Tanks & spheres	572	bbls	12.28	7,024
Pumps	1	ls	1661.00	1,661
VRS	572	bbls	.52	297
Bulks & associated				
equipment (OSBL)	30	pc	317.30	9,519
P/L's to port (unit 90-91)	36	dia-in	190.47	6,857
Electrical (guess from 80-88)	2580	kw	.75	1,935
Subtotal				27,293
Markup	27293	$	.81	22,107
Total				$ 49,400
PROPOSED DESIGN				
Tank	115	bbls	12.28	1,412
Pumps (increase ISBL head)	1	ls	200.00	200
VRS	115	bbls	.60	69
Bulks & associated				
equipment (OSBL) 5-1/2 pc	1	ls	3440.00	3,440
P/L's to port (unit 90-91)	24	dia-in	224.00	5,376
Electrical (orig = 18 pumps)	3	pumps	221.00	663
Subtotal				11,160
Markup	11160	$	1.17	13,057
Total				$ -24,217

SAVINGS

$ 25,183

LIFE CYCLE COST WORKSHEET RECOMMENDATION   NO. P-36

PROJECT: Refinery Projects
ITEM: Combine/Reduce Size Storage/Port Tanks

Discount Rate: 10%
Economic Life: 20 years

PRESENT WORTH ANALYSIS

		Original		Proposed	
		Estim. PW		PW		Estim.
	Factor	Costs	Costs	Costs	Costs
INITIAL COSTS					
Construction	1	49,400	49,400	24,200	24,200
Working capital	1	11,500	11,500	2,900	2,900
Total initial cost		60,900	60,900	27,100	27,100
REPLACEMENT COSTS					
Not included					
Total repl. cost			0		0
ANNUAL COSTS					
Operations	8.51	830	7,063	145	1,234
Total Annual Costs			830		145
Total Annual Costs (PW)			7,063		1,234
TOTAL PW COSTS			**67,963**		**28,334**
					-28,334
LIFE CYCLE PRESENT WORTH SAVINGS					**$39,629**

(Costs all $ x 1,000)

VALUE ENGINEERING RECOMMENDATION NO. E-3

PROJECT: Refinery Projects
ITEM: Revise 115 KV Plant Feed from Underground to Above Ground

---

ORIGINAL DESIGN

A 115 KV plant feed is to be installed underground from the power company substation 4.3 km to the main substation.

PROPOSED DESIGN

Install the 115 KV plant feed above ground. (See attached)

DISCUSSION

Local utility requires 115 KV installation underground. The VE team feels above ground would be less expensive and is suitable for an industrial area. A waiver should be requested to implement this proposal.

LIFE CYCLE COST SUMMARY	Capital	Salvage	Annual O&M
Original	$ 6,347,000	$	$
Proposed	$ 2,047,000	$	$
Savings	$ 4,300,000	$ NA	$ NA

LIFE CYCLE (PW) SAVINGS $ 4,300,000

COST WORKSHEET

PROJECT: Refinery Projects
ITEM: 115 KV Plant Feed

Item	Quan.	Meas.	Unit Cost	Total
ORIGINAL DESIGN				
2 feeders, 3" cable ea (use $25/lf/cable x 6 units)	84,624	lf	25.00	2,115,600
Installation (use $100/lf)	14,104	lf	100.00	1,410,400
Subtotal				3,526,000
Markup indirects (.8)	3,526,000	$	.8	2,820,800
Total				$6,346,800
PROPOSED DESIGN				
2 feeders, 3" cable ea (use $10/lf/cable x 6 units)	84,624	lf	10.00	846,240
Towers at 500' spacing	30	ea	5000.00	150,000
Installation (use $10/lf)	14,104	lf	10.00	141,040
Subtotal				1,137,280
Markup indirects (.8)	1,137,280	$	.8	909,824
Total				$-2,047,104

SAVINGS   **$ 4,299,696**

Master Planning Competition

O ver the years, the author has had the opportunity to participate in several international design competitions. In 1995, he was a consultant in the RFP development for the Master Planning Competition, and he served on the jury for the following competition entry: a large $1 billion hotel, apartment, and shopping complex.[1] The competition offered an opportunity to apply value engineering concepts and techniques.

Development of Request for Proposal

Using the techniques of the Information Phase of the VE Job Plan, the project management (PM) team conducted research into RFPs for similar projects, taking advantage of the resources offered by the American Institute of Architects' library files. The PM team collected a dozen RFPs from large projects in the U.S. and abroad, and developed the competition RFP using these documents, AIA data, and creative input from the project management (PM) team. The development of the RFP was in line with underlying VE methodologies.

In general, *value* is defined in terms of *use, cost, exchange,* or *esteem.* Originally, VE concepts were often unable to temper results with criteria other than cost. However, cost is not always the dominant criterion in selecting alternate design concepts. Over the years, the author developed a weighted evaluation process for selecting the A/E for major projects that would moderate the solely cost-oriented approach of VE. This process weighed cost against other factors, such as experience, availability, and staff. The selection process was modified and adopted for use in VE, and it was implemented in this competition. (See the discussion of weighted evaluation in Chapter Seven.)

The competition evaluation criteria were developed by the PM, and modified by the owner and selected jury members through an exercise in group dynamics. These criteria were incorporated into the request for proposal and were listed under Part II, "Procedural Rules," of the RFP Table of Contents, which is included in this case study.

The Selection Process

A concurrent task involved the selection of jury members. It took months to research and gather the top consultants available at the time and place of the selection. Jury members representing the top professionals in the major areas of the project were chosen.

The agenda was developed according to the Delphi Method and the VE philosophy of applying an organized approach to problem solving. (See Chapter Six for further discussion of the Delphi techniques.) The costing exercises used the budget systems developed in the VE process. Creativity and brainstorming were encouraged throughout, and group dynamics and sensitivity to human factors were key instruments in optimizing the efforts and results.

Results

The results of the process were acclaimed by the owner, the exhibitors (the design teams), and the project manager. The principal comments generated were as follows.

The process was
- well organized,
- based on a set of requirements that was well thought out,
- covered all of the essential elements, and
- resulted in the fairest competition for participants.

Case Study Elements

The items listed below and shown in this case study have been excerpted from an actual VE report. (The Table of Contents on page 275 is one of the excerpts and refers to some documents not listed here or shown in the section.)

[1]The author would like to thank the Abdul Latif Jameel Real Estate Investment Co., Ltd. of Jiddah, Saudi Arabia, for the opportunity to work for them. In particular, General Manager Mohammed Ibrahim Al-Abdan and Engineering & Projects Director Mohammed M. Abdul Qadir were exceptional people to work with.

Case Study Four   Master Planning Competition

Request for Proposal

Hotel, Apartment, and Shopping Center Development Project

Table of Contents

This is the Table of Contents from the actual Request for Proposal. Selected excerpts appear in this case study.

Request for Proposal

Hotel, Apartment, and Shopping Center Development Project

Table of Contents (Continued)

Appendices

A. Profile & Brochure of the Owner

B. Topographic Map

C. Existing Site Infrastructure

D. Property Limits

Video

A. Prepared by the Owner of the Project Site

Photographs

This is the Table of Contents from the actual Request for Proposal. Selected excerpts appear in this case study.

Jury Report

Master Planning Competition

for

Hotel, Apartment, and Shopping Center Development

Table of Contents

* Not included in the excerpts

This is the Table of Contents from the actual Jury Report.
Selected excerpts appear in this case study.

Section I: Overview and Results

1. Summation and Recommendation

In October, the Jury presented the results of their deliberation to the Owner, and their representatives, consistent with the following Evaluation Summary:

Exhibit	A	B	C	D	E
Reference #	721 973	000 111	100 001	010 454	364 805
Score	51	58.9*	55	57.9*	65
Placement	not selected	2	not selected	2	1

Judged a tie by unanimous decision of the Jury members.

2. Review of Exhibits

Table-1 is the evaluation matrices of the five (5) submittals. The evaluation matrix was developed from the key points outlined in the Request for Proposal (RFP). The "scores" on the matrix were "weighted" to provide the following evaluation criteria and weights:

Part I: Master Planning/Concept Design

	Weights
A. General Owner Requirements	10
B. Response to User Needs and Comfort	10
C. Site Planning and Image	12
D. Architectural Planning and Image	16
E. Layout/Staff Operational Efficiency	12
	60

Part II: Technical

		Weights
A.	Cost/Constructability	11
B.	Building Engineering/Operations and Maintenance	12
C.	Schedule Planning	5
D.	Safety	4
E.	Organizational/Manpower Approach	8
		40

The above major criteria areas were further subdivided into forty-six (46) sub-criteria. The scoring consisted of ranking each of the 46 sub-areas, using Excellent = 5, Very Good = 4, Good = 3, Fair = 2, Poor = 1. Subsequently, a weighted value was calculated by multiplying the points for each criteria by its rank, using Excellent = five (5) as total points, Very Good = four (4) as 0.8 times the points, Good = three (3) as 0.6 times the points, Fair = two (2) as 0.4 times the points, and Poor = one (1) as 0.2 times the points. The scores listed in Table 1 represent the average of the seven (7) Jury members' individual scorings.

3. Overview - Jury Members

The Jury for selection of the master planner for the proposed project convened in October, 1995. The Jury members' disciplines and areas of expertise were:

1) Primary focus on building systems and value engineering.
2) Primary focus on architectural and planning of hospitality projects.
3) Primary focus on marketing, operation and development.
4) Primary focus on land utilization and site planning.
5) Primary focus on local urban and master planning.
6) Primary focus on space planning and economic valuation.
7) Primary focus on traffic/transportation engineering and parking.

Sponsor Representatives: The two (2) representatives from the sponsor that participated during the Jury deliberation as **non-voting members** were as follows:

1) General Manager
2) General Manager of Projects

4. Procedure

The agenda followed by the Jury is attached as Figure 2. As per the Agenda, the Jury members initially met with the Owners for overall project objectives. Subsequently, the

Evaluation Criteria	Points Total	Points Dist'd	Exhibit A	Exhibit B	Exhibit C	Exhibit D	Exhibit E
I. Master Planning/Concept Design							
A. General Owner Requirements	10		4.5	6.5	5.2	5.5	6.6
1 Quality Clarify of Submittal		2	2.4	3.6	2.6	3.4	3.7
2 Conformance to RFP esp. Zoning		2	2.1	2.3	2.4	1.9	1.4
3 a) Marketability, Peak/Off peak (Hotel)		2	2.9	3.1	2.0	3.4	4.1
b) Marketability, Peak/Off peak (Apartment)		2	1.7	3.7	3.0	2.6	3.1
c) Marketability, Peak/Off peak (Shops)		1	2.3	3.4	3.7	2.4	4.1
d) Marketability, Peak/Off peak (Food Service & Amenities)		1	2.0	3.9	2.4	2.3	4.3
B. Response to User Needs & Comfort	10		5.3	8.2	5.1	5.4	8.2
1 Response to Needs esp. Elderly/Handicapped		3	2.9	4.3	2.7	2.6	4.6
2 Open Space Treatment		3	2.0	4.7	2.1	2.6	4.4
3 Ability to Provide Widely Varied Support Services		2	3.1	4.0	2.9	3.1	3.9
4 Pleasant below Grade Atmosphere		2	2.7	2.9	2.7	2.7	3.0
C. Site Planning & Image	12		6.8	8.2	6.4	6.8	7.6
1 Site Circulation							
a) Pedestrian		4	2.9	4.3	2.1	3.0	4.1
b) Vehicle		4	3.4	2.4	3.6	3.0	1.6
2 Landscaping Enhancements		2	1.3	4.1	1.6	2.0	4.6
3 Site Utilities/Existing Water Towers Optimization		2	3.0	3.0	3.0	3.0	2.9
D. Architectural Planning & Image	16		6.9	10.6	7.7	7.7	10.8
1 Compatibility with Owner Guidance - Architectural		2	2.6	3.0	3.0	2.9	3.6
2 Conformance to space program		2	1.6	4.1	2.4	2.3	3.6
3 Building massing relative to surrounding		2	1.6	4.1	2.4	2.3	3.6
4 Aesthetics of Facade		2	3.1	3.3	3.0	2.7	4.0
5 Optimization of view		2	2.9	2.9	2.0	3.0	3.9
6 Optimum net to gross & gross area		3	2.3	2.0	2.4	2.4	2.0
7 General integration with neighbors		3	1.3	4.1	1.9	1.6	3.6
E. Layout/Staff Operational Efficiency	12		6.7	6.2	7.2	5.6	9.2
1 Overall response top people & goods flow		3	2.1	1.7	2.9	1.9	3.9
2 Efficiency/Integration of parking		3	3.7	3.0	3.6	1.7	3.9
3 Optimal staff utilization		2	3.0	2.1	3.0	3.3	3.9
4 Operational Efficiency		2	3.0	2.3	3.1	3.0	3.6
5 Flexibility to changing occupancy		2	2.0	4.0	2.1	2.4	3.7
Sub-total	60		30.1	39.7	31.6	31.0	42.3
II. Technical							
A. Cost/Constructability	11		6.2	4.7	6.3	8.2	5.6
1 Ability of submittal to meet budget		4	3.1	1.4	3.1	4.3	1.9
2 Ability to meet owner investment criteria		4	2.6	2.7	2.7	3.4	3.3
3 Constructability aspects		1	3.0	2.1	3.1	3.9	1.4
4 Utilization of local materials/labor		1	3.0	2.7	3.0	3.1	2.9
5 Accuracy of submitted estimate		1	2.4	2.3	2.3	3.4	3.0
B. Building Engineering/Operations & Maintenance	12		5.6	4.8	7.2	8.7	7.6
1 Building system design							
a) Structural		1	3.0	2.0	3.0	3.0	1.3
b) Mechanical		2	2.0	2.1	4.0	3.6	3.7
c) Electrical		2	2.0	2.6	3.0	4.0	3.9
d) Vertical/Horizontal transportation		2	3.0	1.3	1.3	3.0	2.4
e) Security/Special system		1	3.0	2.0	3.0	3.1	2.0
2 Redundancy & maintainability of key operating equipment		2	2.0	1.6	3.1	4.0	3.7
3 Energy optimization		2	2.0	2.3	3.7	4.0	3.7
C. Schedule/Phasing	5		2.0	3.3	3.0	2.8	2.7
1 Ability of submittal to meet construction schedule		2	3.0	2.1	3.4	3.6	2.1
2 Clear & Definitive phasing plan		2	1.1	3.9	3.1	2.3	2.9
3 Flexibility to accommodate changing project, program and market requirements		1	1.9	4.4	2.1	2.1	3.7
D. Safety	4		2.0	2.0	2.0	2.0	1.7
1 Comprehensives of fire protection system		2	2.0	2.0	2.0	2.0	2.0
2 Occupants safety during peak periods		2	3.0	3.0	3.0	3.0	2.3
E. Organizational/Manpower Approach	8		4.8	4.5	4.8	5.2	5.4
1 Hotels & Resorts experience		2	3.0	2.3	3.0	3.9	3.7
2 Quality of curriculum vitae		2	3.0	2.9	3.0	3.0	3.0
3 Comprehensive plan eg.		2	4.0	3.0	2.1	4.0	3.7
a) Companies interface delineated							
b) Balanced resources to management							
c) Involvement of key personnel							
4 Task schedule & manpower adequacy		2	2.0	3.0	4.0	2.1	3.0
Sub-total	40		20.7	19.2	23.4	26.9	23.1
Total	100		50.7	58.9	55.0	57.9	65.4

5: Excellent 4: Very Good 3: Satisfactory 2: Minimal 1: Poor

Jury developed an evaluation matrix, Table 1, for review of submittals. During the initial sessions, the Jury members elected Jury Member #1 as Chairman, who presided over and served as the Jury leader during the judging process. He ensured that Jury deliberations proceeded in a fair and orderly manner. Assisted by Jury Member #6, he prepared the Jury Report. Jurors applied their professional expertise and personal judgment in the prudent deliberation in selection of first-, second-, and third-place winners from among the Master Planning concepts submitted. Reimbursable fees were allocated according to the Jury rankings.

The Jury evaluated the submittals following the Delphi method. The procedure consisted of an initial group discussion, during which the group discussed each project. The discussion included an overview of each exhibit by the designated specialist in the key areas. These were:

* Architectural features	Jury Member #2
* Landscape and Environmental	Jury Member #4
* Transportation and Pedestrian Flow	Jury Member #7
* Building Systems, Costs & Schedule	Jury Member #1

In addition, Jury Member #6 overviewed the general programming elements, Jury Member #3 overviewed marketing and sales aspects, and Jury Member #5 discussed the local custom impact of each exhibit. A jury member was assigned the responsibility to oversee the ranking and development of a narrative for one (1) exhibit.

Subsequently, each Jury member developed a ranking for each exhibit. Again the group was reconvened and differences in evaluations were discussed. Subsequently, each individual again evaluated results. The iterations were repeated until a final consensus was reached. The final day, the selected Jury member developed a Narrative Critique of their assigned Exhibit. The critiques are included in Section II.

5. Technical Advisory Report

The three (3) days prior to the Jury deliberation, the technical advisor started development of the following aids for the jury evaluation:

a. Costs

Development of a baseline cost model (UniFormat) using some eighteen (18) major cost drivers. A compilation in tabulation form of each exhibit was submitted to the Jury. The baseline model was compared to each exhibit, as well as compared to one another. Because of the wide variety of the submitted figures, exhibitors were faxed to send clarifications of their estimates. Their estimates were adjusted after their clarifications were received. The technical advisor then developed their own evaluation of each exhibitor's estimate and constructability aspects.

b. Schedule

Each exhibitor's schedule was listed in a table and compared to the RFP milestone dates and with one another. During the workshop, the technical advisor reviewed each schedule and developed comments as to the accuracy and feasibility of each exhibitor's submittal for Jury guidance in evaluations.

c. Man-month Input Schedule

A table listing all five (5) Exhibits and their man-month projection was developed. The table broke down the local and national firms' labor projections. During the workshop, a baseline labor projection of phases 1 through 6 was developed by a technical advisor for Jury guidance in evaluating each Exhibit's projections.

d. Technical Report Contents

Again, a table of each Exhibit's submitted data was developed assuming some eighteen (18) diverse building elements. Clarification was requested from the exhibitors in the number and types of elevators and escalators, as some drawings were difficult to ascertain the correct numbers.

e. Mechanical Systems

A compilation was assembled of each exhibitor's approach to HVAC, including type of plant, water storage requirements, fire protection concepts, water heating systems, and energy conservation.

f. Electrical Systems

A computation was assembled of each exhibitor's approach to electrical, including power and distribution, lighting, emergency power, and special systems including security.

g. Structural

During the Jury deliberation, a compilation and technical assessment was made by the project manager's structural engineer. This data on each exhibit was used by the Jury for their edification.

Note: It is pointed out that all during the Jury deliberation the technical advisor's staff was available for additional data collection or clarification of collected data. However, during the final evaluation of the exhibits, the Jury acted alone in their deliberation.

6. Conclusion

In conclusion, Exhibit E (Firm No. 364 805) was selected as No. 1 by the Jury. The following are the key criteria used in arriving at this selection:

- Top quality/clarity of submittal
- Best adjudged marketability of design
- Optimum response to user needs and comfort
- Very good site planning/image and best ranked pedestrian circulation and landscape approach
- Ranked No. 1 for architectural planning/image
- Best overall response to layout/staff operational efficiency
- Most comprehensive organization/manpower approach

The Jury unanimously recommended that the Owner award the design of the proposed hospitality development complex to Firm No. 364 805 for Exhibit E.

Section II: Narrative Reports and Findings

(Not included in the Case Study)

Section III: Attachment

Jury Agenda
Master Planning Competition
Hotel, Apartment and Shopping Development Project

---

1. DAY ONE

08:30 AM	Jury Orientation and Debriefing
09:00 AM	Introduction/Agenda/Introduction given by Professional Advisor
10:00 AM	Formation of Jury Team
	* Selection of the Chairperson
	* Breakdown of Jury
10:30 AM	General Overview of the (5) Exhibitors
12:00 Noon	Confirm Sponsor's Objectives
01:00 PM	Lunch
02:00 PM	Technical Advisor Overview
	* Schedule
	* Planning/Programming
	* Costs
	* Financial Projection
04:30 PM	Group (Jury) Review of Exhibitors
	* Master Planning/Concept Design
	* Technical

2. DAY TWO

08:30 AM	Conclude Formal Group Review of Exhibitors
10:30 AM	Individual Evaluation
	* Master Planning/Concept Design
12:00 Noon	Lunch
02:00 PM	Individual Evaluation of Findings (Cont.)
	* Technical
04:30 PM	Group Iteration of Evaluations
	Master Planning/Concept Design
06:00 PM	Adjourn

3. DAY THREE

08:30 AM   Jury Iteration of Evaluation (Cont.)
                    * Technical
10:30 AM   Individual Re-evaluation of Rankings
                    * Master Planning/Concept Design
12:00 Noon Lunch
02:00 PM   Individual Re-evaluation of Ranking (Cont.)
04:00 PM   Develop Preliminary Evaluation
05:00 PM   Adjourn
7-9   PM   Sales & Marketing Brainstorming Session (Night Session)
                    * Dinner/Discussion

4. DAY FOUR

08:30 AM   Review and Finalize Findings -- Group
                    * Master Planning/Concept Design
                    * Technical
12:30 PM   Lunch
02:00 PM   Develop Findings
                    * Outline Presentation of Findings
05:00 PM   Client Briefing of Tentative Findings
07:00 PM   Adjourn
08:00-9:30 Sales & Marketing Brainstorming Session, Dinner with the Client

5. DAY FIVE

08:30 AM   Group Discussion
                    * Finalize Results
                    * Select Winners
10:30 AM   Presentation to Owner
12:30 PM   Lunch
02:00 PM   Preliminary Report Preparation
                    * Narrative Reports of Exhibitors
05:00 PM   Adjourn

Case Study Five

Application to Design Review of Government Headquarters/Complex

In 1996, the author assembled a team and conducted a design review using a two-week formal workshop structured around the VE Job Plan. The team studied 15% design-stage submittal drawings as part of the project management input for a large government agency headquarters/complex in Saudi Arabia estimated at $125,000,000 (U.S.).

Project Description:

Headquarters/complex (including office tower, low-rise office area, parking structure, and auditorium)

Gross building area: 1,500,000 S.F.

Accommodate 2,500 people when complete

Study objective: To assure that the submittal drawings conform to the owner's requirements and to offer value-enhancement suggestions.

During the review, the VE team implemented methodologies that differed from those typically used by the designers/owners, who were following the traditional approach. The key differences were:

- An established scope of work, schedule, and agenda were followed.
- A multidisciplinary, experienced team of noninvolved professionals conducted the review. Maximum effectiveness was realized when the VE team was composed of professionals who had performed a previous study.
- The review team not only looked for typical design review items, it also documented potential value enhancements, such as total cost, quality, time, and constructability improvements.

The VE modified design review was well organized, effective, and resulted in an improved facility. Compared to the traditional design review, the VE modified effort returned to the owner benefits worth several times the cost involved.

Case Study Five   Application to Design Review of Govt. Hdqtrs./Complex

287

Case Study Elements

The items listed below and shown in this case study have been excerpted from an actual submitted report. (The Table of Contents on page 289 is one of the excerpts and refers to some documents not listed here or shown in the section.)

Case Study Five Application to Design Review of Govt. Hdqtrs./Complex

Design Review Report
Headquarters/Complex
Table of Contents & List of Figures

This is the Table of Contents from the actual VE report.
Selected excerpts appear in this case study.

Section I

Introduction

1. General

The design review (DR) team conducted its review on the 15% design stage submittal drawings. The review was conducted at the designer's offices. The objective of the review was to assure that the submittal conformed to the owner's requirements and offered value-enhancement suggestions.

2. Project Description

The proposed project is a building that will be used primarily for the offices of all corporate executive and administrative levels. A large area will be devoted to marketing.

The main elements of the project are the following: office tower, low-rise office area, parking structure, and auditorium. The facility is designed to accommodate a total of 2,500 persons when it is completed. For the sake of convenience and in view of the future needs of the building, the project is divided into three (3) phases -- A, B, and C -- and the construction drawings and bid will be presented in three packages.

Site: Attached is Figure 1.1 -- General Site Plan (Not included in case study.)

Buildings: The gross building area is approximately 1,500,000 S.F., comprising the lower main building, twin towers, auditorium with adjacent training center, cafeteria, lower parking structure, recreation area, warehouse, and utility building.

Design Image and Quality: The proposed building should represent the modern-technology image of the high-level corporate organization and should be functionally efficient. The exterior of the building is designed to be clad in stone/precast panels. The total image should portray one of the most modern designs in the region.

Section II

Procedure

The design review was conducted as part of a continuing program of design review services provided by the Project Manager (PM) for the Owner. This effort represented the first formal project review of the design development (approximately 15%) documents. The agenda for the formal review is attached (see Workshop Agenda). The design review team was comprised of the following professionals:

- Design Review Team Leader/Civil/Costs
- Project Director/Electrical/Costs
- Architectural Designer
- Architectural/ Construction Specialist
- Mechanical Engineer
- Structural Engineer
- Administrative Support/Graphics Specialist

The workshop began with introductions and an explanation of the workshop procedures. This was followed by an overview of the project documents by the Owner and design review team. Following is a list of the twenty-four (24) personnel who were in attendance.

Discipline	Company
Project Manager	Owner
Structural Engineer	PM
Review Team Leader	PM
Mechanical Engineer	PM
Architect	PM
Electrical/Project Director	PM
Structural/Asst. Project Director	PM
Architect	PM
Director of Design	A/E
Report Writer/Illustrator-M.E.	PM
Design	A/E
Project Manager	A/E
Manager of Design Dept.	A/E
Director of Engineering	A/E
Head of Technical Services	A/E
Manager of Q.S. & Estimation	A/E

Case Study Five   Application to Design Review of Govt. Hdqtrs./Complex

291

Discipline	Company
Head of Structural Dept.	A/E
Head of Electrical Dept.	A/E
Head of Plumbing Dept.	A/E
Head of HVAC Dept.	A/E
Project Architect	A/E
Manager of Landscape Architect	A/E
Civil Engineer	A/E
Senior Architect	A/E

The team broke out into discipline areas, and members reviewed details with their design counterparts. The second day was devoted to review of documents and collection of comments. On the third day, comments were collected, reviewed, and discussed with the design/owner team. Discussions as required for clarification, as well as suggestions for potential enhancements to the proposed design, were conducted throughout the formal review process. In addition, the design review team evaluated the project estimate for accuracy, since an estimate should represent a reasonable cost for the proposed project. The team developed comments and suggested changes to improve the overall accuracy of the estimate. These changes were reviewed and discussed with project (A/E) estimators, and the estimate was adjusted. Finally, the comments were documented and plans marked appropriately for evaluation in the report.

During the sessions, considerable time was spent evaluating the net to gross of the design. Because of the two-tower concept and use of atria, the calculated net to gross (65%) was below industry standards. For example, the table below illustrates the ratio goals of the largest building concern in the world, the General Services Administration (U.S.).

Table 3-1: Minimum Net to Gross Ratios

Building Type	Minimum Ratio
Office Building	75%
Courts	67%
Libraries	77%

Source: Data from Chapter 3, *Architectural and Interior Design*, June 14, 1994, PBS-PQ100.1, pages 3-15.

The PM conducted several additional special studies. Because the review team had some initial concerns, a traffic consultant specialist was called in to conduct a traffic study (reported in Appendix B -- not included in this case study). This study, which isolated several points for further clarification, was given to the owner and designer personnel for their review. Design review comments deemed appropriate by the team are included in Section III. Also, an elevator consultant was asked to review the data in the technical report and to conduct some preliminary runs to evaluate the elevatoring of the project. His report, which contained some pertinent comments that would optimize performance and cost (reported in Appendix C -- not included in this case study), was given to the Owner and designer personnel. The A/E used these recommendations to update ongoing elevator studies.

Design Review: Headquarters/Complex

Workshop Agenda

Day 1:

8:30 am	**INTRODUCTION**
	Briefing on Procedure
	Review of Agenda
	Objectives
9:00	**OVERVIEW OF PROJECT INCLUDING CONSTRAINTS**
	By Owner
	By Designer
	Latest Document Status
10:15	BREAK
10:30 - 01:00	**OVERVIEW OF PROJECT INCLUDING CONSTRAINTS (CONT.)**
1:00 pm	LUNCH
2:00	**TEAM BREAKOUT BY DISCIPLINES & PROJECT FAMILIARIZATION**
	Interface with Owner & Design Team
6:00	**ADJOURN**

Day 2:

8:30 am	**TEAM REVIEW OF DOCUMENTS**
	Design Concepts
	Design Analysis
	Program & Requirements
	Any New Submittals
	Drawings
	Costs
	Conformance with code requirements
	Schedule impact & constructability
	1. By Disciplines
	2. By Team
1:00 pm	LUNCH
2:00	**TEAM REVIEW (CONT.)**
4:30	**PROJECT TIME AND STATUS REPORT**
	Overview of Progress
6:00	**ADJOURN**

Day 3:

8:30 am	**METHODOLOGY -- COLLECT AND ANALYZE NOTES**
	Each Discipline
10:00	BREAK
10:10	**METHODOLOGY -- GROUP DISCUSSION**
	Evaluation of Comment
	Discussion of Review Comments by Discipline
1:00 pm	LUNCH
02:00	**DEVELOPMENT OF REVIEW COMMENTS**
3:00	**CROSS FEED OF DISCIPLINES**
	Round-Robin Discussions
4:00	**IDEA EXCHANGE WITH OWNER & DESIGNERS**
	Group Discussion
6:00	**ADJOURN**

Day 4:

8:00 am	**METHODOLOGY & DOCUMENTATION**
1:00 pm	LUNCH
2:00	**PROJECT TIME (CONT.)**
	Documentation by Discipline
3:30	**METHODOLOGY -- DOCUMENTATION REVIEW**
	By Group
	Breakout Group for General Conditions Review
6:00	**ADJOURN**

Day 5:

8:00	**PROJECT TIME -- REPORT**
	Complete Written Comments
	Prepare Oral Presentations
10:30	**GROUP LEADER REVIEW OF COMMENTS**
1:00 pm	LUNCH
2:00	**EXECUTIVE BRIEFING BY DISCIPLINE**
	Oral Presentations
3:30	**CLOSING REMARKS**
4:00	**ADJOURN**

At the conclusion of the formal workshop, the design review team made a brief summary presentation of the key comments generated for the Owner and design team representatives.

Following the five-day formal session, the team returned to the PM's office and developed the final report. During the following week another briefing was held at the Owner's headquarters building. Personnel in attendance are listed below:

Position	Company
Director General	Owner
Director, Projects Department	Owner
Project Designer	Owner
Design Review Team Leader	PM
President	PM
Project Director	PM
Managing Director	PM

The design review team would like to thank the designer's personnel for their hospitality and use of their facilities. Their staff is to be commended for their positive attitude toward the review process. In particular, we especially appreciated the productive input of the Project Manager.

Section IV includes the design review comments that were generated during the formal review. (Note: This case study presents selected excerpts from the design review comments.)

Section III

Conclusion

1. Contract Submittal Issues

The submittal documents were reviewed in detail by the team, and approximately 125 design review comments were generated. The team concluded that the submittal did not fully meet owner requirements. The following key areas of concern were isolated:

- The submittal had not been approved by the municipality.
- The refined space program needed to be accomplished.
- The geotechnical report was not complete but was underway.
- A traffic study was necessary to better define access to site and parking as well as site roadway.
- Major site elements, such as utility building and utility tunnel, thermal energy storage (TES) system, and water storage tank, needed to be better defined and located.
- Especially important--the net to gross of the office areas and parking needed to be improved to represent an efficient facility. Reasonable targets for such a corporate structure are a minimum of 75% net to gross and a maximum of 400 S.F./car for parking spaces.
- Also, clarification was needed for the engineering systems, e.g., location of plant rooms, TES, mechanical penthouse, and required utility shafts.
- Current design of tower atriums did not meet the requirements of the Uniform Building Code (UBC).
- Constructability and construction methods needed to be reviewed for the atrium.
- Wind test needed to be conducted to determine stresses and noise levels on main building.

As for costs, the design review team evaluated the estimate with the project estimators. After several additive adjustments, a revised estimate was developed; the design review team concurred that this represented a reasonable estimate of probable costs. As a further refinement, project estimators agreed to prepare a new estimate using actual project takeoff items before final approval of the 15% submittal.

Note: The project estimate represents the projected cost if all three phases are bid at one time. Escalation costs of Phase B and Phase C, which may be bid 10 to 15 years after the bidding of Phase A, may be from 30% to 100% higher.

2. Approval Process

If the comments are evaluated and implemented to meet owner requirements, the design review team will quickly approve of the submittal.

3. Future Concerns

For future submittals, the design review team would like to have the drawings numbered per American Institute of Architects (AIA) standards, the cost estimate in UniFormat, and a revised design schedule with a milestone, master-type project construction schedule.

Case Study Five Application to Design Review of Govt. Hdqtrs./Complex

295

Section IV: Design Review
General
Headquarters/Complex

No.	UniFormat Element/ Item	Drawing Number, Specification Page or Brief Description	Comment(s)	Action
4.		Contract Item 3a.1.4 Constructability	Contract requires submittal of construction methods. None have been submitted. This requirement should be met, especially for the construction of the towers. See structural for more details.	
5.		Design Contract Item 3a.1 Schedule	Regarding design schedule. Resubmit in accordance with PM letter dated April 7, 1996.	
6.		Contract 3a.2	No structural drawings were submitted. Expected drawings are column layout with approximate sizes, foundation concept should coordinate column location, spans, shear walls, floor height, foundation details and coordination with architectural. See structural for specific basis of design. Report for mechanical should include sizing of major equipment, proposed plant and distribution layout concepts. Major shafts should be indicated.	
7.		Contract 3a.2.6	Basis of design report should include sizing of major electrical equipment. Location and layout.	
8.		Contract 3a.2.1	Municipality written approval must be obtained before approval of 15% submittal. Also, resolution of glass problem (obscured glass) for north and east views needs to be accomplished.	
9.		Contract 3a.2.6,7 & 8	Submittal shall include design analysis and preliminary system selection including materials for major systems. See PM Letter of April 03, 1996.	
10.		AR-01, 02 & 03	Show elevation at ground floor per datum established for site topography.	
11.		Architecture and Engineering Design Criteria 15% stage	Basis of Design Report under General refers to UBC 91 -- should be UBC 94.	
12.		Architecture and Engineering Design Criteria 15% stage	Program: Space allocation and program is not complete. Submittal for Approval required, as well as subsequent determination of room sizes for each department. See # G-2- Arch.2	

No.	UniFormat Element/ Item	Drawing Number, Specification Page or Brief Description	Comment(s)	Action
4.	0620	General	Show typical finishes for various typical spaces. Indicate approximate costs of such finishes as a whole (can be line items in the detailed cost estimate).	
5.	0622	AR-02 & 03	1. Granite or other stone tiles use slip-resistant design. 2. Use carpet tiles only at higher traffic areas. 3. Identify skirting proposed for various floor finish areas.	
6.	0616	AR-02 & 03	Evaluate number of doors at elevator lobby.	
7.	0611	General	Atria requires fire-rated partitions, as per UBC code, Chapter 4, Section 402.	

07 Conveying System

No.	UniFormat Element/ Item	Drawing Number, Specification Page or Brief Description	Comment(s)	Action
1.	0701	See Appendix C* elevator consultant's initial submittal	Consider elevator analysis by independent consultant, not by elevator vendors. *Note: This report was sent to A/E and forwarded to their elevator consultant. Revisions to elevator design are in progress.	

08 Mechanical

No.	UniFormat Element/ Item	Drawing Number, Specification Page or Brief Description	Comment(s)	Action
1.	0811	Hot water supply	a. Study the use of individual electric water heaters (for each toilet room on each floor) of adequate capacity instead of centralized floor electric water heaters and instantaneous type for executive areas. Basis of design and technical report should be clarified. b. Study the use of UPVC pipes instead of copper pipes for hot and cold water supply.	
2.	0811	Cold water supply	Study to use PVC pipe for cold water Check plumbing code?	
4.	082	Outdoor design condition	It is suggested that use of Outdoor: DB = 111°F, WB = 71°F be studied and modified as per official meteorology temperature records. Use 2-1/2% line as recommended by ASHRAE (copy given to A/E). Possible consideration DB 109°F, WB 77°F.	

Case Study Five   Application to Design Review of Govt. Hdqtrs./Complex

297

Section IV: Design Review
Site Work
Headquarters/Complex

No.	UniFormat Element/ Item	Drawing Number, Specification Page or Brief Description	Comment(s)	Action
12 Site Work				
1.	**1221**		Study accesses and parking spaces based on traffic study.	
2.	**1221**	LS - 01	Review sizes and possible combination of visitors parking and auditorium parking lots.	
3.	**1222**	LS - 01	Adjust road entry to protect future expansion of site at the northwest corner.	
5.	**1222**	LS - 01	Main plaza walks and pedestrian areas with patterned marble. Main plaza pavers shall be slip resistant. No vehicle traffic should occur over these areas.	
8.	**1222**	LS - 01	Simplify parking and utility roads around warehouse and proposed utility building.	
9.	**1223**	LS - 01	Provide typical wall section, partial wall elevation and special custom details planned for boundary wall.	
10.	**1223**	LS - 01	Show typical section, water requirements and typical special details required for any water features.	
11.	**1223**	RFP Page 4 Item 9 LS - 01	Designer has indicated a 500-person amphitheater adjacent to the recreation area. This item is not a program element. It was added by the designer at owner's instruction. Review team points out this is an additional program element, which is expensive--a high maintenance item. There were no costs in the estimate for it. Note: Item added to estimate in final validation.	
12.	**1223**	LS - 01	Recreation area is not physically separated by fence/wall from the main headquarters. Suggest evaluation to allow privacy and less interference with other buildings during off-hours.	

Highway Project: South Interchange

T
he VE team conducted a 40-hour modified-task team study for the
1″ = 100′ submittal for a large-city highway interchange project. The
team goals were optimization of the cost impact of design decisions,
simplification of the highway system, and achievement of a grade raise for the
northbound interstate deep-tunnel section.

In final implementation, some 10 proposals out of 15 submitted were carried out.
Initial cost savings of up to $200,000,000 resulted from the study. Follow-on savings
estimates may vary from $3,000,000 to $5,000,000 each year, depending on
alternatives chosen for the final design.

Case Study Elements

The items listed below and shown in this case study have been excerpted from an
actual VE report. (The Table of Contents on page 301 is one of the excerpts
and refers to some documents not listed here or shown in this section.)

Value Engineering Report
Highway Project: South Interchange

Table of Contents

*This is the Table of Contents from the actual VE report.
Selected excerpts appear in this case study.*

VALUE ENGINEERING REPORT
HIGHWAY PROJECT: South Interchange

1.0   SUMMARY INFORMATION

1.1   EXECUTIVE SUMMARY

The VE team conducted a 40-hour, modified task team study for the 1" = 100' submittal for a major highway interchange project.

The team developed a cost model (see Section 3.1), where potential savings targets were isolated through the function analysis performed. The model indicated some six cost elements as potential areas for savings. Approximately thirty ideas were generated during the creative phase, from which ten proposals and five design comments emerged.

The principal proposals recommended elimination of Ramps A and B, modification of Ramp C, and elimination of part of M Street. The team also recommended elimination of the portion of Main Street that passed over the northbound interstate highway as a high-cost, low-value item. Savings for the above are estimated at about $80 million. Implementation of the above changes would permit raising the profile of the major northbound interstate to reduce expensive tunnel construction. This proposal would save an additional $70 million and approximately one year of construction time. In addition, elimination of Ramp D was recommended, based on rerouting some traffic locally. Additional potential savings of approximately $10 million were estimated.

The structural recommendations include review of design criteria for sizing of structural members using load (strength) factor design methods in lieu of working strength, and the use of sheet piling in lieu of slurry walls at selected locations.

The design comments include investigation of the bonding availability for disadvantaged business enterprises, prenegotiation of labor agreements, and analysis of the materials dredged from the proposed channel crossing.

Finally, the VE team expressed concerns about the design of the local channel crossing, which locates the immersed tubes of the crossing within two feet of an existing tunnel. It is recommended that the design be reviewed further to insure that future problems will be avoided. In the event of problems, consider elevating the interstate highway (E-W) over the channel. While this alternative requires relaxation of design constraints and revision to the design schedule, it offers the potential to reduce construction time by two years, initial costs by $140 million, and annual operating and maintenance costs by $2 million. Acceptance of this recommendation would preclude the ability to raise the profile of the major north-south interstate and to realize the savings ($70 million) for that recommendation.

VALUE ENGINEERING REPORT
HIGHWAY PROJECT: South Interchange

1.3 SUMMARY OF POTENTIAL COSTS

NO.	DESCRIPTION	INITIAL COST SAVINGS (000)	ANNUAL O&M COST SAVINGS	TOTAL PW COST SAVING (000)
CIVIL				
C-1	Eliminate Ramp A	64,730	TBD	64,730
C-2	Eliminate Ramp D	11,100	TBD	11,100
C-3	Eliminate Main St. Overcrossing	9,130	TBD	9,130
C-6	Raise Profile of N-S Interstate	69,400	1 million	79,400
C-10	Combine Ramps E and C	26,000	TBD	26,000
C-11	Eliminate Ramp B	4,350	TBD	26,000
C-12	Delete Main St. Connector	800	TBD	800
C-19	Elevate E-W Interstate over Channel and Railroad Yard	145,000	2 million	165,400

Proposals C-6 and C-12 are mutually exclusive.

NO.	DESCRIPTION	INITIAL COST SAVINGS (000)	ANNUAL O&M COST SAVINGS	TOTAL PW COST SAVING (000)
CONSTRUCTION MANAGEMENT				
CM-1	Review insurability of channel crossing		DESIGN COMMENT	
CM-2	Investigate bonding availability for minority contracts		DESIGN COMMENT	
CM-4	Review toxic level and disposal of channel dredgings		DESIGN COMMENT	
STRUCTURAL				
S-1	Review channel crossing		DESIGN COMMENT	
S-2	Change structural design criteria for elevated structures		DESIGN COMMENT	
S-3	Interlocked sheet piling in lieu of slurry walls	29,400	N/A	29,400
S-4	Use of strength and load factor design methods in lieu of working strength	45,600	N/A	45,600

VALUE ENGINEERING REPORT
HIGHWAY PROJECT: South Interchange

2.0 STUDY WORKBOOKS

2.1 NARRATIVE OF POTENTIAL COST SAVINGS

The following is a narrative description of each of the recommendations presented by the VE team. Detailed workshop material and data are included in Study Workbooks Sections 2.2 (General), 2.3 (Civil), 2.4 (Construction Management), and 2.5 (Structures), respectively.

The VE effort for the south interchange area concentrated on (1) cost savings precipitated by budgetary pressures, (2) simplification of the system through greater reliance on local streets to move local traffic, and (3) the underlying goal of achieving a grade raise for the northbound interstate deep-tunnel section.

C-1 Eliminate Ramp A

This proposal eliminates Ramp A. Traffic from south of the city to the northbound interstate may use the shorter and faster route via local Avenue N. The estimated savings is $64.73 million.

C-2 Eliminate Ramp D

This proposal eliminates Ramp D, which only serves as an emergency by-pass ramp for westbound north-south traffic. The savings associated with it is $11.1 million.

C-3 Eliminate Main Street Overcrossing

The VE proposal recommends elimination of the M Street overcrossing and the associated ramp, and rerouting local traffic. This proposal estimates a cost savings of $9.13 million, relieves a congested area, and removes an obstacle to allowing a grade raise for the northbound interstate.

C-6 Raise Profile of Northbound Interstate

This proposal raises the profile of the northbound interstate by passing over railroads, then passing under the main railroad station connector. Implementation depends on acceptance of other proposals, e.g., C-3, C-10, and C-12. The estimated savings in initial costs is $69.4 million.

C-10 Combine Ramps E and C

The VE proposal recommends elimination of Ramp C and combines this function with a realigned Ramp E. This proposal provides an estimated cost savings of $26.0 million, eliminates several undesirable traffic movements, and removes one obstacle to a grade raise for the northbound interstate tunnel section.

C-11 Eliminate Ramp B

The VE proposal recommends elimination of Ramp B, and rerouting local traffic via a local street. This proposal provides an estimated cost savings of $4.35 million.

C-12 Main Street Connector

This proposal recommends the elimination of the Main Street connector between the northbound interstate and local streets, rerouting local traffic via another street. The primary benefit of this proposal is removal of an obstacle to allowing a grade raise for the northbound interstate.

C-19 Raise Profile of East(E)--West(W) Interstate

The VE team has some environmental concerns about construction at the local channel as well as construction feasibility concerns about the impact on the environment of existing tunnels; these situations may require an alternative profile for E-W Interstate. This recommendation was estimated at $145.4 million in initial savings.

CM-1 Contractor Liability -- Local Construction

The VE team expressed concern over the ability of the proposed design of the local channel crossing to insure the integrity of the existing tunnels. As such, the ability of the contractors to realize reasonable liability and property damage insurance coverage should be verified. If problems arise, redesign. Consideration of the VE alternates (see C-19) may be appropriate.

CM-2 Disadvantaged Business Enterprise (DBEs) Bonding

The team recommends initiation of augmented efforts to ensure the ability of DBEs to realize required bonding. With other local projects running concurrently, over $500 million in DBE set-asides will be required. Present methods for securing bonding would be unable to meet the needs in an economical manner. The state needs to resolve the problem before serious consequences result.

CM-4 Disposal of Local Channel Dredgings

VE teams recommend the analysis of proposed dredging to ascertain the nature of the substance(s). The team believes that there is a high probability of the discovery of contaminated material. Disposal and costs (not included in estimate) could adversely impact both the costs and the schedule in this segment.

S-1 Review of Local Channel Crossing

In order to avoid the sensitive design and construction problems associated with assuring the watertightness and structural integrity of the existing tunnels, the team feels it would be better to bridge over the existing channel, rather than tunnel in it.

If it is necessary to proceed with the tunnel scheme as outlined, the team recommends undertaking the following investigations prior to adoption of that scheme:

- Develop a realistic, three-dimensional, structural model of the existing tunnels depicting the soil-structure interaction of the tunnel linings, in their as-built condition, in both transverse and longitudinal directions.
- Using the above model, assess the stress and strain conditions of the tunnel linings through the various stages of construction, taking into consideration the long-term, time-dependent effects.

If the investigation proves, beyond any doubt, that the watertightness and structural integrity of the existing tunnels can be assured, a construction scheme to minimize risk should be developed.

S-2 Structural Design of Elevated Structures

The reference materials provided for this study indicated that:

- The cross sections depicted multicell, reinforced concrete, box-type deck structures.
- The previous designer's estimate assumed an 8-1/2 inch reinforced concrete deck slab supported by A588 structural steel members.

An examination of the site conditions reveals that extraordinarily long spans would not be required. Therefore,

- span lengths could be optimized for both concrete and steel alternates.
- unless aesthetic considerations force the issue, the most economical alternate design can be selected.

S-3 Use of Steel Sheet Piling in Lieu of Slurry Walls

The previous designer's estimate contains 579,650 S.F. of slurry walls at a unit price of $69.71 per S.F. for a total of $40,400,000. An examination of the site conditions leads to the conclusion that, except at very few locations, such as the proximity of a high-rise building, support of excavation could be accomplished with interlocked steel sheet piling. This could effect a savings on the order of magnitude of $29,000,000.

S-4 Use of Strength and Load Factor Design Methods in Lieu of Working Stress Design

Utilizing applicable national codes and design standards, it is recommended that

- instead of the working stress design method for reinforced concrete structures, use the strength design method in accordance with ACI-318, "AASHTO Bridges," and the "AREA Manual."
- instead of the working stress design method for steel structures subjected to highway loadings, use the load factor design method in accordance with "AASHTO Bridges."
- instead of the working stress design method for steel structures at grade, use the load and resistance factor design method in accordance with the *AISC Manual of Steel Construction, First Edition* (1986).`

This will effect a cost saving without sacrificing serviceability, structural integrity, or intended function. Using the figures shown in the present estimate, the order of magnitude of the cost saving is estimated at:

- $16,800,000 for concrete.
- $24,200,000 for reinforcing steel.
- $ 4,600,000 for structural steel.

This results in an approximate total savings on the order of $45,600,000.

C-1 Eliminate Ramp A

SPECULATION PHASE
IDEA LIST

- LIST ALTERNATIVE IDEAS FOR EACH FUNCTION, AND NUMBER IDEAS CONSECUTIVELY.

- USE SEPARATE PAGE FOR EACH FUNCTION.

- <u>DO NOT EVALUATE IDEAS NOW</u>. <u>REFINEMENT COMES LATER</u>.

1. FUNCTION NO. ___1___   __Connect__   __(west) bound to (north) bound__
         (from Form 6)   (verb)   (noun)

Premises

- Constructing Ramp A under local road and tunneling under railroad is costly.

- Driver decision points for ramp take-off are too close.

- Left-hand exit undesirable for local traffic movement.

- Traffic will be minimal since local avenue routing is shorter and faster.

- Direct return movement is missing.

- Traffic assignment is negligible.

Alternative

Eliminate ramp A entirely -- traffic to use local avenue to northbound interstate.

C-1   Eliminate Ramp A

EVALUATION PHASE
FEASIBILITY/SUITABILITY EVALUATION

.. FEASIBILITY:

FOR EACH FUNCTION REVIEW ALL THE IDEAS GENERATED IN THE SPECULATION PHASE. BEFORE YOU ELIMINATE ANY, ASK THE FOLLOWING QUESTIONS: WILL IT WORK? WILL IT SAVE MONEY? WILL IT MEET PERFORMANCE NEEDS?

NOW ELIMINATE ANY UNSOUND, COSTLY, UNACCEPTABLE, OR UNTIMELY IDEAS.

2. SUITABILITY:

SELECT AND LIST BELOW THE MOST FEASIBLE IDEAS OR COMBINATION OF IDEAS FOR FURTHER CONSIDERATION. CHECK ( ) THE BEST IDEA(S). USE A PAGE FOR EACH FUNCTION.

FUNCTION NO. __1__   __Connect__   __(west-to-north) Traffic__
                        (verb)   (noun)

NO.	IDEA	ADVANTAGES	DISADVANTAGES
1.	Eliminate ramp, use alternate route.	Reduces costs. Simplifies left exit. Avoids long tunnel under railroad. Avoids tunnel behind sea wall.	Eliminates free-flow ramp. Eliminates alternate route if local avenue is congested.

C-1   Eliminate Ramp A

DEVELOPMENT PHASE
RECOMMENDED ALTERNATIVE -- VE TEAM SKETCH AND DESCRIPTION

Narrative of Proposed Changes

The current revised proposed action includes the addition of Ramp A connecting westbound interstate with northbound interstate as part of the interchange. The VE proposal eliminates this separate ramp and combines its function with use of local avenue--a shorter, more direct route to the northbound interstate.

Ramp A introduces an undesirable, double, left-hand exit off the roadway, connecting westbound interstate and southbound interstate with decision points only 300 feet apart. The ramp includes costly construction (a tunnel under the border road northbound, and under railroad tracks and east-west interstate).

Negligible traffic is estimated to use Ramp A, since a shorter route (local avenue) is available. Also truck traffic from city to northbound interstate can utilize the connector road and the haul road.

C-1   Eliminate Ramp A

**DEVELOPMENT PHASE
VE COST COMPARISON**

COSTS   [millions (M)]

1. ITEM	2. DESCRIPTION OF MODIFICATIONS	3. BEFORE	4. AFTER	5. SAVINGS	6. TRADEOFFS
C-1	Eliminate Ramp A	$64.7 million	0	$64.7 million	Eliminates emergency alternate.

C-1 Eliminate Ramp A

DEVELOPMENT PHASE
NOTES AND DISCUSSIONS

USE THIS PAGE FOR DISCUSSION, LIFE CYCLE COST CALCULATIONS, COMMENTARY ON AGENCY APPLICATION OF STANDARDS, SPECIFICATIONS, TRAFFIC PROJECTIONS, ETC.

ADDITIONAL NOTES

This major highway interchange is a $1 billion complex connecting two major interstate routes as well as supplying local access to the city. The multiplicity of ramps with closely spaced takeoffs will make signage difficult. Any steps that can be taken to simplify the ramp configuration, such as elimination of Ramp A, will improve operations and safety for future users.

Life cycle cost savings will be achieved through elimination of tunnel ventilation, lighting and maintenance costs for the 2,000 foot long tunnel.

C-1 Eliminate Ramp A

DEVELOPMENT PHASE
SUMMARY AND RECOMMENDATIONS

CONCLUSIONS AND RECOMMENDATIONS

Eliminate Ramp A.

Traffic from south of the city to northbound interstate will use the shorter and faster route via local avenue.

SUMMARY OF SAVINGS

CATEGORY I   = $ <u>64.73 million</u> OR <u>6.5</u> % OF TOTAL PROJECT
CATEGORY II   = $ _____ OR _____ % OF TOTAL PROJECT
CATEGORY III   = $ _____ OR _____ % OF TOTAL PROJECT
CATEGORY IV   = $ _____ OR _____ % OF TOTAL PROJECT

TOTAL POTENTIAL SAVINGS
IDENTIFIED = $ <u>64.73 million</u>   OR   <u>6.5</u>   % OF TOTAL PROJECT

OTHER OPPORTUNITIES FOR VALUE "IMPROVEMENT":

Improves alignment for heavily used Ramp I (1200 vehicles/hour (VPH) in A.M. peak)

IMPLEMENTATION PLAN: (DISPOSITION RECOMMENDED BY PM/DESIGNER)

(Form continued on next page.)

DEVELOPMENT PHASE
SUMMARY AND RECOMMENDATIONS

IMPLEMENTATION PLAN:
(DISPOSITION RECOMMENDED BY PROJECT MANAGER/DESIGNER)

C-1   Eliminate Ramp A

Project Manager agrees with the VE team that Ramp A, as shown on the Revised Proposed Action Plan, includes design features that are somewhat undesirable and costly.

The year 2010 traffic forecast for Ramp A shows A.M. and P.M. peak volumes of 350 VPH and 850 VPH, respectively. These volumes indicate that the ramp would be operating under capacity and may not--alone--justify the movement. However, the movement is justifiable if one considers the positive impact of reducing the over-capacity volumes of ramps in the adjoining project area.

Currently under consideration are design refinements that relocate and improve the design of Ramp A at a substantially reduced cost.

C-1 Eliminate Ramp A

IMPLEMENTATION PHASE
POSITION STATEMENT

FINAL DISPOSITION BY STATE DEPARTMENT OF PUBLIC WORKS (DPW):

The department feels that a successful highway design must include movement from the west on the E-W interstate to the north on the N-S interstate, in order to facilitate commercial activity from the city's industrial area with a desire to go north. Because of the implementation of another proposal that recommends raising the N-S interstate profile, a more direct and substantially less expensive connection was made possible. Therefore, the Project Manager agrees with both the VE team and the design team. However, it still supports the west to north movement, as accomplished in the new alignment.

C-6 Raise Profile of Northbound Interstate

INVESTIGATION PHASE
COMBINE AND RANK FUNCTIONS

1. BASIC FUNCTION OF INTERCHANGE PROJECT:
   - GROUP RELATED FUNCTIONS AND COMBINE COSTS.
   - RANK FUNCTIONS BY COST AND ASSIGN SEQUENTIAL NUMBERS TO EACH GROUP.

2. NO.	FUNCTIONS FROM THE 80% GROUPING	COST
	At Grade	$ 0.08 M
	Boat Section	5.14 M
	Deep Tunnel Section	100.41 M
	TOTAL Northbound Interstate Segment	$105.63 M

3. NO.	FUNCTIONS WITH SIGNIFICANT POTENTIAL COSTS	COST
a.	Deep Tunnel Section	$100.41 M

C-6 Raise Profile of Northbound Interstate

SPECULATION PHASE
IDEA LIST

- LIST ALTERNATIVE IDEAS FOR EACH FUNCTION AND NUMBER IDEAS CONSECUTIVELY.
- USE SEPARATE PAGE FOR EACH FUNCTION.
- <u>DO NOT EVALUATE IDEAS NOW. REFINEMENT COMES LATER.</u>

1.   FUNCTION NO. ___1___   __carry__   _(northbound) traffic_
                                                    (verb)   (noun)

Premises

- Constructing a northbound interstate under the 5 main line railroad tracks approaching the main railroad station will be extremely costly and time consuming, requiring careful underpinning.

- The resulting deep tunnel, also passing under the E-W interstate, will require extensive ventilation and will have high annual operation and maintenance costs.

Alternatives

A high-profile crossing over the railroad and E-W interstate will be less costly to build and less disruptive to rail operations.

C-6 Raise Profile of Northbound Interstate

EVALUATION PHASE
FEASIBILITY/SUITABILITY EVALUATION

1. **FEASIBILITY:** FOR EACH FUNCTION, REVIEW ALL THE IDEAS GENERATED IN THE SPECULATION PHASE AND LISTED ON PAGE 7. BEFORE YOU ELIMINATE ANY, ASK THE FOLLOWING QUESTIONS: WILL IT WORK? WILL IT SAVE MONEY? WILL IT MEET PERFORMANCE NEEDS?

NOW, ELIMINATE ANY UNSOUND, COSTLY, UNACCEPTABLE, OR PERHAPS UNTIMELY, IDEAS.

2. **SUITABILITY:** SELECT AND LIST BELOW THE MOST FEASIBLE IDEAS OR COMBINATION OF IDEAS FOR FURTHER CONSIDERATION. CHECK ( ) THE BEST IDEAS. USE A PAGE FOR EACH FUNCTION.

FUNCTION NO. __1__   __carry__   __(northbound) traffic__
                          (verb)   (noun)

NO.	IDEA	ADVANTAGES	DISADVANTAGES
1	Raise profile to pass over railroad and E-W interstate.	Reduces costs. Easier/faster to construct. Reduces vent. Requirements. Permits lower profile for adjacent northbound interstate elevated structure.	Must eliminate two local streets. Must reroute two ramps.
2	Reroute Ramp C, combining with Ramp E.	Maintains access, but longer distance. Avoids conflict with northbound interstate.	Longer ramp.

C-6 Raise Profile of Northbound Interstate

DEVELOPMENT PHASE
RECOMMENDED ALTERNATIVE -- VE TEAM SKETCH AND DESCRIPTION

Narrative of Proposed Changes

The Revised Proposed Action Plan includes a long, low-level tunnel for the northbound interstate from the vicinity of Main to the northern limit of the south interchange. A long 5.9% downgrade approaches the tunnel from the vicinity of West Street. The VE proposal recommends raising the mainline profile to cross over the railroad tracks and over the north-south interstate. The northbound interstate roadway would then descend a 5.0% downgrade, passing under the main railroad station connector and under a crossing street, rejoining the proposed profile and passing under the railroad line. The profile change would permit the north-south interstate structure south of West Street to be lowered as much as 20 feet. This change will avoid the costly underpinning of the railroad tracks, as well as eliminating ventilation of 1,200 feet of a 3-lane tunnel.

(Note: This recommendation would require the rerouting of two adjacent streets and one ramp.)

C-6 Raise Profile of Northbound Interstate

**DEVELOPMENT PHASE
VE COST COMPARISON**

1. ITEM	2. DESCRIPTION OF MODIFICATIONS	COSTS (000)			6. TRADEOFFS
		3. BEFORE	4. AFTER	5. SAVINGS	
C-6	Raise profile of interstate northbound.	$105,000	$36,200	$69,400	Must remove some ramps and streets.

DEVELOPMENT PHASE
NOTES AND DISCUSSIONS

USE THIS PAGE, AS APPROPRIATE, FOR DISCUSSION, LIFE-CYCLE COST CALCULATIONS, COMMENTARY ON AGENCY APPLICATION OF STANDARDS, SPECIFICATIONS, TRAFFIC PROJECTIONS, ETC.

ADDITIONAL NOTES

To accommodate the raised profile of the northbound interstate, the following changes would also be required:

- Eliminate adjacent streets northbound.

- Eliminate M Street.

- Eliminate Ramp B.

- Reroute Ramp C to take off local traffic and merge with Ramp E in the vicinity of Main Street, joining eastbound interstate with a single, right-hand entrance.

NOTE: This VE recommendation will not be feasible if the alternative recommendation (C-19) for raising the profile of E-W interstate is implemented.

C-6 Raise Profile of Northbound Interstate

DEVELOPMENT PHASE
SUMMARY AND RECOMMENDATIONS

CONCLUSIONS AND RECOMMENDATIONS

Raise profile of northbound interstate to pass over railroad tracks, then pass under the railroad station connector and crossing street.

SUMMARY OF SAVINGS

CATEGORY I   = $ __69.4 Million__   OR __6.9__ % OF TOTAL PROJECT
CATEGORY II   = $ _____   OR _____ % OF TOTAL PROJECT
CATEGORY III = $ _____   OR _____ % OF TOTAL PROJECT
CATEGORY IV   = $ _____   OR _____ % OF TOTAL PROJECT

TOTAL POTENTIAL SAVINGS
IDENTIFIED = $ __69.4__ Million   OR __6.9__ % OF TOTAL PROJECT

OTHER OPPORTUNITIES FOR VALUE "IMPROVEMENT":

There will be a reduction in the number of ventilation fans required in the ventilation building.

IMPLEMENTATION PLAN:
(DISPOSITION RECOMMENDED BY PROJECT MANAGER)

(Form continued on next page.)

C-6 Raise Profile of Northbound Interstate

DEVELOPMENT PHASE
SUMMARY AND RECOMMENDATIONS

IMPLEMENTATION PLAN: (DISPOSITION RECOMMENDED BY PM/DESIGNER)

C-6   Raise Profile of Northbound Interstate

Project Manager agrees with the VE report and design refinements currently under consideration to raise the profile of the northbound interstate.

Previously, the profile of the northbound interstate would work only as a tunnel, due to the Main Street bridge and M Street overcrossing, as the VE report pointed out. These items--C-3 and C-12--have been accepted, allowing this recommendation to be implemented.

C-6 Raise Profile of Northbound Interstate

IMPLEMENTATION PHASE
POSITION STATEMENT

FINAL DISPOSITION BY STATE DEPARTMENT OF PUBLIC WORKS (DPW)

The department concurs with this recommendation. Although a Main Street connection between Frontage Road and Albany Street is desirable, and an M Street connection to Frontage Road would enhance urban design potential, the savings realized by this design change is significant enough to warrant its approval.

S-4 Use of Strength and Load Factor Design Methods in Lieu of Working Strength Design

DEVELOPMENT PHASE
RECOMMENDED ALTERNATIVE -- VE TEAM SKETCH AND DESCRIPTION

A. For design of reinforced concrete structures, strength design method could be used in accordance with ACI-318, AASHTO design specifications for bridges, and the area manual.

The savings could be on the order of 10% for the concrete in sizes and quantity being contemplated, or on the order of $16.8 million.

B. Similarly, by using these design methods, savings are estimated on the order of 25% in amount of reinforcement or $24.2 million.

C. For design of highway steel structures, load factor design method could be used in accordance with AASHTO design specifications for bridges. The savings could be on the order of 7% for a saving of approximately $4.6 million.

The total savings for this proposal are approximately $45.6 million.

S-4 Use of Strength and Load Factor Design Methods in Lieu of Working Strength Design

HIGHWAY PROJECT
STUDY ID: SOUTH INTERCHANGE

**DEVELOPMENT PHASE
SUMMARY AND RECOMMENDATIONS**

CONCLUSIONS AND RECOMMENDATIONS

A. Use strength design method for sizing concrete structures.
   Savings: $16,800,000 or 1.8% of the total project.

B. Use strength design method for sizing up reinforcement required in concrete structures.
   Savings: $24,200,000 or 2.6% of the total project.

C. Use load factor design method for sizing structural steel for elevated highway superstructures.
   Savings: $4,600,000 or 0.5% of the total project.

SUMMARY OF SAVINGS

CATEGORY I   = $ __45.6 million__   OR __4.9__ % OF TOTAL PROJECT
CATEGORY II   = $ _____   OR _____ % OF TOTAL PROJECT
CATEGORY III = $ _____   OR _____ % OF TOTAL PROJECT
CATEGORY IV   = $ _____   OR _____ % OF TOTAL PROJECT

TOTAL POTENTIAL SAVINGS
IDENTIFIED = $ 45.6 million OR __4.9__ % OF TOTAL PROJECT

OTHER OPPORTUNITIES FOR VALUE "IMPROVEMENT":

IMPLEMENTATION PLAN:
(DISPOSITION RECOMMENDED BY PROJECT MANAGER)

(Form continued on next page.)

S-4 Use of Strength and Load Factor Design Methods in Lieu of Working Strength Design

DEVELOPMENT PHASE
SUMMARY AND RECOMMENDATIONS

IMPLEMENTATION PLAN:
(DISPOSITION RECOMMENDED BY PROJECT MANAGER/DESIGNER)

S-4 Use of Strength and Load Factor Design Methods in Lieu of Working Strength Design

Project Manager agrees with the VE study that the strength and load factor design
methods are appropriate for structural elements of this project, as cited. The Design Criteria is
being revised.

S-4 Use of Strength and Load Factor Design Methods in Lieu of Working Strength Design

IMPLEMENTATION PHASE
POSITION STATEMENT

FINAL DISPOSITION BY STATE DEPARTMENT OF PUBLIC WORKS (DPW):

The department concurs with the use of load factor design for all bridge/viaduct structures, whether steel or concrete. Design criteria now reflects this.

The use of load factor vs. working strength for tunnels is currently under review; all indications to date suggest that working stress design is favored.

The department has established that working stress design will be used for buildings and ancillary structures.

VALUE ENGINEERING REPORT
HIGHWAY PROJECT: South Interchange

3.0 DESCRIPTIVE INFORMATION
(Selected data only)

3.1 THE VALUE ENGINEERING TEAM

The value engineering team was organized to provide background and experience in VE and design of related projects. The team reviewed the plans and preliminary data for the current design and followed the general guidelines established by the Job Plan. The VE team members and their assignments are as follows:

Assignment	Area/s of Expertise
VE Team Leader	VE methodology & life cycle costing
Structural Engineer	Bridges and structures
Structural Engineer	Geotechnical & underground structures
Civil Engineer	Highway & traffic engineering
Civil Engineer	Highway construction & costs
Mechanical Engineer	HVAC & utilities

3.9 COST MODEL AND ESTIMATE BREAKDOWN

From the cost estimate provided by the design team, the VE team rearranged the cost to be more responsive to the VE methodology application. The costs were broken out into functional line items, e.g., ramps, Frontage Road, main lines, HOV, and others.

The costs were assembled using the unit costs provided to the team (not included in study) and quantities taken from the site drawing. This estimate was then reviewed, compared with the original project estimate, and adjusted. Ramp A was added in the time since the original estimate was compiled, and its cost has been added into the VE Cost Model (see attached Figure 3.1). Using the same line items as the estimate, a function analysis was performed and target worth figures developed. These figures were placed in the Cost Model. From the model and creative idea listing, the following areas of potential savings were isolated:

1) Main lines N-S	5) Ramp E
2) Main lines E-W	6) Ramp C
3) Ramp A	7) Ramp H
4) Ramp F	

Note: Sections 3.2 through 3.8 are not included in this case study.

A copy of the Masters Schedule Revision 1, the Cost Model, and the VE Cost Estimate Breakdown are attached (not included in study).

Unit Prices for VE Study

UNIT PRICES FOR VE STUDY

Average Unit Prices

Tunnels	1 Way	2 Lanes	$29,000/L.F.
Boat Section	1 Way	2 Lanes	$10,000/L.F.
Viaduct ML	1 Way	2 Lanes	$ 5,000/L.F.
On-Grade Road	1 Way	2 Lanes	$ 500/L.F.
Deep Tunnel N-S			$52,600/L.F.

• Gross number for LCC follow-on cost for maintenance, operational, replacement, etc.

Structures	1% of capital expenditure/yr
Tunnels	5% of capital expenditure/yr

Cost/Worth Model

South Interchange — Schematic

Project:
Location:
Phase of Design: Schematic
Date:
Notes:

Legend:

Component or System	VE Target: In Millions USD	Actual/Estimated: In Millions USD

Mile Post A + Mile Post B + Mile Post C = Main Interchange

Component	VE Target	Actual/Estimated
Main Interchange	690.45	996.08
Mile Post A	89.68	107.76
Mile Post B	39.26	41.61
Mile Post C	561.51	846.71

Mile Post A

Component	VE Target	Actual/Estimated
Frontage Roads	4.73	4.73
HOV Lanes	16.44	16.44
Main Line Lanes	52.00	66.61
Ramp K	4.00	7.47
Bypass Road A	9.47	9.47
Connector A	2.39	2.39
Access Road B	0.65	0.65

Mile Post B

Component	VE Target	Actual/Estimated
Frontage Roads	5.08	5.08
HOV Lanes	4.43	4.43
Main Line Lanes	22.00	24.35
Ramp K	4.43	4.43
Ramp I	3.32	3.32

Mile Post C

Component	VE Target	Actual/Estimated
N-S Lanes	163.56	326.63
E-W Lanes	397.95	520.08

N-S Lanes

Component	VE Target	Actual/Estimated
Frontage Roads	18.29	18.29
HOV Lanes	10.15	10.15
Main Line Lanes	61.50	132.16
Street Line	5.38	5.38
Connector B	12.14	12.14
Ramp A	0.00	64.73
Ramp K	6.10	6.10
Ramp E	30.00	46.50
Ramp C	20.00	31.18

E-W Lanes

Component	VE Target	Actual/Estimated
Main Line Lanes	170.00	243.14
Ramp AA	1.52	1.52
Ramp BB	5.09	5.09
Ramp CE	17.97	17.97
Ramp FF	16.51	16.51
Ramp F	95.00	138.64
Ramp D	37.10	37.10
Ramp FF	6.65	6.65
Ramp G	11.13	11.13
Ramp H	7.13	7.13
Ramp KK	15.50	15.50
Ramp LL	11.15	11.15
Ramp B	0.00	5.35
Ramp Q	3.08	3.08
Ramp U	0.12	0.12

Wastewater Treatment Plant

I n July 1993 a value engineering study was conducted on a proposed wastewater treatment plant (WWTP) Phase 2 expansion program, which required an increase in output from 4.5 million gallons per day (MGD) to 9.0 million gallons per day (MGD). The study also evaluated a larger planned expansion up to 88 MGD.[1] As such, the projected total saving exceeded the estimate for the initial upgrade.

Several reviews with the owner and designer (see Tables 1a and 1b) showed that most of the team's proposals were implemented. Initial cost savings were calculated at $15,000,000 based on progression of the design and related estimates. Follow-on annual savings of over $1,000,000/year were estimated again, based on final design. Savings from the water conservation efforts were not included in these totals.

Case Study Elements

The items listed below and shown in this case study have been excerpted from an actual VE report. (The Table of Contents on page 333 is one of the excerpts and refers to some documents not listed here or shown in the section.)

1. The author thanks both the owner, Regional Municipality of Halton, Public Works Department of Ontario, Canada, and MacViro, local consultants, for their permission to use this project as a case study.

Wastewater Treatment Plant
Expansion Project

Table of Contents

This is the Table of Contents from the actual VE report. Selected excerpts appear in this case study.

Wastewater Treatment Plant
Expansion Project

Executive Summary

A value engineering study was conducted on a proposed wastewater treatment plant (WWTP) Phase 2 expansion from 4.5 million gallons per day (MGD) to 9.0 million gallons per day (MGD). The study was conducted on site in the spring of 1993. The two major objectives of the study were to conduct a VE review of the Phase 2 expansion as recommended in the 1992 Environmental Study Report and to develop a maximum site utilization plan.

Over 180 ideas were developed during the study, from which the team developed approximately 72 proposals, including about 25 design suggestions. Some 25 proposals recommended additional costs primarily oriented toward life cycle savings. These proposals offer over $5,000,000 in potential savings for the present Phase 2 expansion, offset by some $500,000 in costs for performance or life cycle improvements. Life cycle cost savings of $300,000 to $400,000 per year were identified. In addition, over $10,000,000 in potential savings for future expansions beyond 9.0 MGD were identified. These savings would be offset by approximately $13,000,000 of suggested additions for meeting anticipated new standards, performance and life cycle improvements.

VE Proposals

Principal proposals for the Phase 2 plant expansion are:

- haul sludge to centralized sludge storage; convert existing storage tank to a digester; and build storage at CSSF.
- delete additional primary tanks by increasing aeration capacity and adding fine screens.
- reduce aeration tank modules from 4 to 2.
- thicken digested sludge.
- renegotiate Certificate of Approval to reduce need for nitrification and lessen effluent quality criteria.
- reduce size of plant through water conservation.

In addition, several other significant proposals were generated, such as buying a new boiler to utilize plant digester gas, improve handling of grit by using a compactor and auto bagger, raising liquid level in aeration tanks, and seasonal versus continuous disinfection.

For the future expansions beyond 9 MGD, the team generated several significant proposals. These were:

- raise hydraulic profile in the northwest plant.
- recover digester sludge heat.
- use vortex grit removal units.
- use deeper aeration tanks.

- utilize maximum size tanks.

- use chlorine gas vs. hypochlorite, or consider using ultraviolet irradiation.

- reduce need for odor control through utilization of foul air for aeration.

- evaluate alternative digester designs.

- utilize BNR technology.

- thicken waste-activated sludge.

- change to centrifugal blowers for aeration.

The team also recommended the following design suggestions to optimize future expansions beyond Phase 2: procurement of adjoining land for future expansion, conversion of inlet building for greater usage, and utilization of larger 5.5/11 MGD expansion modules.

In July 1993 the draft of this report was reviewed by all VE team members. Tables 1a and 1b summarize the VE proposals that were approved by the team and that are recommended to the region for implementation. The proposals have been grouped under four headings, as follows:

> Table 1a -- Phase 2 Expansion
> > Group 1: Recommended Actions
> > Group 2: Regional Follow-up Actions
> > Group 3: Certificate of Approval Negotiations
>
> Table 1b -- Future Expansion for 9 MGD to 55 MGD
> > Group 4: Recommended Actions

Ultimate Site Capacity

The team combined several applicable ideas and developed a proposed ultimate site development plan. This plan indicates that an 88 MGD plant, with reasonable provisions for possible new standards, appears feasible. Appendix C provides the narrative backup and the proposed plan.

Cost Estimates

(i) Phase 2 Expansion (4.5 MGD to 9.0 MGD)

The cost estimates for the originally proposed Phase 2 expansion, prepared by another firm, are summarized in Table 2. In addition, Table 2 shows the cost estimates developed by the VE team, incorporating the impact of the approved VE recommendations that are detailed in Table 1a under Group 1. Table 2 also shows the differences in capital costs and the annual operations and maintenance savings, resulting from these recommendations.

(ii) Expansion from 9.0 MGD to 55.0 MGD

Construction costs for a single plant expansion program from 4.5 MGD to 55 MGD are estimated at approximately $140,000,000 (see pages 3-4). However, as noted in Appendix C, a staged construction program using 11 MGD expansion modules is recommended. Cost estimates for the various expansion phases are summarized in Table 3. It can be seen that the total estimated costs for the staged construction program for the 55 MGD plant exceed the estimated costs of a single expansion program.

Costs shown for Phase 3 and beyond are of an order-of-magnitude level only. They are based on the VE workshop cost model (pages 3-4) and are prepared by scale-up procedures and/or other data available to the team members during the workshop week. They are presented to introduce, on a preliminary basis, the various construction phases into the region's capital works program.

(iii) Expansion to 88.0 MGD

Construction costs for a single expansion program from 4.5 MGD to 88.0 MGD would be approximately $230,000,000. However, under a continued, staged construction program beyond 55.0 MGD, additional 11.0 MGD expansion modules would be estimated as shown in Table 3.

These costs are based on estimates for similar modules for the 55.0 MGD plant expansion.

Observations

The following obserations can be made on the VE review of the current Phase 2 expansion:

• Cost estimate of the originally proposed Phase 2 expansion	$11,977,000
• The impact of the VE recommendations on the cost estimate include:	
Cost savings	-5,513,500
Costs of additional features to improve operations and reduce annual operations and maintenance costs	+480,400
Update of original cost estimate	+356,100
• Base cost estimate of the VE recommended Phase 2 expansion	$7,300,000
• The base cost estimate includes provisions for off-site sludge storage at the central sludge storage facility.	

Conclusions

The VE recommendations for the current Phase 2 expansion include the following:

• Total capital cost savings	$4,677,000
• Total annual operations and maintenance cost savings (per year)	$69,730
• For budgetary purposes, a contingency allowance of 10% should be included.	
• Total cost estimate (budget)	$8,030,000

Table 1a

Summary of Approved VE Recommendations for Current Phase 2 Expansion

No.	Description	Original Design Cost	VE Design Cost	Initial Cost Savings	Total PW Cost Savings
	Group 1 **Recommended Actions**				
L7	Add unloading facilities for septage & leachate	0	50,000	(50,000)	87,600
L10 L39 PB3 F31	Add screening press and auto-bagger for screenings and grit. Add odour control for headworks	0	93,900	(93,900)	16,100
L11B PH17	Buy methane gas boiler for heating. Consider co-gen in future.	0	150,000	(150,000)	78,200
L32	Minimize landscaping	0	0	0	55,000
L38	Reroute organic return flow	0	15,000	(15,000)	(15,000)
L58 F1	Revise sludge handling design. Haul sludge to CSSF. Pumping for future expansion.	7,235,500	2,200,000	5,035,500	5,035,500
L59	Replace 2 primary clarifiers with one large unit	1,195,000	950,000	245,000	245,000
PD5	Delete primary tanks completely (pending PD7 results). Savings in addition to L59 (above)	Same as L59	Less than L59: (488,000)	488,000	388,900
PE5	Reduce aeration tank modules from 4 to 2	133,000	0	133,000	155,000
PE12	Raise water level in aeration tanks. Delete weir.	100,000	0	100,000	100,000
PG4	Add flow metering for secondary bypass	0	25,000	(25,000)	(52,500)
PI1	Upgrade computers	0	6,500	(6,500)	(15,500)
PI10	Thicken digested sludge	0	100,000	(100,000)	412,000
PI15	Improve sludge loading platform	0	5,000	(5,000)	(5,000)
PI16	Add automatic sampler	0	15,000	(15,000)	(21,200)
PI18	Add chlorination points	0	20,000	(20,000)	(28,300)
	Summary Group 1 Savings Improvements (Costs)* Total (* Note: PD5 not included)	8,663,500	3,630,400	5,513,500 (480,400) 5,033,100	6,573,300 (137,500) 6,435,800

	Group 2 **Regional Follow-up Actions**				
L11C	Consider co-gen at Burlington Skyway Plant	0	670,000	(670,000)	(44,400)
L22	Lease selected site area	0	0	4,000	55,000
L26	Use iron salts in lieu of alum	-	-	-	-
PD7	Conduct settling test in primary tanks	-	10,000	(10,000)	(10,000)
PE3	Conduct O_2 transfer efficiency test	-	10,000	(10,000)	(10,000)
PH12	Pump raw sludge from Oakville Southwest WPCP to Mid-Halton WPCP	-	-	-	-
F15	Reclaim leased property in future	-	-	-	-
F21	Investigate privatization of energy options	-	-	-	-
F28	Follow-up on Water Conservation Program - 9 MGD - Additional 46 MGD	12,287,000 106,239,000	10,450,000 90,305,000	1,847,000 15,934,000	3,272,000 28,268,000
F36	Purchase land on eastern boundary. Consider land purchase east of Pumping Station for new potable water treatment plant	0	750,000	(750,000)	(750,000)
F37	Consider privatization of wastewater operations	-	-	-	-
	Group 3 **Certificate of Approval Actions**				
PE7	Reduce need for nitrification - 9 MGD - Additional 46 MGD	1,733,000 8,850,000	0 4,425,000	1,733,000 4,425,000	2,228,400 6,957,000
PG3	Seasonal vs. continuous disinfection - 9 MGD - additional 46 MGD	- -	- -	- -	185,800 949,000
F24 F25	Lessen stringent effluent quality criteria			significant savings	

Table 1b

Summary of Approved VE Recommendations for Future Expansion from 9 - 55 MGD

No.	Description	Original Design Cost	VE Design Cost	Initial Cost Savings	Total PW Cost Savings
	Group 4 **Recommended Actions.** **Savings Expressed for 55 MGD Plant**				
L2 F12	Revise hydraulic gradient in plant	N/A	N/A	762,000	1,068,000
L3 L4	Consider rectangular clarifiers	Design suggestion			
L5 F8	Evaluate alternative digesters: - deeper tanks - egg-shaped	17,820,000 Design suggestion	18,700,000	(880,000)	1,872,000
L6 L34 F30	Assign area for tertiary treatment. Sell effluent to users.	Design suggestion			
L10	Add odour control to pumping stations	Design suggestion			
L12	Use deeper aeration tanks			30,000	195,000
L13	Minimize size of galleries			120,000	120,000
L16	Use Vortex type grit removal Phase 3: 11 MGD Additional 33 MGD	1,219,000 3,657,000	895,000 2,685,000	324,000 972,000	324,000 972,000
L23	Use precast concrete covers on channels			20,000	20,000
L30	Maintain separate secondary treatment trains	Design suggestion			
L31 F29	Use larger module sizes	Design suggestion			
L52	Assign area for nutrient removal	Design suggestion			
L58	Pump sludge to CSSF	0	2,000,000	(2,000,000)	1,072,000
PB7	Reduce head space at Inlet Building	Design suggestion			
F1	Continue to store (or dewater) sludge at CSSF	Design suggestion			
F2	Maximize existing pumping station - peak flows 60 MGD	Design suggestion			

F3	Construct new pumping station on NW corner of existing site with capacity for average daily flow of 55 MGD (peak flow 105 MGD)	Design suggestion			
F5	Construct new 66 MGD plant on existing Mid Halton site to treat flow from North Halton	Design suggestion			
F9	Provide for interconnection of 22 MGD and 66 MGD plants	Design suggestion			
F10	Provide shared sludge handling and emergency power supply	Design suggestion			
F19	Consider new power supply to Mid Halton site; investigate second grid to reduce requirement for standby power generators	Design suggestion			
F20	Consider ultimate needs for natural gas and potable water	Design suggestion			
F22	Thickening of waste activated sludge vs. co-setting in primary clarifier	31,807,000	23,955,000	7,812,000	5,830,000
F23A F23B	Evaluate alternative disinfection: - UV irradiation - chlorine gas	500,000+ 500,000+	2,000,000+ 1,000,000+	(1,500,000)+ (500,000)+	(14,000)+ 3,078,000+
F32	Evaluate BNR technology	49,200,000	58,800,000	(9,600,000)	16,429,000
F33	Use centrifugal blowers vs. positive displacement	2,520,000	1,800,000	720,000	1,408,000
F39	Consider digested sludge heat recovery	0	200,000	(200,000)	557,000
	Appendix B - Dwg F2 Ultimate Site Development Plan	Design suggestion			
	Summary Group 4 Savings Improvements Total			10,760,000 (13,180,000) (2,420,000)	9,937,000 23,008,000 32,945,000

+ Note: Chlorine gas alternative used in summary.

Wastewater Treatment Plant
Expansion Project

Section 2 -- Project Description

The value engineering study included two main subjects, as follows:

    I.   Value engineering of the currently proposed expansion
    II. Preparation of an ultimate site development plan

I. CURRENTLY PROPOSED EXPANSION PROGRAM
(as recommended in the 1992 Environmental Study Report)

Scope of Work

Expand the plant from its current capacity of 20,500 m^3/d to 41,000 m^3/d. The proposed addition of one 20,500 m^3/d module consists of the following:

- Two (2) primary clarifiers
- Four (4) aeration cells
- Two (2) air blowers
- Two (2) final clarifiers
- New return activated sludge and waste-activated sludge systems
- Improvements to the existing cogeneration system
- One primary and one secondary digestion tank
- One sludge storage tank
- Facilities to receive leachate from the waste management site and sludge hauled from other plants in the area
- Site work, including roads and landscaping
- All associated instrumentation and control systems for integration in the existing SCADA system; all mechanical, electrical, and ancillary items

Estimate

In October 1992 a firm prepared itemized cost estimates for a total construction cost of $11,977,000. Copies of the estimate pages A-2 to A-8 are included in this section as pages 2-3 to 2-9.

II. ULTIMATE SITE DEVELOPMENT

Determine the maximum plant capacity that can be accommodated on the existing site and develop an ultimate site development plan.

The original master plan, prepared by another firm, is attached as Figure 2-1 (page 2-10).

The wastewater treatment plant criteria used during this study are included on pages 2-11 to 2-13.

Wastewater Treatment Plant
Expansion Program

Section 3 -- Value Engineering Analysis Procedure

GENERAL

Value engineering is a creative, organized approach whose objective is to optimize the life cycle cost and/or performance of a facility. In this section we have outlined the procedure followed for the study (1) to present a clear description of our assessment of the project in terms of cost and energy usage, and (2) to explain the approach that we applied to the study.

A multidisciplinary team approach, utilizing applicable value engineering techniques, was used to analyze the project design. It was the team's objective to analyze the project, find high cost areas, recommend alternatives, and estimate initial and life cycle costs for the original design and for each proposed alternative. Other criteria were also used to assure that proposed recommendations did not sacrifice essential functions and timely completion of the project. The actual recommendations derived from the analysis are identified in Section 4 of this report.

PRESTUDY PREPARATION

The success of a VE study is largely dependent on proper preparation and coordination. Information and documents furnished by the owner and designer were distributed to the team in advance of the workshop to prepare them for their area of study. Participants were briefed on their roles and responsibilities during the study. The prestudy effort for this project included the following activities:

- Identification of constraints to the VE study
- Review of project design documentation
- Finalization of arrangements for the workshop

The VE team received excellent support from the owner and designer in the way of information.

VE JOB PLAN

The VE study was organized into six distinct parts comprising the VE Job Plan: (1) Information Phase, (2) Creative Phase, (3) Judgment Phase, (4) Development Phase, (5) Presentation Phase, (6)Report Phase.

Information Phase

Early in the Information Phase, the VE team prepared a cost/worth model for the proposed expansion (see Cost Model 1). The model was broken down by systems and subsystems representing major functions of the project. The numbers in the upper portion of each box represent the design estimate of the cost of construction of the system functions. The numbers in the lower portion of each box represent the VE team's evaluation of the worth of the system functions.

The term *worth* is defined as the lowest cost means possible to achieve an individual function without regard to other systems or functions. Worth is determined by experience of the VE team member, use of data from similar construction, and historical parameter cost data.
The cost/worth model helped to isolate areas of higher potential savings so the VE team could concentrate on those areas. As the model indicates, the major potential for savings occurs in the following areas:

Solids handling	$2,400,000
Architectural	$470,000
Piping/Mechanical	$250,000
Primary Tanks	$200,000
Electrical	$200,000

Overall, the VE team saw a potential cost savings goal of approximately $4 million from the estimated cost of construction.Concurrently, the team collected data on costs and developed an estimate for a plant of 55 MGD. This was done to develop savings estimates for further site development and for budget-planning guidance for the owner. The cost model, (Cost Model 2), was developed. From this model, a total savings potential from VE was targeted at some $20,000,000, with a broad target savings across the total plant.

Next, the VE team analyzed the project documents and prepared a function analysis for the different project components. The functions of any system are the controlling elements in the overall VE approach. This procedure forces the participants to think in terms of function and the cost associated with that function. Preparing the function analysis helped to generate many of the ideas that eventually resulted in recommendations.

This function analysis for the project is included as Worksheet 1. It isolated areas of potential savings and provided backup data to the worth areas selected in the cost/worth model.

Creative Phase

This step in the value engineering study involves the listing of creative ideas. During this time, the value engineering team thinks of as many ways as possible to provide the necessary functions at a lower initial and/or life cycle cost. During the creative phase, judgment of the ideas is restricted. The value engineering team is looking for quantity and association of ideas which will be screened in the next phase of the study. This list may include ideas that can be further evaluated and used in the design.

The creative idea listings are included as Appendix A in this report. They are grouped and numbered by discipline or study team in the following sequence:

L	Layout	59 ideas
P	Process	87 ideas
F	Future	39 ideas

In all, some 185 ideas were listed.

Judgment Phase

In this phase of the project, the value engineering team judged the ideas resulting from the creative session. The remainder of the format provided in Appendix A was used for this phase and results are included on the right side of the worksheet.

The value engineering team ranked the ideas according to the following criteria:

State of the art	1-10	New--existing technology
Probability of implementation	0-10	Low--high chance
Magnitude of savings	0-10	Small--large savings
Redesign effort	0-10	Large--minimal effort
Schedule	0-10	Large--no impact

Advantages and disadvantages of each idea are quickly considered and recorded. Ideas found to be impractical or not worthy of additional study are disregarded, and those ideas that represent the greatest potential for cost savings are then developed further.

The VE team, with help from the owner, created a life cycle model (LCC) to develop a long-range profile for the project. Through interaction with the owner, each cost item on the LCC model was explored to determine its importance. These interactions were quite important for developing a full site utilization approach.

The LCC model, (LCC-1), illustrates the categories addressed by the VE team during the VE workshop. The costs shown are estimated annual costs and the amortized (PP) initial financial expenditure.

Development Phase

During the Development Phase of the value engineering study, many of the ideas were expanded into workable solutions. The development consisted of the recommended design, life cycle cost consideration, and a descriptive evaluation of the advantages and disadvantages of the proposed recommendations.
It was important that the value engineering team convey the concept of each recommendation to the designer. Therefore, each recommendation was presented with a brief narrative to compare the original design method to the proposed change. Sketches and design calculations, where

appropriate, are included in this report with the corresponding recommendations. The individual VE recommendations are included as Appendix B to this report.

Presentation and Report Phase

The last phase of the value engineering effort was the presentation and preparation of recommendations. The major VE recommendations were summarized and presented to the owner and designer at the conclusion of the workshop.

We appreciated the presence of key regional management officials at the oral briefing. At this meeting, we reported a savings for the proposed Phase 2 expansion to 9 MGD of some $4 million, representing some 33%. Based on previous similar studies, implemented savings should be greater than 50% of the savings identified. In addition, annual savings of up to $500,000/yr were also identified.

As for the ultimate site layout, a break-out team was set up and a concurrent study generated. The results of their study are attached as Appendix C.

For the future ultimate site utilization of 88 MGD, annual savings of $2,500,000 were projected which included several areas of additional expenditures of process and life cycle improvements. Annual savings of over $3,000,000/yr were projected if all proposals were implemented.

At the conclusion of the workshop, and before final preparation of this report, each VE recommendation was again reviewed. As a result of that review, some proposals made at the presentation may have been deleted from the report and some may have been added.

Implementation Plan

In accordance with the schedule, an implementation meeting was held on July 1993.

ECONOMIC FACTORS

During the value engineering study, construction cost and life cycle cost summaries are prepared for each element of the project. Economic data and assumptions made for the life cycle cost comparisons were as follows:

Discount rate (for LCC only)	6% (compounded annually)
Analysis period	30 years
Equivalence approach	Present worth converted to annualized method
Inflation Approach	Constant dollars
Present worth annuity factor	13.76
PP Year 30	0.0726
Periodic payment (PP) factor	
Desired payback period	3 to 5 years

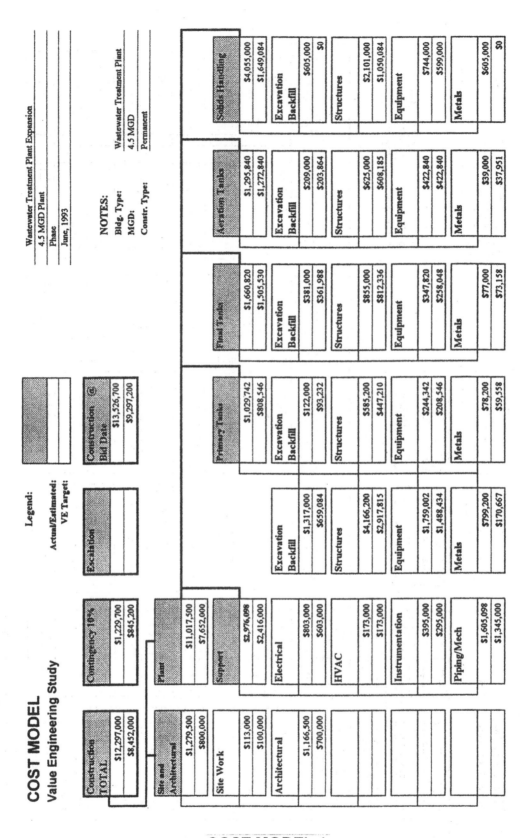

COST MODEL
Value Engineering Study

Wastewater Treatment Plant Expansion
4.5 MGD Plant
Phase
June, 1993

NOTES:
Bldg. Type: Wastewater Treatment Plant
MGD: 4.5 MGD
Constr. Type: Permanent

Legend:
Actual/Estimated:
VE Target:

	Actual/Estimated	VE Target
Construction TOTAL	$12,297,000	$8,452,000
Escalation		
Contingency 10%	$1,229,700	$845,200
Construction @ Bid Date	$13,526,700	$9,297,200
Plant	$11,017,500	$7,652,000
Site and Architectural	$1,279,500	$800,000
Site Work	$113,000	$100,000
Architectural	$1,166,500	$700,000
Support	$2,976,098	$2,416,000
Electrical	$803,000	$603,000
HVAC	$173,000	$173,000
Instrumentation	$395,000	$295,000
Piping/Mech	$1,605,098	$1,345,000
Primary Tanks	$1,029,742	$808,546
Final Tanks	$1,660,820	$1,505,530
Aeration Tanks	$1,295,840	$1,272,840
Solids Handling	$4,055,000	$1,649,084

Primary Tanks
	Actual/Estimated	VE Target
Excavation Backfill	$122,000	$93,232
Structures	$585,200	$447,210
Equipment	$244,342	$208,546
Metals	$78,200	$59,558

Final Tanks
	Actual/Estimated	VE Target
Excavation Backfill	$381,000	$361,988
Structures	$855,000	$812,336
Equipment	$347,820	$258,048
Metals	$77,000	$73,158

Aeration Tanks
	Actual/Estimated	VE Target
Excavation Backfill	$209,000	$203,864
Structures	$625,000	$608,185
Equipment	$422,840	$422,840
Metals	$39,000	$37,951

Solids Handling
	Actual/Estimated	VE Target
Excavation Backfill	$605,000	$0
Structures	$2,101,000	$1,050,084
Equipment	$744,000	$599,000
Metals	$605,000	$0

Totals (Excavation/Structures/Equipment/Metals)
	Actual/Estimated	VE Target
Excavation Backfill	$1,317,000	$659,084
Structures	$4,166,200	$2,917,815
Equipment	$1,759,002	$1,488,434
Metals	$799,200	$170,667

COST MODEL 1

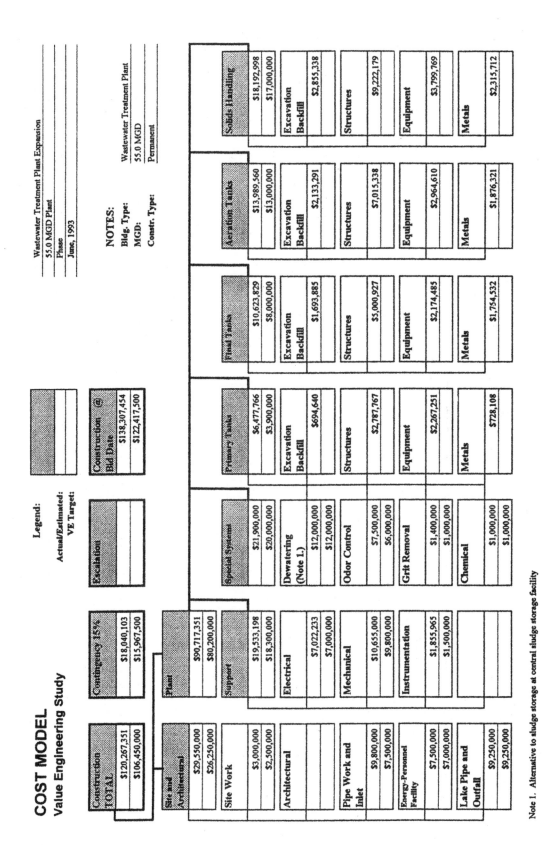

COST MODEL
Value Engineering Study

Wastewater Treatment Plant Expansion
55.0 MGD Plant
Phase
June, 1993

NOTES:
Bldg. Type: Wastewater Treatment Plant
MGD: 55.0 MGD
Constr. Type: Permanent

Legend:

	Actual/Estimated:
	VE Target:

Construction TOTAL
| $120,267,351 |
| $106,450,000 |

Contingency 15%
| $18,040,103 |
| $15,967,500 |

Construction @ Bid Date
| $138,307,454 |
| $122,417,500 |

Excavation

Plant
| $90,717,351 |
| $80,200,000 |

Site and Architectural
| $29,550,000 |
| $26,250,000 |

Support
| $19,533,198 |
| $18,300,000 |

Special Systems
| $21,900,000 |
| $20,000,000 |

Primary Tanks
| $6,477,766 |
| $3,900,000 |

Final Tanks
| $10,623,829 |
| $8,000,000 |

Aeration Tanks
| $13,989,560 |
| $13,000,000 |

Solids Handling
| $18,192,998 |
| $17,000,000 |

Site Work
| $3,000,000 |
| $2,500,000 |

Electrical
| $7,022,233 |
| $7,000,000 |

Dewatering (Note 1.)
| $12,000,000 |
| $12,000,000 |

Excavation Backfill
| $694,640 |

Excavation Backfill
| $1,693,885 |

Excavation Backfill
| $2,133,291 |

Excavation Backfill
| $2,855,338 |

Architectural
| — |
| — |

Mechanical
| $10,655,000 |
| $9,800,000 |

Odor Control
| $7,500,000 |
| $6,000,000 |

Structures
| $2,787,767 |

Structures
| $5,000,927 |

Structures
| $7,015,338 |

Structures
| $9,222,179 |

Pipe Work and Inlet
| $9,800,000 |
| $7,500,000 |

Instrumentation
| $1,855,965 |
| $1,500,000 |

Grit Removal
| $1,400,000 |
| $1,000,000 |

Equipment
| $2,267,251 |

Equipment
| $2,174,485 |

Equipment
| $2,964,610 |

Equipment
| $3,799,769 |

Energy-Personnel Facility
| $7,500,000 |
| $7,000,000 |

Chemical
| $1,000,000 |
| $1,000,000 |

Metals
| $728,108 |

Metals
| $1,754,532 |

Metals
| $1,876,321 |

Metals
| $2,315,712 |

Lake Pipe and Outfall
| $9,250,000 |
| $9,250,000 |

Note 1. Alternative to sludge storage at central sludge storage facility

COST MODEL 2

FUNCTION ANALYSIS WORKSHEET

PROJECT: Wastewater Treatment Plant Expansion
ITEM: Wastewater
BASIC FUNCTION: Treat Waste - 4.5 MGD

B = Basic Function   S = Secondary Function   RS = Required Secondary Function

COMPONENT DESCRIPTION	FUNCTION Verb	FUNCTION Noun	KIND	COST (x 1000)	WORTH (x 1000)	COST/ WORTH	COMMENTS
Primary Clarifiers							
- structures	treat	waste	RS	785	600	1.31	Use one large primary tank with bridge-type collector
	hold	waste	RS	410	350	1.17	
- equipment	treat	waste	B	1,195	950	1.26	
Seration Cells							
- structures	transmit	waste	RS	873	850	1.03	Design aeration tank for plug flows only
- equipment	treat	waste	B	859	859	1.00	Delete cross walls
Final Clarifiers							
- structures	transmit	waste	S	1,403	1,333	1.05	Use rectangular tanks
- equipment	process	waste	B	620	460	1.35	
Solids Handling							
- structures	hold	waste	RS	4,126	2,400	1.72	Use existing digesters pump off-site
- equipment	treat	waste	B	1,943	1,400	1.39	
- architectural	enclose	equipment	RS	1,665	1,000	1.67	
Site Work							
- roads & landscaping	provide	access	RS	113	100	1.13	

Worksheet 1

LIFE CYCLE COST MODEL

11 MGD PLANT MODULE

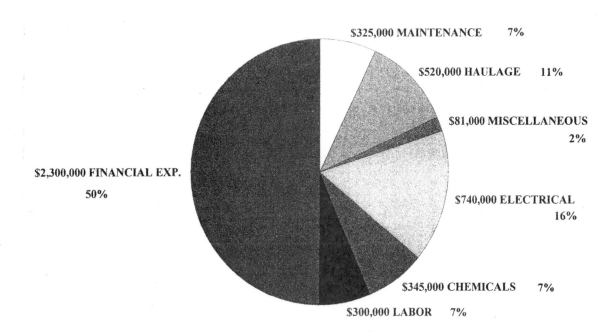

$325,000 MAINTENANCE   7%

$520,000 HAULAGE   11%

$81,000 MISCELLANEOUS   2%

$740,000 ELECTRICAL   16%

$345,000 CHEMICALS   7%

$300,000 LABOR   7%

$2,300,000 FINANCIAL EXP.   50%

Assuming utilization of digester gas in
new boiler and pumping to central
sludge storage facility.

Wastewater Treatment Plant
Expansion Project

Section 4 -- Summary of Results

GENERAL

This section of the value engineering study summarizes the results and recommendations for the study. Ideas that were developed are submitted here as recommendations for acceptance.

It is important, when reviewing the results of the VE study, to consider each part of a recommendation on its own merits. Often there is a tendency to disregard a recommendation when concern is raised about one portion of it. Following is an effective strategy for evaluation of VE study reports: Locate acceptable areas within a recommendation and apply those parts to the final design.

VALUE ENGINEERING RECOMMENDATIONS

The value engineering team developed 72 proposals for change, including some alternates for the same idea, that represented approximately $7,300,000 in value. For clarity, proposals have been separated into groups, as shown below.

Recommendation Category	Reference Code	No. Proposal	Total Initial Savings	Total Annual Savings
Layout	L	27	$4,000,000	$300,000
Process	P	19	800,000	175,000
Future	F	26	2,500,000	3,450,000
TOTALS		72	**$7,300,000**	**$3,925,000**

ADDITIONAL COST SAVINGS IDEAS

Both the owner and designer should carefully review the idea listing provided in Appendix A. The VE team attempted to develop the most significant items, but, time constraints prohibited preparation of recommendations for every savings item possible.

PROJECT: Wastewater Treatment Plant VE
ITEM: Cogen Upgrade

ORIGINAL DESIGN

- Two (2) 150 KW digester--gas engine--generator sets, with 1.2×10^6 BTU exhaust gas boilers (hot water) in the basement of the Energy Building. These units also provide emergency power in the WWTP, using enhanced controls.

- Two (2) 1235 KW (4.2×10^6 BTU) natural gas fired hot water boilers as backup on the grade floor of the same building.

- There appears to be a serious problem with the operability in regard to engine robustness (speed too high at 1800 rpm) and corrosion of engine internals from excessive hydrogen sulphide (2,000 ppm to 3,000 ppm) in the digester gas supply.

PROPOSED DESIGN

Alternative A -- Upgrade Cogen

- Buy new 300 KW engine generators of robust design (1200 rpm, naturally -- aspirated), suitable for <u>digester-gas</u> firing, and add a gas scrubber to reduce H_2S to an acceptable level.

- Sell two (2) existing 150 KW engine-generator sets for <u>natural gas</u> firing only.

Alternative B -- Add Boiler

- Add new small boiler fired by digester -- gas, or replace one existing natural gas fired boiler with a <u>digester gas</u> fired unit. (Avoid modifying an existing boiler with a new digester gas burner; copper tubes are unsuitable for corrosive digester gas.)

- Plan the installation of improved cogeneration for the next increment. Note: Scrubber not required for this alternative.

(Alternative design proposals are continued on the next page.)

LIFE CYCLE COST SUMMARY	CAPITAL	ANNUAL O&M	
Original Design	$	$	
Proposed Design	$	$	
Savings	$	$	
PRESENT WORTH (PS)ANNUAL O&M COST			$
LIFE CYCLE (PW) SAVINGS			$

See attached Life Cycle Costs Analyses.

Alternative C

- Buy 350 KW cogeneration generators of robust design, suitable for digester gas firing and scrubber, if required for Skyway WWTP presently generating gas and not cogenerating.

DISCUSSION

The cogen units are important for energy conservation opportunities involving load-displacement of power and heat at the plant. When the plant reaches the stage that it is developing enough methane gas to support a new 300 KW cogen unit, the savings would be significantly greater for upgrading cogen than for operating the digester gas fired boiler. On this basis, the following are recommended.

1. The wastewater treatment plant's best option is to provide replacement upgraded boiler in the initial phase (see attached LCC based on 150 KW Cogen Unit) and upgrade the cogen at subsequent phases when the gas generation is closer to allowing continuous operation. The existing units can be retained for standby power service using natural gas fuel.

2. In lieu of the region replacing the engine-generators, the cogen system could be privatized with a specialist firm for reduced capital outlay and operating staff labor commitment.

3. A cogen installation at Skyway WWTP would be more suitable based on higher capacity (20 MGD) and existing pressurized gas storage. This could sustain a 350 KW unit.

O&M COSTS

Proposed Alternative A -- Upgrade Cogen

Gross Power Savings	150 KW x $540/KW YR = $81,000/YR	
Maintenance Cost	150 KW x $0.02/KW x 7,000 HR/YR = 21,000/YR	
Heat Savings	250 KWH x 3410 BTU/KW x 1/1000 CF/BTU x	
	7,000 HR/YR x $3.50/1000 CF =	$20,900/YR
Maintenance Cost		$ 2,900/YR
Total Savings		$78,000/YR

Proposed Alternative B -- Smaller Boiler

Based on same gas input as Cogen

Gross Savings	1.4×10^3 BTU/HR x 1/1000 CF/BTU x	
	7000 HR/YR x $3.50/1000 CF =	$34,300/YR
Maintenance		$ 3,300/YR
Total Savings at design flows		$31,000/YR
Total Average Savings		$16,580/YR

COST WORKSHEET

PROJECT: Wastewater Treatment Plant VE
ITEM: Cogen Upgrade

ITEM	UNIT	QTY.	UNIT COST	TOTAL
Proposed Alternative A - Upgrade Cogen				
Buy 300 KW at $1,500/KW	KW	300	$1,500	$450,000
Sell 300 KW at $400/KW	KW	300	($400)	($120,000)
Scrubber	LS	1	140,000	140,000
Installation and Miscellaneous	LS	1	80,000	80,000
Subtotal				550,000
Total				$550,000
Proposed Alternative B - Smaller Boiler				
Special burner	LS	1	75,000	75,000
Digester gas piping	LS	1	75,000	75,000
Subtotal				150,000
Total				$150,000

Note: Use existing cogen as a natural gas emergency unit.

DEVELOPMENT PHASE - LIFE CYCLE COST (Present Worth Method)

Cogen Update
Proposal No. __L-11___ Date _
PROJECT LIFE CYCLE (YEARS)   10
DISCOUNT RATE (PERCENT)   6.000%

			ALT. A Cogen Update (w/scrubber)		ALT. B Small Boiler (w/o scrubber)		ALT. C Skyway (w/scrubber)	
Capital Cost			Est.	PW	Est.	PW	Est.	PW
A) Initial Costs			550000	550000	150000	150000	670000	670000
B)				0		0		0
C)				0		0		0
D)				0		0		0
E)				0		0		0
F)				0		0		0
Other Initial Costs								
A)				0		0		0
B)				0		0		0
Total Initial Cost Impact (IC)				550000		150000		670000
Initial Cost PW Savings								

Replacement/Salvage Costs	Year	Factor						
A)	—	1.0000		0		0		0
B)	—	1.0000		0		0		0
C)	—	1.0000		0		0		0
D)	—	1.0000		0		0		0
E)	—	1.0000		0		0		0
F)	—	1.0000		0		0		0
G)	—	1.0000		0		0		0
Salvage (neg. cash flow)	—	1.0000		0		0		0
Total Replacement/Salvage PW Costs				0		0		0

Operation/Maintenance Cost	Escl. %	PWA						
A) Power Revenue	0.000%	7.360	-81000	-596167	0	0	-90000	-662408
B) Power Maint.	0.000%	7.360	21000	154562	0	0	25000	184002
C) Heat Revenue	0.000%	7.360	-20900	-153826	-34300	-252451	-25000	-184002
D) Heat Maint.	0.000%	7.360	2900	21344	3300	24288	5000	36800
E)		7.360		0		0		0
F)		7.360		0		0		0
G)		7.360		0		0		0
Total Operation/Maintenance (PW) Costs				-574087		-228163		-625607
Total Present Worth Life Cycle Costs				-24087		-78163		44393
Life Cycle (PW) Savings				24087		78163		-44393

PW - Present Worth   PWA - Present Worth of Annuity

VALUE ENGINEERING RECOMMENDATION

PROJECT: Wastewater Treatment Plant VE
ITEM: Revise sludge handling design

ORIGINAL DESIGN

Construct:

1	primary digester	27.5 m dia, 6.2 m SWD
1	secondary digester	27.5 m, 6.9 m SWD
1	digested sludge storage tank	37 m dia, 6.9 m SWD

PROPOSED DESIGN

Convert existing secondary digester to primary digester.
Convert existing storage tank to secondary digester.
Build pump station and force main to central sludge storage facility.
Pumping facilities at central sludge storage facility for supernatant return.
Build storage tanks at CSSF.

DISCUSSION

Advantages:

- No haulage (truck traffic) to central storage.
- Take advantage of lower construction costs and site availability at central facility.
- Lower cost.
- Annual savings: 233,800/yr x 13.76 = 3,218,000 PWA
- Frees up area at northwest corner of site for additional plant capacity.

Disadvantages:

Pumping cost for sludge.

LIFE CYCLE COST SUMMARY	CAPITAL	ANNUAL O&M
Original design	$7,235,000	$278,000
Proposed design	$4,200,000	$54,200
Savings	$3,035,000	$223,800

PRESENT WORTH (PW) ANNUAL O&M COST $3,079,000
LIFE CYCLE (PW) SAVINGS* $6,107,000

*See attached LCC analysis.

Revised July 1993

COST WORKSHEET

PROJECT: Wastewater Treatment Plant VE
ITEM: Revise sludge handling design

ITEM	UNIT	QTY.	UNIT COST	TOTAL
Original Design				
Excavation	LS	1	510,000	$ 510,000
Backfilling	LS	1	95,000	95,000
Structural concrete	LS	1	2,101,000	2,101,000
Process equipment	LS	1	1,200,000	1,200,000
Misc. metal, roofs	LS	1	1,420,000	1,420,000
Mechanical	LS	1	114,000	114,000
Instructional	LS	1	129,000	129,000
Electrical	LS	1	500,000	500,000
Architectural	LS	1	1,166,500	1,166,500
Subtotal				7,235,500
Total				$7,235,500
Proposed Design				
Convert sec/primary tank	LS	1	200,000	200,000
Convert storage sec/primary tank	LS	1	50,000	50,000
Force main, 10 km	LS	1	2,000,000	2,000,000
Pumping facility	LS	1	150,000	150,000
Storage tank (9,000 m^3)*	LS	1	1,800,000	1,800,000
Subtotal				4,200,000
Total				$4,200,000
SAVINGS				**$3,035,500**

*Use $200/m^3
Revised July 1993

DEVELOPMENT PHASE - LIFE CYCLE COST (Present Worth Method)

Revise Sludge Handling Design
Proposal No. __L-58__ Date __

PROJECT LIFE CYCLE (YEARS) 30
DISCOUNT RATE (PERCENT) 6.000%

				ORIGINAL Original Design		ALT. 1 Revised Design	
Capital Cost				Est.	PW	Est.	PW
A)	Initial Costs			7235000	7235000	4200000	4200000
B)					0		0
C)					0		0
D)					0		0
E)					0		0
F)					0		0
Other Initial Costs							
A)					0		0
B)					0		0
Total Initial Cost Impact (IC)					7235000		4200000
Initial Cost PW Savings							3035000

		Year	Factor				
Replacement/Salvage Costs							
A)	Equipment	10	0.5584		0	10000	5583
B)	Equipment	20	0.3118		0	10000	3118
C)		—	1.0000		0		0
D)		—	1.0000		0		0
E)		—	1.0000		0		0
F)		—	1.0000		0		0
G)		—	1.0000		0		0
	Salvage (neg. cash flow)	—	1.0000		0		0
Total Replacement/Salvage PW Costs					0		8701

		Escl. %	PWA				
Operation/Maintenance Cost							
A)	Maintenance	0.000%	13.765	252000	3468737	34200	470757
B)	Operations	0.000%	13.765	26000	357886	0	0
C)	Labor	0.000%	13.765	0	0	10000	137648
D)	Pumping Costs	0.000%	13.765	0	0	10000	137648
E)		—	13.765		0		0
F)		—	13.765		0		0
G)		—	13.765		0		0
Total Operation/Maintenance (PW) Costs					3826623		746054
Total Present Worth Life Cycle Costs					11061623		4954755
Life Cycle (PW) Savings							6106868

PW - Present Worth   PWA - Present Worth of Annuity

Revised July 1993

Case Study Seven Wastewater Treatment Plant

PROJECT: Wastewater Treatment Plant VE
ITEM: Revise hydraulic gradient in new plant

ORIGINAL DESIGN

Hydraulic losses through the existing 4.5 MGD plant is approximately 25 feet.

PROPOSED DESIGN

Raise plant foundation by 5 feet. This raises hydraulic gradient at effluent weirs by 5 feet.

Design for a hydraulic loss through the expanded plant of approximately 6 feet.

Lower hydraulic gradient at inlet works by 14 feet.

DISCUSSION

- New plant assumed to be built to a depth of 5 feet less in shale.
- Typically a loss of 6 feet should be enough for the 66 MGD plant.
- A rise in tanks (primary, aeration, and final) of 5 feet would save cost of rock excavation.
- Savings in energy $22,250/yr, based on reduced head for raw sewage pumps.

LIFE CYCLE COST SUMMARY	CAPITAL	ANNUAL O&M
Original Design	$ 0	$ 22,250
Proposed Design	$ 0	$ 0
Savings	$ 762,000	$ 22,250

PRESENT WORTH (PW) ANNUAL O&M COST $306,000
LIFE CYCLE (PW) SAVINGS $1,068,000

PROJECT: Wastewater Treatment Plant VE
ITEM: Raise hydraulic gradient in new plant

ITEM	UNIT	QTY.	UNIT COST	TOTAL
Proposed Design				
Primaries: 6500 x 1.524 = 9906 m²	m³	9,906	20	198,120
Aerations: 500 x 1.524 = 8832	m³	8,382	20	167,640
Finals: 13,000 x 1.524 = 19,812	m³	19,812	20	396,240
Subtotal				762,000
Total				$-762,000

SAVINGS			$(762,000)	

PROJECT: Wastewater Treatment Plant VE
ITEM: Initiate a Water Conservation Program

ORIGINAL DESIGN

Original plant design is based on projected capital-population flow calculations, using previously established flows.

PROPOSED DESIGN

Augment efforts to implement a water conservation program. Assume 15% reduction in flow to the plant. Reduction will increase strength concentrations to process. Design now for 35 MGD instead of 50 MGD.

DISCUSSION

Savings will be minimally offset by investment in a water conservation program (implementation via community).

Note: Although a 30% reduction in household consumption has been achieved in many areas, the team suggests use of a more conservative factor of 15%. This factor is suggested because infiltration, irrigation, etc., will not be reduced by the water conservation efforts.

LIFE CYCLE COST SUMMARY	CAPITAL	ANNUAL O&M
Original design	$118,536,000	$6,666,666
Proposed design	$100,755,000	$5,666,666
Savings	$ 17,780,000	$1,000,000

PRESENT WORTH (PW) ANNUAL O&M COST	$13,760,000
LIFE CYCLE (PW) SAVINGS	$31,540,000

DEVELOPMENT PHASE – LIFE CYCLE COST (Present Worth Method)

Consider Water Conservation and Design for 35 MGD
Proposal No. __F–28___ Date _
PROJECT LIFE CYCLE (YEARS)   30
DISCOUNT RATE (PERCENT)   6.000%

				ORIGINAL 50 MGD Plant		ALT. 1 35 MGD Plant	
Capital Cost				Est.	PW	Est.	PW
A)	Initial Costs			118536000	118536000	100755000	100755000
B)					0		0
C)					0		0
D)					0		0
E)					0		0
F)					0		0
Other Initial Costs							
A)					0		0
B)					0		0
Total Initial Cost Impact (IC)					118536000		100755000
Initial Cost PW Savings							17781000

		Year	Factor				
Replacement/Salvage Costs							
A)		—	1.0000		0		0
B)		—	1.0000		0		0
C)		—	1.0000		0		0
D)		—	1.0000		0		0
E)		—	1.0000		0		0
F)		—	1.0000		0		0
G)		—	1.0000		0		0
	Salvage (neg. cash flow)	—	1.0000		0		0
Total Replacement/Salvage PW Costs					0		0

		Escl. %	PWA				
Operation/Maintenance Cost							
A)	Maint. & Operations	0.000%	13.765	6666666	91765532	5666666	78000701
B)		—	13.765		0		0
C)		—	13.765		0		0
D)		—	13.765		0		0
E)		—	13.765		0		0
F)		—	13.765		0		0
G)		—	13.765		0		0
Total Operation/Maintenance (PW) Costs					91765532		78000701
Total Present Worth Life Cycle Costs					210301532		178755701
Life Cycle (PW) Savings							31545831

PW – Present Worth   PWA – Present Worth of Annuity

Part Three

VE Workbook

Value Engineering Workbook

The Value Engineering Workbook is designed to guide practitioners through the application of the VE Job Plan. The blank forms and spreadsheet templates, organized according to the structured phases of the Job Plan, provide a framework to assist the team as it works through the VE study process. A list of key questions, techniques, and procedures precedes the forms for each phase, highlighting the objectives and methods for each part of the plan.

An additional feature of this book is a disk with a system of electronic, integrated forms and spreadsheet templates that interface with the workbook. The author developed these digital formats over the course of more than 500 major project VE studies. The disk also includes tools for advanced practitioners, developed especially for use in the VE process. These applications include a parameter-based cost-estimating system tied to the Cost Model and life cycle costing system.

The disk is easily used on IBM-compatible computers with Lotus 1-2-3 or Excel.

Value Engineering Workbook

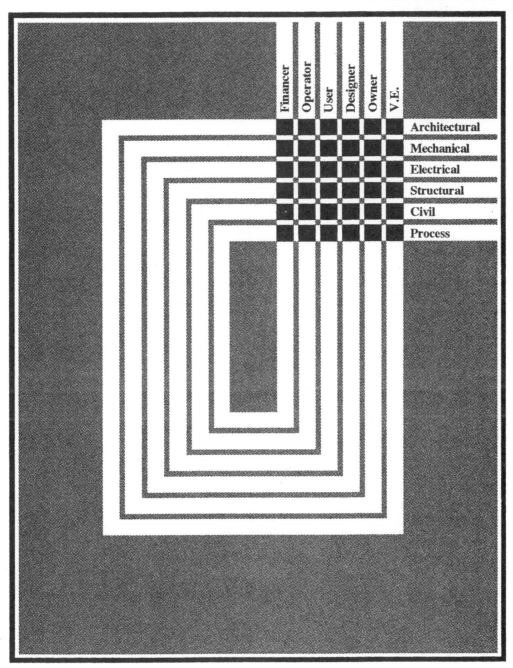

Value Engineering Workbook

Study Title   _____

Date   _____

Study No.   _____

Team   _____

_____

_____

_____

_____

_____

Value Engineering
An organized approach!

Job Plan Phases

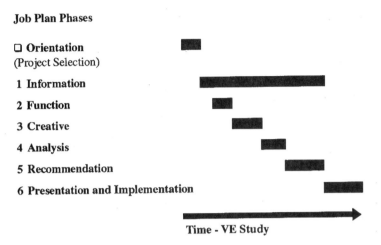

❑ **Orientation**
(Project Selection)

1 Information

2 Function

3 Creative

4 Analysis

5 Recommendation

6 Presentation and Implementation

Time - VE Study

The purpose of this workbook is to guide you through application of the VE Job Plan while performing your study. Feel free to add additional pages of data to the workbook as you collect information. The worksheets are to be used only as necessary for the specific projects. They may be added to, deleted from or modified as necessary.

The list of forms and their projected usage follows:

LIST OF FORMS

Attendance

Project: _____

Location: _____

Item: _____

Date: _____ **Page:** _____

No.	Name	Company	Position	Telephone Number

WS-1

Phase 1
Information Phase

Key Questions

- What is it?
- What does it do?
- What must it do?
- What does it cost?
- What is the budget?
- What is it worth?

Procedures

- Get all the facts.
- Identify all the constraints.
- Determine costs, space, quality parameters.
- Identify functions.
- Develop Models: Initial Costs, Space, Energy, Life Cycle, Quality.
- Set target worth.
- Select functions for value improvement.

Value Engineering Team

Project: _____

Location: _____

Study Title: _____ **Team No.** _____

Study Date: _____ **Sheet No.** _____

I. Team

	Name	Position	Telephone Number
Team Leader			
Team Members			
Part Time Contributors			

II. Describe Problem To Be Studied (existing procedure, design, system)

Information Phase   **Consultation & Document Record**

Project: _____

Location: _____

Study Title:

INFORMATION SOURCE Name, Title, Organization, or Reference Document	Phone No. (If Applicable)	MAJOR POINTS OF DATA

GET INFORMATION FROM THE BEST SOURCES

WS 3

Cost Summary

Project: _____

Location: _____

Study Title: _____

Check one; use separate sheet for each

□ Construction Cost

□ O & M Cost

□ Replacement Costs

□ Energy Cost

ITEM	Major Unit or Item	Original Estimate	New Estimate

GET COST FROM THE BEST SOURCES

WS 4

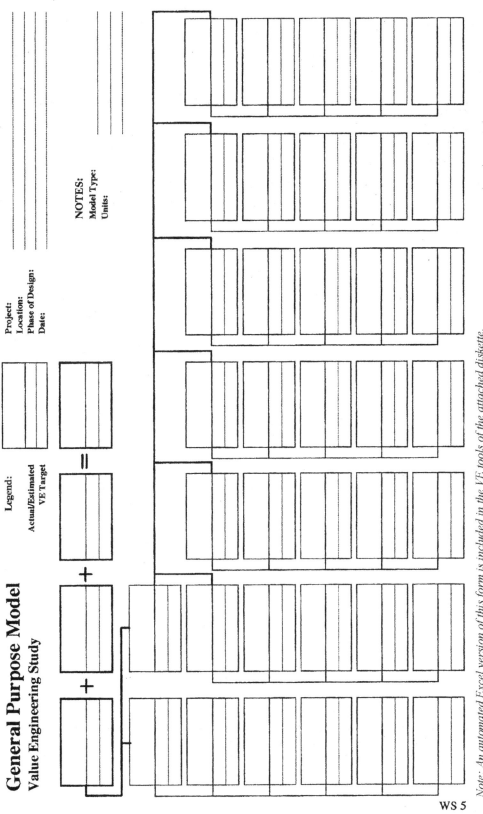

General Purpose Model

Value Engineering Study

Legend:

Actual/Estimated

VE Target

Project:
Location:
Phase of Design:
Date:

NOTES:
Model Type:
Units:

WS 5

Note: An automated Excel version of this form is included in the VE tools of the attached diskette.

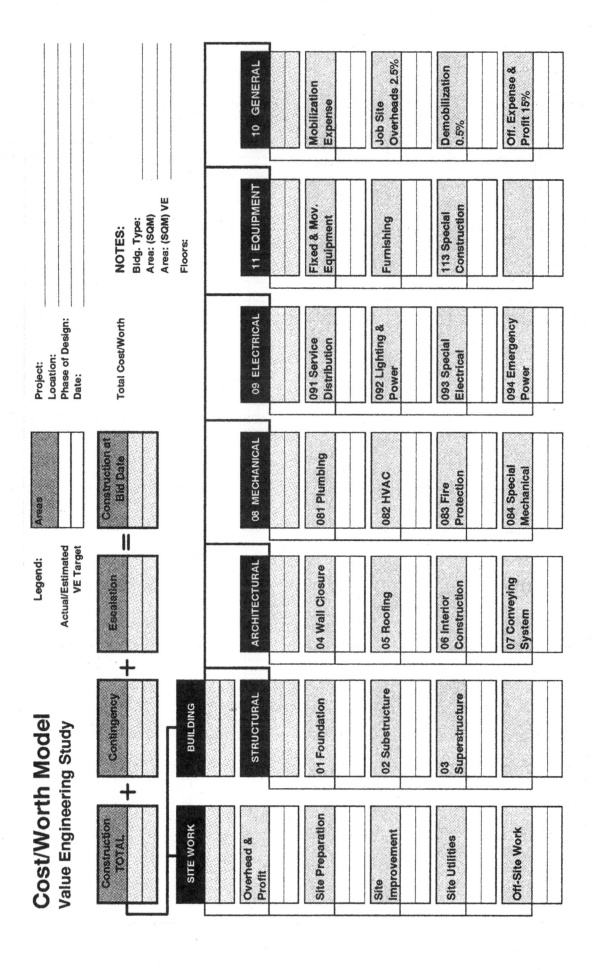

Cost/Worth Model
Value Engineering Study

Legend:

Areas	
Actual/Estimated	
VE Target	

Construction at Bid Date	

Escalation =

Contingency +

Construction TOTAL +

Total Cost/Worth

Project:
Location:
Phase of Design:
Date:

NOTES:
Bldg. Type:
Area: (SQM)
Area: (SQM) VE

Floors:

SITE WORK
- Overhead & Profit
- Site Preparation
- Site Improvement
- Site Utilities
- Off-Site Work

BUILDING

STRUCTURAL
- 01 Foundation
- 02 Substructure
- 03 Superstructure

ARCHITECTURAL
- 04 Wall Closure
- 05 Roofing
- 06 Interior Construction
- 07 Conveying System

08 MECHANICAL
- 081 Plumbing
- 082 HVAC
- 083 Fire Protection
- 084 Special Mechanical

09 ELECTRICAL
- 091 Service Distribution
- 092 Lighting & Power
- 093 Special Electrical
- 094 Emergency Power

11 EQUIPMENT
- Fixed & Mov. Equipment
- Furnishing
- 113 Special Construction

10 GENERAL
- Mobilization Expense
- Job Site Overheads 2.5%
- Demobilization 0.5%
- Off. Expense & Profit 15%

Construction Cost Summary

Project Name: _____ **Date:** _____

Location: _____ **Area:** _____

DIV. NO	SYSTEM	TOTAL COST PER SYSTEM		Sub System	UOM-Unit of Measure	Quant.	Total Cost Per UOM	Total Cost $ US	Cost Per SQF
	DEMOLITION			Demolition					
01	FOUNDATION		011	Standard Foundations	FPA				
			012	Special Foundations	FPA				
02	SUB STRUCTURE		021	Slab on Grade	FPA				
			022	Basement Excavation	BCF				
			023	Basement Walls	BWA				
03	SUPER STRUCTURE		031	Floor Construction	UFA				
			032	Roof Construction	SQF				
			033	Stair Construction	FLT				
04	EXTERIOR CLOSURE		041	Exterior Walls	XWA				
			042	Exterior Doors & Windows	XDA				
05	ROOFING		05	Roofing	SQF				
06	INTERIOR CONSTRUCTION		061	Partitions	PSM				
			062	Interior Finishes	TFA				
			063	Specialities	GSF				
07	CONVEYING SYSTEM		071	Elevators	LO				
			072	Escalators & Others	LS				
08	MECHANICAL		081	Plumbing	FXT				
			082	HVAC	TON				
			083	Fire Protection	AP				
			084	Special Mechanical Systems	LS				
09	ELECTRICAL		091	Service & Distribution	KVA				
			092	Lighting & Power	KVA				
			093	Spec. Electrical System	GSF				
10	GEN. COND. & PROFIT		101	Site Overhead	MOS				
			102	Preliminaries	PCT				
11	EQUIPMENT		111	Fixed Equipment	LS				
			112	Furnishings	LS				
			113	Special Construcion	LS				
12	SITE WORK		121	Site Preparation	SQF				
			122	Site Improvements	SQF				
			123	Site Utilities	SQF				
			124	Off-Site Work	LS				
				Cost Including Office Overhead & Profit					
				Contingencies					
				Escalation					
				Total Estimated Construction Cost					

Abbreviations

AP	Area protected	PSF	Partition Square Footage	LF	Linear Footage
BCF	Basement Cubic Footage	STA	Station	LO	Landing Opening
BWA	Basement Wall Area	TFA	Total Finishes Area	LS	Lump Sum
FLT	Flight	TON	12000 Btu/h	MOS	Months
FXT	Fixture Count	UFA	Upper Floor Area	FPA	Footprint Area
GSF	Gross Square Footage	XDA	Exterior Doors & Window Area	SQF	Square Footage
KW	Kilowatts Connected	XWA	Exterior Wall Area	PCT	Percent

WS 7

Note: An Excel cost program for developing conceptual building estimates is included in the VE tools section of the attached diskette.

Phase 2
Function Phase

- **What does it DO?**
- **What MUST it do?**
- **What does function COST NOW?**
- **What is it WORTH?**
- **Is the function BASIC, SECONDARY or REQUIRED SECONDARY?**

- **Blast (i.e., analyze, break up)**
- **Identify functions: prepare function analysis**
- **Evaluate cost and worth**
- **Compare with simplest known alternative for worth**
- **Classify functions — determine if supporting, unnecessary, etc.**
- **Develop cost visibility — function-wise**
- **Use FAST diagramming (Function Analysis Systems Techniques)**
- **Reduce secondary functions/unnecessary cost**
- **Collect first ideas for value improvement**
- **Prepare Cost/Worth Model**

Function Analysis

Project: _____

Basic Function _____

Date: _____

No.: _____

Subcomponent Description	Function			Initial Cost**	Worth***	Cost/ Worth	Comments
	Verb	Noun	Kind*				

* B = Basic Function
S = Secondary Function
RS = Secondary Function

** Original
Cost Estimate

*** Worth - Least Cost to
Accomplish Function

WS 8

FUNCTION ANALYSIS WORKSHEET

PROJECT:

ITEM:

BASIC FUNCTION:

Date:

COMPONENT DESCRIPTION	FUNCTION VERB-NOUN	KIND	COST	WORTH	COST/WORTH	COMMENTS
B = Basic Function S = Secondary Function RS = Reqd. Secondary Function						
SITE WORK						
Overhead & Profit						
Site Preparation						
Site Improvement						
Off-Site Work						
TOTAL						
STRUCTURAL						
01 Foundation						
02 Substructure						
03 Superstructure						
TOTAL						
ARCHITECTURAL						
04 Wall Closure						
05 Roofing						
06 Interior Construction						
07 Conveying System						
TOTAL						

FUNCTION ANALYSIS WORKSHEET

PROJECT:

ITEM:

BASIC FUNCTION: Date:

COMPONENT DESCRIPTION FUNCTION VERB-NOUN	KIND	COST	WORTH	COST/ WORTH	COMMENTS
B = Basic Function S = Secondary Function RS = Reqd. Secondary Function					
MECHANICAL					
081 Plumbing					
082 HVAC					
083 Fire Protection					
084 Special Mechanical BMS					
TOTAL					
ELECTRICAL					
091 Service & Distribution					
092 Lighting & Power					
093 Special Electrical					
094 Emergency Power					
TOTAL					
EQUIPMENT					
Fixed Equipment					
Furnishing					
TOTAL					
GENERAL					
Mobilization Expense					
Job Site Overheads					
Demobilization					
Off. Expense & Profit					
TOTAL					
OVERALL TOTAL					

FAST Diagram Procedures

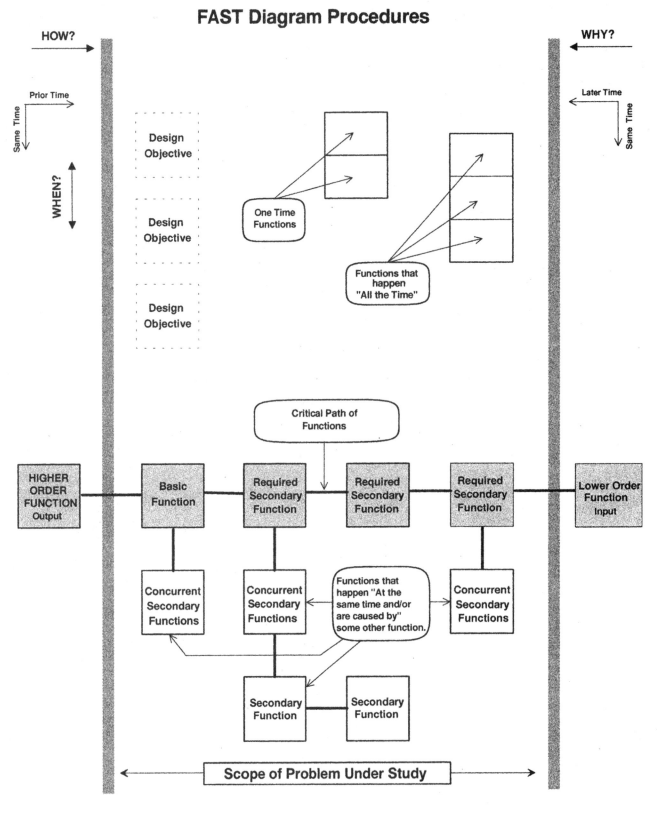

FAST Diagram
Function Analysis Systems Technique

Project Name:

Location:

HOW ? >>>

<<< WHY ?

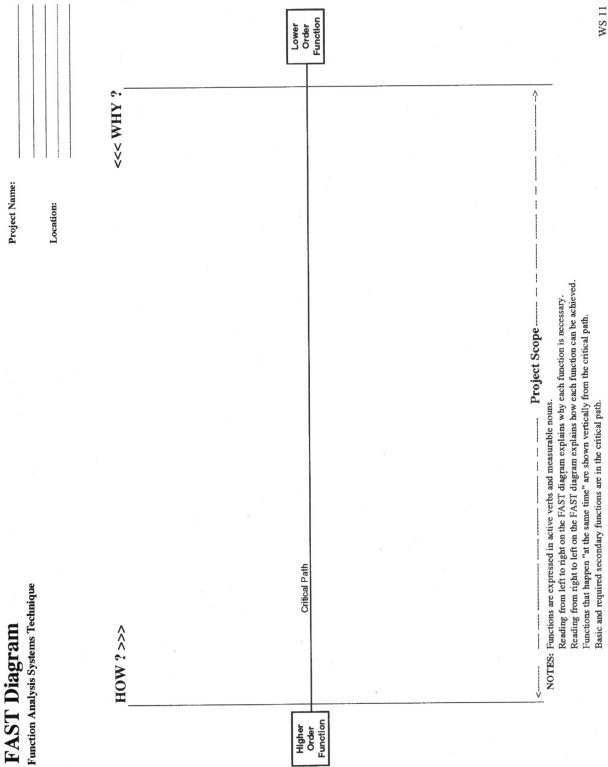

| Higher Order Function |

Critical Path

| Lower Order Function |

<------------------------------- Project Scope -------------------------------->

NOTES: Functions are expressed in active verbs and measurable nouns.
Reading from left to right on the FAST diagram explains why each function is necessary.
Reading from right to left on the FAST diagram explains how each function can be achieved.
Functions that happen "at the same time" are shown vertically from the critical path.
Basic and required secondary functions are in the critical path.

WS 11

Phase 3
Creative Phase

Purpose:

- To generate alternate ideas for providing the NEEDED functions by creative thinking, brainstorming and even speculation.

Techniques:

- Use good human relations.
- Use creative thinking.
- Blast-create.
- Bring new information into the area. (See Idea Stimulator Checklist)
- Eliminate and/or reduce.
- Defer judgment.
- Generate list of ideas.

Key Question:

- What else will do the job?
  (Take ONE function at a time.)

Warning:

- In this phase of a VE study, we want a large QUANTITY of ideas, NOT QUALITY! All ideas are welcomed. When ideas get a laugh, they have contributed. The more ideas, the more welcome they shall be!

- So, ridiculing ideas, judging, criticizing, etc. ➡ are NOT permitted.
  (The time for judgment will come later.)

- Every member must contribute ideas — do not worry whether they are good or bad. The leader should see that no one monopolizes the time and attention of the team to the detriment of others' ideas.

Creative / Evaluation Worksheet

Project: _____

Date: _____

Sheet No. _____

NO	IDEA	ADVANTAGES	DISADVANTAGES	RANK*

*10 = Most Favorable   1 = Least Favorable   DS = Design Suggestion

Note: An Excel worksheet is in the VE tools section of the diskette.

WS-12

Idea Stimulator Checklist

■ ELIMINATE/COMBINE

Can it be eliminated entirely?
Can part of it be eliminated?
Can two items be combined into one?
Is there duplication?
Can the number of different lengths, colors, types be reduced?

■ STANDARDIZE/SIMPLIFY

Could a standard item be used?
Would a modified standard item work?
Does the standard contribute to cost?
Does anything prevent it from being standardized?
Is it too complex?
Can interfaces be simplified?
Is it over-detailed, over-specified or over-controlled?

■ CHALLENGE/IDENTIFY

Does it do more than is required?
Does it cost more than it is worth?
What is special about it?
Is it justified?
Can tolerances be relaxed?
Have drawings and specifications been coordinated?

■ MAINTAIN/OPERATE

Is it accessible?
Are service calls excessive?
Would you like to own it and pay for its maintenance?
Is labor inordinate relative to the cost of materials?
How often is it actually used?
Does it cause problems?
Have users established procedures to get around it?

■ REQUIREMENTS/COST

Are any requirements excessive?
Can less expensive materials be used?
Is it proprietary?
Are factors of safety too high?
Are calculations always rounded off on the high side?
Would lighter gauge materials work?
Could a different finish be used?

THINK OF PURPOSE!
FORCE YOURSELF TO FIND A BETTER WAY!

Figure 1

Phase 4
Analysis/Judicial Phase

Key Questions:

- Will each idea work? (i.e., will it perform the function under study?)
- Will it be implementable?
- How feasible are the selected alternatives?
- What are advantages and disadvantages of each idea?
   Use form from Creative Phase WS-12

Techniques

- Refine
- Use the services of experts
- Use good human relations (Involve owner/designer)
- Use your own judgment

Procedures

- Lay down main criteria to be satisfied
   Filter ideas carefully: drop those that will definitely not
   meet the required criteria, but not before the step below

- Try to refine/develop/build on an idea; freely consult the people who
   may know best about it or about similar products/designs, e.g., you
   may wish to ask the best suppliers in the business or experts in the
   field

- Rank ideas
   Use WS-12 from Creative Phase

- Group similar ideas

Phase 4
Analysis/Judicial Phase: Analysis/Development

Key Question

- **Select top ranked ideas (normally 8 and above)**
- **What is cost impact of ideas?**
- **Consider cost of ownership**

Technique

- **A Life Cycle Cost**

Life Cycle Costing

Form WS-13, the LCC summary, summarizes all the life cycle cost. The present worth costs should be entered in the appropriate space for each design alternative.

The following general instructions for performing the LCC apply:

1. For initial costs, the present-worth factor always equals 1. Therefore, the estimated cost and the present worth are the same and should be so entered.

2. To obtain the present worth of each salvage & replacement cost, refer to Table 4, using the column with the corresponding discount rate. By knowing the building and item life, select the correct factor. Multiply this factor by the estimated replacement cost and enter the value in the present-worth column. For example, a replacement cost of $10,000 equivalent to today's buying power is estimated to occur at the 16th year. The PW factor is 0.2176. The PW of this cost is $2,180.

3. Before the estimated annual cost is converted to present worth, determine if a differential escalation rate is appropriate. Differential escalation rate is the difference one estimates the item will escalate in relation to the devaluation of the currency. For example, if the forecast is that energy will over a 20-year period escalate an average of 5%/year, and devaluation of the dollar ($) is estimated at 3% per year, the differential rate would be 2%. Refer to Table 1, "Present Worth of an Escalation Annual Amount," using a 10% interest factor as recommended by the U.S. Office of Management and Budget. The value PWA escalated for 2% differential over 20 years is 9.934 vs. 8.51 for the nonescalated value. If a differential escalation rate is not necessary, refer to Table 2, "Present Worth of Annuity," for conversion of an annual cost to present worth. By knowing the building life, select the correct factor. Multiply this factor by the estimated annual expenditure. Enter the computed amount in the Present-Worth column.

   For example, the table indicates that, assuming an annual cost of $1 per year at 10 percent interest, nonescalating (0%), the present worth of a 20-year cycle is $8.51.

4. Calculate the difference between the original design and the design alternative's life cycle costs. Enter this figure at the bottom of the form.

5. Attached is Example WS 13 illustrating a typical LCC.

DEVELOPMENT PHASE — LIFE CYCLE COST (Present Worth Method)

		Original		Alternative 1		Alternative 2		Alternative 3	
Proposal No. _____ Date _____									
PROJECT LIFE CYCLE (YEARS) _____									
DISCOUNT RATE (PERCENT) _____									
		Est.	PW	Est.	PW	Est.	PW	Est.	PW
Capital Cost									
A)									
B)									
C)									
D)									
Other Initial Costs									
A)									
B)									
Total Initial Cost Impact (IC)									
Initial Cost PW Savings									
Replacement/Salvage Costs	Year	Factor							
A)									
B)									
C)									
D)									
E)									
F) Salvage (neg. cash flow)									
Total Replacement/Salvage PW Costs									
Operation/Maintenance Cost	Escl. %	Factor							
A)									
B)									
C)									
D)									
E)									
Total Operation/Maintenance (PW) Costs									
Total Present Worth Life Cycle Costs									
Life Cycle (PW) Savings									
PW - Present Worth PWA - Present Worth of Annuity									

WS-13

DEVELOPMENT PHASE - LIFE CYCLE COST (Present Worth Method)

Sample of Typical LCC -HVAC System
Proposal No. _M-1_   Date
PROJECT LIFE CYCLE (YEARS)   20
DISCOUNT RATE (% in decimals)   10.00%

			ORIGINAL Central		ALT. 1 Rooftop		ALT. 2 Split		ALT. 3	
			Est.	PW	Est.	PW	Est.	PW	Est.	PW
Base Cost			816,000	816,000	536,000	536,000	738,000	738,000		
Interface Cost										
A) Electrical			120,000	120,000	100,000	100,000	160,000	160,000		
B)										
C)										
D)										
Other Initial Costs										
A) Owner Supplied Equipment			64,000	64,000	64,000	64,000	2,000	2,000		
B)										
Total Initial Cost Impact (IC)				1,000,000		700,000		900,000		
Initial Cost PW Savings						300,000		100,000		
Replacement/Salvage Costs	Year	Factor								
A) Equipment	8	0.4665			200,000	93,301	20,000	7,710		
B) "	10	0.3855								
C) "	16	0.2176	10,000	2,176	200,000	43,525				
D)		1.0000								
E)		1.0000								
F) Salvage (neg. cash flow)	20	0.1486	(80,000)	(11,891)	(100,000)	(14,864)	(75,000)	(11,149)		
Total Replacement/Salvage PW Costs				(9,715)		121,962		(3,439)		
Operation/Maintenance Cost	Escl..00 %	PWA								
A) Maintenance		8.514	16,000	136,217	25,000	212,839	20,000	170,271		
B) Operations	2.00%	9.934	20,000	198,676	30,000	298,015	25,000	248,346		
C)		8.514								
D)		8.514								
E)		8.514								
Total Operation/Maintenance (PW) Costs				334,893		510,854		418,617		
Total Present Worth Life Cycle Costs				1,325,178		1,332,816		1,315,179		
Life Cycle (PW) Savings						(7,637)		10,000		

PW - Present Worth   PWA - Present Worth of Annuity

Table 1. Present Worth of an Escalating Annual Amount, 10% Discount Rate*

Yrs.	0	1	2	3	4	5	6	7	8	9	Yrs.
1	0.909	0.918	0.927	0.936	0.945	0.965	1.636	1.973	0.982	0.991	1
2	1.736	1.761	1.787	1.813	1.839	1.866	1.892	1.919	1.946	1.973	2
3	2.487	2.535	2.584	2.634	2.684	2.735	2.787	2.839	2.892	2.946	3
4	3.170	3.246	3.324	3.403	3.483	3.566	3.649	3.735	3.821	3.910	4
5	3.791	3.899	4.009	4.123	4.239	4.358	4.480	4.605	4.734	4.865	5
6	4.355	4.498	4.645	4.797	4.953	5.115	5.281	5.453	5.630	5.812	6
7	4.868	5.048	5.234	5.428	5.628	5.837	6.053	6.277	6.509	6.750	7
8	5.335	5.553	5.781	6.019	6.267	6.526	6.796	7.078	7.372	7.680	8
9	5.759	6.017	6.288	6.572	6.871	7.184	7.513	7.858	8.220	8.601	9
10	6.145	6.443	6.758	7.090	7.441	7.812	8.203	8.616	9.053	9.513	10
11	6.495	6.834	7.194	7.575	7.981	8.411	8.868	9.354	9.870	10.418	11
12	6.814	7.193	7.598	8.030	8.491	8.963	9.510	10.072	10.672	11.314	12
13	7.103	7.523	7.972	8.455	8.973	9.530	10.127	10.770	11.460	12.202	13
14	7.367	7.825	8.320	8.853	9.429	10.051	10.723	11.449	12.233	13.082	14
15	7.606	8.103	8.642	9.226	9.860	10.549	11.296	12.109	12.993	13.954	15
16	7.824	8.358	8.941	9.576	10.268	11.024	11.849	12.752	13.739	14.818	16
17	8.022	8.593	9.218	9.903	10.653	11.477	12.382	13.377	14.470	15.674	17
18	8.201	8.808	9.475	10.209	11.018	11.910	12.895	13.985	15.189	16.523	18
19	8.365	9.005	9.713	10.496	11.362	12.323	13.390	14.576	15.895	17.363	19
20	8.514	9.187	9.934	10.764	11.688	12.718	13.867	15.151	16.588	18.196	20
21	8.649	9.353	10.139	11.015	11.996	13.094	14.326	15.711	17.268	19.022	21
22	8.772	9.506	10.329	11.251	12.287	13.454	14.769	16.255	17.936	19.840	22
23	8.883	9.647	10.505	11.471	12.562	13.797	15.196	16.784	18.591	20.650	23
24	8.985	9.776	10.668	11.678	12.822	14.124	15.607	17.299	19.235	21.454	24
25	9.077	9.894	10.819	11.871	13.069	14.437	16.003	17.800	19.867	22.250	25
26	9.161	10.003	10.960	12.052	13.301	14.735	16.384	18.287	20.488	23.038	26
27	9.237	10.102	11.090	12.221	13.521	15.020	16.752	18.761	21.097	23.820	27
28	9.307	10.194	11.211	12.380	13.729	15.291	17.107	19.222	21.695	24.594	28
29	9.370	10.278	11.323	12.528	13.926	15.551	17.448	19.671	22.283	25.361	29
30	9.427	10.355	11.426	12.667	14.112	15.799	17.777	20.107	22.859	26.122	30
31	9.479	10.426	11.523	12.798	14.287	16.035	18.095	20.532	23.426	26.875	31
32	9.526	10.491	11.612	12.920	14.453	16.261	18.400	20.944	23.982	27.622	32
33	9.569	10.551	11.695	13.034	14.610	16.476	18.695	21.346	24.527	28.362	33
34	9.609	10.606	11.771	13.141	14.759	16.682	18.979	21.736	25.063	29.095	34
35	9.644	10.657	11.843	13.241	14.899	16.878	19.252	22.116	25.589	29.821	35
36	9.677	10.703	11.909	13.335	15.032	17.065	19.516	22.486	26.106	30.541	36
37	9.706	10.745	11.970	13.423	15.158	17.244	19.770	22.845	26.613	31.254	37
38	9.733	10.784	12.027	13.505	15.276	17.415	20.014	23.195	27.111	31.961	38
39	9.757	10.820	12.079	13.582	15.389	17.578	20.250	23.535	27.600	32.661	39
40	9.779	10.853	12.128	13.654	15.495	17.733	20.478	23.866	28.080	33.355	40

$$P = A [(1 + e)/(1 + i)] \times [[(1 + e)/(1 + i)^n - 1]/[(1 + e)/(1 + i)] - 1] = PWA_e$$

Table 2. Present Worth (PW)

What $1.00 Due in the Future Is Worth Today

Yrs.	6% PW	7% PW	8% PW	9% PW	10% PW	12% PW	14% PW	16% PW	18% PW	20% PW	Yrs.
1	0.943396	0.934579	0.925926	0.917431	0.909091	0.892857	0.877193	0.862069	0.847446	0.833333	1
2	0.889996	0.873439	0.857339	0.841680	0.826446	0.797194	0.769468	0.743163	0.718184	0.694444	2
3	0.839169	0.816298	0.793832	0.772183	0.751315	0.711780	0.674972	0.640658	0.608631	0.578704	3
4	0.792094	0.762895	0.735030	0.708425	0.683013	0.635518	0.592080	0.552291	0.515789	0.482253	4
5	0.747258	0.712986	0.680583	0.649931	0.620921	0.567427	0.519369	0.476113	0.437109	0.401878	5
6	0.704961	0.666342	0.630170	0.596267	0.564474	0.506631	0.455587	0.410442	0.370432	0.334898	6
7	0.665057	0.622750	0.583490	0.547034	0.513158	0.452349	0.399637	0.353830	0.316925	0.279082	7
8	0.627412	0.582009	0.540269	0.501866	0.466507	0.403883	0.350559	0.305025	0.266038	0.232568	8
9	0.591898	0.543934	0.500249	0.460428	0.424098	0.360610	0.307508	0.262953	0.225456	0.193807	9
10	0.558395	0.508349	0.463193	0.422411	0.385543	0.321973	0.269744	0.226684	0.191064	0.161506	10
11	0.526788	0.475093	0.428883	0.387533	0.350494	0.287476	0.236617	0.195417	0.161919	0.134588	11
12	0.496969	0.444012	0.397114	0.355535	0.319631	0.256675	0.207559	0.168463	0.137220	0.112157	12
13	0.468839	0.414964	0.367698	0.326170	0.289664	0.229174	0.182069	0.145227	0.116288	0.093464	13
14	0.442301	0.387817	0.340461	0.299246	0.263331	0.204620	0.159710	0.125195	0.098549	0.077887	14
15	0.417265	0.362446	0.315242	0.274538	0.239392	0.182696	0.140096	0.107927	0.083516	0.064905	15
16	0.396343	0.338735	0.291890	0.251870	0.217629	0.163122	0.122892				16
17	0.371364	0.316574	0.270269	0.231073	0.197845	0.145644	0.107800				17
18	0.350344	0.295864	0.252490	0.211994	0.179858	0.130040	0.084561				18
19	0.330513	0.276508	0.231712	0.194490	0.163508	0.116107	0.082948				19
20	0.311805	0.258419	0.214548	0.178431	0.148644	0.103667	0.072762	0.051385	0.036506	0.026084	20
21	0.294155	0.241513	0.198656	0.163698	0.135132	0.092560	0.063826				21
22	0.277505	0.225713	0.183941	0.150182	0.122846	0.082643	0.055988				22
23	0.261797	0.210947	0.170315	0.137781	0.111678	0.073798	0.049112				23
24	0.246979	0.197147	0.157699	0.126405	0.101526	0.065882	0.043081				24
25	0.232999	0.184249	0.146018	0.115968	0.092296	0.058823	0.037790	0.024465	0.015957	0.010482	25
26	0.210810	0.172195	0.135202	0.106393	0.083905	0.052521	0.033149				26
27	0.207368	0.160930	0.125187	0.097608	0.076278	0.046894	0.029078				27
28	0.195630	0.150102	0.115914	0.089548	0.069343	0.041869	0.025507				28
29	0.184557	0.140563	0.107328	0.082155	0.063039	0.037383	0.022375				29
30	0.174110	0.131367	0.099377	0.075371	0.057309	0.033378	0.019627	0.011648	0.006975	0.004212	30
31	0.164255	0.122773	0.092016	0.069148	0.052090	0.029802	0.017217				31
32	0.154957	0.114741	0.085200	0.063438	0.047362	0.026609	0.015102				32
33	0.146186	0.107235	0.078889	0.058200	0.043057	0.023758	0.013248				33
34	0.137912	0.100219	0.073045	0.053395	0.039143	0.021212	0.011621				34
35	0.130105	0.093663	0.067635	0.048986	0.035584	0.018940	0.010194	0.005546	0.003049	0.001693	35
36	0.122741	0.087535	0.062625	0.044941	0.032349	0.016910	0.008942				36
37	0.115793	0.081809	0.057986	0.041231	0.029408	0.015098	0.007844				37
38	0.109129	0.076457	0.053690	0.037826	0.026735	0.013481	0.006880				38
39	0.103056	0.071455	0.049713	0.034703	0.024304	0.012036	0.006035				39
40	0.097222	0.066780	0.046031	0.031838	0.022095	0.010747	0.005294	0.002640	0.001333	0.000680	40

$$P = F \times 1/(1 + i)^n = PW$$

Table 3. Compound Interest Factors Present Worth of Annuity (PWA): What $1.00 Payable Periodically Is Worth Today*

Yrs.	6% PW	7% PW	8% PW	9% PW	10% PW	12% PW	14% PW	16% PW	18% PW	20% PW	Yrs.
1	0.943396	0.934579	0.925926	0.917431	0.909001	0.892857	0.877193	0.862069	0.847446	0.833333	1
2	1.833393	1.808018	1.783265	1.759111	1.735537	1.690050	1.646661	1.605232	1.565642	1.527778	2
3	2.673012	2.624316	2.577097	2.531295	2.486852	2.401830	2.321632	2.245890	2.174273	2.106481	3
4	3.465106	3.387211	3.312127	3.329720	3.169865	3.037350	2.913712	2.798181	2.690062	2.588735	4
5	4.212364	4.100197	3.992710	3.889651	3.790787	3.604470	3.433081	3.274294	3.127171	2.990612	5
6	4.917624	4.766540	4.622880	4.485919	4.355261	4.111400	3.888668	3.684736	3.497603	3.325510	6
7	5.582381	5.389289	5.206370	5.032953	4.868419	4.563750	4.288305	4.038565	3.811528	3.604592	7
8	6.209794	5.971299	5.746639	5.534819	5.334926	4.967640	4.638864	4.343591	4.077566	3.837160	8
9	6.801602	6.515232	6.246888	5.995247	5.759024	5.328250	4.946372	4.606544	4.303022	4.030967	9
10	7.360087	7.023582	6.710081	6.417658	6.144655	5.650230	5.216116	4.833227	4.494086	4.192472	10
11	7.886875	7.498674	7.138964	6.805191	6.495061	5.937710	5.452738	5.028644	4.656005	4.317060	11
12	8.383844	7.942686	7.536078	7.160725	6.813692	6.194370	5.660292	5.197104	4.793225	4.439217	12
13	8.852683	8.357651	7.903776	7.486904	7.103356	6.423560	5.842362	5.342334	4.909513	4.532681	13
14	9.294984	8.745468	8.244237	7.786102	7.366687	6.628180	6.002072	5.467529	5.008062	4.610567	14
15	10.712279	9.107914	8.559479	8.060688	7.606080	6.810880	6.142168	5.575456	5.091578	4.675473	15
16	10.105895	9.446649	8.851369	8.312558	7.823709	6.973990	6.265060				16
17	10.347726	9.763223	9.121638	8.543631	8.021553	7.119620	6.372859				17
18	10.827603	10.059087	9.371887	8.755625	8.201412	7.249690	6.467420				18
19	11.158116	10.335595	9.603599	8.950115	8.364920	7.365780	6.550369				19
20	11.409921	10.594014	9.818147	9.128546	8.513564	7.469730	6.623131	5.928844	5.352744	4.869580	20
21	11.764077	10.835527	10.016803	9.292244	8.648694	7.562010	6.686957				21
22	12.041582	11.061240	10.200744	9.442425	8.771540	7.644620	6.742944				22
23	12.303379	11.272187	10.371059	9.580207	8.883218	7.718430	6.792056				23
24	12.550358	11.469334	10.528758	9.706612	8.981744	7.784340	6.835137				24
25	12.783356	11.653583	10.674776	9.822580	9.077040	7.843140	6.872927	6.097094	5.466905	4.947590	25
26	13.003186	11.825779	10.809978	9.928797	9.160945	7.895650	6.906077				26
27	13.210536	11.986709	10.935165	10.026580	9.237223	7.942560	6.935155				27
28	13.406166	12.137111	11.051078	10.116128	9.306567	7.984410	6.960662				28
29	13.590721	12.277674	11.158406	10.198283	9.369606	8.021820	6.983037				29
30	13.764831	12.409041	11.257783	10.273654	9.426914	8.055160	7.002664	6.177200	5.516805	4.978940	30
31	13.929086	12.531814	11.349799	10.342802	9.479013	8.084990	7.019881				31
32	14.084013	12.656555	11.434999	10.406240	9.526376	8.111620	7.034983				32
33	14.230230	12.753790	11.513888	10.464441	9.569432	8.135370	7.048231				33
34	14.368141	12.854009	11.586934	10.517835	9.608575	8.156540	7.059852				34
35	14.498246	12.947672	11.654568	10.566821	9.644159	8.175480	7.070045	6.215337	5.538618	4.991535	35
36	14.620987	13.035208	11.717193	10.611763	9.676508	8.192420	7.078987				36
37	14.736780	13.117017	11.775179	10.652993	9.705917	8.207490	7.086831				37
38	14.846019	13.193473	11.828869	10.690820	9.732651	8.220980	7.093711				38
39	14.949073	13.264958	11.878582	10.722523	9.756956	8.233030	7.099747				39
40	15.046297	13.331700	11.924613	10.757360	9.779051	8.243750	7.105041	6.233500	5.548150	4.996600	40

$P = A(1 + i)^n - 1/i(1 + i)^n = PWA$

Table 4. Compound Interest Factors.

Periodic Payment (PP): Periodic Payment Necessary to Pay Off Loan of $1.00; (Capital Recovery) Annuities (Uniform Series Payments)*

Yrs.	6% PW	7% PW	8% PW	9% PW	10% PW	12% PW	14% PW	16% PW	18% PW	20% PW	Yrs.
1	1.060000	1.070000	1.080000	1.090000	1.100000	1.120000	1.14000000	1.16000000	1.18000000	1.20000000	1
2	0.545437	0.553092	0.560769	0.568469	0.576190	0.591698	0.60728972	0.62296296	0.63871560	0.65454545	2
3	0.374110	0.381052	0.388034	0.395055	0.402115	0.416349	0.43073148	0.44525787	0.45992386	0.47472527	3
4	0.288591	0.295228	0.301921	0.308669	0.315471	0.329234	0.34320478	0.35737507	0.37173867	0.38628912	4
5	0.237396	0.243891	0.250156	0.257092	0.263797	0.277409	0.29128355	0.30540938	0.31977784	0.33437970	5
6	0.203363	0.209796	0.216315	0.222920	0.229607	0.243226	0.25715750	0.27138987	0.28591013	0.30070575	6
7	0.179135	0.185553	0.192072	0.198691	0.205405	0.219118	0.23319238	0.24761268	0.26236200	0.27742393	7
8	0.161036	0.167468	0.174015	0.180674	0.187444	0.201303	0.21557002	0.23022426	0.24524436	0.26060942	8
9	0.147022	0.153486	0.160080	0.166799	0.173641	0.187679	0.20216838	0.21708249	0.23239482	0.24807946	9
10	0.135868	0.142378	0.149029	0.155820	0.162745	0.176984	0.19171354	0.20690108	0.22252464	0.23852276	10
11	0.126793	0.133357	0.140076	0.146947	0.153963	0.168415	0.18339427	0.19886075	0.21477639	0.23110379	11
12	0.119277	0.125902	0.132695	0.139651	0.146763	0.161437	0.17666933	0.19241473	0.20862781	0.22526496	12
13	0.112960	0.119651	0.126522	0.133357	0.140779	0.155677	0.17116366	0.18718411	0.20368621	0.22062000	13
14	0.107585	0.114345	0.121297	0.128433	0.135746	0.150871	0.16660914	0.18289797	0.19967806	0.21689306	14
15	0.102963	0.109795	0.116830	0.124059	0.131474	0.146824	0.16280896	0.17935752	0.19640278	0.21388212	15
16	0.098952	0.105858	0.112977	0.120300	0.127817	0.143390	0.15961540				16
17	0.095445	0.102425	0.109629	0.117046	0.124664	0.140457	0.15691544				17
18	0.092357	0.099413	0.106702	0.114212	0.121930	0.137937	0.15462115				18
19	0.089621	0.096753	0.104128	0.111730	0.119547	0.135763	0.15266316				19
20	0.087185	0.094393	0.101852	0.109546	0.117460	0.133879	0.15098600	0.16866700	0.18682000	0.20535600	20
21	0.085005	0.092289	0.099832	0.107617	0.115624	0.132240	0.14954486				21
22	0.083016	0.090106	0.098032	0.105969	0.114005	0.130811	0.14830317				22
23	0.081278	0.088714	0.096722	0.104382	0.112572	0.129560	0.14723081				23
24	0.079679	0.087189	0.094978	0.103023	0.111300	0.128463	0.14630284				24
25	0.078227	0.085811	0.093679	0.101806	0.110168	0.127500	0.14549841	0.16401200	0.18291900	0.20211900	25
26	0.076904	0.084561	0.092507	0.100715	0.109159	0.126652	0.14480001				26
27	0.075697	0.083426	0.091448	0.099735	0.108258	0.125904	0.14419288				27
28	0.074593	0.082392	0.090489	0.098852	0.107451	0.125244	0.14366449				28
29	0.073580	0.081449	0.089619	0.098056	0.106728	0.124660	0.14320417				29
30	0.072649	0.080586	0.088827	0.097336	0.106079	0.124144	0.14280279	0.16188600	0.18126400	0.20084600	30
31	0.071792	0.079797	0.088107	0.096686	0.105496	0.123686	0.14245256				31
32	0.071002	0.079073	0.087451	0.096096	0.104972	0.123280	0.14214675				32
33	0.070273	0.078408	0.086852	0.095562	0.104499	0.122920	0.14187958				33
34	0.069598	0.077797	0.086304	0.095077	0.104074	0.122601	0.14164604				34
35	0.068974	0.077234	0.085803	0.094636	0.103690	0.122317	0.14144181	0.16089200	0.18055000	0.20033900	35
36	0.068395	0.076715	0.085345	0.094235	0.103343	0.122064	0.14126315				36
37	0.067857	0.076237	0.084924	0.093870	0.103030	0.121840	0.14110680				37
38	0.067358	0.075795	0.084539	0.093538	0.102747	0.121640	0.14096993				38
39	0.066894	0.075387	0.084185	0.093236	0.102491	0.121462	0.14085010				39
40	0.066462	0.075009	0.083860	0.092960	0.102259	0.121304	0.14074514	0.16042300	0.18024000	0.20013600	40

$PP = P [i(1 + i)^n /(1 + i)^n - 1] = PP$

Phase 4
Analysis/Judicial Phase: Analysis/Evaluation

Weighted Evaluation

Weighted evaluation assures optimum decisions. Good decisions are made by placing the proper emphasis on all criteria. During evaluation it is important to discuss the following areas:

- Needs versus desires
- Important versus unimportant
- Design trade-offs versus required functions

Procedure

The recommended procedure for weighted evaluation has been broken down into two processes, the criteria weighting process and the analysis matrix. The criteria weighting process is designed to **isolate criteria and establish their weights or relative importance.**

1. On the criteria scoring matrix all criteria important in the selection of alternatives are listed. Criteria are compared, one against another, this series of comparisons being the simplest way to achieve the evaluation.

   In comparing two criteria, preference for one over the other is scored according to its strength. (That is, 4 = major preference, 3 = above average preference, 2 = average preference, 1 = slight preference). Criteria evaluated as equal are assigned a value of 1 each. Scores are then tallied, the raw scores brought to a common base (normally 10 is used for the evaluation), and the criteria and weights transferred to the analysis matrix.

2. In the analysis matrix, each alternative is listed and ranked against each criterion. The rank and weight of each constraint are multiplied and totalled. The alternatives are then scored for recommended implementation. No alternatives are considered that do not meet minimum criteria.

   For example, if the budget is set, any alternative costing more than the budget is dropped. The same with safety, environment and codes; no idea is listed unless it meets basic project/owner requirements.

   This is to avoid letting one discipline dominate. Typically, the safety engineer will insist that the safer item be selected at any cost; the design architect will insist on his design in all cases; the maintenance engineer will focus on the lower-cost maintenance impact regardless of other criteria; the structural engineer will want the most overdesigned foundation system "to be sure;" the electrical engineer will insist on 100% extra capacity to ensure adequate capacity available in the building for the next 100 years. The mechanical savings energy will wind up becoming the objective of the building, rather than "housing people."

3. Attached as an example, is a weighted evaluation of a car purchase.

Weighted Evaluation

Project:

☐ Architectural   ☐ Structural   ☐ Mechanical   ☐ Electrical

Date: _____

VE No.: _____

Criteria
Criteria Scoring Matrix

How Important:

4 = Major Preference
3 = Above Average Preference
2 = Average Preference
1 = Slight Preference
   Letter / Letter
   No Preference
   Each Scored One Point

A.

B.

C.

D.

E.

F.

G.

	G	F	E	D	C	B	A

Analysis Matrix
Alternatives

	Raw Score								Total
	Weight of Importance (0-10)								
1.									
2.									
3.									
4.									
5.									
6.									
7.									

5 = Excellent   4 = Very Good   3 = Good   2 = Fair   1 = Poor

WS 14

Weighted Evaluation

Project: Car Purchase

☐ Architectural ☐ Structural ☐ Mechanical ☐ Others

Date: _____

Sheet No.: 1 of 1

Criteria
Criteria Scoring Matrix

How Important:

4 = Major Preference
3 = Above Average Preference
2 = Average Preference
1 = Slight Preference
  Letter / Letter
  No Preference
  Each Scored One Point

A. **Cost (LCC)**

B. **Appearance**

C. **Comfort**

D. **Performance**

E. **Safety**

F.

G.

Criteria scoring matrix diagonals:

- A - 2
- A - 2
- B / C   A - 1
- D - 1   A - 1
- D - 1   B / E
- C / E
- D - 1

Analysis Matrix
Alternatives

		G	F	E	D	C	B	A	Total
	Raw Score			2	3	2	2	6	
	Weight of Importance (0-10)			3	5	3	3	10	
1. **Car A (Original)**				9 / 3	15 / 3	6 / 2	6 / 2	50 / 5	**86***
2. **Car B (Alternative No.1)**				9 / 3	10 / 2	12 / 4	9 / 3	40 / 4	**80**
3. **Car C (Alternative No.2)**				12 / 4	25 / 5	15 / 5	15 / 5	10 / 1	**77**
4.									
5.									
6.									
7.									

* Selected based on weighted evaluation

Example

5 = Excellent   4 = Very Good   3 = Good   2 = Fair   1 = Poor

WS 14

Phase 5
Recommendation

Key Questions

- Will it improve value?
- Will it meet all requirements?
- Are there implementation problems?
- What are the advantages and disadvantages?
- What are the differences?

Procedures

- Work on specific changes
- Gather convincing facts
- Determine first and second choices
- Anticipate roadblocks
- Use good human relations
- Prepare life cycle cost analysis
- Generate list of recommendations

VALUE ENGINEERING RECOMMENDATION

Project: *VE Rec. No.*

Item:

ORIGINAL DESIGN

_____

_____

_____

_____

_____

_____

_____

_____

PROPOSED DESIGN (Attach sketch where applicable)

_____

_____

_____

_____

_____

_____

DISCUSSION (Advantages & Disadvantages)

_____

_____

_____

_____

LIFE CYCLE COST SUMMARY	Initial	Replacement	Annual O&M
Original			
Proposed			
Savings			
PW Annual Savings at (Factor)			
TOTAL SAVINGS (Initial + PW Annual)			

Note: Automated workbooks for this sheet and the following cost sheet are included in the VE report Master revised file of the attached diskette.   **WS 15**

COST WORKSHEET

Project: *VE Rec. No.*

Item:

ORIGINAL DESIGN

	Unit	Quantity	Unit Cost	Total
			Total Cost	

PROPOSED DESIGN

	Unit	Quantity	Unit Cost	Total

Remarks   *Total Cost*

                                               Savings

WS 16

SUMMARY OF POTENTIAL COST SAVINGS

Project: _____

Location: _____

Date: _____

Page _____ of _____

ITEM	PROPOSALS	INITIAL SAVINGS	ANNUAL COST SAVINGS	LIFE CYCLE SAVINGS PW

WS 17

Phase 6
Presentation & Implementation

Key Questions

- **What is recommended?**
- **Who has to approve it?**
- **Why should they approve it?**

Procedures

- **Give oral presentation**
- **Use summary list of recommendation**
- **Support it with written executive brief**
- **Be clear**
- **Be concise**
- **Be positive**
- **Anticipate roadblocks**
- **Use good human relations**

  Note: See attached Outline for Team presentations.

I. Introduction

Name — Team Captain
Names — Team Members
Title of Project
Brief Description of Project

II. VE Job Plan Results

A. Information Phase

Results of Function Analysis
Use Graphical Function Analysis Chart
Include Parameter and Total Costs
Include Fast Diagram
Cost/Worth Ratios
Isolated High Cost Areas

B. Speculative Phase

Number of Ideas Generated

C. Analytical Phase

Number of Ideas Selected
Investigative Results
Outside Sources Used
Evaluation Results
Use Weighted Evaluation Sheet Where Applicable
Number and Summary of Proposals
Cost-Out Proposals

D. Proposal Phase

Before/After Sketches
Include:
1 Action Description (Brief)
2 Advantages/Disadvantages
3 Summary of Savings
Number of Proposals by Discipline or Function
Initial Before/After Savings
Life Cycle Savings
4 Implementation Discussion

Figure 2

Appendix,
Glossary and
Index

Web Site Resources

T he following is a list of Web sites, organized by topic, that provide further resource information. These sites will be useful for locating information about, and links to, many cost-related companies and associations worldwide. However, these referenced sites do not represent a comprehensive listing, since new sites are posted on the World Wide Web (WWW) daily, and others disappear. Visit R.S. Means' Web site (**http://www.rsmeans.com**) for updates on relevant WWW resources.

Information Content Providers

ARCAT:	http://www.arcat.com
Construction Market Data:	http://www.comdonl.com
Federal Reserve Bank of New York:	http://www.ny.frb.org
R.S. Means Company, Inc.:	http://www.rsmeans.com

Publications On-line

DesignIntelligence:	http://www.di.net/index.htm
Design Architecture:	http://www.cornishproductions.com
Value Digest:	http://www.valuedigest.com

Codes and Standards

American National Standards Institute:	http://www.ansi.org
American Society for Testing & Materials:	http://www.astm.org
Building Site Network:	http://www.buildingsite.com
Bureau of Reclamation (Interior) Value Program (VA/VE):	http://www.usbr.gov/valuprog
Council of American Building Officials:	http://www.cabo.org
National Institute of Building Sciences:	http://www.nibs.org
Occupational Safety and Health Administration:	http://www.osha.gov

Web-based Resource Referral Services

The Aberdeen Group:	http://www.construct.com
AEC InfoCenter:	http://www.aecinfo.com
Build.com:	http://www.build.com
Building Information Exchange:	http://www.building.org

Associations

American Arbitration Association:	http://www.adr.org
American Association of Cost Engineers:	http://www.eng.hawaii.edu/~aace/
American Institute of Architects (AIA):	http://www.aia.org
The Association for the Advancement of Cost Engineering through Total Management:	http://www.cost.org
Construction Specifications Institute:	http://www.csinet.org
International Construction Information Society (ICIS):	http://www.icis.org
International Cost Engineering Council (ICEC):	http://users.twave.net/icec
International Federation of Surveyors (FIG):	http://www.ps.ucl.ac.uk/figtree
International Project Management Association (IPMA):	http://www.sn.no/ipma
Project Management Institute (PMI):	http://www.pmi.org
Royal Institution of Chartered Surveyors (RICS):	http://www.rics.org.uk
Society of American Value Engineers International (SAVE):	http://www.value-eng.com
Society of Cost Estimating and Analysis (SCEA):	http://www.erols.com/scea
Value Management Research Group:	http://www.reading.ac.uk/~kcrsmstr/home.html

Government

General Services Administration:	http://www.gsa.gov/far

At the GSA Web site, follow this path for value engineering contract information:
Choose Part 52: Solicitation, Provisions & Contract Clauses.
Then select clause no. 52.248-52.300.

HQ, Industrial Operations Command (IOC) Value Engineering:	http://www-ioc.army.mil/ rm/rmv/index.htm
U.S. Army Corps of Engineers Value Program Homepage:	http://www.hq.usace.army.mil/ cemp/e/ev/cemp_ev.htm
U.S. Bureau of Labor Statistics Data:	http://stats.bls.gov/datahome.htm
U.S. Bureau of Labor Statistics, Foreign Labor Statistics:	http://stats.bls.gov/flshome.htm

Appendix B

Value Engineering Services for CM/PM: Typical Scope of Work

Objective

To utilize a systematic approach that identifies and provides the required functions of the project at an optimum cost, while maintaining or improving the basic design objectives. The proposed value engineering services will be a time-phased process that ends only when the final results are ascertained. The VE Program will ensure that the project objectives will meet or exceed the standards established by the owner and will include:

a) Value Engineering

b) Life Cycle Costing

c) Constructability

d) Operations and Maintenance

VE Workshops

Value Engineering Workshops will follow the Standards of the Society of American Value Engineers (SAVE). The workshops will be conducted by a team managed by the Value Engineering Team Coordinator (VETC). The team will be multidisciplined and include such professionals as architects, traffic, signals and controls, civil, structural, mechanical, electrical and cost engineers relevant to the disciplines being studied. Management of the Value Engineering study through the leadership of a Certified Value Specialist (CVS) is a major factor. Application of VE methodology and coordination of the VE study activities make the difference in implemented ideas and improved performance of the facility. Experience has shown that project studies performed by a team with limited VE experience will sometimes steer in the direction of a design review. The team may find errors in the plans, but may not increase the cost savings and operations reliability. Therefore, the qualifications and experience of the VETC and the team are critical to meaningful results.

The team approach used for the VE study is comprised of three specific phases:

1. Pre-Workshop Activities

2. VE Workshop

3. Post VE Workshop: Presentation & Report

The team approach also encourages the owner's representatives and the A/E to participate in the study effort, allowing them an opportunity to apply their past experience to the analysis of the project. It is expected that members of the owner's staff, including key management representatives, will attend as part of the VE team.

Pre-Workshop Activities Phase

Coordination of the VE effort is vital to the project's success. Its prime importance lies in developing the proper rapport with the A/E and the owner's representatives so that each recognizes his or her responsibility in the VE effort.

The Certified Value Specialist (CVS) will meet with the owner and the owner's consultants to discuss the workshop and assemble/organize logistics. Required data includes the following:

- Design Standards (Owner, etc.)
- Design Drawings
- Program Requirements
- Design Criteria
- Alternate Designs Considered

- Pertinent Regulations and Codes
- Outline Specification
- Design Calculations
- Construction Estimate
- Preliminary Construction Schedule

Deliverables: Memo on VE Job Plan & Logistics

VE Workshop Phase

Value Engineering is a systematized approach for isolating high-cost areas in a design and arriving at a balance between cost, performance, and quality. The best VE Job Plan will be used as the framework for conducting each study. The Job Plan consists of the following stages:

- Information
- Creative
- Analysis/ Development
- Presentation/Post

1. Information Stage

- Gather all the available facts, such as drawings, specifications, cost estimates, cost targets, project goals, strategies, schedules, and contracts.
- Build a cost model that includes the reasonable anticipated costs for each component of the project based on historical data, and compare it to the current estimates. For civil projects, cost parameters would be earthwork, pavements, drainage structures, rails, electrical distribution, etc.
- Select those systems, components, spaces or items that the model(s) indicate have the highest potential for cost savings, typically those where the estimate varies the most from the cost model target values.
- Analyze the functions of the identified items. Since the purpose of VE is obtaining the required function(s) of an item at the lowest total cost, functional analysis is a key component of VE.

  a. List the function of each item being studied using two words—a verb and a noun.

  b. Determine if the function is basic, e.g., must do; secondary, e.g., not essential, but desirable; or unnecessary. More complex functions will be analyzed using Function Analysis System Techniques (FAST) to define the problem scope by diagramming all functions with respect to each other.

- Allocate the current estimated cost to each function to determine the worth of the basic functions (e.g., the least expensive reasonable solution to perform the basic function).

- Select the basic functions for in-depth study which have the best cost-saving potential because of high cost and/or high ratio of cost-to-worth.

2. Creative Stage

- Generate a wide variety of ideas to provide the basic functions and any required secondary functions using brainstorming and other advanced creativity techniques. Brainstorming techniques will also be utilized to generate alternative design proposals.

3a. Analysis Stage

Ideas generated during brainstorming will be evaluated on a life cycle cost basis, utilizing cost estimates that approach the same level of detail as the current cost estimate available for the existing design.

- Consider each of the alternatives generated during the speculative phase.
- Estimate the cost of each alternative.
- Make sure the alternative will perform the basic functions.

The alternatives will be converted into proposals for presentation.

3b. Development Stage

- List all the alternatives or combinations of alternatives that have significant cost savings potential and meet the basic functional requirements. Note the advantages and disadvantages of each as well as areas requiring further investigation to evaluate the alternative.
- Obtain additional information and seek technical assistance from suppliers and specialists.
- Develop proposals for each selected alternate, including total cost impact (M&O) and impact on noncost-definable areas as applicable.

4. Presentation/Post Stage

The team will conduct a presentation of results on the last day of the workshop. In some cases, an effective approach is to have the VETC prepare a preliminary VE report summarizing the study results and present the recommendations to the owner and designer. The owner will respond and make a decision to accept, reject, or modify each proposal. The consultant shall keep minutes for inclusion in the final report.

The report will include the following:

- Executive Summary
- Introduction
- Project description, including:
    Goals and objectives
    Scope of work
- VE study recommendations, each with:

    Description of the change, including advantages/disadvantages.
    Supporting sketches and computations, as appropriate.
    Estimate of initial cost savings.
    Estimate of life cycle savings, as appropriate.
    Acknowledgment of contributions by others.
    Summary statement of reasons for accepting and actions
    required for implementation.

    Deliverables: Preliminary VE report
                Minutes of presentation meeting

After the presentation/implementation meeting and submittal of the preliminary report, the VETC and other VE team will be available to confer with owner representatives and the A/E, to provide further explanation, and to discuss actions on the VE proposals.

The edited initial submittal and the designer/owner response becomes the Final VE Report.

Deliverables: Final VE Report

Glossary of Terms

AACE American Association of Cost Engineers

ACEC American Consulting Engineers Council

accounts, code of 1. A set of numbers used to categorize major components of the whole product or components of general company overhead, 2. A set of numbers used in estimating group costs, 3. In construction, a hierarchical set of numbers used to represent the whole project (e.g., the 16 Division CSI set or the 12 System UniFormat set).

A/E architect/engineer

AFC automatic fare card

AGC Associated General Contractors of America

AIA American Institute of Architects

alternative, function A different method or way (in terms of a product) to achieve the desired result.

Amp. ampere

analysis, function 1. The study of product performance using two words—a verb and a noun, 2. The methodology of value analysis.

analysis, functional A mathematical technique originated by Vito Volterra in 1887 involving the use of integro-differential equations.

analysis, future value An economic technique to accumulate costs occurring at various points in time to their equivalent value at a specified future point in time.

analysis, life cycle cost The comparison of acceptable alternatives on the basis of their contribution to life cycle costs using present value or annualized cost methodology.

analysis, present value An economic technique to discount costs occurring in future years to their equivalent current value and sum them.

analysis, value 1. A method for enhancing product value by improving the relationship of worth to cost through the study of function, 2. A methodology using an organized approach (Job Plan) with an organized effort (multidisciplinary team) to provide required functions at the lowest overall cost consistent with achieving required acceptance or performance, 3. The determination of the value of product functions as perceived by the user/customer in the marketplace.

analyst, value One who uses value analysis methodology to study a product and search for value improvement.

ASPE American Society of Professional Estimators

assurance, value See *analyst, value.*

AVS Associated Value Specialist

benefit, function The life cycle advantages, income, or revenue attributable to the provision of a particular function.

BOMA Building Owners and Managers Association

BTUH BTUs per hour

burden, indirect See *cost, indirect.*

characteristics, essential The minimal or necessary operational, maintenance, safety, performance, and reliability needs of the customer which must be fulfilled.

chart, PERT A project evaluation and review technique. A schedule that charts the activities and events anticipated in a work process.

CIAPB Capitalized Income Approach to Project Budgeting

CIP cast-in-place

CM Construction Manager

COE Army Corps of Engineers

control, value See *analyst, value.*

cost, acquisition The price paid to procure a product not produced in house.

cost, annualized An economic technique to convert any defined set of present value costs to an equivalent uniform annual amount for a fixed period.

cost, application See *cost, customer.*

cost, break-even 1. The point, for a given quantity of product, where the cost to purchase the product is the same as the cost to manufacture it in-house, 2. The quantity at which two competing acquisition alternatives are equal in cost.

cost, conversion The money expended to convert raw material, or an unfinished product, into the desired usable end product.

cost, customer The price of product acquisition paid by a customer.

cost, development 1. The amount spent on product research, design, models, pilot production, testing, and evaluation, 2. Cost normally considered product overhead and distributed as fixed cost over an estimated number of products to be produced.

cost, differential The difference in the life cycle cost between two competing alternatives.

cost, direct 1. Cost that is directly identifiable with and attributable to the production of one specified product, 2. Cost that cannot be allocated to more than one product.

cost, direct labor The amount expended for salaries and wages to provide a product.

cost, essential All cost necessary to provide a basic function.

cost, factory See *cost, manufacturing.*

costs, fixed 1. Cost incurred which is not dependent upon the quantity of products produced, 2. Costs that do not vary with the volume of business, such as property taxes, insurance, depreciation, security, and basic water and utility fees, 3. Expenses for labor, material, equipment, and tools to produce the first product.

cost, function 1. The proportion of product cost allocated to functions performed by the product, 2. All costs directly associated with the performance of a particular function, 3. Costs required for the realization of a function.

cost, general and administrative A special classification of overhead cost normally apportioned to products and including salaries for executives, managers, administrative and clerical staff as well as general office supplies and equipment, and marketing, which may also include, as specified, advanced design, research, and other administrative costs.

cost, incremental Also referred to as *variance cost.* 1. The difference in product cost between established incremental levels of product performance, 2. The add-on, alternative, accessory or choice cost which takes into account the availability of existing resources when adding a new system.

cost, indirect Also called *indirect burden.* See *cost, overhead.*

cost, indirect labor The amount expended for employee benefits, i.e., retirement, health insurance, vacation, other leave, unemployment compensation, and bonuses.

cost, investment The initial costs of product development, excluding sunk (past expenditure) costs, which are assumed to occur as a lump sum in a base year.

cost, labor The sum of direct labor cost and indirect labor cost.

cost, life cycle 1. The sum of all acquisition, operation, maintenance, use and disposal costs for a product over a specified period of time, 2. The sum of all costs for the development, procurement, production, and installation of a product, as well as for its financing, taxes, operation, logistic support, maintenance, modification, repair, replacement, and disposal over the period of its useful life, 3. In manufacturing it is also referred to as the sum of development, production, and application cost, 4. The economic measure of value.

cost, logistic support 1. The cost of spare and replacement parts and equipment with associated installation labor, 2. The cost of periodic maintenance and repair, 3. The cost for those activities necessary to plan for and provide support programs, such as logistics, field engineering, publications, supply support, spares, training, administration of logistic functions, and repair coordination, 4. In the military, the cost for details embracing the transport, quartering, and supply of troops.

cost, lowest total The lowest life cycle cost.

cost, manufacturing The sum of the costs expended for direct material, direct labor, and factory overhead costs for a product.

cost, material 1. The cost expended for raw or purchased materials needed to produce a product, 2. Normally includes the cost for packaging, inspection, shipping, and delivery of purchased materials.

cost, nonrecurring 1. Items of cost that represent one-time expenses at predicted times in the future, 2. Normally includes the cost for packaging, inspection, shipping and delivery of purchased materials.

cost, overhead Also called *indirect costs* or *burden.* 1. Costs apportioned to products from overhead accounts, 2. Costs which cannot be specifically and directly charged to a single product as being solely incurred by that product, such as development, supervision, tooling, maintenance, heat, power, light, buildings, taxes, and financing, 3. Usually fixed costs.

cost, ownership 1. The cost to acquire, operate, maintain, repair, and dispose of the product during its period of use, 2. The cost to possess the product including all finance charges, taxes, insurance, and loss of product use when it is out of service.

cost, prevention The elimination of unnecessary cost during the development stages of design or operations.

cost, product 1. The sum of manufacturing, general and administrative, and selling costs, 2. The total expense to produce a product, 3. The transfer of money, labor, time, or other personal items to achieve an objective, 4. One component of price.

cost, production See *cost, manufacturing.*

cost, recurring 1. Repetitive production costs that vary or occur with the quantity being produced, 2. Cost expressed in terms of a recurring direct unit cost of production of an item consisting of labor, direct burden, materials, purchased parts, expendable tooling, quality control, test, inspection, packaging, and shipping, 3. Costs which are repetitive throughout a product's useful life.

cost, relative 1. Differential costs between various products or functions rather than actual or absolute costs, 2. Costs which show order of magnitude only and the order of expense from greatest to least.

cost, replacement Future costs to replace a product or product component which is expected to occur during the product life.

cost, retrofit The cost to incorporate a product improvement or necessary change into an older product.

cost, standard 1. Cost calculated on accepted productivity and material rates used as a norm against which to compare actual performance, 2. Costs accepted as the basis for budgeting or allocation of funds.

cost, supplier The price a manufacturer pays for generally off-the-shelf purchased parts, materials, and supplies as contrasted with *subcontractor costs* which generally include some degree of added input such as, connection and/or product manufacturing.

cost, total 1. All costs for someone to acquire, use, enjoy, maintain, and dispose of a product, plus the time, effort and risk of buying. See *cost, life cycle*.

cost, unnecessary 1. Costs for functions not desired, 2. Cost for quality or performance above that needed by the user, 3. Any cost which does not contribute to value, 4. That portion of the cost of a product which does not contribute to essential functions, required performance, or marketability.

cost, variable Direct or indirect costs which change directly with the quantity of, or conditions under which, products are produced, as distinguished from *fixed costs*.

cost, variance See *cost, incremental*.

cost, vendor See *cost, supplier*.

CRF capital recovery factor

CSI Construction Specifications Institute

CVS Certified Value Specialist

Delphi See *Method, Delphi*.

DOD Department of Defense

DOE Department of Energy

dollars, constant Economic value expressed in terms of the purchasing power of the dollar in the base year; both inflation of cost and the time value of money are reflected through use of a discount rate.

dollars, current Economic value expressed in terms of actual prices each year, including inflation; i.e., present or future value of current dollars is determined by using the time value of money rather than a discount rate.

DOT Department of Transportation

ECC estimated construction cost

EDRC estimated design and review cost

EMIC estimated management and inspection cost

engineer, value One who uses value engineering methodology to study a product and search for value improvement.

engineering, value 1. The same as value analysis except with emphasis on application during product development and/or design, 2. The incorporation of functions into products considered by the user to be of value.

ERC estimated reservation cost

ESC estimated site cost

estimate, cost 1. A product representing the art and science of predicting cost or price, 2. The summation of unit quantities of labor and material multiplied by unit costs of labor, material, overhead and profit for providing a product under a specified set of conditions.

ETPC estimated total program costs

factor, discount A multiplication number for converting cost and benefits occurring at different times to a common basis.

FAST Function Analysis System Technique

FAST, customer The same as a technical FAST Diagram except the same four supporting functions (assure dependability, assure convenience, satisfy user, attract user) always appear immediately to the right of the left scope line.

FAST, technical 1. A diagramming technique that graphically shows the logical relationships of the functions of a product, 2. Product functions displayed horizontally in diagram form using the following rules: higher-order functions appear to the left answering *why* a function occurs; lower-order functions appear to the right answering *how* a function occurs; functions occurring at the same time appear vertically below one another; scope lines indicating the scope of the value study are placed vertically; and basic function of the product is defined immediately to the right of the left scope line.

function, aesthetic Also referred to as *esteem value*. 1. Esteem value rather than use value, 2. A function attributable to pleasing the user rather than contributing to performance, 3. A function that indicates product features that exceed its technical utility or performance requirement.

function, basic Also called *primary* or *essential function*. 1. That which is essential to the performance of a user function, 2. The function describing the primary utilitarian characteristic of a product to fulfill a user requirement.

function, critical A combination of the basic and selected required secondary or dependent functions defining the means used to achieve workability of the product.

function, critical path One of the set of basic and dependent functions that meet the *how* and *why* logic on a FAST Diagram, forming a path of essential functions without which the product would not perform.

function, dependent 1. Lower order functions, to the right of each other on a FAST Diagram, that are successively dependent on the one to its immediate left for its existence, 2. A function that depends on a higher order function for its existence, 3. A function that exists or is chosen in order to achieve a basic function.

function, essential Also called the *necessary* or *required function*. A function describing a characteristic that is absolutely necessary to a product's ability to perform the user function.

function, esteem See *function, aesthetic*.

function, higher-order 1. A function that is a goal rather than an objective, or an objective rather than a task, 2. A function that is more abstract than specific (i.e., *feed people* is a higher-order function than *distribute food stamps*).

function, independent 1. A function that does not depend on another function or on the method selected to perform that function, 2. A function that occurs *all* *the time* (e.g., a part or assembly may have to *resist corrosion*, regardless of what other basic or secondary function that part is performing.)

function, lower-order The opposite of a higher-order function (tasks rather than objectives, specific rather than abstract).

function, necessary See *function, essential*.

function, nonessential See *function, unnecessary*.

function, primary See *function, basic* or *function, essential*.

function, required See *function, essential*.

function, required secondary A secondary function that is essential to support the performance of the basic function, 2. A function that may result from specified design criteria.

function, secondary 1. The manner in which the basic function was implemented, 2. A function indicating quality, dependability, performance, convenience, attractiveness, and general satisfaction beyond that needed to satisfy minimum user needs, 3. Includes supporting unwanted, unnecessary, and required functions.

function, sell 1. A function that provides primarily esteem value (such as *improve style* or *enhance decor*), 2. A function that may result from specified design criteria.

function, supporting Also called a *sell function*. 1. A function required by the user to make a product sell, 2. A function that increases acceptance, 3. A function to assure dependability, assure convenience, satisfy user, or attract user.

function, task See *function, user*.

function, unnecessary Also referred to as a *nonessential function*. A function not contributing to the utility or desirability of the product.

function, use See *function, work*.

function, user Also referred to as a *task function*. 1. That function performed by a product that causes its purchase by a user, 2. The function performed by an employee for the company.

function, unwanted Also called an *undesirable function*. 1. A negative function caused by the method used to achieve the basic function (e.g., such as heat generated from lighting, which often must be cooled).

function, work Also called *use function*. 1. A function which is essential to make the product or service perform as intended, 2. A function that provides use value.

GDMW General Directorate of Military Works (Saudi Arabia)

GSA General Services Administration

GSF gross square foot

HEPA high-efficiency particulate air filter

HEW Department of Health, Education and Welfare

HVAC heating, ventilation and air conditioning

ICEC International Cost Engineering Council

improvement, value The same as value analysis, except with the emphasis on application to improve existing products.

index, value 1. The monetary relationship of function worth to function cost (expressed as $V1 = FW/FC$) where V1 is never greater than unity, (e.g.; $V1 = 0.79$), 2. Sometimes expressed as function cost ($V13 = FB/FC$).

investment, return on In value analysis, the ratio of the dollars saved versus the cost of performing and implementing the study (normally expressed similar to the following; ROI = $8:1).

Job Plan Also called *VE Job Plan*.

kWh/yr kilowatt-hours per year

KV kilovolt

KVA kilovolt ampere

Law, Pareto's Economic theory attributed to Vilfredo Pareto, an Italian economist and sociologist. The distribution of incomes tends to remain the same in spite of changes in governmental policy (e.g., taxation).

LCC life cycle cost(s) or costing. See *cost, life cycle*.

LCK L.C. Kingscott and Associates

life, economic 1. The period of time over which an investment is considered to be the lowest-cost alternative for satisfying a specific need, 2. The period of time used to justify obtaining a product, from a financial point of view as reflected by a contract period, lease, mortgage, loan agreement, statutory limitation, warranty, depreciation, method, and so forth.

life, design The period of time intended by the designer for product use; under expected levels of use, maintenance and repair, before product disposal and/or replacement.

life, product The period of time the product is actually used, maintained, and/or repaired before being taken out of service.

life, useful The period of time during which the customer needs to use a product.

LPG low-pressure gas

management, value *Value analysis*, with emphasis on application as a management technique. See *analysis, value*.

MBM McKee, Berger, and Mansueto

Method, Delphi An idea-generating technique that may also be referred to as *Delphi patterns* or *Delphi technique*.

methodology, value The study of the relationship of cost and worth to function for any product, in a prescribed manner, using the Job Plan.

mismatch, value When function cost does not fit or match user/customer function attitude for a given function.

MODA Ministry of Defense and Aviation (Saudi Arabia)

model, cost 1. A diagrammatic representation of cost, based on a hierarchical structure (often work breakdown structure) of product components or functions, 2. A model which sums to the total cost of the product.

model, energy 1. A diagrammatic representation, in a hierarchical structure, of the quantity of energy consumption caused by each of the product's components or functions, 2. A model which sums to the total energy used by a product.

model, LCC 1. A diagrammatic representation, in a hierarchical structure, of the present worth or annualized expenditures relating to a product for a specified period of time, 2. A model which sums to the total life cycle cost for a product.

model, space 1. A diagrammatic representation, in a hierarchical structure, of the square foot (or other unit of measure) of area or space allocated to each component of a facility, 2. A model that sums to the total amount of area or space in a building.

model, time A diagrammatic representation, in a linear form, of the duration to perform all tasks associated with obtaining a product, 2. A model that sums to the total length of time to obtain a product and accounts for overlapping time(s) of concurrent effort, i.e., a PERT chart. See *PERT chart*.

model worth A second set of numbers, in the same units of measure, superimposed on the same format used for a cost model, energy model, LCC model, space model, or time model that represent the worth of that model element, 2. A model that sums to the total worth of a product for the resource measured.

MSB main switchboard

NAVFAC Naval Facilities Engineering Command

nomograph Also known as *nomogram*. A chart that consists of several scaled lines that are arranged so that by connecting two known values on two lines, an unknown value can be read at the point of intersection of a third line.

NSPE National Society of Professional Engineers

objective, value 1. The same or necessary performance or acceptance at lower cost, 2. Better performance at the same cost, or at a higher cost, if a greater market share is thereby obtainable.

OMB Office of Management and Budget

ownership, cost of See *cost, life cycle*.

parameter-based A type of cost estimate.

Plan, Job A sequential approach for conducting a value study, normally consisting of an information step, and/or a function analysis review or implementation step, and an optional follow-up or measurement step.

planning, value Value analysis, with emphasis on application to strategic directions of new product development, organization strategic planning, or filling market niches. See *analysis, value*.

PP periodic payment

price, customer 1. The fixed sum of money or amount of service given or required to transfer ownership of products, 2. Normally the sum of product cost plus profit.

profit, product The difference between product price and cost, where price = cost + profit.

program, quality control/value assurance A system of procedures and standards by which a constructor, product manufacturer, materials processor, or the like, monitor the properties of the finished work.

program, value A stated plan or procedure that uses value methodology as its basis for optimizing total cost.

Projacs A company that offers consulting services for project management in the Middle East, VE, LCC, and cost control. The author is president of Projacs USA, a subsidiary of Saudi Projacs.

proposal, value change Also called a *value engineering proposal* (VEP). A change submitted by in-house personnel to improve the value of a product.

proposal, value engineering Another term for value study proposal. See *proposal, value study* and *proposal, value change*.

proposal, value engineering change (VECP) A change submitted by a contractor, pursuant to a contract provision, for the purpose of reducing the contract price or life cycle cost of the product under contract.

proposal, value study A recommendation, determined by utilizing value methodology, to change a product to achieve greater value and/or reduce overall cost.

PW present worth

PWA present worth of annuity

PWF present worth factor

quality, required The minimal level of product performance necessary to satisfy the customer (not to be confused with the word *value*).

rate, discount The rate of interest reflecting inflation and the time value of money that is used in the discount formula to convert costs and benefits occurring at different times to a common time.

RFP request for proposal

ROI return on investment

ROR rate of return

SAVE Society of American Value Engineers

SJVE Society of Japanese Value Engineers

technique, Delphi See *Method, Delphi*

technology, value The specific method or process of value analysis for handling a cost problem. This term is used in the science or art of applying value methodology.

TES thermal energy storage

TQM Total Quality Management

UPS uninterruptible power supply

VA Veterans Administration

value, aesthetic See *value, esteem.*

value, annual Past or future costs or benefits expressed as an equivalent uniform annual amount, taking into account the time value of money.

value, cost Archaic terminology. See *value, use.*

value, economic 1. The relationship of benefits (utility) to cost as seen by the user, 2. The life cycle benefits as related to the cost of ownership, use, and disposal of a product. The components of economic value are the following: use value, esteem value, and exchange value.

value, esteem Also referred to as *aesthetic value.* 1. The monetary sum a user is willing to pay for functions providing prestige, appearance, and/or other nonquantifiable benefits, 2. The relative value a user places on the aesthetic functions provided by a product, 3. The monetary measure of the functions of a product, which contribute to its desirability or salability, but not to its required functional performance, 4. The motivated desire to possess for the sake of possession.

value, exchange 1. The monetary sum for which a product can be traded, 2. The market value of a product at a given point in time.

value, function The relationship of function worth to function cost. See *index, value.*

value, future The equivalent value, at a specified time in the future, of estimated recurring and replacement costs expected during the life of a product.

value, good 1. That which occurs when a product has reasonable cost and desired performance, as determined by the user, 2. The lowest life cycle cost to reliably accomplish a function, 3. A relative economic comparator, as determined by the user and measured by profit and sales.

value, market The sale price of a product under the voluntary conditions of a willing buyer and a willing seller.

value, maximum The lowest life cycle cost to reliably accomplish the minimum required performance.

value, perceived The user's view of benefits received and the price of acquiring the product.

value, poor The condition that occurs when function cost exceeds function worth by a significant amount.

value, present The economic procedure to account for the time-equivalent value of past, present, or future costs at the beginning of a base period.

value, product 1. The relationship of benefits to cost, which conforms to a user's desires and resources in a given situation, 2. A specific combination of use, esteem, market, and exchange values.

value, salvage 1. The residual value of a product, net of disposal costs, that may derive from removal or replacement of the product during the study period, 2. Also the residual value from the sale of the product during or after the study period.

value, use 1. The monetary measure of the functional properties of a product that reliably accomplishes a user's needs, 2. The life cycle cost (worth to cost relationship) considering user function only.

VAV variable air volume

VE value engineering

VECP Value Engineering Change Proposals

VETC Value Engineering Team Coordinator

VI value index

visibility, cost 1. The display of all costs for a product in one format at one time, 2. The breaking down and identification of costs hidden through aggregation, 3. Obtained through use of a cost model.

workshop, approved VE A workshop, approved by the Society of American Value Engineers, that meets the minimum training requirements and may be credited toward a certification as a Certified Value Specialist (CVS).

workshop, VE A group meeting to carry on the work of conducting a value study of a product.

worth, function 1. The lowest overall cost that is required to perform a function, 2. The least cost attainable through the use of a functional equivalent, 3. The cost of a function without regard to the consequences of failure, 4. Referred to as the value of a function in some texts, but not a preferred usage.

worth, present See *value, present*.

year, base The year to which all future and past costs are converted when the present value method is used.

Index